YOU'RE THE JUDGE!
How To Understand Sports, Torts & Courts

by JOHN M. FOTIADES

E&N EDGEWORTH & NORTH BOOKS
WORCESTER, MASSACHUSETTS

Library of Congress Cataloging in Publication Data

Fotiades, John M., 1946-
   You're the judge!

   Includes index.
   1. Sports--Law and legislation--United States--
Popular Works. 2. Liability for sports accidents--
United States--Popular works. I. Title.
KF3989.Z9F67   1989   346.7303'22   89-1430
ISBN 0-926565-00-1   347.306322
ISBN 0-926565-01-X

Attention Organizations and Corporations: Quantity discounts are available for bulk purchases of this
book for sales promotions, premiums or fund raising. Special books or excerpts can be created for special needs. All inquiries should be addressed to Edgeworth & North Books.

Published by Edgeworth & North Books
Post Office Box 812
West Side Station
Worcester, Massachusetts 01602-0812
(508) 799-9860

Printed and Bound in the United States of America

DEDICATION

In loving memory of my mother, Marion.
Also to my father, Michael, with love and admiration.

IN APPRECIATION

Thanks to my wife Valla Dana, for her many hours of assistance in the research and completion of *You're The Judge!*

Thanks to Tom and Marilyn Ross and Clyde McVicar for their invaluable help with this book.

Thanks to New England School of Law and the University of Miami School of Law for the use of their libraries, and; to Richard Gibson at Nova Law School for his assistance.

Special thanks to Alex Gazonas who took my art work and illustrations and, with his unique touch, gave them life, and; to Jim Canada for his imaginative help in the book's design.

CONTENTS

Chariots & Complaints! traces the history of sports—as a means for man to feed and protect himself and his possessions—and the law—rules to be followed for an orderly society. This chapter explains how people's rights and the law developed, and further details both their influences on sports. Do you know how a court or a jury decides a legal dispute that comes before it?

Amateurs & Eligibility spells out amateurs' rights and responsibilities regarding their eligibility to participate in amateur sports for their school or in other competitions. These rights and responsibilities govern both the athletes' and the schools' conduct, covering areas from recruiting and the granting of scholarships to grades, conduct and awards. What is "redshirting"? Do amateur athletes have to be well-groomed?

Due Process & Equal Protection goes into the effect that the Fourteenth Amendment to the Constitution, and its requirements, has on the enforcement of rules and regulations by amateur athletic organizations. A sample Complaint highlights the issues that are examined. Can student-athletes be deprived of the right to an education or the right to participate in sports without the opportunity for a fair and impartial hearing? Should all athletes be treated alike?

Discrimination discusses attempts to discriminate or differentiate in favor or against athletes or others in sports on the basis of prejudice because of the race, sex, color or disability of the person. Are girls physiologically inferior to boys? Should girls be permitted to participate in contact sports (football) on the same team as, or against, boys?

Athletes & Injuries discusses and comments on personal injuries to professional and amateur athletes which are caused by intentional misconduct (**assault and battery**), or by non-intentional misconduct (**negligence**). Injuries to amateur athletes may occur while they are participating for a school or other organized team, or while just playing around. There are defenses to the charges of assault and battery or negligence. In addition, this chapter covers injuries at work and those caused by extraordinary risks or conditions "not fit for play." Do injured athletes assume the risk of injury or are they guilty of contributing to their injury when they are aware of the dangers of the sport in which they are participating? Are parents responsible for the conduct of their children?

CONTENTS

ABOUT THIS BOOK

You're The Judge! — How To Understand Sports, Torts & Courts is an indispensable book for anyone with an interest in sports, either as a participant, spectator, parent, teacher, coach, or in any of the many other ways that people are involved with sports. In easy to understand language, this book will help you interpret sports and the laws, rules and regulations that control and affect them. These same laws will apply to many similar situations that occur in everyday life.

In recent years, the law and judicial scrutiny by the courts have emerged to play a major role in controlling the affairs of sports and its activities.

Sports, with their games and contests, have been moving from the playing fields and sports arenas to a very different arena. This one is comprised not of bases, end zones and baskets, but of judges, juries and lawyers; of "Hear Ye! Hear Ye!" instead of the National Anthem; of lawsuits and damages instead of cheering and booing, and; of guilt or innocence instead of victory or defeat. Today, the issues aren't tickets, programs, snackbars or replays—but instead, complaints, legal defenses and legal decisions.

In a court of law, the stakes are higher and the play is very real. The law—decisions of courts, regulations and rules established to make it easier for us to live with one another—has been increasingly applied

to sports activities in order to determine one's rights and duties. Additionally, the law determines whether or not there has been a violation of these rights or duties which caused injury to another.

You're The Judge! can be easily read, understood and enjoyed by all. It contains law for the layman, law which is not technical, but explanatory and informational. *You're The Judge!* has over 1,000 pieces of art and cartoons. This is not an attempt to make light of the seriousness of some of the cases described here, but to point out the humor in some situations.

Over 1,000 cases, each with a set of facts followed by a decision where **YOU'RE THE JUDGE!,** are presented so you can understand how the law affects sports and how to protect yourself and others. For example:

> FACTS: While attending a baseball game, you were hit in the head and injured by an errant baseball.
>   Manny, the leftfielder for the Tiajuana Tacos, mad at having dropped a fly ball, admitted, "I threw the ball into the stands." Did you assume the risk of such an injury? Could you recover damages against Manny or his team? **YOU'RE THE JUDGE!**
>
> DECISION: Had the ball slipped, there would be no recovery. You would have assumed the risk of such an injury as being an injury common to the game of baseball. However, Manny intentionally threw the ball into the stands. His team was liable for your injury.

Occasionally, the legal decision is omitted. This may be because the case was either hypothetical to illustrate a legal point, or because there was no decision. Such cases will stimulate thought and allow you the fun of deciding the ruling or verdict on your own.

Many of the names of the plaintiffs or defendants in lawsuits have been changed to protect their privacy. The goal of the book is not to glorify or vilify athletes or others involved in sports, but to point out how the laws, rules and regulations concerning sports affect you and everyone else in everyday life.

Because of the nature of this unique reference work, you will find the same sports discussed and explored throughout all of its pages. The same legal terms and the same or similar case histories may appear more than once because they apply to and serve as examples for different situations.

In reading the case histories the reader may feel that the masculine image was overused. The simple fact is that many of the case histories involved males. Real names—when not actually used—were merely substituted with ones of the same sex and seemingly similar ethnic origins. No slights to either females or ethnic groups were intended in the choice of names and gender.

You're The Judge! begins with the history of sports and law, and shows how a legal controversy proceeds: from an injury, to a complaint, and then to a decision or settlement.

Each chapter generally concludes with an *Odds & Ends* section where miscellaneous or non-serious, comical situations are discussed, followed by a brief closing comment. Occasionally, a summary or further discussion of an important issue is presented.

How did sports and law begin? Do you know what a personal injury is? Who would be liable if you were injured by an errant ball or "slipped bat?" Who would be liable if a seat or a protective barrier was defective and, as a result, you were injured? Do you assume the risk of injury in certain situations? Can a participant be liable for an injury? What about his team, the operator of a facility, a manufacturer of sports equipment, a teacher, coach, school, city, or a property owner? If you are injured during a lunchtime game at work, is your employer liable?

Do you know what a "redshirt" is? Do you know how an athlete's eligibility is determined or can be affected by outside activities, such as by accepting gifts or money, or by transferring to another school? What's a nuisance? Libel? Slander? Is discrimination permitted in sports? What's a conspiracy or monopoly? Who decides what unsportsmanlike conduct is? How are "wars" between leagues settled? Are you entitled to privacy? Are athletes entitled to equal protection? Can you waive your rights to recover damages for any injury you received? Can you be denied admission to a sports event even if you have a ticket?

> FACTS: You left your car at a parking lot while attending a baseball game; it was stolen. You left your tennis racket at a repair shop and it was destroyed in a fire. Who would be liable?

DECISION: **YOU'RE THE JUDGE!**

You're The Judge! answers all of these questions and many, many more concerning any involvement in sports by participants, spectators and others. Many of these situations concern the small guy or fan, the one who is hit by a ball, injured at an autorace, hurt in a high school game or practice, or injured in a pick-up game.

Sports, both amateur and professional, have become big business. Because of television and masses of spectators, professional athletes (after successful collegiate careers) now command and receive lucrative contracts.

This increased financial stake for players, as well as for schools, teams, leagues, cities and others, has provided an increased concern about decisions affecting these parties. Therefore, when misfortune occurs, those aggrieved will more likely resort to the courts. In turn, this has led to significant changes both in the law as it affects sports and in how amateur and professional sports are conducted and played.

This book covers laws, rules and regulations as they affect participation in any sport. And it covers other than participants—such as spectators, parents, schools, cities, manufacturers, promoters, officials, operators of sports facilities, doctors, the media, owners, teams, coaches, instructors, landowners and many others involved with sports.

You're The Judge! does not have to be read from front to back, although you can. It is meant to serve as a sort of encyclopedia of sports and law where you can read about those topics that presently interest you most. It is a vast storehouse of information that can be referred to as needed or desired. As topics come up from reading the sports page or a magazine, from watching TV, or from participating in or watching a sport, you can then find that topic and read about it.

These days you almost have to be a lawyer to interpret the sports page. Instead of just reading about the home team's chances for the upcoming season, or of nostalgic stories about teams or players past, you now read of contract negotiations, strikes, law suits, arbitration awards.

FACTS: Why is understanding the law and rules and regulations concerning sports so important? **YOU'RE THE JUDGE!**

DECISION: Because it affects the lives, occupations, safety and enjoyment of almost everyone, whether or not you or your children or friends participate in or just watch sports.

Sports and its legal implications affect everyone: from the ticket taker to the sports facility construction workers, from the athletes to those who benefit from their contributions. Those who support teams by buying tickets, cities and schools who take part in and benefit from the revenue that sports generates, manufacturers who make sports equipment, and those responsible for protecting participants and spectators from injury are also affected. So are those who promote, officiate and control sports events, those who care for the injured, those who set up rules and regulate participation in and admittance to sports events, and those who interpret and enforce such rules, regulations and the law as they relate to sports.

Many legal and other important words and terms (in bold) are defined and discussed as they appear. To locate these, see the page reference in *Words & Terms* or the *Index*. These words and terms and others used generally throughout *You're The Judge!* are defined in *Words & Terms*. Every attempt has been made to present information and terms in a way which will be clearly understood. If a term requiring defining appears elsewhere in another chapter, such as negligence or the defense of assumption of the risk, then the term is again discussed and illustrated. There is no need to refer elsewhere.

> FACTS: What law applies to sports? Is it different from other law? What is the law's purpose? **YOU'RE THE JUDGE!**

> DECISION: The law that applies to sports is the same everyday law that is applied to other similar situations. The same law applies to personal injuries whether it involves someone in an auto accident or fight or to an athlete or spectator hit by a participant.
> Law consists of the entire body of principals that govern conduct and the observance of which can be enforced in court. The purpose of the law is to provide order, stability and justice—to inform everyone of their rights and duties concerning the interaction between themselves and others—and to change as the needs and values of society change.

Although the principles upon which all laws are founded are the same, laws may vary from state to state depending on a particular state's needs. Federal laws will be the same no matter where applied.

However, even where it may appear that the facts are the same or quite similar, a different decision may be reached for a number of reasons. For example, a jury, court or other tribunal (such as an arbitrator) may interpret or weigh evidence or facts differently, or the witnesses or presentation of the facts or evidence may sway others to reach a different verdict. And one state or locale may find certain behavior more or less tolerable than another.

Any decision or information given in *You're The Judge!* is not intended to be a substitute for proper legal or other advice. This book does not, nor can it, guarantee similar results, for the reasons stated above. It is suggested that you use the book as an informational guide only; then seek out competent legal or other advice as necessary.

ENJOY!

1

CHARIOTS & COMPLAINTS!

WHAT'S IT ABOUT?

Chariots & Complaints! traces the history of sports—as a means for man to feed and protect himself and his possessions—and the law—rules to be followed for an orderly society.

This chapter explains how people's rights and these laws developed, and further details both their influences on sports. Do you know how a court or a jury decides a legal dispute that comes before it?

Long before the Olympic Games, sports—from the Latin word desport meaning to carry away, or a diversion or amusement—began as a religious cult and in preparation for life. Its roots were in man's desire to protect himself and his tribe, crops, cattle and territory.

For self-defense, man learned to "run and jump, to project spears by hand and later by bow, and also to defend himself by what is now called wrestling, judo or boxing." New sports evolved, not from this early training, but from the basic need for existence and not as a diversion or a pastime.

Most importantly though, sports began as a "rite to ensure productive crops by the return of the rains, sun and favorable winds."

Competing groups represented the earth and the heavens. And as no one would dare cheat or challenge the gods, referees were unnecessary.

When, in Egypt and Mesopotamia, self-preservation ceased to be man's constant preoccupation, sports became more of an avocation.

SPORTS & LAW

The Olympic Games, which began in 776 B.C., were governed by special **laws**—sets of rules to be followed as a means to an orderly society—subject to penalties meant to preserve peace and guard the honor of the Games.

Athletes and trainers swore by Zeus to "obey the rules and compete fairly." And as Zeus was a terrible and avenging God, competitors generally obeyed. If they did not, penalties consisting of exclusion from the Games, fines and flogging were imposed. Judges' power was nearly absolute. Whipbearers kept order amongst the spectators and peddlers.

> FACTS: The Olympia Women's Club decided that they wanted to attend and compete in the Olympic Games. Several women wanted to compete in the foot races. Was this permitted? **YOU'RE THE JUDGE!**

> DECISION: Most women, at least until late in the pre-Christian era, were not only prohibited from competing, but under penalty of death, were prohibited from even attending the Olympics!

Footraces were the first events at the Olympics. Later boxing, chariot and horse races, wrestling and other events were added.

> FACTS: The year was 706 B.C. You were at the Olympics, at the stadium in the sacred city of Olympia, Greece, built in honor of the Greek God, Zeus. You went to see the foot and chariot races and other sporting events.
> You explained what happened next, "It was a beautiful day... but not for long. As the first chariots and their warriors, with all their metal gleaming in the bright sun, passed in front of the viewing stands, there was a thunderous crash. Chariot parts flew through the air, striking me and breaking my nose." What were your rights? Could you recover damages for your injury?

> DECISION: **YOU'RE THE JUDGE!**

Boxing, the most brutal of the sports, was ferocious. Blood was encouraged by the spectators. Death was a certain risk to the boxers!

> FACTS: Igor and "Max the Ax" squared off for the Mediterranean Boxing Championship.
> The referee explained what happened, "In the third round, Igor went down from a hard right. Max was the winner. But as Igor attempted to regain his feet, Max again began to pummel the defenseless Igor. Max killed him." Did Igor assume the risk of such an injury? Could Igor's family recover damages from Max? **YOU'RE THE JUDGE!**

> DECISION: There was no right to sue for injuries, let alone recover damages. When death came to one of the participants, the offender—although not jailed—was required by law to make amends to the bereaved family by the payment of "blood money."

Although the world relied on the Code of Hammurabi and, from 1200 B.C., the Ten Commandments, these laws dealt mostly with criminal matters. They did not allow for the obtaining of relief or

monetary damages for personal injuries.

In 450 B.C., the Romans published The Twelve Tables, a set of moral principles and practices. However, their influence did not reach the Olympic Games.

By 146 B.C., when Greece was conquered by the Romans, the Olympic Games no longer bore any meaningful relationship to the values that athletics had represented to the ancient Greeks.

Hellenic News	
Summer	144 B.C.

BLOOD & BRUTALITY!

"Events were staged to satisfy the crowd's thirst for blood and brutality. Athletes were not chosen from amongst native-born sons of proven virtue. But instead, gladiators were criminals, or slaves from conquered lands. Their reward for fighting and winning was freedom, but only if they pleased the crowd with bravery and skill.

The Games consisted of contests between unarmed combatants and also with unfed lions. Friends and brothers fought to the death, only to be spared if the tyrant saw fit to withhold the arbitrary gesture of 'thumbs down!'

The Olympic Games and gladiator contests ended as Christianity was establishing itself in Rome. For centuries to come, sports was looked upon as a symbol of religious decay."

Around 560 A.D., all laws were brought together into a Body of Civil Laws. The most complete collection of laws to that time, this had an enormous influence on the development of law. As the Roman Empire gradually fell apart, much of the Roman law became the canon law of the Catholic Church.

The English began developing their own legal system after the invasion by the Normans in 1066. They won their basic rights in the Magna Charta from King John in 1215, and for the rest of their rights, a system began to develop which would later become the foundation for modern American law.

Common Law & The Jury

FACTS: Long before the English, the Greeks tried legal cases before citizens whom we now call a jury. These juries, together with early courts and occasionally from acts of Parliament, began to make what was called common law. What is a jury? What was the common law? **YOU'RE THE JUDGE!**

DECISION: A **jury** is a "group of people selected to hear evidence and decide the matter before them." **Common law** was law developed from "custom, tradition, decisions by judges and juries and from acts of Parliament."

By the 14th century, underground popularity for sports spread This was so, even against laws (especially in England) created to make the playing of certain sports illegal. People began to see sports as a "way to fill leisure time and obtain some measure of importance."

Although at this time, participation in sports was frowned upon, laws pertaining to the playing of sports were now beginning to emerge. These laws, combined with the emerging common law, now gave an injured participant or spectator at least an opportunity to seek damages for injuries or other wrongs.

FACTS: Shawn was injured during a boxing match. He complained, "My opponent, Jake, attacked me from behind before the fight started." Although no one, as yet, had thought of suing to recover for such injuries, suppose Shawn sued, alleging that Jake intentionally violated the rules. "Could I recover?" asked Shawn. **YOU'RE THE JUDGE!**

DECISION: Although Shawn may have been permitted to bring an action, there was not, as yet, any law permitting recovery.

The common law developed in England would become the single most important root of the American legal system. It would become two different kinds of law: **case law**—that law based on earlier court decisions (precedents), and; **statutory law**—that law which comes from written acts of federal, state, or local legislation.

Puritans in early Massachusetts sought to limit participation in sports by the colonists. Again, religion played a major role. The Sabbath was strictly enforced and religious conformity was fostered. Laws passed in the 1600's were designed to "ensure obedience, prevent drinking, gambling and other conduct which would weaken the morals of society." Sports were promoted to fulfill military training needs.

Do you know what "blue laws" are?

FACTS: The Puritans sought to control sports by the enactment of Sunday **"blue laws"**—laws regulating religious and personal conduct. The colonists wanted to "play baseball on Sunday afternoons, our only day off from work." Were they allowed to play? **YOU'RE THE JUDGE!**

DECISION: The blue laws specified which sports were legal, and that any such sports were to be played without disturbing other people or their property.

Playing areas, out of the general public's way, had not yet been well defined. Certain sports, such as baseball, were prohibited in public. Later, when the blue laws were amended, recreation, as well as baseball, was allowed in municipal parks on Sunday.

In 1776, with the advent of the Declaration of Independence, an entirely new legal system had to be developed. This led to the U .S. Constitution in 1789, which—along with its amendments (Bill of Rights) and state constitutions—became the principal source of individual rights. Certain other basic rights were derived from the old English common law.

From this new constitution evolved the basic rights of the opportunity for an aggrieved person to be heard, and the right to a jury trial.

Should I Sue?

Into the 1960's, if participants received injuries from competing in sports, they just didn't sue. It wasn't the thing to do.

But, as people became more conscious of their rights, and as the courts began to hand down decisions in favor of those injured, attitudes changed.

FACTS: Tommy was injured by a "late hit" during a high school football game. He sued, charging, "I wouldn't have been hurt if the tackle was proper."

The opposing player and school defended, "Tommy assumed the risk of injury from conduct which was part of the game of football."   Could Tommy recover for his injury? **YOU'RE THE JUDGE!**

DECISION: Although Tommy assumed the risk of injury from ordinary risks of the game, such as a proper tackle, he did not assume the risk of injury from an intentional "late hit," as was encouraged by the opposing coach to intimidate players. Tommy could recover damages for his injury.

The awareness that negligent conduct might lead to liability brought about dramatic changes in sports, such as improved safety in equipment, supervision, facilities and medical care, and in laws protecting participants, spectators and the public from negligent conduct.

FACTS: After being injured by that flying chariot wheel, you left the stadium and saw a healer. He said, "You'll always have pain and a scar from your injury."

Suppose that the present judicial system was in place back in 706 B.C., what would have been the **procedure**—process for enforcing rights and seeking redress—for seeking damages for your injury?

DECISION: **YOU'RE THE JUDGE!**

Plan of Attack

Arbitration—process where a dispute is submitted to an impartial party for resolution—will not be used. You will seek relief through the court, leaving open the possibility of a **settlement**—agreement settling the matter without the further need for a decision by the court.

Depending on the type of action, parties involved, amount in dispute, and other matters, you might file a complaint in either a federal, state or local court.

To help in explaining the civil process, assume that Greece was a state in this country and present-day law ruled.

Complaint & Summons

You filed a **complaint**—document setting forth the facts on which you base your claim for relief. You named Yani (the driver of the chariot), Mikali (the owner of the chariot and sponsor of the race), and Greco (the manufacturer of the chariot), as **defendants**—persons against whom your complaint is brought. You, as the complaining party bringing the action, are the **plaintiff.**

FACTS: In part, your complaint alleged, "Each of the defendants—Yani, Mikali, and Greco—breached their duty to insure my safety. As a result of their breaches, I was injured. What court should I file my complaint in? " **YOU'RE THE JUDGE!**

DECISION: The **small claims court**—which handles claims below a specified monetary limit and where, generally, a lawyer is not needed—is out as your claim will exceed its limit. If the defendants were residents of states different from the one in which you lived, **diversity of citizenship** would exist and you might bring this action in the federal court.

However, assuming all of the defendants lived in your state, then the **jurisdiction**—power of the court to hear and adjudicate your claim—will be in the state court. The **venue**—geographical place where you filed the complaint—will be the county where you live.

Your complaint was served on the defendants—Yani, Mikali, and Greco—by way of a **summons**—written order requiring the defendants to answer the complaint against them.

Answer & Defenses

The defendants all filed an **answer**—document answering a complaint, and containing any denial and listing any defenses.

They contended, "You were never injured. But, if you were, we're not negligent."—**general denial.** "You assumed the risk of,

and contributed to, your injury by attending the Games and sitting in a seat too close to the track."—**specific denial.**

Mikali alleged, "I didn't know of Yani's reckless driving."

"We were not negligent in making the chariot," Greco added.

If you had violated the **Statute of Limitations**—statute limiting the time in which an action must be brought—or had unreasonably delayed filing the complaint to the detriment of a defendant—**laches,** then the defendants might have asserted either of these as a defense.

Also, the defendants could make motions regarding the correctness of the complaint, jurisdiction, or possibly for a more definite statement or explanation of your complaint. They might also include in their answer any **counterclaims**—claims that they might have against you. Possibly, you owed one of them money. What next?

Discovery!

FACTS: How would you go about discovering and obtaining evidence to use in presenting your case to the court—**discovery? YOU'RE THE JUDGE!**

DECISION: Discovery may consist of **depositions**—testimony of a witness recorded outside of the court for use at trial.

You may want to ask Yani questions such as, "Is that how you always drive?"; to Mikali, "Were you aware of Yani's reputation as a driver?" or; to Greco, "Did you know of the ease with which the chariot would fall apart?"

You might want to have an engineer inspect the chariot or the stadium racecourse.

Some of these **interrogatories** could be taken at the trial, but it simplifies the trial and lessens the time needed—as well as takes out any element of suprise—when answers have been obtained before trial and there is an opportunity to check into the validity of any information given.

To discover your injuries, the defendants could request that you submit to a medical examination. You will also have a report from your own doctor.

Trial

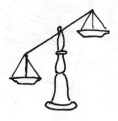

If a settlement cannot be reached then a trial, which may be some time in coming, will follow.

Voir dire—the method by which a jury is selected—is conducted after a case has been called and the parties are present and ready to proceed.

The right to a jury trial is guaranteed by the Constitution but may be waived, thus allowing the court—through the judge—to make a decision based upon the facts of the case.

FACTS: Because you brought the action, it is your job, through your attorney, to persuade the court of the merits of your case. You bear the burden of proof. How convincing does your evidence have to be for you to recover? **YOU'RE THE JUDGE!**

DECISION: It is your duty in a civil case (as opposed to a criminal case) to establish the truth of your claim by a clear "preponderance of the credible evidence"—that is, by presenting evidence having a more convincing effect on the jury than does the defendant's.

Your attorney makes his **opening statement** to the court—telling of your injuries and that he will prove that the defendants are all guilty of **negligence**—a breach of their duty to care for your safety—which breach caused your injury and damages.

The defendants (each with their own attorney) present their opening statements. They all deny any negligence and tell what their evidence will later prove.

Each side now presents its case to the court. You go first. Your attorney calls his witnesses—fellow spectators who witnessed the accident, your doctor, the engineer, and you. The engineer presents the physical evidence showing how the chariot wheel was defectively manufactured. Can your witnesses be cross-examined?

FACTS: The defendants' attorneys may **cross-examine**—ask questions of your witnesses—after they testify. What may they question your witnesses about? **YOU'RE THE JUDGE!**

DECISION: They must restrict their questions to the coverage of the original testimony by your witnesses.

Next, the defendants present their cases, calling their own doctor, engineer and themselves. They attempt to refute your testimony and show they are not negligent. You also have the opportunity to cross-examine their witnesses.

Now, assuming that there is no **rebuttal**—reexamination of your witnesses in an attempt to refute their testimony—or that any motions for summary judgment without further evidence, mistrial or dismissal of the case have been denied, then, you are ready for your **closing statement.**

Your attorney summarizes to the court what he feels he has proved and then asks the court "to find for us in an amount that you feel is just and necessary."

Of course, the defendants tell the jury "The plaintiffs have not proven their case and, therefore, should not recover any damages."

Burden of Proof

The court then instructs the jury on: what the law is regarding negligence; the **burden of proof**—your duty to prove those facts necessary to win a judgment by a clear preponderance of the credible evidence; and the rules to be followed in deciding the case.

The jury then deliberates until it has reached a **verdict**—decision by court or jury of issues—and finds for a party on each issue submitted to them by the court.

The losing party may, with certain restrictions, appeal any decision. Any appeal will extend the time necessary to complete the procedure from the filing of a complaint to a final decision.

ODDS & ENDS....

You versus Yani, Mikali & Greco - Could You Recover?

FACTS: Your complaint alleged in part:
"While I was attending the chariot races, the defendant, Yani, negligently drove and crashed his chariot, causing me severe and permanent injuries.

The owner of the chariot, Mikali, was negligent in that he was aware of Yani's propensity for reckless driving, but made no effort to prevent such driving.

Greco was negligent in the manufacturing of the chariot. Had he taken proper precautions, the wheel would not have come off and injured me."

The complaint also alleged that Greco had been notified of several other crashes of his defective chariots.

The stadium had no wire screening to protect spectators from flying debris. Could you recover damages for your injuries? **YOU'RE THE JUDGE!**

DECISION: "The defendants are all negligent," the court held. "They breached their duty to insure your safety: Yani by driving recklessly, Mikali by fostering such reckless driving (and further by not constructing proper screening to protect the spectators), and Greco by manufacturing defective chariots."

The defendants' breaches caused your injuries and damages. That is, you would not have received the injuries but for their negligence. You were awarded damages for your pain and suffering, medical expenses and lost pay from missing work due to the injuries.

You now have a basic understanding of how a legal dispute or controversy winds its way through the legal system.

2

AMATEURS & ELIGIBILITY

WHAT'S IT ABOUT?

Amateurs & Eligibility spells out amateurs' rights and responsibilities regarding their eligibility to participate in amateur sports for their school or in other competitions.

These rights and responsibilities govern both the athletes' and the schools' conduct, covering areas from recruiting and the granting of scholarships to grades, conduct and awards. What is "redshirting?" Do amateur athletes have to be well-groomed?

Podunk University
1211 University Drive
Justice, Georgia 22220
Member NCAA

Dear Student-Athletes:

Congratulations! You've been accepted to Podunk University, home of the "Fighting Wabaws."

As recent changes in the law have made amateur sports increasingly subject to judicial scrutiny, it is important that you become aware of your rights and responsibilities.

In the past, amateur sports were more recreational in nature. Now, due to television and the increased attraction by spectators and participants, amateur sports have become "big business." Although amateur sports and money are not supposed to mix, money does have a definite effect upon your future and your rights.

If you are successful in athletics, prosperity may lie ahead in pro sports, however slim the chance. Thus, you have a significant financial stake in the decisions and events affecting your eligibility.

Therefore, in order to protect your rights, you should be aware of amateur status and eligibility. For more information, refer to your college's manual or to the rules of your high school athletic association.

Best of Luck,

President, Podunk University

WHAT IS AN AMATEUR?

The International Olympic Committee (IOC) states that an athlete, to be an **amateur**—"must pursue athletic activity as an 'avocation' (hobby), not as a 'vocation' (occupation), and must engage in sports solely for the educational, physical, mental, and social benefits obtained." Simply put, the athlete must compete for fun, not for pay.

> FACTS: Jim Thorpe competed in the 1912 Olympic Games, winning gold medals in the pentathlon and decathlon events. Two years earlier he had competed, for pay, in a semi-pro baseball league. Should Thorpe have been ruled a professional and "stripped" of his medals? **YOU'RE THE JUDGE!**

> DECISION: Thorpe was stripped of his medals for having competed while a professional.
> In 1985, the IOC restored Thorpe's medals to his family. This was due, in part, to the fading distinction—in the eligibility rules for Olympic athletes—between an amateur and a professional.

Professionals are now allowed to compete in some Olympic competitions.

This could signal the end of the rule holding that an athlete is ineligible to take part in amateur sports "if he enters into a contract or agreement to compete as a professional athlete."

Some amateur athletes, including Olympic hopefuls, may now receive funds for traveling, training and living expenses, as well as for product endorsements. Some of the funds are placed in trust until the athletes no longer compete as amateurs.

The National Collegiate Athletic Association (NCAA) definition of an amateur differs from that of the IOC in several respects.

The NCAA permits athletes to compete professionally in one sport and yet retain their amateur status in others.

This change would have allowed Thorpe to compete as a professional in baseball, but still retain his amateur status in track and field.

> FACTS: Al and Babe were professional baseball players while attending Sports U. (where they wanted to play tennis and golf). Could they compete with or against amateurs? **YOU'RE THE JUDGE!**

> DECISION: These professional student-athletes can compete with or against amateurs in both intercollegiate tennis and golf, but not in baseball.

None of these definitions of an amateur, however, are binding upon the courts in deciding cases relating to amateur athletics.

THE NCAA

The National Collegiate Athletic Association (NCAA), a voluntary organization of almost all major colleges and universities, was formed in 1906 to regulate and supervise collegiate athletics in the U.S.

The most powerful of the associations regulating college athletics, the NCAA is divided into three divisions (based in part upon the school's or its athletic facility's size). All divisions are subject to NCAA rules and regulations governing education and athletics in their division.

The rules cover admittance requirements, academic standing and recruiting and eligibility. They also provide for enforcement and sanctions.

FACTS: "I was improperly recruited to attend Ames U," confessed Joe. Could Joe, the school, or both be penalized? If so, what penalties? **YOU'RE THE JUDGE!**

DECISION: The rules apply to schools as well as to athletes. Sanctions to the athlete may be temporary or permanent ineligibility. Sanctions to the school may be: probation, loss of television appearances, forfeit of television or post-season proceeds or a loss of scholarships.

In addition, any school (on probation for violations in a sport) which is found guilty of additional violations in that sport within five years will be given the **"death penalty"**—they may have to drop that sport for a minimum of two years.

Ames U. was prohibited from giving football scholarships and playing football for one year. In addition, they could only play road games during the second year, and were banned from post-season play for two years.

LET'S HAVE A CONFERENCE

Although collegiate conferences, such as the Athletic College Conference (ACC) or Big Ten, generally have rules and regulations that are the same as, or similar to, those of the NCAA to which they belong, such rules may differ.

FACTS: Bubba Jackson, a star collegiate football player, accepted an airplane ride from a pro football team interested in drafting him. According to his college conference's rules, this made Jackson a professional. He was declared ineligible to compete for the school's baseball team.

The NCAA permits a college athlete to be a pro in one sport

while competing as an amateur in another. Could Jackson continue to play for the college baseball team? **YOU'RE THE JUDGE!**

DECISION: No. A student-athlete must abide by his school's conference rules as well as those of the NCAA. Jackson could not play on the college baseball team.

SCHOLARSHIPS

Typically, student-athletes receive **financial aid**—school funds such as scholarships, grants, loans or on-campus work—over which the school has some determining authority.

Scholarships are awarded on a one-year basis and are renewable for up to four years. Renewal is not automatic, but is based upon athletic and educational performance. Exceptions relate to academic awards and some loans. Prospective student-athletes may be denied an athletic scholarship unless they meet certain minimum academic standards.

Generally, the amount of financial aid a student-athlete may receive without jeopardizing his eligibility is based upon the total amount necessary for tuition and fees, room and board and required books and materials.

Student-athletes are prohibited from receiving financial aid other than from the school (boosters), if it is related to athletic ability or participation. This prohibition does not apply to any earnings as a pro in a sport other than the athlete's college sport.

FACTS: "I was offered money from a local booster club to help pay expenses for attending and playing football for Aztec U," admitted E.Z. Smith. "The help was offered because of my athletic ability." If E.Z. accepted the money, would it jeopardize his eligibility as a student-athlete? **YOU'RE THE JUDGE!**

DECISION: Yes. This would be aid based upon athletic ability other than from the school. E.Z. would be ineligible to compete as an amateur.

A major difference exists between the IOC and the NCAA regarding financial aid.

FACTS: Bob received financial aid from his college in return for playing football. If he became ineligible or left the sport for personal reasons, the aid could be cancelled.

Bob quit the football team and asked, "If I decide to prepare for the shotput for the upcoming Olympics, will I have an eligibility problem? " **YOU'RE THE JUDGE!**

DECISION: Under the IOC standard, Bob may receive assistance, but it cannot be because of his athletic ability, as it may with the NCAA. Therefore, if the IOC definition of an amateur were rigorously enforced, Bob would be ineligible for Olympic competition

Therefore, even though the IOC now allows certain professionals to compete in some Olympic sports, an aspiring Olympic athlete should insure that his financial aid arrangement is structured to resemble an educational grant, with receipt dependent upon fulfillment of scholastic obligations, not athletic ability.

Could the way athletic scholarships are viewed by the courts present a problem?

FACTS: A prospective college basketball player, "Hoops," was awarded an athletic scholarship. It was withdrawn, however, when the college learned that his high school grade point average was miscalculated, thus making him ineligible for the scholarship under NCAA rules.

Another high school athlete, Marston, was also awarded a college athletic scholarship. It too, was revoked after Marston—who originally did not participate because of low grades—raised his grades but then did not report for football.

Hoops and Marston sued their colleges. "We would like to keep the scholarships," they declared. "Receiving them was not contingent on our being able to play basketball or football. Can we keep our scholarships?" **YOU'RE THE JUDGE!**

DECISION: The courts treated the relationship between the athletes and their schools as contracts (agreements)—the schools would award the scholarships if the athletes played. Because the athletes could not live up to their agreements to play, they were denied the scholarships.

If the scholarship is treated as a contract—where the athlete must participate in return for the consideration of the scholarship—then the athlete may be considered to be playing the sport as a vocation (occupation) rather than as an avocation (hobby), thus jeopardizing amateur status!

FACTS: Tony and Dan received scholarships to attend Quinsigamond U. The scholarships were contingent upon the athletes' athletic performance for the school's football team.

A new tax ruling held that the total amount of the scholarships, including room and board, must be considered income for tax purposes. Will this make Tony and Dan pros for receiving money to play football? Will they lose their amateur status?

DECISION: **YOU'RE THE JUDGE!**

If the courts treated these arrangements as educational grants, the grant would be viewed as a gift, under the condition that the athlete maintain eligibility, but without the risk of loss of amateur status.

FACTS: The players and coaches of the Correcto University badminton team did not file disclosure affidavits listing all financial aid and benefits received—from the school or others—and also listing anything promised to them. Were the players and the school declared ineligible for the NCAA championships? **YOU'RE THE JUDGE!**

DECISION: Yes, both were declared ineligible. The affidavits help the NCAA make sure that schools comply with financial aid rules. Individual athletes or a team will lose their eligibility if they or their head coach fail to complete the affidavits.

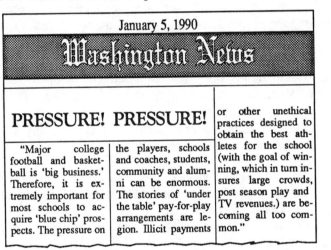

January 5, 1990

Washington News

PRESSURE! PRESSURE!

"Major college football and basketball is 'big business.' Therefore, it is extremely important for most schools to acquire 'blue chip' prospects. The pressure on the players, schools and coaches, students, community and alumni can be enormous. The stories of 'under the table' pay-for-play arrangements are legion. Illicit payments or other unethical practices designed to obtain the best athletes for the school (with the goal of winning, which in turn insures large crowds, post season play and TV revenues.) are becoming all too common."

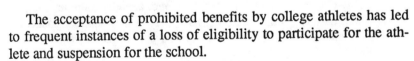

The acceptance of prohibited benefits by college athletes has led to frequent instances of a loss of eligibility to participate for the athlete and suspension for the school.

FACTS: Davis was thrown off his college football team for accepting money from boosters. As he no longer was eligible to play amateur football, could Davis immediately play as a pro? **YOU'RE THE JUDGE!**

DECISION: The National Football League's (NFL)"Red Grange Rule" prohibited Davis from playing both collegiate and pro football in the same season.

One case is somewhat different from the normal situation. This is where an athlete or prospective player accepts aid in the form of money or otherwise.

FACTS: "Skates," while playing "amateur" hockey in Canada, accepted compensation for three years while in high school, and also for two years between high school and college. Was he ineligible to play in college? **YOU'RE THE JUDGE!**

DECISION: Skates was ineligible. Compensation for the two years between high school and college was not in connection with his obtaining an education. This may mean that had he not accepted the pay for the intervening two years, he would have been eligible, as the other three years pay was in conjunction with his obtaining an education.

NON-APPROVED CAMPS

Rules denying eligibility to athletes participating in events not approved by their school (summer camps or clinics) will generally be upheld as long as they have a legitimate purpose. A few such purposes include: preventing undesirable consequences (exploiting the athlete) or promoting academics and equal opportunity for all athletes. Thus, participation in post high school athletic competitions must be approved. Furthermore, participation in events after enrollment in college is also restricted.

However, the rules must be reasonable and must only affect those whose conduct it is necessary to control.

FACTS: To prevent athletes from receiving pay for playing, all athletes were prohibited by their schools from playing in all-star games, unless given permission.

Jorn said, "Without approval, I played in an all-star basketball game to raise money for charity."

Ray played in an all-star baseball game, attended summer camp where baseball clinics were held and played in a summer basketball league. Were Jorn and Ray still eligible to play as amateurs? **YOU'RE THE JUDGE!**

DECISION: Jorn would probably still be eligible as it may be unreasonable to prevent him from playing in a charity event. Ray would lose his eligibility if he had not been approved to participate in his activities.

FACTS: Tom was a member of his school's hockey team. A school rule read: Students may not "participate in hockey during the off-season, attend non-approved camps or clinics or participate on independent hockey teams."

Tom wanted to play on such a team. He contended, "The rule is unreasonable. It denies me my constitutional right to equal protection—that is, to be treated like the others who will be permitted to play." Was the rule unreasonable? **YOU'RE THE JUDGE!**

DECISION: The rule was not unreasonable. Tom could become a member of an approved hockey team, or he could attend an approved camp or clinic.

FACTS: Several parents challenged a rule suspending varsity athletes for attending "special" summer camps. They claimed, "The rule's objective of fostering interschool competitions as an aid in the preparation for life, interferes with our authority in child rearing, family choice, private life and right to send our children to camp." Could the parents send their children to camp? **YOU'RE THE JUDGE!**

DECISION: No. The rule was reasonable. It did not interfere with parents sending their children to camps giving an over-all activity program, but only restricted attendance at those camps specializing in football or basketball.

The purpose of the rule was to control over-zealous parents, teachers and coaches and to achieve competitive balance with those who could not attend and to avoid undue pressure on the students.

HOW LONG MAY I PLAY?

To prevent schools from retaining athletes until they are either needed, or have matured athletically, certain rules restricting the time within which an athlete is eligible to compete (generally to four years in high school) exist. The object of such rules is to prevent **"redshirting"**—the intentional retention or keeping back of athletes.

Such rules may only apply to students who want excess eligibility in order to continue participating athletically.

FACTS: John passed the eighth grade. But because his parents felt their son was not ready for the ninth grade, he was forced to repeat the eighth.

After competing for the school football team in the ninth-eleventh grades, John was declared ineligible. He wanted to play, and asked the the court to "allow me." What was the court's decision? What if John had failed the eighth grade? What if he had dropped out of school to help his family overcome a desperate financial problem? **YOU'RE THE JUDGE!**

DECISION: A rule providing that a student repeating a grade which he has passed loses his fourth year of eligibility in high school would be upheld.

However, if John had failed the eighth grade, he then would not lose his fourth year of eligibility. But John could not compete the first semester after failing. This "forced" time off would allow him time to study. And if John had dropped out of school to help his family, the rule probably would not be applied to deny his competing after four years.

FACTS: Guy was 19 at the start of his fourth year of high school. He wanted to play for the football team but his school had a rule prohibiting students turning 19 before Sept. 1 from competing. "Can I play?" Guy pleaded. **YOU'RE THE JUDGE!**

DECISION: No. As long as such a rule has a legitimate purpose related to the school's interest in assuring fair competition and minimizing the risk of having its high school athletes compete against older, more skilled athletes, it will be enforced.

Maturity may also be considered in deciding eligibility. Some states have eligibility standards which allow students with "advanced, or slower, rates of maturity" to compete at team levels best suited to their stage of maturity. This allows certain students to play above or below their age group. It may also extend their period of eligibility.

REDSHIRTING & HARDSHIP

Redshirting—the intentional retention or keeping back of athletes—is a practice also used by most colleges. The NCAA allows this practice under what is called the "five-year rule." This may be done solely to allow an athlete to continue to compete for the school.

FACTS: Andy was a promising freshman quarterback, but the team already had Peter, a potential All-American. Could Andy be redshirted for his freshman year—making it possible for him to spend his first year on scholarship without playing—and then, still have four years eligibility remaining? **YOU'RE THE JUDGE!**

DECISION: Yes. Andy could be redshirted for his freshman year, thus taking five years to use his four years of eligibility for football. Although he would attend school his first year, he would not play football until the second year.

Had Andy attended a junior college or transferred to another four year school after two years, the same rule would apply. He could take three years to use two years eligibility.

A student-athlete may be granted an additional year of eligibility for reasons of hardship (unless the athlete had been redshirted), such as an incapacity resulting from an injury or illness. The injury or illness, as long as it occurs after the athlete has reported for team practice, does not have to result from athletics. It could, for instance, happen while the athlete was working or while just walking across campus.

FACTS: "I broke my toe," moaned Frank. He was injured in the sixth football game of an eleven game schedule.

"I fractured my ankle," groaned Tom. He was injured in the fifth game of a twenty-seven game basketball schedule.

Both would not play for the remainder of that season. Could either of them ask for a hardship ruling, and thereby retain that year of eligibility? **YOU'RE THE JUDGE!**

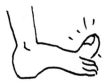

DECISION: If Frank or Tom had not played in more than 20% of their teams games (including scrimmages with outside competition), or had not played in more than two events, whichever figure was greater, and the injury or illness occurred in the first half of the season, then hardship would apply.

The sixth game would leave five remaining. Therefore, Frank's injury occurred in the second half of the season. He could not be granted hardship.

Tom's injury occurred in the first half of the season and he had not played in 20% of his teams games (20% of twenty-seven games equals the sixth game). Tom could apply for hardship to save that year's eligibility.

"BONA FIDE" TRANSFERS

Students transferring between high schools or colleges are subject to rules generally requiring that residency requirements and grades be considered. These rules are designed to discourage ill-advised transfers and prevent improper recruiting.

The NCAA requires that a student-athlete maintain certain minimum grades for eligibility. In addition, student-athletes may be required to attend the school that they are transferring to for up to one year before becoming eligible to participate in intercollegiate sports competition for that school.

FACTS: "My school was placed on probation," objected Lou.

Bill complained, "My school did not have a football team." Both transferred to Sports U. Will they have to sit out a year if they want to play football there? **YOU'RE THE JUDGE!**

DECISION: There are exceptions to the one-year residency rule. One applies to college students transferring from schools placed on probation. These students may be eligible immediately.

In addition, students transferring from a school which has dropped the sport (or never sponsored it to begin with) generally do not have to sit out a year before being allowed to participate.

Athletes attending a college which is not an NCAA member will not be governed by NCAA rules.

FACTS: Archie, the football coach at M.V. State, was leaving to coach at Arkansas-Pine Bluff. Fifty of his players wanted to transfer there to continue playing for Coach Archie. Will the players have to sit out a year before becoming eligible to play football at Pine Bluff? **YOU'RE THE JUDGE!**

DECISION: Pine Bluff is a member of the National Association of Intercollegiate Athletics (NAIA), which permits transferees to become eligible to play immediately.

High school transfers are also subject to the one-year transfer rule. Generally, unless a transfer is due to the student-athlete's parents making a **bona fide**—good faith—move from one school district to another—or for some other "unavoidable circumstance" (health, compelling personal reason, work)—such a student will be required to sit out one year before being allowed to participate.

FACTS: A high school football player, Walter, said dejectedly, "After having married, I was required to transfer due to a rule prohibiting attendance by married students. After transferring, my parents moved into our new apartment." Was this a bona fide move, which would enable Walter to play football without waiting a year? **YOU'RE THE JUDGE!**

DECISION: The high school association declared that the parents move was not a bona fide or good faith move and declared Walter ineligible. This was unfortunate in that Walter had no choice but to transfer.

Most often, unless a student's transfer is to a legitimate guardian (not to a relative's or friend's home with the intention of circumventing the transfer rule), eligibility will be denied. But, where the move is necessary, eligibility will not be denied.

FACTS: John moved with his family from Vermont to Texas. His father was transferred in his job.
   Although John had played basketball in high school in Vermont, he was not recruited to play in Texas. "When I enrolled in school, I was declared ineligible to play ball because of the one-year transfer rule," muttered John. "Could I play immediately without sitting out a year?" **YOU'RE THE JUDGE!**

DECISION: Yes. The rule's purpose was to prevent recruiting, not to unfairly deprive John and his family of important rights—the right to travel and the right to privacy in family matters.

Warren moved to Indiana to live with his brother, who was appointed Warren's legal guardian. The move was due to "demoralizing and detrimental conditions" existing Warren's home and school environment in Florida (friends and teammates involved with drugs and ten sisters living in a two bedroom home). He was declared ineligible to participate in sports for one year. When Warren brought suit, the court held, "Although the school's objective in preventing recruitment and 'school jumping' was a proper concern, Warren's move was because of unavoidable circumstances." Warren could participate immediately.

If a school district has such a rule, would it have be applied to all of the schools in that district?

> FACTS: Seven students, after graduating from a Lutheran parochial school wanted to attend the only Lutheran high school available to them.
>
> One of them explained what happened, "Upon transferring to this school in another district, we were declared ineligible to participate athletically for one year. Unless we are allowed to transfer and retain our athletic eligibility, we will be denied the right granted others— to participate." Could the students retain their eligibility after transferring? **YOU'RE THE JUDGE!**

> DECISION: Yes. Because some schools were exempted from its coverage, the rule was found unconstitutional. To be found constitutional, the rule would have to apply to all schools in the district.

> FACTS: Susan said, "After finishing the ninth grade, I transferred to another school but was declared ineligible to compete in interscholastic athletics for one year."
>
> Susan and her parents felt, "The decision to transfer had nothing to do with athletics; Susan was not recruited. She only wanted to attend a school that would better prepare her for college." Susan wanted to play field hockey. Could she? **YOU'RE THE JUDGE!**

> DECISION: The transfer rule carries out the state's interest in protecting students from recruiting. The students were aware of the rule. Only in a situation in which the student has no control, such as a family work transfer, will the rule be waived.

Everyone has a fundamental right to freedom of travel. If a transfer rule attempts to restrict that right, the rule—to be upheld—must be supported by a compelling interest (such as to prevent improper recruiting).

AM I STILL ELIGIBLE?

Between the completion of high school, and while in college, a student-athlete must be concerned with eligibility rules. Student-

athletes must sign (under penalty of loss of eligibility), a statement submitting information related to eligibility, recruiting, financial aid, amateur status and gambling.

FACTS: Charles said, "Prior to enrolling at Aztec U., I signed a contract with an agent, obtained a loan which did not have to be paid back, received benefits and services due to my athletic ability and not available to other students, received excessive expenses for reporting to and visiting the Zumbas pro volleyball team and signed a pro contract to play for pay with the Zumbas." Did any of these activities affect Charles' eligibility when he enrolled at Aztec U.? **YOU'RE THE JUDGE!**

DECISION: All of the activities were in violation of NCAA rules. Charles was not eligible to participate in athletics at Aztec U.

FACTS: Bob, Susan, and Cheryl participated, respectively, in track and field, golf and tennis competitions. They received expenses based upon how they finished. Depending on how well they did, expenses may have exceeded the actual and necessary expenses allowed. Was this permitted? **YOU'RE THE JUDGE!**

DECISION: No. Receiving such expenses would be considered taking pay for participation. That is not permitted.

FACTS: Edgar attended Gonzo U. He explained what happened. "A local booster club outside the school, and an agent, liked my athletic ability. They paid my expenses for attendance. Did this affect my eligibility?" **YOU'RE THE JUDGE!**

DECISION: Yes. Financial assistance, based upon athletic ability, paid by an outside source, is not permitted. Edgar lost his eligibility to participate.

FACTS: All of the members of the Wilder U. football team received tickets to home games. Some of the guys decided to sell the tickets.

The price printed on the ticket was $10. John sold his for $5; Bob sold his for $15. Sam sold his for $10, while Gabe traded his for a free round of golf. Was the eligibility of any of these players jeopardized? **YOU'RE THE JUDGE!**

DECISION: Yes. They all used their athletic skill for pay and have received extra benefits not available to the general student body.

FACTS: Wearrite Sports Co. donated equipment to Aqua U. athletes and then publicized that fact in their ads in the local newspaper. Was the eligibility of the athletes jeopardized? **YOU'RE THE JUDGE!**

DECISION: No, provided the students names or pictures were not used, either in the ads or on any equipment or other commercial items, such as T-shirts or posters.

The students would forfeit their eligibility only if their names and/or pictures were used with their permission.

FACTS: Judson, a football player at All-American U., signed autographs at a prep rally held at the local mall. Did this jeopardize Judson's eligibility? **YOU'RE THE JUDGE!**

DECISION: Yes. An athlete cannot use his name for any commercial business. According to NCAA rules, by signing the autographs, Judson became a pro! He forfeited his remaining eligibility.

A student-athlete, or the athlete's parents, cannot accept any gift or "extra benefit" of value from an agent, company or team unless the same is offered to all of the students at that school.

FACTS: Vinnie, a star athlete at Aqua U, listed what he was offered from local businesses. "I was offered, free of charge: movie tickets, dinners, use of rental cars, sports equipment and legal and medical services at a reduced cost." Could Vinnie accept any of these without jeopardizing his eligibility? **YOU'RE THE JUDGE!**

DECISION: Unless these same products and services were available to the general student body under the same conditions, Vinnie could not accept any of them without jeopardizing his eligibility.

FACTS: Two hockey players received room, board, book and other expenses while playing as prep players in Canadian amateur hockey. They were declared ineligible to compete in college hockey in the U.S. due to receiving this assistance. Did the court require the school to declare them eligible? **YOU'RE THE JUDGE!**

DECISION: "Conditions were much different in Canada than in the U.S. The athletes were required to play for teams often a considerable distance from home, but received no more assistance than would players in the U.S. In order to not deprive these athletes of the opportunity to play, they were allowed to accept such assistance and still maintain eligibility for collegiate play in the U.S."

RECRUITING BY SCHOOLS

The NCAA provides rules concerning the recruiting of prospective student-athletes—athletes who have not enrolled in a college and have not exhausted their high school eligibility, but who have been contacted by a college. Contact for recruiting, with certain limitations, may be by providing transportation to the college, entertaining the athlete or his family, or by telephone contact or visits to the athlete or his family.

The rules also allow for physical exams of prospective student-athletes, reimbursement of expenses and the exchange of financial aid information. All of these areas are strictly covered by rules intended to insure proper recruiting.

FACTS: Alan stated, "I was given financial aid by a college. A booster club gave me cash, a car, clothes and special discounts. Also, they bought my football tickets for a higher price than printed on the ticket." Did this jeopardize Alan's eligibility to participate in athletics for his college? **YOU'RE THE JUDGE!**

DECISION: Yes. The rules do not permit financial aid, such as: improper inducements, cash, promises of work, special discounts, use of autos or clothing. Alan was declared ineligible to participate.

Also, NCAA rules do not permit: contacts (other than as allowed—whether with the athlete or his school), certain publicity and press conferences, nor do they allow certain entertainment of the athlete, his family or friends.

RECRUITING BY PROS

The NCAA has specific rules that apply to amateur eligibility for athletes who are considering competing as professionals.

FACTS: "I was paid to play pro football for the Wreckers, but I'd still like to play on my college baseball team," said Joe.

Before enrolling in Charles College, Joe tried out with the Wreckers, received expenses for the tryout and was employed to give instructions. Was Joe still eligible to play baseball for his college? **YOU'RE THE JUDGE!**

DECISION: Joe could take pay in one sport and still be eligible in another. He could retain his eligibility as long as the try-out was not against another team and as long as he only received necessary expenses. However, Joe could not try out during school.

Joe's school's or conference's rules may differ.

Joe would not be eligible for baseball if he had taken or accepted a promise of pay for baseball, had negotiated or entered into a contract to play pro baseball, had requested to be placed on the pro baseball draft list, or if he had received any salary, expenses (not permitted) or other financial assistance based upon his athletic ability or participation.

FACTS: Joe agreed to be represented by an agent, Herman. Also, Joe was paid to promote and to allow his name and picture to be used for an ad for "Joe's Fly-Fast Tennis Shoes." Was Joe's eligibility jeopardized? **YOU'RE THE JUDGE!**

DECISION: Yes. Joe could not agree to be represented by an agent for baseball and still be eligible to compete as an amateur in other sports unless such representation was for only that one sport. If Joe agreed to be represented generally, he would be ineligible in all sports.

Joe forfeited his eligibility in all sports by accepting pay and for allowing his name and picture to be used commercially.

FACTS: Shelton, while attending State U. signed a pro contract with the American Basketball Association (ABA). Despite a void—no good—contract, the school declared him ineligible to participate.

Shelton argued, "The contract was unenforceable because I was induced by fraud and was pressured. The school should let me play." Should Shelton have been allowed to play? **YOU'RE THE JUDGE!**

DECISION: The court held, "The rule requiring ineligibility was reasonable in attempting to preserve amateurism in college athletics. Furthermore, the school would have no way of knowing whether or not the contract was void. If they allowed this, then anyone could sign a contract, then allege that the contract was unenforceable and play in college while having the option of entering the pros at any time."

All participants in Division I, NCAA basketball tournaments are required to sign an affidavit stating that they have not signed with an agent, nor will they during a tournament.

This action allows the NCAA to not just penalize the athlete's school, but to pursue the player and his agent for any damages which the school might suffer (fine for playing an ineligible player).

NCAA schools have counseling panels to give student-athletes information about careers, schools, representation, determination of worth and rules. These panels may not accompany an athlete in meeting with a pro team, nor may their assistance result in a contract.

Lee News   December 12, 1978
AMATEUR SPORT'S ACT

"In the 1972 Olympics, because of improper medications, missed starting times, improper conduct and officiating, medals were lost or forfeited by U.S. Olympic Team athletes. The U.S. Olympic Committee was charged with having inadequate authority, insufficient experience and a great reluctance to change—selecting committee members without consideration to merit."

Out of all the controversy brought about by these problems, the Amateur Sport's Act of 1978 was born. Its goal is to promote, develop and support physical fitness, safety and participation in U.S. amateur athletics, and to resolve disputes and coordinate athletic activity by U.S. amateurs.

LETTER OF INTENT

Prospective college student-athletes may sign a National Letter of Intent to attend a certain college. Generally, this signing takes place during recruiting.

FACTS: "Switch," after signing a letter of intent to attend and play volleyball for G.U., decided to transfer to another school.

Could he do so without a loss of eligibility? **YOU'RE THE JUDGE!**

DECISION: The letter committed Switch to attending and participating for G.U. After the letter was signed, only G.U. was permitted to have contact with him. Switch may be faced with up to two years of ineligibility should he transfer to another school.

Exceptions would be where his school was either placed on probation, or dropped that sport and students then transferred. In such situations, the students would not lose their eligibility.

For a National Letter of Intent to be official, the signature of a parent or legal guardian, or whomever is looking after the student's best interests at that time, is required (unless the student has reached the age of eighteen or other legal age).

REPORT CARDS & CREDITS

The primary objective of schools should be the encouragement and support of scholastic, not athletic, achievement.

FACTS: A state rule barred public school students from extracurricular activities for six weeks if they failed any course. This was called the "no-pass, no-play rule."

Affected students sued their schools, arguing, "The rule discriminated against us by not allowing us to play, but allowing others to." Should the students who failed a course have been allowed to play before the six weeks were up? **YOU'RE THE JUDGE!**

DECISION: The court held, "No. Grade maintenance rules, designed to insure academic achievement, which may prevent participation by those unable to perform academically—either before acceptance to, or while attending, college—will generally be upheld."

Admissions to college are governed by rules requiring a certain grade point average and fulfillment of a specified number of credits. These rules are intended to insure that only academically qualified student-athletes become eligible to participate in sports. This will prevent athletes, thought to have little or no chance of academic success, from attending.

FACTS: Barbara was declared ineligible to participate in intercollegiate athletics. Her high school, in computing her grade point average, excluded her mark in physical education. Without that mark, her grade point average fell below the average required for participation. Should the school have included the physical education mark? **YOU'RE THE JUDGE!**

DECISION: "The policy of the NCAA not to interfere with a high school clearly furthers the objective of admitting and allowing to participate individuals who will be students first and athletes second," said the court.

Barbara will have to improve her grades before she will be eligible to participate.

Students must meet the NCAA's "satisfactory progress" guidelines to remain eligible to participate in intercollegiate sports.

These rules must be reasonable and must only affect those unable to maintain academic requirements. Thus, where students were not allowed to participate even after maintaining suitable grades, the rule was held unenforceable. The students were allowed to participate.

Other decisions based on similar facts did not allow students to participate.

FACTS: Five high school basketball players were recruited to play in college. The college was warned that the players did not qualify under the NCAA's grade point average rule. The athletes were nonetheless granted scholarships and continued to play.

When the NCAA declared both the athletes and their college ineligible to participate in post-season play, the school asked a court to decide if the students could play. How did the court decide? **YOU'RE THE JUDGE!**

DECISION: The court decided, "The NCAA's rule requiring athletes to possess and maintain a certain grade point average was a reasonable rule, intended to insure academically prepared students before allowing them to participate in athletics. Neither the school nor the athletes could participate in post-season play."

The courts felt that if they allowed these students to participate, then schools would recruit academically unqualified .

In order to become eligible, the students would have to "sit out" until they improved their grades.

FACTS: Ben played for the TriCity College football team. After attending summer school, he was told by TriCity, "These credits will allow you to remain eligible for the football team." But Ben was then declared ineligible when the school decided not to accept the credits.

"The school lied to me. Because I didn't have a chance to impress the scouts, I was not drafted in a higher round," Ben complained. Was the school responsible? **YOU'RE THE JUDGE!**

DECISION: If TriCity knew that the summer course would not help Ben retain his eligibility, and failed to warn him of this, then they would be liable for any loss in potential earnings.

However, if Ben knew that the summer course was not acceptable, then the school would not be liable.

In any event, there is no way of knowing how Ben would have performed had he played. It might well be too speculative to determine what his damages, if any, would have been.

PERSONAL CONDUCT

Podunk University
1211 University Drive
Justice, Georgia 33323

Dear Parents, Student-Athletes & Concerned Citizens:

There have been many recent court decisions involving the conduct, grooming and marriage of student-athletes. Further decisions concerning sanctions, expulsions and awards in amateur sports are also noteworthy.

Issues, which in the past were not subject to judicial scrutiny, now are. The law is playing an increasingly major role in controlling the affairs of amateur sports.

As eligibility may be jeopardized, it is in your best interest that you become familiar with these issues and decisions.

Furthermore, these issues have (and will continue to have) an effect on student and community opinion and morale in amateur sports.

Thanking you for your attention,

School Board 12, State Athletic
Conference and Podunk U., member of NCAA

A COACH'S AUTHORITY

A coach has the most frequent and direct contact between an athlete and his school. While a coach may be granted broad authority to control an athlete's athletic life, this control must be reasonable.

Such authority includes the power to establish and maintain health and training rules, direct and conduct practices, issue instructions during practice and games and impose penalties for violations.

Can a coach control an athlete's private life?

FACTS: Zephyr High and its football coach adopted several rules. All players had to be dressed properly, according to standards set by the school, and had to "hustle" during practices.

The coach determined that Bob and Gary "did not hustle during the last practice, and they dressed improperly during the school vacation." Could the coach impose a penalty? **YOU'RE THE JUDGE!**

DECISION: If the school and coach had authority to adopt these rules, the hustling rule probably would be upheld as being necessary to prepare the team for competition. However, the rule would have to be reasonable.

The dress code might be necessary while the students were in school or traveling to athletic events, but would not be upheld for a violation taking place outside of school during an athlete's private life.

One court was asked to rule on whether or not a coach's authority extended to allowing a radio receiver in a quarterback's helmet. The court said, "No." The coach was suspended, the school's victory forfeited and the school was fined.

FREEDOM OF EXPRESSION

Two cases involving the limits of the school or coach's authority had to do with armbands.

In the first case, students who wore armbands to school in protest of the Vietnam war were expelled for violating a school policy.

The court held that this action deprived the students of their First Amendment right to freedom of expression. There was no evidence that the wearing of the armbands would cause a disruption. The second case had a different result.

FACTS: Coach Jones instituted a rule prohibiting "the players participating in demonstrations or protests."

A group of players informed the coach, "In protest of the policies of our opponent and their church, we intend to wear armbands to the next game." When the athletes did so, they were dismissed.

The school reasoned, "It was our intention to protect an invasion of the rights of others (fans) by avoiding a hostile expression by the athletes." Was the school's reasoning in dismissing the players proper? **YOU'RE THE JUDGE!**

DECISION: No. This was not enough to allow the school to dismiss the players. The school had to show that the wearing of the armbands would potentially cause disruption. Nevertheless, the students were not allowed to wear the armbands during the game.

A coach has authority to control his players as long as any rules are reasonable and do not affect a player's rights of freedom of expression or conduct. If these rights are affected, then—to enforce the rule—the school must show that any violation of the rule will cause disruption or otherwise substantially affect the operation of the school.

BENCHED!

FACTS: Two football players at Red U. were "benched" for missing practice. Xavier was benched for one game, Lora for five. Before the benchings, should they have been given an opportunity for hearings to determine if the penalties were warranted and proper? **YOU'RE THE JUDGE!**

DECISION: Lora should been given a hearing for such a severe penalty. Xavier's discipline was short. It did not require a hearing.

As the length of any disciplinary action increases, so too does the need for a fair and impartial hearing, with representation, to determine if the penalty is justified and proper.

HAVE YOU BEEN BEHAVING?

Good conduct rules—rules requiring appropriate conduct under penalty of sanctions—are often adopted by schools.

Generally, such rules will be upheld so long as they "notify the athletes of the conduct expected of them, and are related to a legitimate, athletics-concerned objective."

FACTS: Brenton High School had a rule providing:

"Anyone discovered using alcohol, drugs or tobacco will be expelled from athletic competition."

Five of the school's athletes were expelled for being at a party where there was drinking. However, they had the right to appeal and to due process—a fair and impartial hearing with representation. Should the athletes have been expelled? **YOU'RE THE JUDGE!**

DECISION: The court stated, "Seeking to deter athletes from using liquor was a legitimate and reasonable goal." The students were also afforded due process. They all had adequate notice of the rule and had admitted guilt. The purpose of such rules is to protect the health and welfare of the athletes.

Other similar cases have produced different results. In one, an athlete lost eligibility for violating a "beer rule"—providing for suspension for possession, consumption, or transportation of alcohol or drugs. The athlete was stopped, during the off-season, in a car containing beer. He brought suit to enjoin enforcement of the rule.

"The rule was unenforceable," ruled the court. The rule was too broad in that it presumed guilt for merely being present in the car.

Rules prohibiting smoking on school grounds generally have been

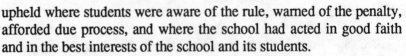

upheld where students were aware of the rule, warned of the penalty, afforded due process, and where the school had acted in good faith and in the best interests of the school and its students.

What if the students were not aware of another's violation of such a rule?

FACTS: West High School had a rule, "Anyone using or transporting drugs, alcohol or tobacco, in the presence of another, will be suspended." Was this rule too broad? Might it discipline someone not intended to be disciplined? **YOU'RE THE JUDGE!**

DECISION: The rule would probably be considered too broad. An athlete might be in the presence of someone carrying drugs, but without being aware of it. To expect one athlete to be responsible for others' violations would be stretching what otherwise may be a valid and enforceable rule.

In addition, the rule would not cover the situations where a drug was bought "over the counter" and had no effect on an athlete's ability to perform, or was taken under the direction of a physician.

Generally, subjecting an athlete to blood, urine or saliva testing for drugs will be in violation of the Fourth Amendment's prohibition against unreasonable search and seizure, as well as against the Fifth Amendment's privilege against self-incrimination. Such tests may also be an invasion of the athlete's privacy.

FACTS: Sharon, after failing a drug test, was declared ineligible to participate in the NCAA diving championships. He challenged the NCAA test as an invasion of her privacy. Did the court allow Sharon to participate? **YOU'RE THE JUDGE!**

DECISION: Yes. The court concluded, "The NCAA's drug testing as an eligibility rule was too broad. It did not show evidence that drugs would enhance performance. The test was ruled an invasion of privacy.

However, other courts have held that the testing was not an invasion of privacy of student-athletes' rights. Athletes, amateur and professional, continue to be asked to submit to such tests as are thought necessary to detect the use of banned drugs—which such athletes are prohibited from using. A player refusing to submit to such testing generally may be banned from participating.

For fighting in an NCAA college basketball game, a player will be ejected for that game. For a second offense, the player will be suspended for one additional game. But for a third offense, the penalty is suspension for the remainder of the season.

MARRIAGE & GROOMING

FACTS: A state high school association rule read:

"MARRIED STUDENTS SHALL NOT BE PERMITTED TO
PARTICIPATE IN ANY SPORTS."
Rule 203 D.F. S. School Board

This rule was adopted in an attempt to exclude married students
not only from athletics, but also from extracurricular activities. Did
the rule discriminate against married students? Could it be enforced? **YOU'RE THE JUDGE!**

DECISION: Even though the rule did not prohibit unmarried athletes from participating, no discrimination was found. The rule
could be enforced.

Such exclusionary rules have generally been upheld by the courts.
Reasons given have been that married students have responsibilities,
financial obligations and an essential need for an education greater
than that of other students. In addition, married athletes influence
other athletes. The married athletes may be held in some esteem and
their actions often emulated by other students. Furthermore, approval
of participation by married athletes might indicate that the school
condones teenage marriages.

Do you think that married athletes should be prohibited from participating in sports?

FACTS: Harold, a married student, hoped, "By playing football, I
might get a college scholarship."

A school district rule prevented married students from participating in athletics.

Harold felt that he was being discriminated against and should
be allowed to participate as were unmarried students. Should he
have been permitted to play?

DECISION: **YOU'RE THE JUDGE!**

FACTS: John was married and an excellent baseball player. "I
want to play in the pros," he said. Several colleges were interested
in granting him a scholarship. John's high school board prohibited
married students from participating in athletics.

John argued, "I am being deprived of the fundamental right of
marital privacy." Should John have been allowed to play?
YOU'RE THE JUDGE!

DECISION: Both school boards were enjoined from enforcing
marriage exclusion rules. Both athletes were permitted to participate.

LONG HAIR & EARRINGS!

Rules attempting to regulate the length and style of hair worn by athletes have also come under attack.

Reasons given by public school boards have been: interest in teaching hygiene, instilling discipline, compelling uniformity, and enhancing school and community spirit.

If a rule prescribing length or style of hair applies to all students and is a reasonable means of furthering a concern in the appearance and health of its students, then the rule will probably be upheld. Otherwise, it will not be enforceable.

> FACTS: Members of a high school tennis team were dismissed by their coach because of a violation of a grooming code regulating the length of hair and sideburns. The code only applied to athletes. "The length of our hair did not affect our playing ability," said the players.
>
> Another coach attempted to enforce a hair code during the off-season. Were the grooming codes enforceable? **YOU'RE THE JUDGE!**
>
> DECISION: The courts held, "The rules were violations of the athletes' fundamental rights to determine their own hair style and personal appearance." There was no compelling necessity for the rules.

May a school prohibit students from wearing earrings while attending class?

> FACTS: Kevin and Andy, members of their high school football team, bragged, "We wore earrings to class."
>
> Their school district banned them from wearing earrings while attending classes. The district reasoned, "Earrings might indicate youth gang activity." Was such a ban enforceable? **YOU'RE THE JUDGE!**
>
> DECISION: The court found that the school district had the right to enforce the ban as necessary to ensure the safety and welfare of the school's students.

Private Schools

Constitutional requirements do not apply to wholly private schools. Therefore, if a private school adopts a grooming code, it may be upheld. This is because the Constitution only applies to schools where the state is involved with its activity. States generally are involved with public (not private) schools. Therefore, rights granted by the Constitution, such as equal protection, due process (right to hearing and representation), and protection of fundamental rights (personal grooming and marriage privacy) do not apply to wholly private schools.

FIRST PRIZE IS....

The NCAA permits personalized awards that do not exceed specified amounts. The awards must be approved by the school and the school's conference.

> FACTS: The coach of the champion "Fighting Tiger" football team asked, "May the players be given TV's for awards?" **YOU'RE THE JUDGE!**

> DECISION: Awards that cannot be personalized, such as gift certificates, televisions, appliances or club memberships, and which may exceed a specified amount, may not be awarded.

Student-athletes enrolled in NCAA member schools or high schools, who accept unapproved awards for a sport, jeopardize their eligibility—not only for that sport—but for all sports.

> FACTS: The Polar Bears, a high school football team, had an outstanding year and was honored by the community. Team members were awarded lettered jackets and a book of religious testimonials by famous athletes. The price of the jackets was within the limits allowed of acceptable awards, but the book was not. When the team found this out, they returned the books. Should the school have been placed on probation? **YOU'RE THE JUDGE!**

> DECISION: Even though the team returned the books, the school was still placed on probation for three years!

Generally though, medals, letters, trophies, and other awards not exceeding a nominal value may be accepted.

The interest is in preserving amateur status and preventing "pro athletes" from competing in high school sports. A rule declaring that any student who receives an award of more than a nominal value is considered to be a professional is reasonable. Otherwise, athletes could be paid simply by giving them awards, which they could exchange for money.

Can a grammar school student-athlete be considered a pro?

> FACTS: Andy won the 60-meter dash in a grammar school track competition and was given a candy bar as a prize. Did such an award jeopardize Andy's eligibility? **YOU'RE THE JUDGE!**

DECISION: Although the prize was of nominal value, officials claimed that the prize made Andy a professional. He was banned from further competition

These cases point out the need to be aware of which awards are acceptable without jeopardizing the eligibility of either the athlete or the school.

ODDS & ENDS....

It's A Tie?

FACTS: Georgia's high school athletic association adopted a curfew calling for weeknight basketball games to end by 9:00 P.M., even if there was time on the clock, and even if the game was tied. If a player was fouled at 9:00 P.M., could he take the free throws? **YOU'RE THE JUDGE!**

DECISION: The controversial rule was rescinded.

Speaking Out!

FACTS: Jan, an instructor at G. U., alleged, "My right to free speech was violated when I was fired for 'speaking out' against the school's policy of academic favoritism and preferential treatment for student-athletes in an attempt to keep them eligible."

Testimony revealed that academic standards were lowered for some athletes while others were promoted without meeting grade requirements.

If Jan's dismissal was in retaliation for her speaking out against these practices, could she recover back pay and other damages? **YOU'RE THE JUDGE!**

DECISION: A jury found that Jan's "...right to free speech, as guaranteed by the First Amendment, was violated." She was awarded back pay and damages, including punitive damages.

Are We Pros?

FACTS: Eric, a high school senior, won a sports car in a field-goal kicking competition after a random drawing at a pro football game.

"Stick," also a high school senior, won money by throwing in a three quarter court length basket after a random drawing at a pro basketball game.

If either kept their prize, would they be ineligible to compete in college? **YOU'RE THE JUDGE!**

DECISION: "Accepting the car or money would make Eric and Stick pros and thus ineligible to compete at any NCAA school." However, they may compete at a smaller college division school.

All amateur athletes desiring to compete in organized amateur sports should fully understand their rights and responsibilities concerning elegibility.

3

DUE PROCESS
& EQUAL PROTECTION

WHAT'S IT ABOUT?

Due Process & Equal Protection goes into the effect that the Fourteenth Amendment to the Constitution, and its requirements, has on the enforcement of rules and regulations by amateur athletic organizations A sample Complaint highlights the issues that are examined. Can student-athletes be deprived of the right to an education or the right to participate in sports without the opportunity for a fair and impartial hearing? Should all athletes be treated alike?

John & Susan, plaintiffs
v.
Z. University, defendant

4th Circuit, Essex County, RI

COMPLAINT

The plaintiffs, John & Susan, allege as follows:

1. that they were student-athletes on athletic scholarships at ZU; John a member of the football team, Susan a member of the tennis team;
2. that, due to alleged violations, their scholarships and team memberships were terminated;
3. that certain of their rights were violated, namely:
   a. rules were applied discriminatorily, treating them differently than others similarly situated, a violation of the **Equal Protection Clause;**
   b. they have been deprived of the right to develop athletically, thus greatly diminishing their potential worth, and lessening their chances of becoming pros;
   c. that their scholarships were terminated without **Due Process**—the opportunity for a fair and impartial hearing with representation;
   d. that as a result of the termination of their scholarships, plaintiffs will not be able to continue work towards a degree, and;
   e. that the defendant "exploited" plaintiffs, using their athletic skills without regard to educational needs and desires, and dismissing them when they were no longer needed in advancing the athletic pursuits of ZU;
4. that as a result of ZU's actions, John & Susan have suffered, and will continue to suffer, immediate and irreparable harm and economic loss;

WHEREFORE, John & Susan ask:
1. that ZU be enjoined from terminating their scholarships and team memberships;
2. that they be given a hearing and opportunity to defend themselves, and;
3 that they be awarded damages in an amount that the court deems necessary and appropriate for injuries suffered and to be suffered.

IMPROPER ACTS

The enforcement of rules and regulations by amateur athletic organizations consists of the investigation of alleged improper acts and, if necessary or required, a fair and impartial hearing. Such proceedings to determine violations, if any, must be conducted within the organization's power and authority.

FACTS: For fighting in a game, Ally and Ben were suspended for five games. This was their first violation of the "no fighting" rule. The rule provided for a two game suspension, but the school decided to "set an example" in an attempt to prevent further fighting. Was the discipline fair? Should Ally and Ben have been given an opportunity to defend themselves? **YOU'RE THE JUDGE!**

DECISION: The discipline was improper. Furthermore, the severity of the sanction required minimum due process—a fair and impartial hearing with representation.

RULE-MAKING BY PRIVATE SCHOOLS

The essential difference between public and private schools is the extent of state involvement in their activities.

Schools, public or private, which are affected with **state action**—state involvement in providing "public" education, such as public schools—are bound by the requirements of the Constitution (due process and equal protection).

If a private school is not affected with state action, then they are only bound by their given authority.

A private group of people or associations, combined to achieve a common goal, is usually considered voluntary. Such membership is a privilege rather than a right. Thus, a private association may adopt rules and conditions for eligibility that will not be subject to constitutional requirements, as long as they are not in conflict with state or federal laws.

FACTS: John was a student-athlete at T.R.U., a private school not affected with "state action." His eligibility and athletic scholarship were terminated for fighting and destroying school hockey equipment. In addition, there was a question about his transfer from another college. "What are my rights and the school's duties?" asked John. **YOU'RE THE JUDGE!**

DECISION: If John's scholarship was viewed as an implied contract—a scholarship in return for athletic participation—then the court would look to see if both parties had lived up to the agreement.

The court would consider the student-athlete's inferior "take-it-or-leave-it" position.

Although John's eligibility and schooling may be terminated for fighting and destroying equipment, he may not be declared ineligible for any of the following reasons: because he transferred from a junior college, had taken the last year off, had transferred from a school without a hockey team or one on probation, or had not previously competed in hockey.

When a court decides to interfere in a school's affairs, it attempts to strike a balance; both between the interests of the parties (and similarly situated persons), and the potential harm to the parties (and whether the court can grant meaningful relief).

If John had the potential for becoming a professional hockey player, would the courts look more closely at any attempt to terminate his eligibility?

Loss of an education or eligibility, where a student-athlete may have the potential for a professional career, requires that courts scrutinize the actions of the association to determine if its rules and their objectives are reasonable. They may not assume that students have only "privileges" and no rights relating to sports activities.

THE CONSTITUTION REQUIRES....

Rule-making by associations that are "affected" with "state action," whether public or private, is governed by the Fourteenth Amendment to the Constitution. It requires that:

> **"No state shall ... deprive any person of life, liberty, or property, without due process of law; nor deny to any person ... the equal protection of the laws."**

If a student-athlete is declared ineligible due to a rule's violation, due process may be required—that is, the opportunity for a fair and impartial hearing with representation. The court will decide what process is due.

Cases where the Fourteenth Amendment is not an issue, or where it has already been resolved, will be decided by state or common law, or by the school's rules.

Must a student-athlete whose eligibility has been terminated be given due process?

FACTS: John's school explained, "Without giving any reason, John missed seven games. We declared him ineligible and took away his athletic scholarship to Sun Tan U." Should John have been given a hearing before being declared ineligible? **YOU'RE THE JUDGE!**

DECISION: The loss of eligibility for missing practice, although a severe sanction, did not require a hearing. The rule clearly provided for ineligibility, unless a reason were given and a hearing was requested within thirty days. John did neither, even after being notified of his rights.

In a case like this, a sanction will generally be upheld as long as it is reasonably related to the rule violated and to the severity of the offending conduct.

State Action

"No *state* shall ... deprive any person of life, liberty, or property, without due process of law; nor deny to any person ... the equal protection of the laws."

Student-athletes wishing to claim their right to due process or equal protection must show that the NCAA (or whatever association or conference governs their school) is involved in state action, meaning state involvement in providing "public" education.

Several cases have held that regulation of college athletes by the NCAA did not involve state action as it was not an activity "traditionally reserved exclusively to the state."

FACTS: Coach "K," the football coach at U.N.V.L., was ordered suspended by the NCAA for two years for alleged rules violations. The state court ruled that the coach had not been given his due process rights during the NCAA's investigation. The NCAA appealed. Did the NCAA have to give the coach a fair and impartial hearing during its investigation before imposing any sanctions? **YOU'RE THE JUDGE!**

DECISION: No. The Supreme Court held that the NCAA is not a state entity bound by the Constitution, but that it acted as a private entity, an agent of its member schools. It did not have to give the coach a hearing.

Although this case may discourage lawsuits involving alleged violations of due process, it is generally thought that the NCAA, high school athletic associations and college conferences are all "affected" with state action.

FACTS: The state government authorized, encouraged and delegated its authority to associations, schools and conferences to carry out the state's duties to provide education, including athletics.

The schools received public funds. Also, the state, allowed the use of publicly owned facilities for athletic events. Were such actions by the state considered state action? **YOU'RE THE JUDGE!**

DECISION: Yes. All of the affected associations, schools, and conferences will be governed by the U.S. Constitution.

Will a court interfere where a private association treated a student-athlete unfairly?

Courts may intervene in the affairs of private associations—at least where the plaintiff can show substantial injury resulting from the association's actions. Such intervention would not be based on constitutional grounds, but might be based on grounds of equality or fairness.

Give Me Liberty....

"No state shall ... deprive any person of life, *liberty*, or property, without due process of law; nor deny to any person ... the equal protection of the laws."

What is liberty? The most obvious meaning of liberty would be freedom from bodily restraint. But liberty also includes the freedom to be educated and the freedom of opportunity.

FACTS: A football player at a major university, Mark, asked, "Does liberty include the freedom to keep an athletic scholarship that could ensure me an opportunity for an education or an opportunity to expose my athletic ability that might lead to a pro career?"

DECISION: **YOU'RE THE JUDGE!**

It's My Property!

"No state shall ... deprive any person of life, liberty, or *property*, without due process of law; nor deny to any person ... the equal protection of the laws."

After showing state action, a plaintiff or student-athlete, alleging an improper loss of eligibility, must show that he has a right to participate.

May property be defined here, not as land or an object, but as a right to participate?

High School

Courts have generally found that a high school student-athlete does not have a **property interest**—a right to participate—in athletics.

FACTS: Chico was suspended without a hearing for slugging a teammate. "The suspension of my right to participate will injure my chances of becoming a pro. I have a property right to an education. Sports is a part of that!" argued Chico. Did Chico have a right to participate in athletics that required a hearing when suspended? **YOU'RE THE JUDGE!**

DECISION: No. Although Chico may have had a property right in the whole educational system, he did not have a property interest in each separate part, such as athletics.

High school athletes are not pursuing careers, have not yet sufficiently developed, and the opportunities for their exposure are minimal.

But there are cases holding that high school athletes have a separate property interest in athletics that can be protected.

One court commented, "If classes such as physical education are a required part of a student's curriculum, then athletic participation should be given the same protection. If one were declared ineligible from a required course, such as physical education, due process would apply. It, therefore, should also apply to sports participation."

College

Participation in collegiate athletics may be quite different.

FACTS: For fighting in a college basketball game, Alonzo— without a hearing—was declared ineligible. He challenged the dismissal. "Shouldn't I have been given a fair and impartial hearing?" he asked. **YOU'RE THE JUDGE!**

DECISION: The court held that the right to participate in athletics was a valuable right that could not be denied without due process. The chance to display their athletic prowess in college stadiums and arenas may be worth more in economic terms than the chance to get a college education.

Despite some language of a few courts to the contrary, college athletes do have a constitutionally protected property right to participate in sports. This right entitles them to participate and to given due process safeguards to ensure that their interest in participation is properly protected.

There's No Process Like Due Process!

"No state shall ... deprive any person of life, liberty, or property, without *due process* of law; nor deny to any person ... the equal protection of the laws."

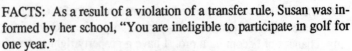

COURT ROOM
5

FAIR
AND
IMPARTIAL
HEARING

FACTS: As a result of a violation of a transfer rule, Susan was informed by her school, "You are ineligible to participate in golf for one year."

Susan was denied the opportunity to show that the rule did not apply to her because she had already sat out a year. Should she have been allowed to participate? **YOU'RE THE JUDGE!**

DECISION: Susan had already sat out a year before transferring. An earlier hearing would have revealed that fact and she then would have been allowed to participate.

Due process would require: notice of the proceedings to declare her ineligible; the opportunity to prepare, to have representation and to obtain discovery—the information that the action is based on and who furnished such information—and; the opportunity to be heard—a fair and impartial hearing.

How Much Process Is Due?

YOU'RE
THE JUDGE!

If an attempt to convince a court that a protectible interest has been deprived is unsuccessful, then no due process is available. If, however, a liberty or property interest is involved, the court must then decide what protection the plaintiff should be given.

FACTS: For "goofing around," Jerry was benched for one game. Sara was declared ineligible for one year after being accused of "cheating in a golf match." Who was entitled to more "protection" from their loss of eligibility? **YOU'RE THE JUDGE!**

DECISION: The length, severity and reason for ineligibility required that Sara be given much more substantial protection, such as a hearing.

Generally, as the length and severity of any potential loss becomes greater, required safeguards become more necessary to fulfill the requirements of due process.

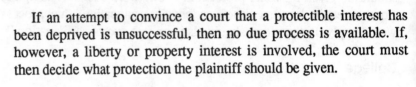

REPORT CARD

SUSAN D. SMYTH

ENGLISH	D
MATH	F
HISTORY	D
SCIENCE	F

FACTS: Because of poor grades, Susan was declared ineligible to participate in athletics for one semester; at which time she would be reinstated provided she improved her grades. She complained, "The rule is unfair." What process was Susan due?

Suppose Susan decided to challenge the procedure used to calculate her grades, or felt that there was personal bias by one of her professors? Or what if she maintained her low grades were punishment for allegedly stealing a book and that she was declared ineligible for three years? What process would be due now? **YOU'RE THE JUDGE!**

DECISION: The first situation would only require modest procedural safeguards. But when Susan challenged the method for calculating her grades, the personal bias, and the charge of stealing—it became much more important for her to have a fair and impartial hearing with representation.

If a court found a school's tribunal to be fair and impartial, then the right to representation would be diminished.

Equal Protection

"No state shall ... deprive any person of life, liberty, or property, without due process of law; nor deny to any person ... the *equal protection* of the laws."

As with the due process clause, the equal protection clause requires state action; it does not apply to any action of wholly private associations.

The equal protection clause prohibits discrimination in either laws or their administration. It is intended to insure that "all persons similarly situated shall receive no different or greater penalty. They shall be treated alike."

It strikes down overly-broad rules that sweep or catch into their nets individuals who are not intended to, or should not, be included within the reaches of these rules.

FACTS: A transfer rule read, "Any transfer athlete shall sit out one season in their sport." The rule was intended to prevent improper recruiting.

Bob transferred to Eastern U. from Western U. He did not play football at Western. He further took a year off before transferring. Bob was declared "ineligible to play football for one year from the transfer." "Shouldn't I be allowed to play immediately?" asked Bob. **YOU'RE THE JUDGE!**

DECISION: Yes. The rule was intended to prevent improper recruiting. As Bob was not recruited, did not play at Western, and sat out a year—declaring him ineligible would be a violation of the equal protection clause as "sweeping" too broadly by including him in the class of athletes intended to be covered by the rule.

TRANSFER

There are two tests that may be applied in determining whether a rule is a violation of the equal protection clause.

The first is the **rational basis test.** This was what Bob's case was decided upon. It requires, "The rule or classification must be reasonable, not arbitrary, so that all persons similarly situated are treated alike."

The second is called the **strict scrutiny test.** It requires, "Where a 'suspect class' (race, sex, color) or 'fundamental interest' (marriage, interstate travel) is involved, the rule will be unconstitutional unless there is a compelling interest to be protected or promoted."

FACTS: Susan transferred to Tutten High from out of state. She wanted to try out for the boys' golf team (there was no girls' team), but was denied because, "Girls are not allowed to play on boys' teams."

Also, she was declared "ineligible to participate in any sport for one year due to the transfer rule." Susan did not play golf at her previous school. She transferred because her father was transferred from his job. Should Susan have been permitted to try out? **YOU'RE THE JUDGE!**

DECISION: The refusal of a tryout was based on sex. The transfer rule discriminated against interstate travel for a valid reason (work transfer). Both were subject to the strict scrutiny test. Neither served to promote any compelling reason for their discrimination. Susan was denied equal protection. She was permitted to try out for the boys' golf team.

Some schools reason: "Boys are bigger and stronger than girls." Are these compelling enough reasons to deny equal protection?

FACTS: What if there had been a girls' golf team or what if Susan had wanted to participate on the boys' football team? Would your decision be any different? **YOU'RE THE JUDGE!**

DECISION: The school's reasons for not allowing Susan to play on the boys' golf or football teams were, "There is a girls' team for golf, and football is too rough for girls." They cited the differences in size, strength and ability, and the chance to compete against others of the same sex and abilities.

A court might well feel these are "compelling enough reasons" to deny Susan's claim of denial of equal protection.

Due process and equal protection by the laws can only be demanded where there is a "protectible interest"—such as the right to interstate travel. A court may nevertheless deny a claim where due process has already been given or equal protection of the laws has not been denied.

PUBLIC REGULATION OF SPORTS

Most states have athletic commissions which regulate specific sports. If self-regulation has failed or the interests of those involved requires review, public regulation may be necessary.

Generally, the sports requiring public regulation are: horse, dog and automobile racing, boxing and wrestling.

Athletic Commissions

An **athletic commission**—a group of appointed officials—attempts to prevent abuses that may be a part of a sport and promote and protect the interests of the public in having sportsmanlike conduct. A commission, created by law, becomes—in effect—an agent of the state, subject to judicial review.

> FACTS: Some of these sports, particularly boxing and horse racing, have attracted gamblers, criminals and "fixing" of results. In addition to establishing rules and regulations, what may commissions do to help insure proper conduct? **YOU'RE THE JUDGE!**

> DECISION: To insure proper conduct, the commission will issue licenses and provide rules, regulations and enforcement.

Do You Have A License?

With certain exceptions, anyone desiring to take part in one of the sports requiring regulation will be required to obtain an appropriate license. This requirement includes participants, referees, owners, trainers and sponsors. What will the applicants be questioned about?

Applicants must submit information regarding their conduct, training, character, physical and financial condition, and past activities.

Numerous courts have concluded, "A commission's authority may be broad and exclusive. Their decisions concerning rules will not be overturned unless there is a clear abuse of authority. A commission may only reject a license for good and reasonable cause."

> FACTS: Because of his conviction for refusing to be inducted into the armed services, Ali was denied a boxing license. Was the boxing commission's action reasonable? **YOU'RE THE JUDGE!**

> DECISION: No. The court observed, "Many others had been issued licenses before and after being convicted of crimes." These facts were overwhelming proof that the commission's denial of Ali's application for a boxing license was unlawful, arbitrary, unreasonable, and a violation of the equal protection clause, guaranteeing the same treatment received by others similarly situated. The commission was enjoined from denying Ali a license.

Courts have also held that denial of a license application may require due process—notice, hearing, and the opportunity for the applicant to answer and defend any charges used as a basis for its denial.

The Rules Are....

The authority to make and enforce rules and regulations is included in the law creating the commission.

Whether a court will review any enforcement of a commission rule will depend upon whether the claimant is attacking the rule itself or whether he is challenging the interpretation of the rule.

> FACTS: Vinnie was denied a promoter's license for boxing. He alleged, "The rule requiring promoters to be licensed was invalid. If it did apply to me, I was exempted from needing a license because I only promote fights for charitable purposes for local fairs." Should Vinnie have been exempted from the license rule? What authority did the court have? **YOU'RE THE JUDGE!**

> DECISION: The court could decide if the rule was within the boxing commission's power, whether it was issued pursuant to the proper procedure and if it was reasonable. The court can substitute its judgment for that of the commission in interpreting the rule. However, the court will not question the boxing commission's decision on the facts.
>
> The rule was not invalid, but Vinnie could be exempted from the license requirement because he only promoted fights for charitable purposes.

Conduct & Character

A state has an interest in determining whether an applicant possesses the necessary character and fitness for certain professions. The types of conduct and character considered for a license will, in part, depend upon what profession the applicant desires to enter.

Rules must be reasonable and must only affect those persons whose conduct it is necessary to control.

> FACTS: Al and Manuel were convicted of stealing. Will such action affect their applications for a promoter's or jockey's license? **YOU'RE THE JUDGE!**

> DECISION: Al, convicted of stealing, may be denied a license to promote. However, this fact may have little bearing on Manuel becoming a jockey—at least not enough to deny his application.

EXPLOITATION

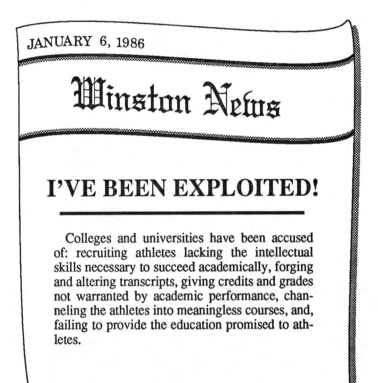

JANUARY 6, 1986

Winston News

I'VE BEEN EXPLOITED!

Colleges and universities have been accused of: recruiting athletes lacking the intellectual skills necessary to succeed academically, forging and altering transcripts, giving credits and grades not warranted by academic performance, channeling the athletes into meaningless courses, and, failing to provide the education promised to athletes.

FACTS: Curtis, a former collegiate basketball star, sued the colleges he attended, and the coaches and officials. Curtis was recruited, and transferred, from a school for slow learners to a regular school where he did not receive the special attention he needed. He was "passed" through school without passing work and induced into attending college. Yet, he could not read or write well enough to fill out the application! (The coach filled it out!) Cheating and other improper acts were used to maintain his eligibility.

Curtis was taunted and insulted mercilessly. He had a mental breakdown, requiring constant medical attention. Was this exploitation of Curtis' athletic abilities to the detriment of his educational needs? Could Curtis recover damages?

DECISION: **YOU'RE THE JUDGE!**

Some former student-athletes have charged that colleges and universities exploited them by using them for their athletic ability—with no concern for their educational advancement—and later discarding them when they no longer could help the school athletically. These student-athletes alleged that such exploitation was done solely to advance the interests of the school.

FACTS: Eight basketball players sued their college for "depriving us of a legitimate education." They claimed, "We wasted our careers on courses designed only to keep us eligible for basketball. There was fraud and misrepresentation on the part of the school. We were denied access to adequate counseling." Were these students exploited for their athletic ability?

DECISION: **YOU'RE THE JUDGE!**

FACTS: Several football players at Big Time U. were advised by their academic advisor, "Certain summer courses will be accepted for credits needed to retain your eligibility next season."

After being declared ineligible, the students alleged, "We were exploited for our athletic abilities to the detriment of an education." Was this exploitation?

DECISION: **YOU'RE THE JUDGE!**

Whose fault is it for the system's failure to provide students with an education? Is the university obligated to provide an education to a scholarship athlete?

Each case has to be treated separately, but maybe the reasoning lies in the court's handling of a case where a basketball star was declared ineligible by his school because he had "not met academic standards." The player took the school to court to win reinstatement. The judge commented:

Orevill News

"...athletes... are given little incentive to be scholars and few care how they perform academically. The talented student-athlete is led to perceive athletic programs as farm teams for pro sports leagues. It may well be that a good academic program for the athlete is made virtually impossible by the demands of sports at the college level. If this situation causes harm to the university, it is because the schools have fostered it, and the school, rather than the individual, should suffer the consequences.

New academic standards have to be strictly enforced. Admission requirements have to be tightened. Proof must be required that shows real and substantial progress towards a degree."

ODDS & ENDS....

Old Age!

When is an athlete too old to participate?

FACTS: John, 27, said, "I went from playing high school basketball to working in the coal mines of Pennsylvania, playing only city basketball during those years. When I wanted to play college basketball, I was declared ineligible. Should I have been eligible?" **YOU'RE THE JUDGE!**

DECISION: An NCAA rule reads, Participating in "...any organized competition after an athlete is age 20 will count against his college eligibility."

This prevents older, more experienced players from dominating. It also promotes equality in competition and discourages students from delaying entrance to college in order to develop their skills. Each year of such competition counts as one year of college eligibility. Had John played fewer than four years of city basketball he would have had eligibility remaining.

Sweatpants?

May student-athletes wear clothing, other than their "standard" uniform, while playing in competition?

FACTS: Lisa, a member of her college basketball team, wore a scarf and sweatpants while playing. This was in conflict with dress code rules prohibiting the wearing of such articles of clothing. "I wore the scarf and sweatpants for religious reasons." explained Lisa. Should Lisa have been prohibited from playing? **YOU'RE THE JUDGE!**

DECISION: Because her religion prohibited showing physical beauty, Lisa was granted an exception to the dress code rules. She could wear the clothing and continue to participate.

The rights to due process (the opportunity for a fair and impartial hearing), and equal protection (intended to insure that all persons similarly situated shall be treated alike), will apply to numerous situations in everyday life, not just those involving the right and opportunity to an education and the right to participate in sports.

For example, where a suspect class (race, sex, color) or fundamental interests (marriage, interstate travel) is involved, any law or rule will be unconstitutional unless there is a compelling interest to be protected or promoted, such as the protection and safety of those affected.

4

DISCRIMINATION

WHAT'S IT ABOUT?

Discrimination discusses attempts to discriminate or differentiate in favor or against athletes or others in sports on the basis of prejudice "because" of the race, sex, color or disability of the person.

Are girls physiologically inferior to boys? Should girls be permitted to participate in contact sports (football) on the same team as, or against, boys?

SEX DISCRIMINATION

FACTS: Sally wanted to try out for the boys' basketball and tennis teams at All-Am High. The school had a girls' basketball team, but not a girls' tennis team.

As other schools in the area did not have girls' basketball teams, All- Am's girls' team only played a few games against local pick-up teams. The boys' basketball team played mostly other small, local schools. Before transferring to All-Am after her family moved, Sally was a star basketball player for North High's girls' team.

Jack wanted to try out for the girls' volleyball team. There was no boys' team.

The eligibility rules for the school's sports program were pinned to the bulletin board outside the athletic office. One rule in particular read:

ELIGIBILITY RULES
"Girls shall not be permitted to participate
in athletic games against boys,
either as a member of a boys' team
or as a member of the girls' team
playing against a boys' team.
Girls' teams shall not accept
male members."

When Sally found out that the State High School Association was responsible for the rule, she asked for an explanation. She received a letter which read, in part:

> "The separation of males and females in athletic competition is necessary to achieve equitable competition.
>
> Due to their physiological superiority, males outperform females. This superiority makes it necessary to separate the two in order to prevent psychological injuries to females, and to allow for the development of female athletic programs.
>
> Furthermore, the separation of males and females in sports is a 'tradition'...."

"Those rules are nothing more than old prejudices and myths," complained Sally. "I'm being discriminated against because of my sex. Can I enjoin the school from enforcing the eligibility rule?" she asked. Should Jack have been allowed to try out for the girls' volleyball team?

DECISION: **YOU'RE THE JUDGE!**

A number of our nation's documents and laws prohibit discrimination. The most important are the Constitution, the Equal Rights Amendment (ERA) and Title IX.

EQUAL PROTECTION

The Fourteenth Amendment to the Constitution provides:

"No state shall ... deny to any person ... the equal protection of the laws."

This is called the Equal Protection Clause. It prohibits laws or rules that are either discriminatory, or are applied in a discriminatory manner.

Where a state is sufficiently involved, by either conducting, encouraging, authorizing, administering, or participating in private conduct (such as by delegating its duty to provide an education), to a school or athletic association, then the Equal Protection Clause applies to the rule or conduct of the private association. This is called **state action**. It must exist. The Equal Protection Clause does not apply to actions of wholly private schools or associations.

Any rule, and its purpose, must be fair and reasonable. All persons similarly situated must be treated alike.

Must eligibility to play be based on ability and not on a student-athlete's sex?

FACTS: Cynthia and Peggy wanted to try out for the boys' tennis team at their high school.

Antoinette wanted to try out for the boys' skiing and cross-country running teams.

All of the girls' high schools had rules "prohibiting mixed athletic teams. Males are physiologically superior to females." Further, such rules were necessary for the development of female athletic programs, of which there were none. Did the rules discriminate against girls? **YOU'RE THE JUDGE!**

DECISION: Yes. In both cases, the court found that "the rules discriminated against the girls solely because of their sex. Such rules are arbitrary, unreasonable, and in violation of the Equal Protection Clause." Separating males and females is not necessary to achieve equitable competition. Eligibility to play must be based upon ability, regardless of sex.

If the court determines that a rule is based on a "suspect" classification (sex, color, race), then such a rule is unconstitutional unless there is a "compelling" reason for it.

FACTS: Natalie wanted to enter a men's boxing tournament. A "MEN ONLY" rule denied women permission to enter boxing competitions. "I want to be treated like the boys and allowed to box," grumbled Natalie. "Can't I box?" **YOU'RE THE JUDGE!**

DECISION: The court found that the "MEN ONLY" rule did not violate the Equal Protection Clause because the Boxing Federation was an entirely private organization not involved in "state action." Even if there had been state action, the law permitted gender classification in contact sports.

The Equal Protection Clause has led many schools to accept girls on boys' teams, especially in non-contact sports.

The challenges to the segregation of the sexes in sports arose in two main types of situations: girls who wanted to play on boys' teams where there were no girls' teams, and where outstanding female athletes wanted to play on boys' teams (even where there was a separate girls' team) because the male team better suited their athletic ability.

But girls were not always allowed to play on the boys' teams!

FACTS: As there was no girls' team, Maria wanted to try out for the boys' high school track team.

Sandra Lynn, an outstanding swimmer, wanted to try out for the boys' team. There was a girls' swim team.

The Athletic Conference's rule forbids girls on boys' teams, reasoning that the rule reflected "custom and tradition." Also, the rule was intended "to prevent psychological damage to both males and females." Did the rule discriminate against girls? **YOU'RE THE JUDGE!**

DECISION: The court found no discrimination. "Boys will get no thrill from defeating girls. The challenge to win, and the glory of achievement would become nullified. Athletic competition should build character in our youth. We do not need that kind of character (born of constant defeat) in our girls, the women of tomorrow."

Courts began to recognize the absurdity of this position.

JoBeth qualified for the boys' high school golf team, there being no girls' team. She was not permitted to play due to a rule "prohibiting male and female students from competing on the same team or against each other." The court decided, "The rule denied girls the opportunity to participate with boys in non-contact sports solely because of sex. JoBeth must be judged solely on her ability." The court also noted that had there been a separate team for the girls, then there would be no discrimination in prohibiting JoBeth from participating on the boys' team.

FACTS: Tammie and Carolyn wanted to participate on the boys' high school cross country teams. There was no girls' teams. Although they were qualified, a school rule denied them the opportunity to participate. Should they have been allowed to participate on the boys' teams? **YOU'RE THE JUDGE!**

DECISION: Yes. "The rule discriminated against the girls by not treating them in the same manner as the boys, that is, to judge them on ability, and not prohibit their participation solely because of their sex," held the court.

These suits were, in part, responsible for a number of states passing laws requiring that girls be allowed to compete for positions on boys' teams in non-contact sports where there was no girls' team.

What if a girl wanted to try out for a boys' team even where there was a girls' team?

FACTS: Maria and some of her girlfriends wanted to play little league baseball. They were qualified, but were prohibited from playing because of a rule prohibiting girls "because of physical differences between the sexes. Girls were more likely to be injured in the game, which is played with a hard ball, than boys."

The girls charged, "We're being treated differently than the boys. That's a violation of the Equal Protection Clause." Was it? **YOU'RE THE JUDGE!**

DECISION: Yes. Girls of this age group were not subject to a greater hazard of injury, while playing baseball, than boys of the same age group. Medical evidence showed that girls of ages 8 to 12 are at least as strong as their male peers, with no less reaction time. They can compete safely and as successfully as boys in the game.

The little league had to allow girls to play, if they were capable.

This decision became part of state law. Congress then revised the Little League's charter to permit girls to play, and deleted that passage which said the purpose of little league was to instill manhood. Sportsmanship became the goal.

Athletic Segregation At Any Age?

Brenda, 12, and Nichole, 13, were permitted to play on their school's boys' football teams. The courts decided that they should not be denied the opportunity to play unless they lacked the required physical ability.

However, other high school girls have been ruled ineligible to play football because "they were more likely to get hurt than boys."

One doctor testified, "Whether you like it or not, God made women the weaker sex." Under similar reasoning, girls have also been prohibited from playing on boys' hockey teams, but not on boys' baseball teams.

FACTS: Jo Ann, 17, wanted to play on the boys' high school baseball team. There was no girls' team. At first, after cutting her hair, she was allowed. Later, she was informed, "You cannot participate. Baseball is a contact sport and you would be subject to an unreasonable risk of harm."

Jo Ann alleged, "I was being denied the right to play because of my sex." Could Jo Ann enjoin the school from preventing her from playing? **YOU'RE THE JUDGE!**

DECISION: Yes. Jo Ann was denied the right to play solely because of her sex. She had the physical ability to play.

When Susan and Nina, both 16, were denied the opportunity to try out for the boys' baseball and soccer teams at their high school, the court found discrimination and ordered the schools to either drop the sports, establish girls' teams, or allow the girls to try out.

Separate Seasons

FACTS: Classical High School established separate seasons of play for male and female athletic teams in order to allocate limited facilities and to maximize participation by both sexes.

Several girls argued, "Because the weather and competition was better for tennis in the spring, we were not being treated like the boys. The rule discriminated against us." Did it? **YOU'RE THE JUDGE!**

DECISION: No discrimination was found. Neither season was so substantially better than the other that equal protection of the laws was denied the girls.

EQUAL RIGHTS AMENDMENT (ERA)

Sex discrimination in sports has also been litigated under state Equal Rights Amendments. A typical state ERA provides:

"Equality of rights and responsibility ... shall not be denied or taken away ... on account of sex."

FACTS: Commerce High School's sports eligibility rule read: "Girls shall not compete or practice against boys in any athletic contest." Did the rule violate an ERA prohibition against sex discrimination? **YOU'RE THE JUDGE!**

DECISION: The court found that the rule violated both the ERA and the Equal Protection Clause. "The notion that girls—as a whole—are weaker, more injury prone and less skilled, cannot justify such a rule."

Even where there are separate teams for boys and girls, the most talented girls should have the opportunity to play at that level of competition which their ability warrants.

Every student is guaranteed, and should have, an individual determination of qualification to play on school sports teams. Especially where, concerning girls, the school provides no corresponding girls' team. Girls can be protected from physical injury by appropriate equipment.

Discrimination Against Boys!

The Equal Protection Clause and Equal Rights Amendment have also allowed boys to play on girls' athletic teams, at least where there was no corresponding boys' team.

FACTS: The Massachusetts ERA required that any classification by sex must serve a compelling purpose. A high school athletic association rule read: "To protect the welfare and safety of all students participating in athletics, no boy may play on a girls' team, but a girl may play on a boys' team if that sport is not offered for the girl."

Several high schools that permitted boys to play on girls' teams in volleyball, softball, swimming, tennis, and basketball, where there were no boy's teams, challenged the rule.

One school—with only a few boys—could not field teams exclusively for boys.   Could the boys play on the girls' teams? **YOU'RE THE JUDGE!**

DECISION: The court ruled, "Yes. Any rule which classifies by sex alone is subject to close examination." The problem of boys playing on the girl's team was marginal. Where the problem becomes more acute as by girl's sports being overrun by boys, it can be met by measures less offensive and less sweeping than a complete sex barrier.

Although one state prohibited boys from playing on a girls' field hockey team for safety reasons, a Massachusetts high school (David Hale Fanning) allowed the boys to play on the girls' field hockey team. "To show their dedication to the sport, the boys wore blue plaid kilts while playing!"

DISCRIMINATION IN EDUCATION

Title IX of the Educational Amendments Act provides:

"No person … shall, on the basis of sex, be excluded from participation in, be denied the benefit of, or be subject to discrimination under any education program or activity receiving federal financial assistance."

Title IX was intended to eliminate inequalities and discrimination in sports by requiring equal funding for both men's and women's programs, encouraging athletic participation by females, and increasing the number of sports offered to women. The goal is to elevate women's competition.

FACTS: Football U. wanted to spend more on its men's football program than on the women's intramural touch football program. Would such unequal spending violate Title IX? **YOU'RE THE JUDGE!**

DECISION: Title IX permits nonequivalent spending in certain spectator sports, such as football, provided that the difference results from nondiscriminatory factors. In the case of football, equipment, injuries and needed facilities and their maintenance make football expensive. Therefore, schools are justified in spending more on this traditionally male sport.

Contact Sports

Title IX regulations make a crucial distinction between contact and non-contact sports. In the case of contact sports, such as basketball, football, wrestling, and ice hockey, a school may operate single-sex, "separate-but-equal" teams.

FACTS: "I wanted to play for the boys' basketball team," declared Karen. She was not permitted. She had been given the opportunity to play on the girls' basketball team, but refused to try out. The girls' team and their schedule were top-rated. Was this discrimination? **YOU'RE THE JUDGE!**

DECISION: No. The equality of the teams and her voluntary refusal to try out for the girl's team lessened her claim of injury.

The rationale seems to be that in rough sports, it isn't reasonable to expect boys and girls to compete equally. Therefore, a school does not have to let a girl try out. Her only recourse would be to gather enough girls and start their own team. The school would be obligated to support them as long as girls were limited in that sport and there was sufficient interest, ability and a reasonable expectation of competition. Would this be true for all schools?

FACTS: Susan wanted to play on the boys' high school baseball team. There was no girls' team. She had the required ability.

Sherry wanted to play basketball and football, but there were no girls' teams in those sports at her high school. Should Susan and Sherry have been permitted to play on the boys' teams? **YOU'RE THE JUDGE!**

DECISION: Yes. The court held that there was no specific prohibition on girls playing on boys' teams in a contact sport. Girls must be allowed to try out for the boys' team, even if it was the football team. They must be judged on ability and not discriminated against because of their sex.

Would the decision have been different had the girls wanted to play on college football and basketball teams where the boys are bigger and stronger, and the game rougher?

Non-Contact Sports

In non-contact sports, schools can offer separate teams for sports such as tennis, golf, swimming and track. If there are teams for boys and girls in all these sports, there generally will be no problems. The exception is where there is no girls' team, or where one of the girls possesses unique ability.

FACTS: "I want to try out for the boys' track team. There is no girl's track team," said Tammie.

Helena, the state's 100 yard dash champion, wanted to run for the boys' track team even though there was a girls' track team. Would they be allowed the try-out? **YOU'RE THE JUDGE!**

DECISION: The court held that the girls must be permitted to try out for the boy's track team. The same would hold true for tennis, swimming, or golf.

Until Congress intervened in 1988—where a school's athletic program did not receive federal assistance—Title IX could not be used to prohibit discrimination in the school's selection process for that team or in providing unequal funding for women's and men's sports programs. Now, regardless of whether or not a school's athletic program receives federal assistance, if a public or private school receives federal assistance, equal funding for both women's and men's athletic programs is required with no discrimination (football is an exception).

SEX DISCRIMINATION ON THE JOB

Claims for wages, based upon sex discrimination, have had mixed success.

Where coaching duties are substantially similar, coaches of girls' and boys' sports must receive pay on an equal basis without regard to the coach's sex or the students coached. Laws prohibiting such discrimination may also require other equal terms and conditions of employment concerning hiring and assignment.

FACTS: Melissa, a sportswriter, sued the commissioner of baseball, stated, "He ordered all major league baseball teams to take a 'unified stand' against the admission of women sportswriters into major league clubhouses. Because of that order, I was excluded from the Blue Sox clubhouse. Did they discriminate against me?" **YOU'RE THE JUDGE!**

DECISION: Other pro sports admitted women sportswriters to their locker rooms. Adequate steps could be taken to ensure the necessary privacy of the players. The custom of refusing to allow female reporters into the locker room was discrimination. Such discrimination violated Melissa's right to equal protection (to be treated as male reporters were treated), and unreasonably interfered with her right to pursue her profession. The Blue Sox were enjoined from refusing her admission to the locker room area.

To accommodate all reporters, professional teams set aside a room where the players would go to be interviewed. Thereby, they could still retain their privacy.

DISABILITY

"No otherwise qualified handicapped individual ... shall, solely by reason of a handicap, be excluded from participation in, be denied benefits of, or be subject to discrimination...." in athletics.

This is the Rehabilitation Act. As in Title IX, it covers any athletic program or activity receiving federal financial assistance.

Handicapped athletes have been prevented from participating where a school would be forced to make substantial modifications to accommodate a handicapped athlete, or where the public school system acted pursuant to its **loco parentis** (acting as parents) powers to protect the well-being of students not old enough to weigh the risks involved and make a mature, informed decision.

What if there is no substantial risk of serious injury related to the handicap?

FACTS: "Tank," with an artificial leg below his left knee, wanted to run the 40 yard low hurdles for his school's track team. The school said, "No." Could Tank participate? **YOU'RE THE JUDGE!**

DECISION: In ruling "Yes." the court commented, "No athlete should be denied the opportunity to participate solely because of a handicap. Hard work and dedication can and have overcome enormous odds."

Disabilities alleged by professional athletes are not covered by the Rehabilitation Act.

FACTS: Pierre, a pro hockey player, was barred from playing when it was discovered that he was blind in one eye.

Charlie, a jockey, was denied a jockey's license because of blindness in one eye. Although both athletes had performed satisfactorily in the past, they were ruled medically unfit to continue playing. Were Pierre and Charlie discriminated against? Should they have been allowed to participate?

DECISION: **YOU'RE THE JUDGE!**

A Massachusetts little league faced the loss of their charter unless they banned three teams of physically and mentally handicapped players from competing.

FACTS: The little league organization felt that the handicapped children should not compete since they were not covered by insurance and, also, because they were not coached by professionals, but by volunteers. Would such a ban be discrimination?

DECISION: **YOU'RE THE JUDGE!**

RACE OR COLOR -
CIVIL RIGHTS ACT OF 1964

"All persons shall be entitled to the full and equal enjoyment ... of any place of public accommodation ... without discrimination or segregation on the grounds of race, color...."

This is to eliminate "the inconvenience, unfairness and humiliation of racial discrimination."

A place of public accommodation may be a sports arena, bowling alley, golf course, YWCA, health club, skating rink, public or private swimming area open to the public or any other place of entertainment open to the general public.

FACTS: Lake Nixon Amusement Club had recreation facilities including: swimming, boating, dancing, miniature golf and a snack bar. It advertised in a magazine and on the radio. Whites who patronized the club were routinely furnished "membership cards" for a small fee.

Blacks were denied admission. They alleged that they were being discriminated against solely because of their race. They asked the court for an injunction prohibiting the club from denying them admission. Was this a violation of the Civil Rights Act? **YOU'RE THE JUDGE!**

DECISION: Yes. The court held that Lake Nixon was not a private club. It was "open in general to all of the public who are members of the white race." The club, in violation of the Civil Rights Act, discriminated against Blacks. It was enjoined from continuing the practice.

The Civil Rights Act applies whether patrons are spectators or participating in a sport or other activity.

Therefore, where membership to an athletic program or team was denied solely due to race, the Civil Rights Act was used to prohibit such discrimination. And where a school refused to promote a coach, solely because of his race, the court found racial discrimination and ordered that he either be promoted or compensated as if he were.

Are public golf courses covered by the Civil Rights Act?

FACTS: An ordinance made it unlawful for Black people to use parks owned and maintained by the city for use of white people, and unlawful for white people to frequent or use any park maintained by the city for the use and benefit of Black persons.

Holmes argued, "Me and other Black citizens couldn't use the golf courses run by the city. They did that because of our race and color. It was discrimination." Did the ordinance discriminate against Blacks? **YOU'RE THE JUDGE!**

DECISION: Yes. The court held that segregation of public facilities could not be justified. The city was enjoined from refusing to allow Holmes to play golf on any golf course that it ran.

Justice Douglas of the U.S. Supreme Court, in addressing the problems of discrimination, declared: "Segregation of Negroes... is a relic of slavery. It is a badge of second-class citizenship. It is a denial of a privilege... of national citizenship and of the equal protection guaranteed by the Constitution...."

PRIVATE CLUBS

Private clubs that discriminate against females and racial minorities, and whose goal is to "permit exclusive membership to gather together away from public view," have become very controversial for condoning such "impermissible snobbery."

Now, a growing number of cities have passed ordinances requiring many men-only or whites-only clubs to accept women and minority members.

FACTS: John, Tom and Andy joined the Lago Lake Club, a pri-

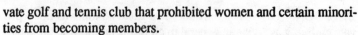

vate golf and tennis club that prohibited women and certain minorities from becoming members.

Their wives (who also wanted to join the club but were refused membership) protested, "The club is discriminating against us!"

State's Attorney Warren filed a discrimination suit against the club, arguing, "The club's tax breaks, lease of city property at a reduced rate and the IRS's allowance of membership-costs as a business deduction all make the club 'public.' The public is paying for those savings."

Furthermore, Warren explained, "When a club provides a place where business is transacted, then the club must not discriminate. As are other businesses, it must be open to all who desire membership."

The husbands pleaded, "The Constitution guarantees us the right of free association, to associate or not with whomever we please." Should the club be allowed to continue prohibiting women and minorities as members?

DECISION: **YOU'RE THE JUDGE!**

ODDS & ENDS....

Ladies' Night!

FACTS: Bruce and his wife went to a Supersonic's basketball game. It was "Ladies' Night." Bruce requested to pay the same admission price (a 50% discount) for himself as that paid by female spectators.

"The ticket seller refused to allow this," said Bruce. Was Bruce discriminated against? **YOU'RE THE JUDGE!**

DECISION: The Court concluded that "Ladies Night" ticket prices constituted sex discrimination. Men could not be charged more than ladies. The injustice would be easily recognized if it arose concerning race. It would be inconceivable to have a "Blacks' Night" or a "Whites' Night" or a "Filipinos' Night."! The Court suggested a "Spouses' Night" as a way to promote the ladies' attendance.

Similarly, discrimination was found where other professional teams held a "Ladies' Day" with discount prices for women only.

Weight For Me!

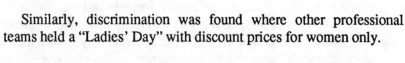

FACTS: "I wanted to march in the school band!" cried Peggy.

Sue wanted to play basketball. They were both told that they could not participate because they were overweight. Their school imposed the weight restrictions for performance and to avoid heckling by the fans. "Were we discriminated against?" asked the girls. Will it depend upon how overweight they were? **YOU'RE THE JUDGE!**

DECISION: There were no such restrictions applying to boys. This was sex discrimination in violation of the equal protection clause. Even if the restriction applied to boys, discrimination might still be found where it could be shown that a loss of weight might be injurious to health, or that the extra weight would not affect performance.

The prohibitions of discrimination in the Constitution, Equal Rights Amendment, Title IX and The Civil Rights Act apply equally to all, not just athletes.

5

ATHLETES & INJURIES

WHAT'S IT ABOUT?

Athletes & Injuries discusses and comments on personal injuries to professional and amateur athletes which are caused by intentional misconduct (assault and battery), or by non-intentional misconduct (negligence). Injuries to amateur athletes may occur while they are participating for a school or other organized team, or while just playing around. There are defenses to the charges of assault and battery or negligence.

In addition, this chapter covers injuries at work and those caused by extraordinary risks or conditions "not fit for play."

Do injured athletes assume the risk of injury or are they guilty of contributing to their injury when they are aware of the dangers of the sport in which they are participating? Are parents responsible for the conduct of their children?

"They were playing soccer." said John. "Bob intentionally kicked Gil, fracturing his jaw!"

"I didn't mean it. I was only trying to tackle him. It was an accident," cried Gil.

This is a case of personal injury—someone was hurt. It can happen in any sport. It doesn't matter if you're a pro, an amateur in school, or just playing around.

If you're hurt, you can claim damages for your injury. But there are defenses. Anyone you sue might claim that you contributed to your injury by participating, or that you assumed the risk of getting hurt. You have to prove that they were at fault.

FREE seminar!
Learn all about personal injuries
and YOUR RIGHTS...

ASSAULT & BATTERY

FACTS: Some neighborhood boys were playing soccer. John explained what happened, "Tempers were growing short when Gil was on the ground, wreathing in pain. Just moments before, he and Bob were eye to eye. I think Bob threatened Gil."

Gil was taken to the hospital and treated for a fractured jaw. After finding out he might have a permanent speech defect, Gil filed a complaint charging Bob with negligently causing his injuries. In addition, Bob might be charged with assault and battery. Was Bob guilty of assault and battery? Was Bob's conduct negligent?

DECISION: **YOU'RE THE JUDGE!**

Although most cases involving injuries to participants during sporting events are based on **negligence** (an unintentional act), some may be the result of **assault and battery** (an intentional act).

For Bob to be found guilty of a **tort**—a civil wrong committed against an individual—certain things have to be proven.

What if Bob had threatened Gil with harm? Gil was a better player and maybe Bob hoped to intimidate him. If Gil was aware of Bob's conduct, and was also reasonably apprehensive, fearing that Bob intended to immediately cause him injury by contact (hitting him), then Bob would be liable for **assault** upon Gil.

Would it still be an assault if Bob pushed someone else onto Gil?

FACTS: "Bob committed harmful and offensive contact, intending to hurt me. That's a **battery!**" charged Gil.

"I didn't hit you, Harry fell on you," Bob yelled.

Sam said, "Bob knocked Gil down and then pushed Harry, who fell on Gil."

If Bob intended to push Harry onto Gil, was Bob still liable for battery on Gil, even though he didn't directly hit Gil? **YOU'RE THE JUDGE!!**

DECISION: Yes, Bob would be liable. He would not have to touch Gil if he intended to hurt him, but could do so indirectly by, pushing someone into Gil, hitting him with an object or touching something Gil was holding.

DEFENSES TO ASSAULT & BATTERY

Bob insisted, "Gil gave his **consent** to the contact. He challenged me, 'You wanna fight, come on, let's go!'"

Gil denied this, contending that he "only consented to reasonable contact within the rules of soccer."

Next, Bob claimed **self-defense.** "After Gil hit me first, I defended myself, only using enough force to prevent Gil from harming me. If anyone else was hurt, I'm not liable for those injuries either. I didn't intend to hurt them."

Lastly, Bob argued, "Gil was beating up on Harry and Tom, so in **defense of others,** I used that force that they could have used to defend themselves."

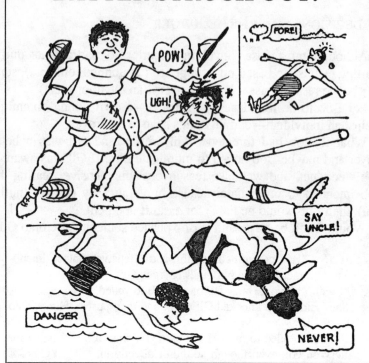

Boston Times SPORTS **September 12, 1987**

BATTER STRUCK OUT!

In a semi-pro baseball game last month, Lyle, the Lookouts' shortstop, had his jaw fractured. He was the batter when Earl, the Vols' catcher, struck him on the jaw. Was Earl liable? Yesterday, after listening to testimony, the court reached a decision.

Lyle explained in court what had happened, "I was up once before and Lane threw me curve balls outside. So the next time up, after the catcher gave his sign, I stepped up to try to hit the pitch before it broke. The ball almost hit me."

The pitcher then shouted, "Nobody does that to me. If you do it again I'll stick it in your ear!"

Lyle continued, "Well, I stepped forward and was hit. I knew that he was throwing at me. So, I started to throw the bat towards him, but held up and dropped it. That's all I remember."

Then, Earl, without any warning, struck Lyle with his fist, fracturing Lyle's jaw. Was Earl's team liable for the act of its player—vicarious liability?

The court found that, "Although Earl may have been personally liable for the injury to Lyle, the team was not. Earl was not performing his job when he hit Lyle. The team had no knowledge of any such previous conduct."

BURDEN OF PROOF

How convincing would the evidence have to be to prove assault and battery?

In a civil case involving negligence, the **plaintiff**—party bringing an action—has the **burden of proof.** He must prove to the judge or jury that the defendant is guilty by a mere majority of the clear and convincing evidence.

However, in a criminal case, such as one charging assault and battery, the prosecuting attorney must prove that the defendant is guilty beyond all reasonable doubt before there can be a conviction.

In other words, if the jury is more than 50% sure that the evidence shows that Bob was guilty, then they must return a verdict in Gil's favor and against Bob.

> FACTS: Bill Smith threw a punch while tackling Jay Jones during a football game. After the pile-up, he punched Jones again, causing a severe eye laceration.
>
> Jim Kirby, during a basketball game, struck Wally Shaw in the face with his fist, causing lacerations and broken teeth.
>
> Hank Lovel, a softball coach, beat an opposing coach with a bat.
>
> When assault and battery charges were brought against Smith, Kirby and Lovel, they defended by stating, "They gave their consent to the contact. We acted in self-defense, only using enough force necessary to stop them from hurting us." Were the defendants guilty of assault and battery? **YOU'RE THE JUDGE!**
>
> DECISION: Yes. The acts of Smith, Kirby and Lovel were intentional acts of misconduct—assault and battery.

Would the courts use a different approach for a pro game, knowing that professional players play for their livelihood, that the game is rougher, and that fighting may be more a part of the game, and therefore accepted?

ASSAULT & BATTERY IN PRO SPORTS

Northfield News
June 24

VIOLENCE ON THE FIELD!

Injuries in professional sports, where there is fault, may be due to either intentional or negligent conduct. Those that are intentional—assault and battery—are often referred to as acts of violence.

"As far back as 70 A.D., spectators at the games in Pompeii broke into wild sword fights. Centuries later many people were killed in riots set off by chariot racing."

Soccer matches have turned into mayhem and many other acts of violence have taken place between fans, and even between players. Is there a connection between spectator violence and violence on the field?

Pressure from teammates, coaches and fans may encourage athletes to take part in "generally accepted" violence during a game. Violence may be looked upon as a legitimate "part of the game." Leagues may accept and condone the use of violence while the media exploits it.

The fear of being labeled for not "performing," or of being waived, cut or traded helps to carry on this "macho code," leading to violence and injury.

Winning becomes the sole criteria for success. Violence has its part in determining that success… or lack of.

To review, the elements for cases involving intentional torts—assault and battery—that cause personal injury are: intentional, impermissible, and harmful or offensive contact to a person or something in his control. The defenses available to a defendant are consent, self-defense and defense of others.

Assault and battery may occur in numerous situations involving different sports.

Hockey

FACTS: The Town Crier newspaper reported, "There was a scramble in front of the hockey net. Danny, an NHL pro hockey player, in attempting to clear the puck away, hit Walt in the face with his stick. Walt, reacting quickly, swung his stick like a baseball bat, striking Danny on the bridge of his nose."

Injury to Danny: broken nose, concussion, facial lacerations. Danny sued Walt and the owner of Walt's team, alleging assault and battery and negligence. Did Danny assume the risk of such an injury? **YOU'RE THE JUDGE!**

DECISION: Judgment was for the plaintiff, Danny. Walt's conduct was intentional, impermissible and harmful, to which Danny did not consent. Danny only consented to that contact reasonably expected to be part of the game. Nor was the contact in self-defense. In addition to actual damages, Danny was awarded **punitive damages**—intended to serve as a deterrent to the defendant and others in preventing such conduct in the future.

Hockey may well produce the most violence. Insufficient suspensions for violent conduct and the general lack of enforcement of its rules by the NHL, have been severely criticized. Brawls have led to criminal actions. The fans expect violence; the teams and leagues condone it.

FACTS: Jay, an announcer, told of another fight in the NHL. "Matty and Brown pursued the puck behind the net. A skirmish developed. Brown struck Matty in the face with his glove. Matty retaliated by striking Brown in the stomach with his stick. After a penalty was called, a stick fight broke out. It was unclear who struck the first blow. Matty was struck near the shoulder and Brown was struck with a blow that resulted in a fractured skull."

Criminal assault charges were brought against both players by the district attorney. Both claimed that they were "acting in self-defense," and that the other player had "consented" to the injury by voluntarily playing hockey. Did the players consent to their injuries? **YOU'RE THE JUDGE!**

DECISION: The court concluded, "No athlete should be presumed to accept malicious, unprovoked, or overly violent attack." Nevertheless, both players were acquitted—found not guilty.

The court felt Matty consented to being struck by the glove because that was a common practice in hockey and not likely to result in serious injury. The court also felt that Brown's action was in self-defense and reasonable under the circumstances. No civil complaints for damages for personal injuries were ever filed.

Could a hockey stick be considered a deadly weapon when used to injure a player?

FACTS: Jacques and Pierre were assessed penalties after Jacques attacked Pierre. Upon serving out the penalties and leaving the penalty box, another fight broke out. Jacques allegedly assaulted Pierre from behind, striking him with his hockey stick and pummeling him with his fists. Jacques was charged with aggravated assault with a deadly weapon, a criminal charge. Was this aggravated assault? **YOU'RE THE JUDGE!**

DECISION: The jury could not agree upon a verdict (**hung jury**) and a **mistrial**—no decision—was declared. Unless the criminal charges were dropped, there would be a re-trial. No civil charges were filed.

Soccer

Soccer can also be a violent sport. Although play may be even rougher in the stands, leading to riots (especially after unfavorable officials' decisions), play on the field may lead to injuries for the players.

FACTS: A soccer player, Mario, was "dribbling" the ball toward his opponent's goal. When an opponent appeared in his path, Mario kicked the ball away. The opponent then jumped in the air and struck Mario in the stomach with his knee, rupturing Mario's intestines. When Mario died the next day, manslaughter charges were brought. Was this an assault and battery? **YOU'RE THE JUDGE!**

DECISION: In a criminal action, the court remarked, "If the defendant was acting within the rules, not motivated by any malicious motive which he knew could result in injury, then there was no crime. If he acted outside of the rules, intending to cause harm, was indifferent and reckless, the act would be unlawful."

The court concluded that, "There was not enough evidence to show that harm was intended." The accused player was acquitted.

What is the standard of proof in a criminal action? What must the plaintiff prove to the court?

In a criminal action, the jury must find, after hearing the evidence, that there was intent and "guilt beyond a reasonable doubt." That is much more difficult to prove than in a civil action, where the standard of proof is "by a mere majority of the clear and convincing evidence."

FACTS: Mario's wife brought suit for the death of her husband. Could she prevail in a civil action for damages?

DECISION: **YOU'RE THE JUDGE!**

Baseball

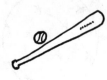

Baseball has perhaps the most lethal weapon in all of sports, the "beanball." This occurs when the ball is intentionally thrown at a batter's head. An umpire has the power—within certain guidelines (warning)—to eject a pitcher for intentionally throwing toward or at a batter. This may be a deterrent. However, it has not put an end to the beanball.

FACTS: Sam, a pro baseball player, was at bat and was hit by a pitch. When Sam threw his bat at the pitcher, he was struck by the catcher, Bob. Sam's jaw was fractured. He sued Bob and Bob's club for his injury.

Bob claimed assumption of the risk and self-defense of others as defenses. Bob pleaded, "I was defending the pitcher from being assaulted." "Was Bob liable for my injuries?" asked Sam. **YOU'RE THE JUDGE!**

DECISION: Yes. As the batter, Sam, made no further attempt to injure the pitcher. The pitcher was not in imminent (immediate) danger. Therefore, Bob did not have to defend Sam. Bob's act was intended to cause harm and did.

The court held that, "The club was not liable." reasoning that the assault was not performed within the **scope of employment**—Bob was not doing things normally permitted as part of his job. The club had no **vicarious liability**—liability for another's negligent acts.

How far can a player go in claiming that he was acting in self-defense when injuring another player?

FACTS: Another catcher, Gluefingers, in throwing the ball back to the pitcher, hit the batter—who happened to be the opposing pitcher. The batter hit the catcher over the head with his bat causing serious injuries. Was the batter acting in self-defense? **YOU'RE THE JUDGE!**

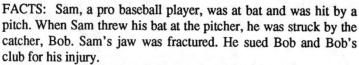

DECISION: There was no self-defense. Hitting the batter was unintentional and caused no damages. The defendant batter was suspended and fined; the suit was settled out of court. Gluefingers received money damages.

Basketball

In an attempt to keep things in order on the court, there have been many fights in pro basketball. Penalties for fighting may include fines and suspension, but they are not mandatory.

May an injured player recover damages against the team of the player who injured him?

FACTS: Adam and John got into a fight. Rudy, not involved in the fight, was struck in the face by Adam as he came toward the two. Rudy suffered fractures of the face and skull, a concussion, severe lacerations, a loss of teeth and a separated jaw.

As one witness testified, "The punch sounded like a watermelon being dropped on a cement floor!"

Rudy sued Adam's team, alleging vicarious liability–team liability for its players' actions. "The team was responsible for Adam's acts." Was the team liable for Adam's conduct? **YOU'RE THE JUDGE!**

DECISION: Yes. The jury found that Adam acted as an employee of his team. The team had failed to train him adequately so as to avoid such violence. Knowing his "dangerous" tendencies, the club did nothing to prevent the violence which occurred. The acts were a battery and reckless disregard for the safety of another person. In addition to actual damages, punitive damages were awarded. The case was settled before appeal.

Football

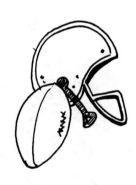

Football, like hockey, is an aggressive and, sometimes, violent sport. Rules have been changed in an attempt to lessen excessive violence. But physical contact and intimidation remain part of the game.

FACTS: After attempting to block Jim, Hank remained on one knee watching the play. The facts given to the court explained what happened next. Jim, acting out of anger and frustration but without specific intent to injure, struck the back of Hank's head and neck with his right forearm.

It was discovered that Hank had a serious neck injury. In addition to having pain and suffering, he felt that his career had been shortened. Hank sued Jim and Jim's team under vicarious liability. Who was liable? **YOU'RE THE JUDGE!**

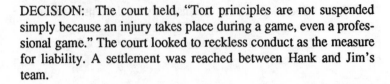

DECISION: The court held, "Tort principles are not suspended simply because an injury takes place during a game, even a professional game." The court looked to reckless conduct as the measure for liability. A settlement was reached between Hank and Jim's team.

NEGLIGENCE

The most frequent allegation and claim for relief when a participant is injured will be, "Someone was negligent. Their conduct, or lack of conduct, fell below that expected of an ordinary and responsible person in similar circumstances."

FACTS: If Jones, Shaw and the battered coach–all assaulted and battered–each brought separate actions to recover damages for their injuries, could a jury find the defendants negligent for their conduct? **YOU'RE THE JUDGE!**

DECISION: The defendants' conduct was below that expected of them. They breached their duty to care for the plaintiff's safety. They were negligent and, therefore, liable for damages.

The elements of **negligence** are: a **duty** owed to the plaintiff by the defendant (such as to play by the rules to insure everyone's safety), a **breach of** that **duty** by the defendant (the **injury** would not have happened **"but for"** the act of the defendant), and an injury resulting in **damages.**

The defenses that may be used by a defendant are: **contributory negligence**—the plaintiff contributed to his injuries by participating, **comparative negligence**—where a plaintiff's own negligence may reduce any amount that he recovers for injuries, and **assumption of the risk**—the plaintiff assumed the risk of injury from a known danger.

FACTS: The teams had warmed up for the state championship football game. The Fighting Wabaws won the toss.

Paul received the kickoff for the Polar Bears and headed up the field. In a sea of bodies, crunching and groaning, the play came to an end. The players unpiled; all except Paul.

X-rays revealed that Paul had a sprained neck. It could have been much worse.

"It could get worse when he gets older. Paul should no longer play football," the doctor warned his parents.

Paul missed work, incurred medical expenses and will always have pain and suffering from the injury. He brought an action against Billy, the player who tackled him, and Ray, the opposing coach. Who was at fault? Do you have enough evidence to decide if there was fault?

DECISION: **YOU'RE THE JUDGE!**

Paul must show by a majority of the clear and convincing evidence that one, or both, of the defendants was guilty of negligence (an unintentional tort—a breach of a duty of care) that caused his injury and damages.

Duty Of Care

Coach Ray had a duty to teach his players the proper way to tackle. Billy had a duty to tackle in the proper manner.

Their **duty of care** was to act as reasonable people would act under the same circumstances, considering the potential harm, and considering the precautions that were available. That is the duty owed by an adult. Billy, participating in an adult activity, is treated as an adult.

If Billy was a minor, would he have the same duty? A minor may be held to a lesser duty of care.

Breach Of Duty

FACTS: Paul accused Billy, "You breached your duty of care by tackling with your head."

Paul further charged, "Coach Ray taught Billy and his teammates to use their heads and helmets to tackle, or at the least, he did not discourage the practice." Would such conduct be negligent? **YOU'RE THE JUDGE!**

DECISION: Tackling, by using one's head, was a violation of safety rules and therefore, negligent. The coach had a duty to protect Paul from unreasonable risks of injury, such as that caused by head tackling.

"But For...."

Paul contended, "Billy's and Coach Ray's breach of duty was the **proximate cause** of my injury and damage. That is, 'but for' their actions, I would not have been hurt."

In other words, had Coach Ray taught the proper way to tackle, and had Billy tackled properly, Paul would not have been injured.

Injury & Damages

Paul must prove his injury and show damages. These may be **special damages**—all medical related costs and loss of earnings (real or potential), or **general damages**—pain and suffering and loss of enjoyment of life.

Paul can't recover **punitive damages**—damages which are meant to punish and penalize the defendant—unless he shows that one or both of the defendants were grossly negligent and acted with **malice**—recklessness or evil intent.

DEFENSES TO NEGLIGENCE

What defenses may the defendants claim against the action by Paul to recover damages for his injury?

The defendants claimed **contributory negligence**. "Paul was aware of the danger and risk involved. He contributed to his injury by playing and by lowering his own head."

FACTS: Tom was injured during a pick-up football game. "I stepped in a hole in the field," he said. Tom had played there many times before and was well aware of the condition of the field. Did he assume the risk of injury? Was he guilty of contributory negligence? **YOU'RE THE JUDGE!**

DECISION: Tom cannot recover for his injury. He assumed the risk of, and contributed to, his injury by playing there. He violated a duty to protect himself.

In addition, the defendants argued, "Paul had the **last clear chance** to avoid the injury, didn't, and he should be guilty of contributory negligence, preventing any right to recover."

The defendants also felt that **assumption of the risk** should prevent Paul from recovering any damages. "Paul knew the risk of being injured existed and was common to the game. He voluntarily proceeded anyway."

FACTS: Paul said, "I only assumed the ordinary risks of the game. I did not contribute to the injury. Furthermore, I didn't assume extraordinary risks, such as from head tackling. Nor did I assume the risk of injury from such an unforseeable violation of the rules. Can I recover for my injury?"

DECISION: **YOU'RE THE JUDGE!**

Billy and Coach Ray thought that because Paul lowered his own head, that Paul's **comparative negligence** should be compared with theirs. If they were found guilty, any recovery by Paul should be reduced because of his own negligence.

If an injury is from an unavoidable **pure accident**—unforseeable or could not be prevented by reasonable caution—it may be unavoidable and not actionable. Assumption of the risk will be a valid defense.

FACTS: One baseball player was injured when a ball curved around a screen. Another was injured when a ball bounced off a wall and into the dugout. This had never happened before.

A football player who was run out of bounds lamented, "I was so mad, I ran far past the sideline and was hurt when I tripped over a tree stump in a lot next to the field." Did the players assume the risk of such injuries? **YOU'RE THE JUDGE!**

DECISION: If an injury is unforeseeable (pure accident), or could not be prevented by reasonable caution, it may then be unavoidable. Both players assumed such risks and could not recover damages.

Assumption of the risk or contributory negligence may arise where a participant is clearly aware of the risk or danger involved and, yet, voluntarily proceeds to encounter that danger.

FACTS: Tom played for the Aztec U. basketball team. He explained, "I know that it gets rough under the hoop, so I decided to play rough myself. While trying to grab a rebound, my nose was broken by someone's elbow." "Did I assume the risk of injury? Was I guilty of contributory negligence? " asked Tom. **YOU'RE THE JUDGE!**

DECISION: Tom assumed the risk of injury and—by knowing of the danger, but continuing the rough play—he was also guilty of contributory negligence.

Where a player receives injuries from accidents that are a result of normal or reasonable conduct, there will be no liability.

FACTS: Robert, while playing in a pick-up football game, injured his knee. He charged, "There was no preparation for the game, no equipment and inadequate supervision. They piled on me. Also, I was encouraged at too early an age, 15, to play." Did Robert assume the risk of injury? **YOU'RE THE JUDGE!**

DECISION: Robert assumed the risk of injury from the normal and reasonable conduct of the game. There was negligence for no preparation and equipment, but that didn't cause the injury, nor did being encouraged to play at too early an age. Robert was aware of the danger.

As long as play is in pursuit of the normal and accepted goals of the game, then any injuries arising from contact may be considered as from ordinary risks of the game.

But what if a player, whether intentionally or not, pursues the game in a way which creates a risk that it is not a normal and expected risk of participating in that game?

FACTS: A softball player, Lucky, was injured when a runner, Spikes, "rounded second, ran out of the base path and intentionally dove head first into me, injuring my knee."

"Was that a normal or ordinary risk of the game?" questioned Lucky. **YOU'RE THE JUDGE!**

DECISION: Ordinary risks are assumed, but not where another acts intentionally and in violation of the rules. This was a breach of Spike's duty to care for Lucky's safety.

What if the injured was a voluntary participant, such as a ball boy?

FACTS: A basketball coach, Ishy, was injured. "I slipped on the floor and fractured my ankle." he groaned.

A ball boy, Wally, while at a baseball game, was hit and injured by a foul ball.

A caddy, Bobby, was struck by an errant golf shot which broke his wrist. He had gone ahead of the players to watch where the balls landed. Could any of the three recover for their injuries? **YOU'RE THE JUDGE!**

DECISION: No. Voluntary participants and others, who in some way are involved in a sports activity, assume all the ordinary risks of that sport, so long as the activity is played in good faith and the injury is not the result of intentional misconduct.

Where accidents are so many that a game is too dangerous to continue without change (such as where accidents on an auto racetrack were numerous and continuous), assumption of the risk may not be a valid defense.

Also, where risks are created by the negligence of third persons—such as medical personnel, a referee or a coach—assumption of the risk may not be a valid defense.

FACTS: A hockey player, Francis, sued his team for breach of its duty to care for his safety. "I was ordered to play while I had a separated shoulder. The team knew about my injury," said Francis. A check by an opposing player then left him with permanent injuries to his spinal cord. Were his team and coach liable for the injury? **YOU'RE THE JUDGE!**

DECISION: Yes. Francis' club was vicariously liable for the coach' negligence. In addition to actual damages, punitive damages were assessed against the team for conduct "such as to merit condemnation."

In determining if there is liability by a defendant, courts use a two-step process. If the first duty, owed by the defendant to the plaintiff is violated, the plaintiff should recover. However, if the plaintiff has violated the second duty—that of using reasonable care to protect himself—this will prevent any recovery for damages for a resulting injury.

REVIEW! REVIEW!

There are two general rules concerning injuries to participants in sports activities.

First, the owner or operator of a sports or public amusement facility is not an insurer of a participant's safety.

The owner or operator is bound to exercise "ordinary and reasonable" care for the safety and protection of his patrons; that is, the care which an ordinary, prudent, careful and cautious person would have exercised under the same or similar circumstances.

Second, athletes assume all ordinary and inherent risks of an activity, but do not assume extraordinary risks, unless they know of and voluntarily assume them.

Defenses that owners or operators may assert in defense of charges of negligence against them will be assumption of the risk, and contributory or comparative negligence.

Negligence resulting in injuries to athletes may occur in many different sports, activities and situations.

BOXING

Where there are no laws prohibiting boxing, courts have held that a person who engaged in, and consented to, a boxing or "prize" fight, generally cannot recover from an opponent for injuries he suffers. Assumption of the risk and consent to the contact will be valid defenses.

If there is a law making boxing unlawful, then participants can file complaints against each other for assault. Here, consent will not excuse any act resulting in injury.

BOWLING

Bowling premises are to be kept in a reasonably safe condition. There is a duty to warn of dangerous conditions of which the proprietor is or should be aware.

Does a proprietor of bowling premises have a duty to inspect the premises for defects which can cause injuries?

The proprietor must inspect the premises at reasonable intervals and correct any dangerous conditions within a reasonable time, or warn patrons.

A bowler assumes the ordinary risks of bowling and may be con-

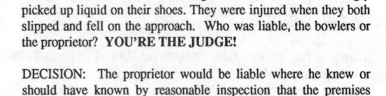

tributorily negligent if aware of an unsafe condition, but still exposes oneself to it.

> FACTS: One bowler was called to the control stand, another went to the bathroom before returning to bowl. Both unknowingly picked up liquid on their shoes. They were injured when they both slipped and fell on the approach. Who was liable, the bowlers or the proprietor? **YOU'RE THE JUDGE!**

> DECISION: The proprietor would be liable where he knew or should have known by reasonable inspection that the premises were unsafe.

But where it could not be proven how long the substance was there, and the bowler knew that there were drinks in the area, the proprietor will not be liable for any resulting injury.

Where it is alleged that there was a substance present, the plaintiff must also prove that the injury was as a result of the substance and not due to some other cause, such as worn shoes or the condition of the bowler (drunk). But if the worn shoes, rented from the proprietor, caused an injury, the proprietor may be responsible for not properly inspecting and replacing them.

If an injury is the result of a "faulty" approach, of which the bowler was not aware, liability will be based on either a failure to discover the defect, or on a failure to correct it.

Who would be liable where a bowler selected a house ball and was injured when it "stuck" in her hand?

> FACTS: Mary selected a house ball and began to warm up for the bowling league.
> "When her fingers stuck in the ball, she slipped to the floor, injuring her hip," explained Sue. Mary alleged negligence on the part of the proprietor for not inspecting the ball. "Was the proprietor at fault? **YOU'RE THE JUDGE!**

> DECISION: No. Although the proprietor has a duty to inspect for defects and unsafe conditions, it would be burdensome to require the constant checking all of the balls. Of course, if the proprietor knew of the condition, but didn't correct it, and the bowler could not know of the consequences until actually using the ball, the proprietor may be liable.

ROLLER & ICE SKATING

The owner or operator of a skating rink does not insure a patron's safety. However, he must exercise reasonable and ordinary care. This duty includes inspecting the premises and maintaining them in a reasonably safe condition.

Participants must exercise reasonable care for their own safety, and they assume the ordinary risks and dangers of the sport.

FACTS: Several skaters were injured when they tripped over holes and soft spots on the ice. They were "fooling around" when injured. Was the proprietor liable for these injuries? **YOU'RE THE JUDGE!**

DECISION: No, unless the proprietor had enough time to discover the defects, and either knew or should have been aware of them.

Negligence has been found where skaters unknowingly skated into a pile of litter and ice scrapings and were injured, and were cut from glass doors that were too close to the rink.

Negligence was not found where a skater was injured while skating in an off-limits area (an entrance) or where a skater tripped over a railing necessary for the protection of patrons to separate the rink from the walkway.

Does a proprietor have a duty to furnish safe equipment?

FACTS: A proprietor furnished skates which were loose, falling apart, or otherwise defective. The skaters were either not aware of the defects, or were encouraged to use the skates nonetheless. Who would be liable for any resulting injuries? **YOU'RE THE JUDGE!**

DECISION: Some risks may be ordinary ones, such as a broken shoelace. For these, the skater assumes the risk, as he also will when using equipment improperly. Otherwise, the proprietor may be negligent if he furnishes equipment which he either knew, or by reasonable inspection should have known, was defective and such equipment causes an injury.

Does a proprietor have a duty to protect patrons where he either knew or should have known that another's conduct might cause injury?

A proprietor may be liable for improper supervision which results in an injury if he allows rowdy conduct: skaters going too fast or into an area reserved for less experienced skaters, too many skaters on the rink, or allowing known "rowdies". on the ice.

An operator may not be liable where an injury occurs from an ordinary risk of the sport (unintentional bumping), or if a skater participated in unpermitted activity.

FACTS: "John and Jack, weaving in and out, were skating too fast. They crashed into Susan, injuring both her and Jack," noticed Tony.

The proprietor was not aware of this "sudden" breach of the rules. Who was liable for the injuries? **YOU'RE THE JUDGE!**

DECISION: Jack assumed the risk of and contributed to his own injury. Both John and Jack were liable for Susan's injury. This was not an ordinary risk of the sport.

SWIMMING & WATER SKIING

The duties imposed upon operators of premises used for swimming or water skiing, and the responsibility of participants and others, depends upon whether the facilities are regarded to be public or private.

Public Facilities

Operators of facilities open to the general public are bound to use ordinary and reasonable care for the safety of the public. This includes the duty to provide and exercise proper supervision. These duties may be affected by laws and the age of a child.

Will greater care be required for younger children?

FACTS: Greg, 12, drowned at a public pool in the neighborhood park. There was no lifeguard on duty when the incident occurred (2:00 P.M.). Was the operator of the pool liable? **YOU'RE THE JUDGE!**

DECISION: Yes. The operator had a duty to provide a lifeguard, especially where younger children used the pool.

If a drowning occurs due to either the non-presence or inattentiveness of a lifeguard, liability will be found.

However, if a lifeguard would not have been able to save a swimmer, or the swimmer placed himself in a position of danger (such as jumping or swimming into water known to be too deep, especially after being warned), there may be no liability by the operator the facility.

Unexplained drownings also may not impose liability, unless the drowning occurred at a crowded pool where there was an insufficient number of lifeguards, or they were inattentive.

Negligence may also be found where there was a delay in a rescue, or where it was improperly attempted, or with improper rescue equipment.

What if a swimmer was injured during "horseplay?"

FACTS: "Johnnie jumped into the water, struck his head on the bottom and was then cut by broken glass. Frankie was pushed in on top of Johnnie and Bob jumped on top of them," testified Sherry. All were injured. Was the operator liable for these injuries? **YOU'RE THE JUDGE!**

DECISION: If Johnnie jumped into the shallow water after he knew, or should have known, its depth, there will be no liability by the operator. The operator should have known of the glass by inspection. He was negligent.

If there was a lifeguard on duty to warn of the danger from horseplay, and the warning was not heeded or if the injury happened suddenly, there will be no liability to the operator. There would be liability if a lifeguard was not present, was inattentive, or did not try to prevent such conduct. That would be improper supervision.

Patrons are held to assume the ordinary risks of the sport. If an accident was either unavoidable, or if the patron contributed to his injury, assumption of the risk and contributory negligence will be valid defenses.

Private Facilities

A patron at a private swimming facility must exercise ordinary care for his own safety. If he either knew, or should have known, of a danger, but proceeded anyway to place himself in danger, he may be held to have assumed the risk of venturing into water too deep and contributed to any injury.

Private operators (such as a hotel, resort or private club) of premises used for swimming have a duty to use ordinary and reasonable care for the safety of patrons.

> FACTS: Bill injured his neck diving into a pool unmarked for depths; Joe cut himself on glass in the pool; Mary was injured when other kids piled on top of her after coming down the water slide; Jeremy was injured when bumped into by some kids fooling around in the bathhouse. What were the operator's duties? **YOU'RE THE JUDGE!**
>
> DECISION: The operator has a duty to: mark the varying depths of the water, keep it clear of dangerous substances, warn of unsafe conditions, provide adequate and attentive supervision where required, and properly control the patrons and maintain the premises. These duties extend to the bathhouse or shower rooms.

Water Skiing

Operators of premises used for water skiing must exercise reasonable and ordinary care to maintain the premises in a reasonably safe

condition. Water skiers and others involved assume the normal risks of water skiing. If they place themselves in a perilous or dangerous condition, they may be guilty of contributory negligence.

FACTS: Henry was injured while water skiing. "I was forced to dive to the side to avoid a swimmer!" he testified.

Kirk was also injured while water skiing when he hit a rock in shallow water fifty feet from shore. There was no notice of the shallow depth, and Kirk did not know of it. What were the operator's duties? **YOU'RE THE JUDGE!**

DECISION: The operator of the premises should provide a separate area for both swimmers and water skiers. This area should be clearly marked and a proper warning, either oral or by sign should be given. Shallow water should be properly marked where it would not be apparent, and notice should be given as to the acceptable speed limit in such an area.

What duty does the operator of a boat used for water skiing or in the area of swimmers have?

The operator of a towing, or other, boat has the same duty of due care for the safety of those using the water. He may be responsible for a sudden start without warning or before the skier is ready or for not providing a necessary lookout and signals.

FACTS: Sue charged, "I was getting ready to be towed. Without warning, the driver intentionally accelerated the boat, injuring me!"

Leona, sunbathing on a float, drowned after she was knocked off the float by a tow rope. The water skier attempted to flip the rope over her as he passed between her and the shore. Did Sue or Leona assume such risks? **YOU'RE THE JUDGE!**

DECISION: No. These were not ordinary risks inherent to using the water. The conduct of the drivers was in reckless disregard for the girls' safety. In addition to actual damages, punitive damages were awarded—to punish the drivers and water skier.

A water skier may be guilty of contributory negligence when aware of the danger involved, such as an inexperienced driver, shallow water or the speed of the boat.

An operator of another boat in the area may be liable for failure to exercise ordinary care, such as when coming too close to a waterskier, going too fast, or being inattentive (thereby causing an injury).

Boating Laws

Laws governing the use of boats may have a provision prohibiting operating a boat:

"...in a reckless or negligent manner so as to endanger the life, limb, or property of any person...."

"Reckless or negligent manner" prohibits: excessive speed, overloading, improper—or a lack of—safety equipment, improper passing, operating under the influence, "buzzing" of other boats or persons, using dangerous waters, standing in the boat, and generally failing to take proper precautions on approach of bad weather or other situations involving risk of safety.

SKIING, SNOWMOBILES....

An operator of premises used for winter skiing and other activities is not an insurer of a participant's safety. However, the operator must exercise ordinary and reasonable care in maintaining the premises and in giving proper and adequate warning of possible dangers.

Participants are held to assume the ordinary risks and dangers involved in such activities.

An operator may be held liable where he breaches his duty of care, such as by permitting snowmobiles in the same area as skiers, failing to properly inspect and maintain the premises, or where proper and adequate warnings of dangers are not given.

> FACTS: A novice skier, Holly, fell and became entangled in brush concealed by loose snow. She was rendered a permanent quadriplegic. She sued the operator at the ski resort for failure to provide a safe place to ski. Was the operator liable? **YOU'RE THE JUDGE!**

> DECISION: The operator was found liable for Holly's injury. This was a breach of the operator's duty to provide and maintain premises safe for their intended use.

However, where the risk is obvious, assumption of the risk may be a valid defense.

> FACTS: A skier, Walter, struck a utility pole, which allegedly was not properly padded, and was injured. A state statute read: "The skier accepts the dangers that are inherent in skiing." in reference to obvious dangers. "Did I assume the risk of injury?" asked Walter. **YOU'RE THE JUDGE!**

> DECISION: This case established assumption of the risk as a defense. The skier was, or should have been, aware of the obvious danger. Walter assumed the risk of injury.

Unless an operator is negligent in providing supervision, the operator may not be liable for injuries occurring as a result of collisions

between skiers. The operator may be liable where different areas are necessary, but not set out for different levels of skill.

As between two skiers, they both assume the ordinary and inherent dangers of the sport. But they will not assume extraordinary dangers, such as where a more experienced skier "cut off" one less experienced, or where the general rules of the slope (right-of-way) were not obeyed and injury resulted.

Competitors may assume ordinary risks within their control. Therefore, where a ski-jumper was blown out of position by the wind, he assumed the risk of injury.

What if, to mark off a course, an operator used improper equipment which resulted in an injury?

> FACTS: Several skiers were injured when they collided with poles used to mark off a racecourse. There were other thinner, less dangerous poles available. Was the operator liable for the injuries? **YOU'RE THE JUDGE!**

> DECISION: The operator was liable for using improper poles. The injuries would not have happened but for the negligence of the operator.

Foresight and caution in guarding against dangers involving chair lifts are also required of the operator. This generally will involve proper maintenance and supervision.

A skier must exercise care for his own safety, both in the use of chair lifts and on the slopes.

Does an operator have a duty to inquire of the experience of those renting his equipment?

> FACTS: Novice renters of skis and snowmobile equipment said, "We were injured when we went out of control. We did not know how to use the ill-fitted equipment." They sued the operators, alleging a neglect of a duty to give proper instructions for using the equipment. Was the operator liable? **YOU'RE THE JUDGE!**

> DECISION: Yes. When an operator rents out equipment to be used in skiing, snowmobiling or other winter activities, he has a duty to insure that it is fit for its intended use and that the user is given proper instructions. Through inquiry, the operator should have known that the skiers were novices.

As to the use of snowmobiles, skimobiles, sleds and toboggans used in racing or otherwise, care must be taken to: inspect the area to be used, give adequate warnings to participants and spectators, use barriers where necessary, and, to properly mark off-limit areas.

An operator will not be an insurer of a participant's or other's safety. Participants and others must use proper precautions for their own safety and will assume the ordinary risks involved.

GOLF

What is the duty of the operator of a golf course?

The operator of a golf course has a duty to exercise reasonable care for the safety of others, both in the supervision of play, and in maintaining the premises and equipment under her control in a safe condition.

However, she is not an insurer of a patron's safety. Golfers will assume the risks of injury from the ordinary and usual hazards inherent in the game. She will not assume liability from extraordinary risks brought about by others.

Who would be liable where an operator employs a starter or ranger to help in supervising play, and an injury results?

FACTS: At the instruction of the starter to "Go ahead." Ray and John teed off. They both struck and injured players in the same and adjacent fairways. Who was liable for the injuries? **YOU'RE THE JUDGE!**

DECISION: If a golfer "tees off" at the instruction of a starter, liability by the starter can be established where the injured player was on the same hole, in front of the golfer teeing off and not yet out of range.

If Ray and John were aware that a player was within their range on the hole they were playing and, nevertheless, teed off and injured that player, the golfer and the operator may share liability.

If the injury occurs to one in an adjacent area, the golfer teeing off may be liable if a warning is not given, if required and which may have prevented the injury.

The operator of a golf course has a duty to maintain the golf course and surrounding premises.

Who would be liable where a golfer did not know of an incorrect yardage and therefore, in hitting the ball, used "too much club," injuring another golfer?

FACTS: Ivan was teeing off on the eighth hole at Orchard Country Club. Not having played there before, he checked the card — 315 yards. When the group in front of him reached the green, Ivan teed off. His drive struck Joe, who was pulling the pin out of the hole.

After the accident, Ivan said disbelievingly, "I just can't understand how I could hit a ball that far." In fact, the hole was only

225 yards long. Joe sued Ivan for striking him, and the golf course for incorrectly stating the yardage. Who was liable for Joe's injury? **YOU'RE THE JUDGE!**

DECISION: The club was found liable for Joe's injury. The manager of the golf course, in a conversation with Ivan's wife, admitted, "Two years ago, we moved the green forward. We got a lot of cards left here. When we print them up again, we'll probably change them."

Where screens or fencing, designed for the safety of players, are not properly maintained, liability may be established if an injury is a result of such negligent maintenance.

An operator has a duty to exercise due care in maintaining equipment, ensuring that it is fit for its intended use. Therefore, if the brakes on a cart are not properly inspected and an injury results, the operator may be liable.

FACTS: Rental golf clubs were not inspected. A reasonable inspection would have revealed a loose or broken clubhead. As a result, Guy was injured when his partner swung a club and the head flew off, striking him. "Who was liable, the proprietor?" asked Guy. **YOU'RE THE JUDGE!**

DECISION: Yes, particularly where the danger was not apparent to the user. A renter of equipment has the right to assume that the equipment is fit for the use intended.

If a golfer yells "Fore!" after hitting an errant shot, is he relieved of liability for any resulting injury?

FACTS: Paul hit a golfer in another fairway with an errant shot. He saw the other player when he hit the ball. Was Paul liable? What if he yelled "Fore"? **YOU'RE THE JUDGE!**

DECISION: Paul had a duty to give a timely and adequate warning to the other player. If he did so, he would not be liable. The other player would have assumed the risk as one ordinary to the game. The exception might be where Paul intended the ball to start in the direction of the other golfer, hoping to "draw" or "fade" the ball. Here, he will be held to have at least waited until the other player was out of range.

In holding that an injured golfer assumed the risk of injury from an errant golf shot, one judge stated, "Generally, it is well known that a slight deviation of the club head may send the ball in a most unexpected direction. To hold that a golfer is negligent merely because his ball did not go in a straight and intended line would be to impose a greater duty of care than the creator endowed him with faculties to carry out."

What if a golfer is "waived on" by a golfer up ahead and he then hits that golfer?

FACTS: John, 36, teed off after he was waived on by the players ahead of him.

His ball struck Mike, 24, one of the players who waived him on. Did Mike assume the risk of such an injury? **YOU'RE THE JUDGE!**

DECISION: Mike assumed the risk of injury after waiving John through. He was also guilty of contributory negligence.

What if Mike was only 10 years old? Who would be liable then?

Where a player up ahead is very young and not mindful of the danger involved, an older, more experienced golfer may assume the responsibility and liability.

Who would be liable for injuries from a reckless swing or a caroming ball?

FACTS: Barney, frustrated over hitting two balls into the woods, took a reckless swing. His club "flew" twenty feet and struck his partner, Tim, in the face. "I didn't assume the risk of such an injury, did I?" asked Tim. **YOU'RE THE JUDGE!**

DECISION: No. Barney breached his "duty to exercise reasonable care in controlling his golf club." He was liable for Tim's injury.

FACTS: Andy's ball caromed off a tree, injuring a golfer in another fairway. Was Andy guilty of negligence? **YOU'RE THE JUDGE!**

DECISION: Their was no liability. Such a result could not reasonably be anticipated.

Where a caddie or groundskeeper voluntarily went "up ahead," or worked in an area known to be within the range of errant golf shots and was injured, assumption of the risk will prevent any recovery.

This will not be the case where a golfer was aware of the presence of others, but did not give a timely or adequate warning which could have prevented the injury.

Generally, the operator of a driving range will be responsible for properly supervising "play"—ensuring that golfers are hitting from and to a permitted area.

FACTS: The operator of a driving range hired several young junior high school boys to "shag" balls from the range. He told the golfers to hit "away" from the boys.

An errant shot struck one of the boys, Stevie, who then sued the golfer and the operator. Who was liable? **YOU'RE THE JUDGE!**

DECISION: The operator had the duty to protect the boys by whatever means were necessary, including stopping golfers from practicing until the boys were done. Any golfer, although encouraged to continue, may share such liability.

"RACK 'EM UP"

The operator of premises used for pool or billiards is not an insurer of a patron's safety. However, he must exercise reasonable care in supervising and in keeping the premises and equipment reasonably safe for its intended use.

FACTS: A patron at a pool hall was injured when a fight spread to the area he was playing in. The operator yelled, "Break it up!" but it was too late. The operator had ample notice and time.

Another injury resulted from flying splinters, where there was no advance notice of the disturbance. Were the operators liable for these injuries? **YOU'RE THE JUDGE!**

DECISION: The first operator was negligent and liable for the injuries. The second operator did not have notice. He was not liable, although the patron causing the injury may have been.

JOGGING, CYCLES, SKATES....

The general duty owed to pedestrians, "joggers," cyclists and others is one of reasonable care and maintenance of public ways. However, those in charge of such ways are not insurers of pedestrian's and other's safety. Generally, pedestrians and others will assume the ordinary and inherent risks involved in using or traveling a public way. They will not assume extraordinary risks or dangers.

Pedestrians, cyclists, joggers, skateboarders, and rollerskaters, while using public ways, are subject to and shall: obey traffic signals, use sidewalks, use that side of the roadway facing traffic where there is no sidewalk, yield and be yielded the right of way—depending on the circumstances—and cross only in marked walkways and in a proper manner.

FACTS: John and Valla were out for a walk. They decided to walk in the street instead of on the sidewalk. When crossing the street, they didn't use the marked crossing area.

Kevin, out for a jog, ran through a red light.

Jimmy rode his bike with the flow of the traffic where there was no sidewalk. He also rode at night without using reflectors. Were any of these practices prohibited? **YOU'RE THE JUDGE!**

DECISION: All of the practices were prohibited. John and Valla are required to use the proper areas set off for walking and crossing the street.

Jimmy is required to have reflectors on his bike when riding at night.

Kevin was given a $17 citation by a police officer, but the judge reduced the fine to $7 when he discovered that he could run a faster mile than Kevin. "He saved $10 for being slower than me," chuckled the judge.

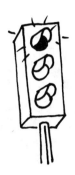

Where private property or public ways are "set aside" for pedestrians for walking, jogging or for marathons, is a higher degree of care required to maintain the way?

FACTS: "I was hurt when I fell after my bike hit a hole in the bike path. I never saw the hole," muttered Henry. Did Henry assume the risk of his injury? **YOU'RE THE JUDGE!**

DECISION: The town was liable. They had notice of and opportunity to attend to the hole or other defects not readily apparent to users. However, the town could not be sued. Sovereign immunity—which may apply to some towns—prevented any recovery.

Runners in a race, such as a marathon, may generally assume that the course is in the condition required for its intended use. A runner will assume the risks and dangers ordinarily inherent in running, such as from other runners, or cars (if not in a race).

Motorcyclists have the same rights and duties as those of the driver of any other vehicle.

Does a bicyclist have those same rights and duties?

Yes. Therefore, a cycle may only carry that number of people that it is equipped to carry while being ridden: it cannot be attached to a vehicle, it must be kept to the right except when passing, making a turn or to avoid an accident; one hand must be on the handlebars at all times, and pedestrians must be given the right-of-way on a sidewalk.

What about using radio headsets?

FACTS: Tom and Maria, with their radio headsets turned on, went out for a bicycle ride. They raced down the sidewalk past all of the stores on Main Street. Right behind them on skateboards were Jorni and "T.J." "Were we doing anything wrong?" they asked. **YOU'RE THE JUDGE!**

DECISION: Yes. All persons operating a bicycle or skateboard shall not ride on a sidewalk within a business district, or where otherwise prohibited.

Bicyclists, motorcyclists, rollerskaters and joggers may be prohibited from wearing radio headsets as this gear could restrict the necessary ability to hear.

TENNIS

The operator of a tennis facility, in supervising and in maintaining the premises, will be held to exercise reasonable care for the safety of others.

However, an operator is not an insurer of the participant's safety. Participants and others will assume the ordinary and inherent risks of the game, but not extraordinary ones.

FACTS: Andy, in disgust at his play, threw his racket. It hit Tom and broke his nose! Who was liable for Tom's injury? **YOU'RE THE JUDGE!**

DECISION: The injury was not from an ordinary risk of the game. Andy was liable for the injury.

Where an operator had forewarning and notice of improper conduct, he will be liable for injury caused by improper supervision.

FACTS: John was injured when he was struck in the eye with a tennis ball. He claimed, "Peter intentionally tried to hit Hank in the face after he screamed 'Eat this!' But the ball hit me instead."

Peter and Hank had been screaming at each other for some time before the injury to John. Who was liable? **YOU'RE THE JUDGE!**

DECISION: John assumed normal risks, not extraordinary ones. Peter and the proprietor, for allowing the improper conduct to continue, shared liability.

GYMNASTICS

Is supervision required where a proprietor has a trampoline on the premises?

At Sarge's Trampoline Center, a notice read, "Patrons use the trampoline at your own risk."

A patron, Paul, 18, was injured while jumping on the trampoline. Could he recover damages?

Paul assumed the risk of injury. The trampoline was not in a defective condition and the danger was obvious. Furthermore, in this situation, supervision was not required. If Paul was only ten years old (or the trampoline was at a school), would supervision then be required?

HUNTING

The basic rule for hunters is that a hunter "must not pull the trigger without ample assurance that he is shooting only at game."

Therefore, where a hunter shot at something which turned out to be a man picking berries, the hunter was liable for negligence. He breached his duty to exercise reasonable care for the safety of others. A hunter must handle his gun with extraordinary care.

> FACTS: Johnson left the safety off of his gun. The gun discharged when he fell from a wobbly duck blind. A companion was hit in the leg. Did the injured hunter assume the risk of injury? **YOU'RE THE JUDGE!**

> DECISION: No. Johnson, who must handle his weapon with extraordinary care, was found negligent. He was liable for the injury.

No liability was found for an injury resulting from a hunter firing in a direction where any experienced bird hunter would not be without having given warning of his changed position.

PICNICS

> FACTS: Henderson chided his friends at a picnic, "You can't throw me in the lake!" In the roughhousing which followed, he was severely injured when someone fell on top of him. Who was liable? Could he recover for his injury? **YOU'RE THE JUDGE!**

> DECISION: No. Recovery was denied. It was reasonably foreseeable that injury might occur during the horseplay. Henderson assumed that risk. Furthermore, he was guilty of contributing to his own injury.

Had Henderson not invited or consented to the contact, then there would be liability for "unconsented contact."

Also, if someone had consented to contact, but the contact was beyond that normally expected, liability may also attach. This would be especially so where the injured, after first consenting, later retracted that consent ("Cut it out!") and was injured.

CAMPS

Generally, in part due to the age of the participants, there will be a greater than normal duty to use reasonable care in supervising most

activities at camps. Some degree of risk will be assumed, but not excessive or unpermitted force, nor injury from extraordinary hazards.

> FACTS: Jan sobbed, "I dove off the platform as I had many times the previous year. I cut my head on a rock." Was the operator of the camp liable for the injury? **YOU'RE THE JUDGE!**

> DECISION: Yes. The platform had been moved during the winter. This created an extraordinary hazard for which the operator was liable. He should have inspected the premises beforehand.

Operators of camps must also maintain the premises in a satisfactory condition, considering its intended use. Premises may include the water, trails, general play areas and any housing accommodations.

GO-CARTS

> FACTS: John and Robby were injured when their go-carts collided and tires, stacked up to prevent the cars from leaving the track, fell on them.
> Jennifer was injured when her brakes wouldn't function after she hit a puddle. Their parents asked, "Can we recover damages?" **YOU'RE THE JUDGE!**

> DECISION: John and Robby assumed the ordinary and inherent risks of the sport, such as an unintentional collision or falling tires after a collision.
> Jennifer could recover damages. She did not assume extraordinary risks, such as oil or water on the track, where there was notice and opportunity for the operator to correct such a danger.

An operator has a duty to properly supervise such an activity and to maintain the premises in a safe condition.

FISHING

Does a weather bureau have a duty to properly forecast oncoming inclement weather?

One court ruled that they did. The court held a weather bureau liable for the drowning deaths of three fishermen. They drowned when a sudden and violent storm struck.

Will one fisherman be liable for "hooking" another?

> FACTS: Gary, in his excitement to get his pole in the water, paid no attention to Lou, who was baiting his hook. "I didn't see him," said Gary. Gary "hooked" Lou in the mouth. Did Lou assume the risk of such an injury? **YOU'RE THE JUDGE!**

DECISION: No. Gary owed Lou a duty of reasonable care for his safety. By casting with indifference as to where Lou was, Gary was liable.

AUTO RACETRACK

The owner, promoter or operator of an auto racetrack may be liable for an injury to a participant where there was negligence in the construction or maintenance of the racetrack, when the owner or operator knew, or should have known, of the defect.

FACTS: "Cannonball" Jones was injured in an auto race when his car skidded off the track and hit a retaining wall.

"Cannonball was injured during the first lap. The oil from a previous accident had not been cleaned up as required," explained an attendant. Was the owner or operator of the track liable for Cannonball's injury?

DECISION: **YOU'RE THE JUDGE!**

There will be no liability where negligence was not the proximate (but for) cause of any injury. Therefore, where an auto racer's car went out of control, due either to unavoidable circumstances or the driver's neglect, the driver was held to have contributed to, and assumed the risk of, such an injury.

It is a a common practice in racing to "ride" the bumper of a car in front. Injuries arising from such conduct are accepted as normal risks of the sport.

Pit crew members are treated, in most instances, as a driver is, with the same rights and responsibilities.

THEY'RE AT THE GATE!

FACTS: A jockey, Gene, sued the racetrack operator for injuries received when the horse he was riding "bolted through a removable railing." The railing was at the location where horses were accustomed to leaving the track. Gene contended, "The railing should have been painted a different color than the rest of the infield fence." Was the track operator liable for my injuries? asked Gene. **YOU'RE THE JUDGE!**

DECISION: The court ruled, "The track operator did not maintain the race track in good condition. It violated a safety regulation by providing inadequate and unsafe fencing around the track infield."

Gene's injuries would not have occurred "but for" the negligence of the racetrack. Horses are color blind and can only distinguish between black and white. All other colors appear gray. Therefore, because the railing, through which the horse bolted, was

COMMISSIONER

not painted white, it may have visually blended with the gray in-field. Coincidentally, that was the location where the horses were accustomed to leaving the track.

Injuries received by jockies when "cut off" are generally as-sumed risks, due in part to the sometimes uncontrollable nature of a horse. To recover, a jockey would have to show reckless, wanton or intentional conduct (malice) by another jockey.

The defense of assumption of the risk will be a deterrent to most actions for damages for injuries to professionals. Professionals are acutely aware of the dangers and risks inherent in their sports. They will not be able to pass along that responsibility to others except in those situations where an injury was as a result of the negligence or intentional misconduct of others.

WORKMEN'S COMPENSATION

May an athlete, injured while performing duties for his team, re-cover damages against his own team for an injury?

> FACTS: Ellis, a pro football player for the Pushovers, injured his knee during a football game. He sued an opposing player for mak-ing an improper tackle. He also sued his own coach and team. "They played me while I was injured," charged Ellis. Could Ellis recover damages from his team? **YOU'RE THE JUDGE!**

> DECISION: No. Where workmen's compensation applied, Ellis' only remedy against his own team (not an opponent's) was provid-ed by workmen's compensation. Ellis could not sue his coach. He could sue an opposing team or player, as they would not be his em-ployer.

When an athlete is injured while performing a duty for his em-ployer, relief may be available under **workmen's compensation statutes.**

These statutes provide that employees, with certain exceptions, "may receive compensation for injuries which are related to their em-ployment."

In effect, each side (the team and the players) gives up rights in return for others. The employer gives up any defenses he may have in return for limited liability. The employee gives up the right to bring an action in negligence against the employer (but not against others) and, in return, receives limited compensation for any injuries.

Injured parties must prove they are employees and their injuries resulted from work (or activities related to work) and under the em-ployer's control and direction.

Professional Athletes

FACTS: Al, a pro baseball player, broke his ankle sliding into third base.

Pat, a pro football player, was injured while driving from his home to a game.

Carlo, a pro basketball player, slipped and broke his hip while doing team promotional work at a local mall. Were any of these athletes covered by workmen's compensation? **YOU'RE THE JUDGE!**

DECISION: Al and Carlo, performing duties for their teams, were covered. Pat was on his way to a game, and not yet covered.

Are all professional athletes covered by workmen's compensation?

Professional athletes may be excluded from workmen's compensation coverage because participation in pro sports is "highly dangerous." Additionally, professional team athletes generally receive their salaries for the remainder of the year under their contracts.

In addition, some states—although covering athletes under workmen's compensation—have denied benefits where the injury was not an "accidental" injury, even though occurring as a result of a legitimate physical contact.

FACTS: "Killer" McGee, a linebacker for the Devils, injured his shoulder making a vicious tackle.

The team doctor, on orders from the owner, told Killer, "Your shoulder is fine, you can play." when, in fact, it was not. Killer permanently injured the shoulder during the next game. Was the team owner liable for Killer's injury? Could Killer recover workmen's compensation? **YOU'RE THE JUDGE!**

DECISION: An employer may be liable for aggravating injuries where an employer—or the employer's agent—fraudulently conceal the existence of injury to the player, who then is injured further by playing, not knowing of the injury. The team's owner was liable.

Had the employer been found not liable, Killer could recover workmen's compensation benefits.

FACTS: What if Killer, while traveling to the next game, injured the shoulder when he slipped and fell in the airport. Could he recover workmen's compensation? **YOU'RE THE JUDGE!**

DECISION: Injuries occurring while traveling with the team between games are covered. Killer was engaged in activities related to his work for his employer.

Independent contractors—athletes or others working solely and entirely for their own benefit—are not covered under workmen's compensation.

Jockeys may, or may not, be considered employees, depending upon any agreement with an owner of a track or horse.

Other athletes, such as pro tennis players or golfers, will only be covered by any applicable workmen's compensation statutes if they are working for an employer, under the employer's control and for the employer's benefit, and while engaged in the employer's employ and not playing for part of a purse, where they keep anything that they earn.

FACTS: A pro golfer, Ian, represented a golf club. He worked there on occasion, but mainly went out on the tour fending solely for himself. While playing in a tournament, he slipped and injured his back. Was he covered by workmen's compensation?

If he was injured while not on tour, but while working for the employer at the club, would he then be covered? **YOU'RE THE JUDGE!**

DECISION: Ian would not be covered while playing entirely for himself. But while working at the club, he would be covered and could receive workmen's compensation benefits.

University & College Athletes

As a general rule, a college or university athlete will not be considered an employee because of the receipt of an athletic scholarship. However, where the performance of athletic services is required for the scholarship, the athlete will be an employee for purposes of workmen's compensation coverage.

FACTS: An athlete, Sam Vanderly, was killed in a plane crash returning from an away game for his college football team.

His family claimed, "Sam's scholarship and rent money, received from the school, was payment for his playing football. He was an employee of the school." Could his family recover workmen's compensation benefits? **YOU'RE THE JUDGE!**

DECISION: Yes. The court held, "The scholarship and rent money received by Vanderly were payment for his football activities. Therefore, he was an employee and his family could recover workmen's compensation benefits."

However, in most instances, receiving a scholarship will not be dependent upon an athlete performing athletically. He can receive the scholarship even if he no longer participates in the sport for which he was granted a scholarship. In these situations, if the athlete is injured while participating in athletics, he will not be able to collect workmen's compensation benefits.

> FACTS: Clark Reddon, while playing football for Indian St. on an athletic scholarship, was injured during practice. The injury left him a quadriplegic. Could he recover workmen's compensation benefits? **YOU'RE THE JUDGE!**

> DECISION: The court found, "Reddon was not an employee of the college. He could not recover benefits."
> The court considered the student's financial aid arrangement, which included the NCAA bylaw that sports was viewed as part of the educational system and that taking pay was prohibited, subject to a loss of eligibility. Furthermore, Reddon did not report the scholarship as income.

Athletic Activities On The Job

Employer sponsored or sanctioned athletic activities may range from pick-up games (played mostly during lunch breaks) to athletic teams. Whether these athletes will be covered under workmen's compensation statutes for injuries received during these activities will depend upon whether the athletes are employees and, if so, whether their activities were related to work, for the employers' benefit and under their control.

As a general rule, an employee's activities may be considered within the course of employment when the activities occur on the employer's premises and during work hours.

> FACTS: While at work, Warren, attempting to catch a pass during a lunch hour touch football game, was injured when his hand went through a glass window. The game was on the employer's premises. Warren filed a claim for workmen's compensation benefits. "Can I recover?" he asked. **YOU'RE THE JUDGE!**

> DECISION: Yes. "The injury was within the course of employment. The accident happened during lunch hour and on the employer's premises. Warren could recover benefits," ruled the court.

An employee's activities will also be within the course of his employment when an employer requires participation or is responsible for organizing activities, such as softball games and golf tournaments. And this is especially so where an employer provides transportation to the activities, or has them on his premises.

Compensation may be denied where an activity takes place outside of an employer's premises, not during working hours, not under his control or encouragement, and where employees furnished their own transportation.

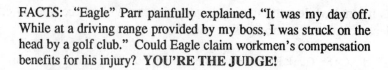

FACTS: "Eagle" Parr painfully explained, "It was my day off. While at a driving range provided by my boss, I was struck on the head by a golf club." Could Eagle claim workmen's compensation benefits for his injury? **YOU'RE THE JUDGE!**

DECISION: "The accident was not incurred in the course of employment. Additionally, it was not a required part of his employment to enjoy recreation on his day off—the employer did not require his presence there and received no benefit." commented the court.

EQUIPMENT

Injury to a participant in a sports activity may arise out of the misuse of equipment.

FACTS: "John was injured when Pierre intentionally swung his hockey stick!" said a teammate.
   In a baseball game, an on deck batter was injured when struck by a baseball bat which slipped from the batter's hands. Were Pierre and the batter liable for the injuries they caused? **YOU'RE THE JUDGE!**

DECISION: Pierre was liable. He intentionally, and without regard for the safety of others, caused John's injury.
   The batter was not liable. Such a risk will be assumed as one ordinary to the game.

GREAT DANGER!

What if a participant continues to encounter an unreasonably great risk. Would that be contributory negligence? Will he be able to recover damages for any resulting injury?

FACTS: Wayne was injured during a fight in a hockey game with an opposing player, Niko. Niko screamed, "Wayne was guilty of contributory negligence. He can't recover damages." Can he? **YOU'RE THE JUDGE!**

DECISION: No. Courts use a two step process. If the first duty, owed by the defendant to the plaintiff, is violated, the plaintiff should recover. However, if the plaintiff has violated the second duty, that to ensure one's own safety, that will prevent recovery.

As a general rule, voluntary participants, including coaches, bat and ball boys, caddies, and others involved in sports contests, assume all of the ordinary and inherent risks of that sport, so long as the activity is played in good faith and the injury is not the result of intentional misconduct.

HIDDEN DANGER!

If any dangers common to a particular sport are hidden, unobserved or so serious as to require safety precautions, the general rule of assumption of the risk for injuries received during voluntary participation in that sport may not apply as a valid defense.

Such may be the case where there are holes in a ball field, or where the danger of a ride at an amusement park cannot be observed, and—in either case—a participant, unaware of the defect, is injured.

Will assumption of the risk be a valid defense where accidents have been so many that a game or activity is too dangerous to continue without change?

FACTS: Before high school basketball practice, the boys played "Mexican basketball," a brutal game in which fouls were not called.

The bumper cars at an amusement park consistently went too fast, causing injuries to many riders.

In a "paddle" football contest, paddles were lined up at the 50 yard line, with freshmen and sophomores at opposing goal lines. The goal was to get the paddles back to your end zone. There were no rules. Were these games too dangerous to continue without change? If participants were injured playing these games, could they recover damages for their injuries against their schools or the amusement park?

DECISION: **YOU'RE THE JUDGE!**

FACTS: The "Slasher," known for crushing his roller derby opponents into the railings, was seriously injured. "A weak guardrail gave way, and I crashed to the floor," he related.

Randy was hospitalized when, during a skydiving competition, "I landed in the target circle and was severely stung by a colony of red ants!"

"Big Pappa" crashed his drag racer into a briar patch after completing the quarter mile. The stopping area was too short.

Were the dangers in these sports hidden, unobserved or serious enough to warrant safety precautions for the participants? Did the participants assume the risk of such injuries, or were the operators or supervisors of the events liable?

DECISION: **YOU'RE THE JUDGE!**

PRESSURE! PRESSURE!

Volition (voluntary exercise of free will) of a participant to assume a risk of injury from participation in a sports activity may be overcome in extreme situations where there has been undue pressure.

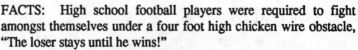

FACTS: High school football players were required to fight amongst themselves under a four foot high chicken wire obstacle, "The loser stays until he wins!"

Another high school football player was injured during a practice session in a game of "jungle football"—a rough version of touch football, played without equipment.

"You can't play without participating in these practices," warned the coaches. Did these players voluntarily assume the risk of injury? **YOU'RE THE JUDGE!**

DECISION: No. Volition may be robbed by the disciplinary authority of a coach, or by pressure to play from fellow players and schoolmates.

The courts held, "The players did not play voluntarily. They did not assume the risk of injury from negligent or reckless conduct by other participants or coaches. The risks involved were not ones ordinarily inherent to the game of football.

FACTS: John, a star football player for Emerson High, had not yet recovered from an ankle injury. His personal doctor recommended that he not play, "Any play before you're fully healed could jeopardize your future in football."

John's coach cautioned, "You must play if we are to win the play-offs. Don't forget, your play could get you college scholarship offers. And your teammates are depending on you."

John played, seriously reinjuring his ankle. John then sued the coach and school for "pressuring" him into playing. John asked, "Can I recover against the coach and school for negligence?" **YOU'RE THE JUDGE!**

DECISION: Yes. John's volition was robbed by the "pressure and disciplinary authority" of the coach. He did not voluntarily assume the risk of injury. He could recover from the school and its coach.

GOOD FAITH COMPETITION?

Where other than good faith competition is involved, or risks are not ordinary and part of the sport, participants will not assume the risk of injury.

What if conduct is negligent, but unintentional?

FACTS: Two high school teams squared off in a soccer match. Julian, a goaltender, received a pass in the penalty area, and then crouched, hugging the ball to his chest. Bill, an opposing forward, unintentionally kicked Julian in the head, causing a fractured skull and permanent brain damage.

A safety rule prohibited any contact with the goalie in the penalty area. Could Julian recover for his injury? **YOU'RE THE JUDGE!**

DECISION: The court ruled for Julian, remarking, "Players have a duty to refrain from conduct forbidden by safety rules which are included to protect players from serious injury. Players assume the normal risks of the game, but do not assume the risk of unintentional, but negligent, conduct."

Conduct, in violation of a safety rule, if either deliberate, willful, or with reckless disregard for another's safety (malice) may be negligent.

FACTS: Barry, a second baseman on his high school baseball team, received a fractured jaw when a baserunner—who had been on first base—ran into him full speed in an attempt to prevent a double play. Did Barry assume the risk of such an injury? **YOU'RE THE JUDGE!**

DECISION: No. Although Barry assumed ordinary risks (such as being spiked), he did not assume the risk of injury from unexpected and unsportsmanlike conduct. Testimony revealed, "The runner ran five feet from the base and hit Barry under the chin with his arm." The runner breached his duty to play in a sportsmanlike manner.

POOR JUDGMENT!

FACTS: Mary, a little league player, was injured when she was struck by lightning. Her parents sued, contending, "The game should have been stopped earlier when it was obvious that the storm was worsening." "Isn't the coach responsible for not stopping the game?" they asked.

DECISION: **YOU'RE THE JUDGE!**

NOT FIT FOR PLAY!

The most important risk that will not be assumed by participants will be any risk created by a breach of duty by owners or operators of sports facilities.

FACTS: Playing on a baseball field for the first time, Johnson stepped in a hole in the base path and was injured. He sued, claiming, "They neglected their duty to keep the field safe."
The defendant, operator of the field, maintained, "Johnson didn't use reasonable care for his own safety. He should have seen the hole." Did Johnson assume the risk of injury? **YOU'RE THE JUDGE!**

DECISION: The holes were hidden from view by grass. By knowingly maintaining the holes on the base path which players had to use, the defendant breached his duty to maintain the premises in a reasonably safe condition.

ARE PARENTS RESPONSIBLE?

Under common law, parents are not responsible for the acts of their children. But many states have passed laws which may impose potential limited liability on parents for the acts of their children.

Where such laws exist, parents are generally held responsible until a child reaches age 18, but may not be responsible if the child is under a certain age (varies from 7-13).

The kinds of torts committed by children for which their parents may be responsible are intentional or malicious acts.

> FACTS: While playing in a football game, Wade, 13, received permanent injuries when he was beaten up by Jason, 14. Wade had not consented to the contact. Jason had been in many fights before. Were Jason's parents liable for Wade's injuries? **YOU'RE THE JUDGE!**

> DECISION: In finding Jason's parents liable, the court stated, "The better rule is that parents be held to a requirement of reasonable care concerning their child's conduct when it might lead to serious injury."

When will parents be responsible for their child's conduct? Parents will be responsible for their child's conduct if:

- they are aware that their child has a "vicious propensity" to commit acts injuring others and fail to restrain and control him, or;
- they are present when a fight takes place and do nothing to stop it (if they had the time and opportunity), or;
- they—in any other way—direct, consent or approve of their child's conduct, or;
- the child is acting as his parent's agent in committing the act (this may apply if the child were on an errand for his parents).

FOSTER PARENTS

Although not related through blood or legal ties, foster parents raise their foster children and give other parental care. Are they responsible for their foster child's conduct?

> FACTS: Jennifer and Jeff, foster parents, were sued when their foster child, Eddie, beat up an opposing player during a high school football game. "Are we liable for Eddie's conduct?" they asked. **YOU'RE THE JUDGE!!**

> DECISION: Where foster parents are found to be "agents of the state," that is, acting for or on behalf of the state, they will not be held responsible for the acts of their foster child.

However, this immunity from liability may not extend to where the foster parents have willfully neglected or improperly supervised their foster children.

ODDS & ENDS....

FACTS: "Stash The Masher," a local wrestling favorite, sued his opponent, "Bimp The Wimp," for injuries Stash received during their wrestling match.

Stash claimed, "Bimp went outside of our 'choreographed' script where no one was supposed to be trying to hurt each other. We were supposed to be 'faking' it. I didn't know that Bimp would be really trying."

Bimp defended that Stash assumed the risk of injury from such a "dangerous" sport. Further, that he contributed to his own injury by competing. Did Stash assume the risk of such an injury, or was Bimp guilty of negligence by not following the choreographed script?

DECISION: **YOU'RE THE JUDGE!**

Robert, after finishing football practice, was hungry. So, when the walk-in section of a local fast food restaurant was closed, he drove his bicycle up to the drive-through lane.

He was told, "The drive-through lane is only for cars."

"It's unfair!" griped Robert. There was no mention of no bicycles on the drive-through's sign.

Because bicyclists are subject to the same laws as vehicles where Robert lives, he felt that he should have been served. Should he have? The police thought otherwise.

The most frequent allegation and claim for relief when a participant is injured will be, "Someone was negligent. Their conduct, or lack of conduct, fell below that expected of an ordinary and responsible person in similar circumstances."

There are two general rules concerning injuries to participants in sports activities.

First, the owner or operator of a sports or public amusement facility is not an insurer of a participant's safety.

The owner or operator is bound to exercise "ordinary and reasonable" care for the safety and protection of his patrons; that is, the care which an ordinary, prudent, careful and cautious person would have exercised under the same or similar circumstances.

Second, athletes assume all ordinary and inherent risks of an activity, but do not assume extraordinary risks, unless they know of and voluntarily assume them.

Defenses that owners or operators may assert in defense of charges of negligence against them will be assumption of the risk, and contributory or comparative negligence.

6

DID I WAIVE MY RIGHTS?

WHAT'S IT ABOUT?

Did I Waive My Rights? details attempts by those controlling some sports activities, such as an amusement park, auto racing, skiing and golf, to limit their liability for injuries to participants by having them accept or sign a waiver or otherwise surrender their right to recover damages for an injury.

Are waivers effective? Are they effective if signed by a minor, a minor's parents, or by another for a participant? What happens if a waiver isn't signed?

WAIVER

It was the summer. You gleefully declared, "I'm going to do all of the things that I've never done before: enter an auto race, play golf, go rollerskating, scuba dive, go to the amusement park and join a health club!"

Several of the sponsors or operators of these activities wanted you to sign or accept a waiver. This would relieve them from any liability for any injuries to you.

Therefore, to participate in some of these activities, they told you, "Sign this waiver!"

WAIVER

I hereby release the operator or owner from any duty to care for my protection and safety and from all liability for any injuries that I may receive while participating. I assume full responsibility for any injuries to me, promise not to hold anyone else liable, and will not sue for any such injuries. I HAVE READ, UNDERSTAND, AND VOLUNTARILY AGREE TO THIS WAIVER OF LIABILITY.

_____ Date _____

FACTS: Some of these activities did not require a waiver to be signed, but included it on the back of the admission ticket. What would happen if you signed this waiver, or used a ticket with such a waiver on it, and were then injured? Would the waiver prevent you from recovering damages for any injuries?

DECISION: **YOU'RE THE JUDGE!**

A **waiver** or release—which may be inferred from one's conduct—is a voluntary surrender of a right (right to recover damages for an injury) with both knowledge of its existence and an intention to surrender it.

What effect does a waiver have on an injured participant who accepted a waiver?

A waiver alters ordinary negligence principles that would otherwise apply—that is, that one should be responsible for his negligent acts that cause injuries to others.

FACTS: Tony played for his company's softball team, Astra Tools. Right before the league championship game, the company's owner told the players, "Sign this waiver or you can't play!" They all signed.

Tony told how he was injured. "I ran into the fence attempting to catch a foul flyball. I broke my foot." "Can I seek recovery of damages or workmen's compensation benefits?" asked Tony. **YOU'RE THE JUDGE!**

DECISION: Yes. A waiver or release must be voluntary. If it comes out of a relationship with unequal bargaining power, such as between an employer and employee, then such a waiver is invalid.

In addition, for a waiver to prevent liability for an injury to a participant, the participant must have had actual (knew) or constructive (should have known) knowledge of the waiver or release.

FACTS: Vic signed an agreement before competing in a football tryout. It contained a waiver. Vic could have read it before signing, or kept a copy and taken time to read the waiver after signing. But before competing he did neither. When injured, he sued the promoter of the tryout. "Did I have knowledge of the waiver?" asked Vic. **YOU'RE THE JUDGE!**

DECISION: Vic knew or should have known of the waiver. He had both the time and opportunity to read the waiver before participating in the tryout.

Furthermore, it must be shown that a participant had the intention to sign and thereby waive any right to a claim for injuries.

What if a participant intended to sign an agreement, but didn't know that a waiver or release was included?

FACTS: When several semi-pro basketball players showed up for a summer clinic, they were asked to sign, as in the past, an attendance sheet. Only this year, a waiver clause had been added to the back of the sheet.

Emil signed without seeing the waiver. Stan, before signing, asked about the waiver. The director of the clinic replied, "Just a requirement, go ahead."

When Emil and Stan were injured and sued, the director defended, "They signed the waiver." Did Emil and Stan intend to release the director of any liability? **YOU'RE THE JUDGE!**

DECISION: No. Ignorance negates the waiver, as does consent given under mistake or misapprehension of fact.

For any waiver or release to be valid, it may be necessary to support it with consideration. That is, each party must give up something—such as the right to enter or participate—in return for admission or pay.

Therefore, when Rick, a participant, was issued a free pass to compete in a "Beat The Goalie" contest and was injured, the waiver on the pass did not release the operator from liability for his negligence in allowing Rick to play without proper equipment. Because the pass was free, the operator gave no consideration.

Auto Racing

FACTS: An auto racer explained, "I was hurt when a wheel from another automobile struck me while I was working in the pit area."

Another racer was injured when a car went out of control after hitting a piece of a fender on the track after an accident. The racers, who had signed waivers to obtain their racing licenses, sued. Could they recover damages for their injuries? **YOU'RE THE JUDGE!**

DECISION: No. The court held, "An agreement between the racers and the promoter—providing that the racers, in consideration for obtaining a racing license, would release the promoter from all liability due to his negligence—would be upheld."

Would such a waiver be upheld if it was contrary to safety regulations?

A waiver will not be enforced—where it is against public policy—because it renders safety requirements, prescribed by law, ineffective.

One court held that a stock car racer, McCarthy, could recover despite a signed waiver. He was injured when his car burst into flames. The sponsor failed to inspect the car, which did not comply with safety regulations.

Other courts have also questioned waiver agreements.

FACTS: Adamson, a stock car driver, was rendered a quadriplegic following an accident. The announcer told what happened. "His car swerved off the course, crashed through a guardrail and struck a utility pole."

Rescue personnel, attempting to put out the fire, sprayed Adamson with chemicals, resulting in brain damage. He sued the track owner and race promoter for inadequate and improperly trained rescue personnel.

The defendants produced a waiver which Adamson had signed, releasing them from liability. Did the waiver release the owner and sponsor from liability? **YOU'RE THE JUDGE!**

DECISION: No. Waivers containing very broad release clauses will only prevent claims within the understanding of the parties. The improper rescue operations were not within the agreement.

Moreover, waivers will not be enforceable where injuries are the result of intentional or reckless misconduct (such as where a track owner did not fill barrels with sand, as necessary to slow down out of control cars, and thus protect pit crew workers).

How Old Are You?

Is a waiver or release valid if it is signed by a minor? And what if the minor lied about his age?

FACTS: A waiver was signed by a minor, Kirk, who was then injured when his car turned over in a demolition derby. He knew what he was signing, but misrepresented his age. "I'm twenty-one," he lied.

When he sued the track owner for his injuries, the owner defended by producing the signed waiver. "Can I still recover?" asked Kirk. **YOU'RE THE JUDGE!**

DECISION: When Kirk, a minor, reaches majority (18-21), he may disaffirm the waiver, thereby creating liability for the track owner. This would be so even if Kirk misrepresented his age in signing the waiver.

Toboggans & Snowmobiles

Nor did the waiver (by itself), signed by a minor, Marie, release an operator from liability when the toboggan sled, in which Marie was riding as a paying customer, tipped over and she was injured. Although she disaffirmed the waiver upon reaching majority, the operator was found not negligent.

Another participant, Jenkins, signed and kept a copy of a "Notice To Patrons," which he knew included a release of liability for the owner of the toboggan ride. He was bound by the release and could not recover for injuries.

What if a participant signed a paper which contained a release, but didn't get a copy?

FACTS: A participant, Johnson, signed a receipt which contained a similar waiver. He swore, "I didn't get a copy!" When he was injured due to the owner's negligence and sued, the owner of the snowmobile ride produced the signed waiver. Did the waiver prevent Johnson from recovering damages for his injury? **YOU'RE THE JUDGE!**

DECISION: The waiver did not relieve the owner from liability for Johnson's injury. The participant had no actual (knew) or constructive (should have known) knowledge that the receipt contained a release.

Parents

Parents cannot sign away the rights of a minor. If parents sign a form releasing a school, coach or any other party from liability for any negligence for injuries to their child, the form is either illegal or may be disaffirmed by the minor upon his reaching majority.

FACTS: Lanny's father said, "I was required to sign a waiver so that Lanny could attend football summer camp." When he was injured and sued, the camp defended with the waiver. Did the waiver prevent Lanny from recovering? **YOU'RE THE JUDGE!**

DECISION: The court found, "It is doubtful that a parent could waive a child's right for damages from an injury due to the negligence of the camp." There also was unequal bargaining power between the boys and the camp.

Even if the father could waive any right to recover by his child, the waiver relieving the camp of liability would be frowned upon by the public.

Skiing, Horses & Scuba Diving

FACTS: A ski jumper, Garretson, was injured when blown out of position, allegedly due to adverse weather conditions. As he had done for previous competitions, Garretson read and signed an "Entry Blank" releasing the sponsors of the competition from any liability for injuries to participants. Could he recover for his injury? **YOU'RE THE JUDGE!**

DECISION: No. Garretson voluntarily signed the waiver with both knowledge of its release and an intent to give up the right to recover.

A like decision was reached after a rider, Peter, was injured after he knowingly signed a waiver upon renting a horse. Hewitt, a scuba diver who hit his head on a rock and drowned (after signing a waiver from "inherent or ordinary dangers") was similarly denied.

Would your answer be different if it was known that a participant was inexperienced?

A waiver signed by another equestrian, Palmquist, did not release the riding academy, from where he rented a horse, of liability. The academy "knew of Palmquist's inexperience and yet gave him a dangerous horse, from which he was thrown and injured." That was gross negligence.

Hidden Waivers

Golf

FACTS: Marvin sued for an injury to his shoulder. He was thrown out of a moving golf cart. "The cart tipped over when the brakes stuck," said Marvin. He had signed a receipt which contained a waiver on the back. Can I still recover?" asked Marvin. **YOU'RE THE JUDGE!**

DECISION: The "not liable" clause was "hidden" in the receipt. It was void as against public policy. It would be unconscionable to allow the lessor to exclude himself from liability by the use of an agreement which "tends to injure the public," commented the court.

Health Club

Another court had the same problem where a waiver on a health club membership form was buried in fine print on the back of a form which the plaintiff had signed.

But at gyms, where one woman slipped near the pool and another in the shower room on a smooth spot, and they sued for negligent

maintenance, the courts held that their membership contracts excused the gyms from liability. "The language was clear. Their applications were voluntary and they had time to read them and, they agreed to the terms."

Amusements & Beach Clubs

Any agreement between a patron and an amusement operator, which exempts an operator from liability, must be fairly and honestly negotiated and understandingly entered into. If it is, then it will be valid.

However, such agreements will be closely scrutinized and strictly interpreted against the operator.

> FACTS: Two patrons, Jones and O'Connell, were thrown from their horses and injured, allegedly due to the negligence of Wally World management.
>   The waiver, which they knowingly signed, read in part:
>
> I AGREE TO ASSUME THE RISKS INHERENT IN HORSE-BACK RIDING. I WAIVE ALL CLAIMS THAT I MAY HAVE AGAINST WALLY WORLD FOR INJURIES RECEIVED WHILE HORSEBACK RIDING.
>
> Jones and O'Connell wanted to recover damages for their injuries. Could they? **YOU'RE THE JUDGE!**
>
> DECISION: The court found that the waiver did not prevent them from suing for the park's negligence, as the language in the release did not indicate the intent to release the park for its own negligence.

A similar decision was reached where a swimming club member was injured when he fell off the gangplank leading to a dock. The court held that the words: "WAIVE CLAIM FOR ANY PERSONAL INJURY" was not sufficiently clear or explicit to relieve the club from liability for its own negligence.

Waiver Signed For Patron

A waiver read that an applicant to a beach club, Michaels, would "waive all claims for injury occurring in the use of the club." A friend had signed it for him. Would this prevent Michaels from recovering for an injury caused by the club?

The waiver did not release the club from liability for its own negligence. Even if the waiver were valid, it would not bind Michaels as he did not sign it, and the friend who did was not his agent—one authorized to act for another.

Unsigned Waivers On Tickets

Unsigned waivers, as sometimes appear on the back of admission tickets, generally will not release an operator from liability for injuries which are due to the operator's negligence.

FACTS: A waiver on the back side of a rollerskating rink admission ticket stated that patrons "assume the risk of any injury." The tickets were collected immediately at the door.

When O'Brien, who had skated at that rink many times, was injured and sued, the operator defended with the waiver on the ticket. Did the waiver relieve the operator of liability? **YOU'RE THE JUDGE!**

DECISION: No. The warning was not properly brought to O'Brien's attention. Otherwise, it may have been effective to relieve the operators of liability for their negligence in causing O'Brien's fall and injury.

Even if O'Brien had read it, she could not be held to have understood the implications of the waiver.

Similar decisions resulted where waivers on tickets and on signs, such as at an amusement park's roller coaster ride, were not properly brought to the attention of patrons.

ODDS & ENDS....

FACTS: You decided to try riding "Boltin' Benny," the mechanical bull at a local country nightclub. After you had had a few too many, you signed this waiver:

WAIVER

I, an aspiring cowboy, assume the risk of any injuries that I may receive while attempting to ride the mechanical bull. I release the operator from any claims for injuries and of any liability for negligence on his part.

Signature —————————————————— Date ——————

You got on "Boltin Benny." After success at a slow pace, you bellowed to the operator, "Turn 'er all the way up!!" He did, and you fell. You got back on and were again thrown. You bounced off the mats and crashed into the wall. Result: separated shoulder and broken ankle.

When you sued, the club defended, "He signed this waiver!" Would the waiver prevent you from recovering for your injuries? **YOU'RE THE JUDGE!**

DECISION: You could not be held to have understood the implications of such a waiver, especially in your condition, which the operator knew or should have known of.

The club was negligent for allowing you to ride while in such condition, and, furthermore, for not providing proper protection for your safety—the bull was too close to the wall.

It is important to remember that to effectively waive any right you may have to recover damages for an injury received as a participant in a sports activity, you must know of and voluntarily surrender that right.

7

CITIES & SCHOOLS - IT'S THEIR DUTY!

WHAT'S IT ABOUT?

Cities & Schools—It's Their Duty! outlines a school's or municipality's (city or town) duty to exercise reasonable care for the safety of those either under their control or using their facilities, such as ballfields or swimming pools.

But there are defenses to allegations, such as for negligent supervision or improper instructions. One of those defenses, sovereign immunity, originated out of the belief "The King can do no wrong." Can he?

AND NOW...
INTRODUCING!

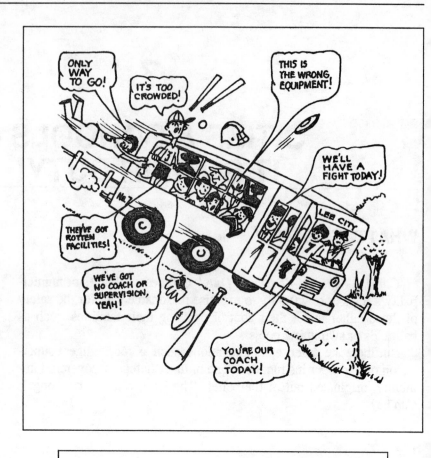

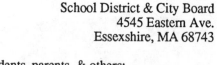

School District & City Board
4545 Eastern Ave.
Essexshire, MA 68743

Dear athletes, students, parents & others:

Sports activities and sports related injuries occur most often on the fields and in the gyms and at other facilities of cities, towns & schools.

In the interest of having everyone understand who may be responsible for these injuries, and in the hopes of minimizing or eliminating them, we would like you to read the following material. It discusses the rights and duties of schools and municipalities (cities and towns) and of the athletes, who come under the school's or municipalities' control or guidance, or anyone using their athletic facilities.

Yours truly,

School District & City of Essexshire

YOU HAVE A DUTY TO....

FACTS: Several roller and ice skating participants were injured at city and school owned skating rinks. The injuries were due to: accidents, defective barricades and equipment, and, as one skater put it, "There was no supervision. Everyone just raced around and knocked me over." What were the city's and school's duties? Did they neglect these duties?

DECISION: **YOU'RE THE JUDGE!**

Schools and municipalities (cities and towns) have a duty to exercise ordinary and reasonable care for the protection and safety of those either under their control or using their facilities. They must provide proper supervision where necessary, insure that facilities are safe and correct any defects which are known or, by inspection, should be known of. This is particularly important as regarding hidden hazards or defects.

There can be no liability for a school or municipality unless all of the elements of negligence are present.

What must a plaintiff show in order to succeed on a charge of **negligence** against a school or municipality?

A plaintiff must show: a duty owed by the school or municipality, a breach of that duty which was the cause of an injury, and damages. That is, that the injury would not have occurred but for the school's or municipality's conduct or lack of conduct.

FACTS: Bauer was injured during a soccer game on a town field. "I stepped in a hole that was hidden by uncut grass. I didn't see it," he complained.

Williams was injured at the town swimming pool by a group engaged in "roughhousing." "I wasn't involved," he moaned.

Did the town have a duty to inspect and correct the field? Did they have a duty to provide supervision at its pool?

DECISION: **YOU'RE THE JUDGE!**

For school sponsored sports activities taking place on municipal property, the school has the primary duty to provide instruction and supervision. Both the school and the municipality in control of the property have a duty to ensure that the property is free from any hazards or defects.

A school's or municipality's duty to those to whom they owe a duty is to protect them from unreasonable risks of injury that are foreseeable and that can be reduced by proper care.

Should consideration be given to the type of activity or the age of the participants?

Consideration must be given to the type of activity, and to the participant's age and experience. Younger or less experienced participants require more care than older or more experienced participants.

FACTS: Johnny, 8, was injured when, "Some kids jumped in the town pool and landed on me." This conduct had been going on for some time without any warning from the authorities.

Jason, 18, was injured during a "pile-up" in a rough football game with the town's rival. Could either of the boys recover damages for their injury? **YOU'RE THE JUDGE!**

DECISION: The court held, "The town's breach of its duty to provide proper supervision was the cause of Johnny's injury. The age of the children demanded stricter supervision."

Jason was older and playing a more inherently dangerous sport. He "assumed the risk of, and, by playing, contributed to, such an unintentional injury."

General supervision is required where participants are engaged in activities which are not usually dangerous, such as soccer or baseball.

Specific supervision is required where activities are unusually dangerous, or where the activity is not familiar, such as football or gymnastics.

For activities taking place at, or under the control, of a school, a participant may assume that proper instruction, supervision, equipment and facilities will be given.

However, for sports activities taking place at a municipal facility, most of the activities (with the exception of swimming pools and municipally run park's programs—which demand the same duty as that expected of a school) will not be supervised.

In these instances, will participants have a duty to protect themselves?

Where there is no required supervision, participants have more of a duty to exercise ordinary and reasonable care for their own protection and safety than do those participating in a supervised activity.

FACTS: Hogan explained, "I was hurt when I was tackled in a pick-up football game at the town field. We had no equipment." Did the town have a duty to provide equipment and supervision? **YOU'RE THE JUDGE!**

DECISION: No. As the game was not under the control of the town, the town had no duty to provide equipment or supervision. Hogan assumed the risk of and contributed to his injury by playing.

Participants assume all of the ordinary and common risks in a sport. A school or municipality does not insure a participant's safety.

They may only be held liable for their own negligent acts, or for those committed by one for whom they are responsible, such as a teacher, coach or instructor.

DEFENSE! DEFENSE!

A school or municipality may (in addition to the **Statute of Limitations**—which bars any action not brought within a specified period of time) have certain legal defenses available which may prevent a participant from bringing a suit or from recovering damages in part or fully.

Immunity For The King!

"The King can do no wrong." It was thought in England, in the 1700's, that the king or sovereign could do no wrong. Therefore, as the courts received their powers from the sovereign, they did not have the power to hold the ruler liable.

Are schools or municipalities **agents** (one appointed to act for another) of the sovereign? This idea of **sovereign immunity** was adopted in this country and eventually was extended to include as immune from liability, municipalities and schools, both as agents of the sovereign.

Others saw immunity as a "convenience to the people, who, when carrying out their governmental powers, should use school or municipal funds solely for those purposes." Therefore, they should not be sued.

Did this mean that a school or municipality could not be found liable for an injury even where they were negligent?

FACTS: School officials used unslaked lime to line a football field. Johnson sighed, "I had my face pushed into the lime, causing a permanent loss of sight in one eye and severely damaging the other." Johnson sued the school for not protecting his safety. Was the school negligent? Could Johnson recover damages? **YOU'RE THE JUDGE!**

DECISION:: The immunity doctrine acted as a complete defense to Johnson's suit. Even though the school may have been negligent, he could not recover.

Because of such harsh results from the immunity doctrine, states began to chip away at it, thus making municipalities and public schools liable to those injured because of the municipality's or school's negligence.

Could a coach or other person responsible for an injury be held liable?

Even where a school or municipality was immune from liability, an individual supervisor, teacher, instructor or coach involved could be subject to liability.

> FACTS: Several football players on a town sponsored team were injured when their coach instructed them to participate in tackling drills without equipment. "Was the coach responsible?" asked the players. **YOU'RE THE JUDGE!**

> DECISION: Yes. The town was protected by sovereign immunity. But the coach, due to the improper instruction and supervision, was liable for the injuries.

Save-harmless

Where an injured plaintiff may be prevented from bringing an action against the school, he could sue the teacher or coach personally.

"Save-harmless" statutes may be used to grant immunity from liability by indemnifying school personnel (teachers and coaches) for judgments rendered against them.

> FACTS: Richardson, a little league baseball player, "misjudged a fly ball and was struck in the face and injured." His parents sued the coach and his assistant—another parent—alleging that they were negligent in instructing Richardson how to play. Could Johnnie recover damages for his injury? **YOU'RE THE JUDGE!**

> DECISION: Yes. Although an out of court settlement was reached, later legislation—save-harmless statutes—now offers some protection for coaches, parents and others associated with civic sports programs. Had Richardson been older, he may have been held to have assumed the risk of such an injury as one ordinary or common to the game.

Charitable Immunity

Charitable immunity, which may apply to charitable organizations, such as the Little League, YMCA, YWCA, and other non-profit organizations, provides a shield of protection from liability similar to that of sovereign immunity. The theory here was that since funds were for charitable purposes, they should not be diverted for other uses, such as to pay damages for injuries to participants.

This doctrine also came under criticism and therefore, has been widely rejected. Those engaged in charitable activities are not, for that reason alone, immune from liability.

> FACTS: Sarah was injured during a little league baseball game. "I tried to slide into home and crashed head first into the catcher."

she explained. She sued, alleging that the coach "did not properly instruct me how to slide. He never said I couldn't make head first slides." The little league claimed the defense of charitable immunity. Did this defense relieve the league or coach of potential liability? **YOU'RE THE JUDGE!**

DECISION: No. Charitable immunity did not protect the league or the coach.

Assumption Of The Risk

Assumption of the risk will apply as a defense if a participant knew of the risk or danger as one ordinary to the sport, but then proceeded voluntarily to assume that risk.

What if a participant is required to participate, such as in a gym class? Is that voluntary participation?

Assumption of the risk is less likely to be used in defending against an injury from a physical education class. This is because students are required to participate, and therefore there may be no voluntariness of assuming any risk. But, not always.

FACTS: Hanson, during a gym class, was instructed in the proper method to jump over the horse. He was also told, "It's dangerous. You shouldn't try if you don't think you can do it."

Hanson attempted the jump, was injured, and then sued the school for negligence. Although it was a mandatory class, the school claimed, "Hanson assumed the risk of injury."

"Whose fault was it?" asked Hanson. **YOU'RE THE JUDGE!**

DECISION: Although the class was mandatory, Hanson was given the option of not participating. In trying the jump, Hanson assumed the risk of injury and, therefore, relieved the school of any liability.

When considering whether a participant understood and appreciated a risk, consideration must be given to his age and experience, and to the nature of the activity. However, if the injury is the result of another's negligence, there can be no assumption of the risk.

FACTS: Susan, 12, was injured when the go-cart she was driving at a city owned facility crashed. She said, "I went through the retaining barrier into a wall." Had the retaining barrier been properly installed, it would have prevented Susan from hitting the wall. Was the city negligent? **YOU'RE THE JUDGE!**

DECISION: Susan only assumed the risk of the ordinary and inherent dangers of the sport, not of the city's negligence.

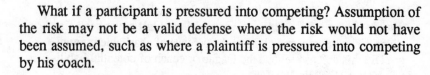

What if a participant is pressured into competing? Assumption of the risk may not be a valid defense where the risk would not have been assumed, such as where a plaintiff is pressured into competing by his coach.

> FACTS: "Tank" tried out for the school wrestling team. He was warned by the coach of the risk of injury, but nevertheless, agreed to try out.
> Similarly, John was warned when trying out for the football team. When both were injured during the normal play of the sport, they sued the school.
> "Pig," nicknamed for his enormous appetite and size, had never wrestled. Although skeptical about trying out for the wrestling team, he was talked into doing so by the coach. He was injured during his first practice. Were any of these participants pressured into competing? **YOU'RE THE JUDGE!**

> DECISION: Tank and John assumed the risk of injury; their consent was voluntary. Pig's consent was by undue pressure. He may recover for his injury, the others may not.

Contributory & Comparative Negligence

Participants in sports activities are held to a duty of exercising ordinary and reasonable care for their own protection and safety. That is, that care which an ordinary or reasonable person would exercise in the same or similar circumstances. Participants may be guilty of **contibutory negligence** where they are aware of a risk or danger, but proceed anyway and are then injured.

The question becomes, "Did the participant have sufficient knowledge, awareness and appreciation of the danger?"

Many school-related injuries involve minors. The standard of care to which the minors are held is that of an ordinary and reasonable child (of the same age and capacity) to appreciate and avoid danger in the same—or similar—circumstances.

> FACTS: Jimmy, 14, and Frankie, 15, asked their school's physical education teacher if they could try boxing. He said, "Sure, put the gloves on and give it a go!"
> Frankie, much the bigger of the two, hurt Jimmy. Jimmy sued the coach and the school, alleging improper instructions and no supervision. The school defended, "He contributed to his injury by participating. He can't recover." Could he?

> DECISION: **YOU'RE THE JUDGE!**

May a participant who contributed to his injury still recover?

Some states have **comparative negligence**—where any recovery by a plaintiff may be reduced by the amount of his own negligence. Or the plaintiff can recover for that amount of the defendant's negligence. Comparative negligence statutes vary from state to state. In some, if the plaintiff's negligence is equal, to or exceeds, the defendant's, there can be no recovery. In others, any negligence on the part of the plaintiff will completely bar recovery.

FACTS: Kenny and Stan were injured in school football games. They sued their schools, which were not protected by sovereign immunity.

Both were guilty of contributory negligence, but Kenny's school was in a state with comparative negligence. The school was found to be 40% at fault and Kenny 60% at fault. Could either Stan or Kenny recover for their injuries? **YOU'RE THE JUDGE!**

DECISION: Because Stan was guilty of contributory negligence, he could not recover.

In some states, Kenny could not recover because his degree of fault exceeded the school's. In such a state which reduces Kenny's award by the amount of his own negligence, he would have to be less than 50% at fault to recover.

In other states, Kenny would recover, but only the 40% that the school was found to be at fault; or, if the school were 60% at fault and Kenny 40%, Kenny could recover the difference, which would be 20% of the total negligence award.

In the following discussion, assume that there is no immunity from liability for a municipality or school for any negligence which causes an injury to a participant.

MUNICIPAL LIABILITY

Municipalities (cities and towns) have a duty to exercise ordinary and reasonable care for the protection and safety of those using their facilities.

It may be sufficient to charge a municipality with negligence where the municipality had an opportunity to discover unsafe conditions by inspection (or had knowledge of these conditions, or allowed a lack of supervision) and injuries followed.

FACTS: Lou and Richie were injured when they fell after hitting pot holes on the town's paved bicycle trail. Richie said, "I knew that the path was in need of repair, but Lou didn't." The holes had washed out after a heavy rain a few weeks earlier. Could the town be charged with negligence? **YOU'RE THE JUDGE!**

DECISION: Lou knew of the danger; he assumed the risk. As to

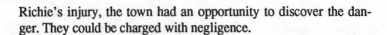

Richie's injury, the town had an opportunity to discover the danger. They could be charged with negligence.

A municipality also has a duty to warn the public of any lack of supervision or of a defective condition at one of its facilities. This could be done by posting a warning.

What if the warning is removed? If a warning is removed, the municipality may still be charged where an inspection would have revealed the missing warning.

Will a warning protect a municipality from liability where further action is necessary?

FACTS: A large hole had been left on a municipal ballfield with a sign warning: DO NOT USE THIS FIELD. Several grammar school children were playing kick ball when one of them fell into the hole and was injured. Was the municipality negligent for not taking further precautions? **YOU'RE THE JUDGE!**

DECISION: The failure to either fill in the hole or take other more necessary precautions to protect children was negligence. The children's age negated any contributory negligence or assumption of the risk.

Ballfields

Participants using municipal ballfields have a right to assume that those facilities will be free from any hazards or defects, and that necessary warnings will be posted alerting them to any hidden dangers.

Participants assume ordinary and inherent risks, such as from running into fences or bleachers. In addition, participants may assume risks inherent in playing a particular game on a specific field.

FACTS: Jerry was injured chasing a foul pop-up in a pick-up softball game. "I tripped over the curbing of a surrounding track and sidewalk and then fell over the concrete bench near the field," he testified. Jerry, who had played on this field many times before without injury, sued the city, complaining that the field was negligently designed and constructed. Was the city liable for Jerry's injuries? **YOU'RE THE JUDGE!**

DECISION: No. Although the field was not in the condition that could reasonably be expected, Jerry had played on the field before and was aware and had knowledge of the condition. He assumed the risk of, and contributed to, his injury.

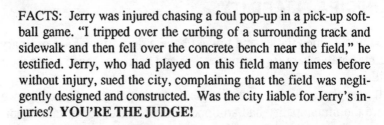

Unless it had posted a conspicuous sign warning of the dangerous condition, the city may have been held liable even if Jerry not played on the field before.

FACTS: Hank, running out for a pass in a pick-up touch football game, fell and broke his ankle. "My foot got caught in a hole hidden by long grass. And I cut myself on a broken bottle." Hank sued the town which owned the field. Was the town liable for Hank's injuries? **YOU'RE THE JUDGE!**

DECISION: If the hole was open and obvious, Hank would have assumed the risk of injury. But where the hole was hidden because of the failure of the town to either cut the grass or fix the hole, the town was liable. Hank had no knowledge or appreciation of the danger.

As to the cut, Hank was held to have contributed to his injury by playing on the field without making at least a visual inspection, which would have revealed the broken bottle.

Similarly, where a town did not warn of a defective fence surrounding their facility, they were held liable when a player unintentionally ran into the fence, which then collapsed, injuring him. Here, even an adequate warning may not have been enough. The town should have either fixed the fence or prohibited use of the field until the fence was fixed.

What if the player had noticed the defective fence before playing there?

Even if the player had noticed the fence's condition, temporary forgetfulness while in the heat of the game, might have excused him from assuming any risk of injury. It would be up to a judge or jury to decide if the player had forgotten.

If a city or town furnishes equipment, it must be in proper condition. Liability may attach where any equipment has a hidden or unknown defect. However, liability will not attach where a player knew of the defect.

Will a potentially dangerous game broaden a municipality's duty of care?

FACTS: A town issued gear to the neighborhood boys for a football game. Because of a cracked helmet, one of the boys was injured and sued the town. Did the town have a responsibility to issue proper equipment, or provide either instruction, supervision, or both? **YOU'RE THE JUDGE!**

DECISION: The town would not only be responsible for issuing equipment in the proper condition, but may also have a duty to instruct or warn the boys of the dangers, and to provide supervision to ensure their protection and safety.

Swimming

A municipality has a duty to exercise ordinary or reasonable care for the protection and safety of those using municipal swimming facilities. This duty includes giving proper warnings concerning the use of a facility and known hidden hazards (as well as the inspecting and cleaning up of all foreign substances on the grounds and in and around any protective barriers.)

This duty extends to bathhouse and changing areas. There is also a duty to have required safety equipment in proper condition.

> FACTS: John, while walking next to a city owned and supervised pool, slipped and fell into the pool. Jay held out the safety hook, "It fell apart." he said. John went under. Attempts to resuscitate him were unsuccessful. John's family sued the city "for negligently operating its swimming pool." Was the city negligent? **YOU'RE THE JUDGE!**

> DECISION: Yes. The city breached its duty to provide proper safety equipment. This breach was the cause of John's death.

A city's duty to keep its swimming facilities in proper condition may not extend to unsupervised, unimproved public property. Such might be the case where a city was either not aware of a water's use or had posted warnings.

> FACTS: Keith drowned when, at a local pond, he jumped out of a tree and landed on a rock along the bank. His family sued the city for "not preventing the kids from using the pond." They asked, "Was the city liable?" **YOU'RE THE JUDGE!**

> DECISIONS: Keith contributed to and also assumed the risk of such an injury. He knew, or should have known, of the condition. The city is not an insurer of a user's safety. Nor can it guarantee, or be held liable for, the safety of all users.

A municipality's duty to care for the safety of its users may extend to other situations which could result in injuries (such as by having inattentive, or an insufficient number of, lifeguards).

What if a lifeguard uses improper life-saving techniques or none at all in attempting a rescue?

> FACTS: Will, a lifeguard at a city-owned swimming facility, was giving instructions in life-saving techniques. Susan, a beginning swimmer, ventured into the deep end, but started thrashing about when she realized where she was. She drowned. Efforts to revive her were unsuccessful.
>
> The city claimed that the lifeguard was giving necessary instruc-

tion to other swimmers. "He could not be held liable to protect everyone in the pool at every moment. Susan assumed the risk of drowning." Was the city liable for Susan's death? **YOU'RE THE JUDGE!**

DECISION: Yes. Although the city may not have been negligent where an injury was the result of an unexplained tragedy (no one's fault), this tragedy happened because the lifeguard was improperly supervising the pool. Had he been observant as required, Susan would have been under the water for a much shorter time and, in the view of medical opinion, saved.

If facilities are off-limits, then there is a duty to provide adequate safeguards, such as a barrier and posting as such. This duty extends to periodically inspecting the area to ensure that the barrier is intact.

FACTS: Several kids were using the diving board at the city pool. Frank hit the bottom, severely spraining his neck. Upon inspection, it was found that, although the marking on the side of the pool showed the depth to be 8 feet; the actual depth was 6 1/2 feet.

Testimony was given, "Had the pool been 8 feet deep, it is unlikely that the injury would have occurred." Frank sued the city for not warning him of the depth of the water. Did Frank assume the risk of such injury? **YOU'RE THE JUDGE!**

DECISION: No. Although had Frank known of the shallower water, he may have assumed the risk, it was not evident that the water was shallower than marked. The city was held liable.

Basketball, Tennis & Rinks

Any defective conditions in basketball or tennis courts, or a skating rink—such as holes, cracks, broken supports or unmended fences—will most likely be open and obvious. Therefore, assumption of the risk will bar recovery for such conditions, even if there is no warning. Is supervision necessary at such facilities?

FACTS: The neighborhood kids were playing a three-on-three basketball game at an outdoor court. "J.D. and Slammer collided while going for a loose ball," explained another player.

J.D. was injured and sued the city. Was the city liable for not providing supervision? **YOU'RE THE JUDGE!**

DECISION: No. The court held, "J.D. assumed the risk of injury. Even if the city had provided supervision, it could not be shown that such supervision would have prevented injury from an ordinary and inherent risk of the game."

If, however, supervision was given and a supervisor knew (or should have known) of rough play that could lead to injury, then a city may be held to have been on notice of such potential injury and could be found responsible for not taking proper safety measures.

Golf

As it is well known that injury may result from an errant golf shot, assumption of the risk is a widely used and successful defense to actions alleging negligence for such an injury.

For a hazard, other than a normal hazard on a golf course, there may exist a duty to warn by an appropriate sign or barrier and to make periodic inspections.

Who is liable for injuries to passersby from errantly struck golf balls?

FACTS: Moe, Larry and Curly were injured while driving their cars on the road next to the city owned, Highlands Golf Course.

Moe was struck by a ball that went through a hole in the fence; Larry was hit by a ball which sailed over the fence; Curly was hit by a ball where there was no fence.

Moe and Larry were aware of the course and its danger, Curly was not. He insisted, "I never drove on that road before." Was the city liable for the injuries? **YOU'RE THE JUDGE!**

DECISION: Larry assumed the risk of being struck by an occasional errant ball, but would not assume the risk if the city was aware, or should have been aware, of this being more than a common occurrence.

Moe and Curly did not assume the risk of injury due to the city's negligence in not repairing the fence, or in not constructing one where it was needed to protect the public.

Racing

Where a participant or an observer of either unauthorized or prohibited drag racing of cars on public streets is injured, contributory negligence and assumption of the risk will generally be successful defenses.

What if a city knew or should have known of such conduct, but did nothing to prevent it?

FACTS: Robinson, using a city park, was injured when he was struck by a vehicle which was drag racing on an adjacent street. The city was aware of the prohibited racing, but found it difficult to control. Was the city liable for Robinson's injury? **YOU'RE THE JUDGE!**

DECISION: The city was not liable. A city has a duty to maintain its streets in a reasonably safe condition. However, where a city makes an acceptable effort to prevent such racing, recovery for any resulting injury may be barred, at least as against the city.

Trampoline

An 11-year-old, Marie, while bouncing on a trampoline at a city park, lost her balance, fell, and fractured her jaw on a metal pipe near the trampoline.

When she sued the city, the court held, "At the least, there should have been instructions, adequate warning and properly placed equipment." The city-run trampoline center failed to exercise reasonable care. But, what if Marie were older?

FACTS: Daniel, 35, and college educated, was injured using a trampoline at a city gym. Signs were posted telling patrons to: ASK FOR INSTRUCTIONS, IF NEEDED. Warnings were also given. Did Daniel assume the risk of injury? **YOU'RE THE JUDGE!**

DECISION: Daniel assumed the risk of his injury from using the trampoline. He was old enough to understand the warning and the risk of using the trampoline.

SCHOOL LIABILITY

School authorities owe to those who participate for a school or on school property, the duty to exercise ordinary and reasonable care for their protection and safety.

Schools, however, are not insurers of safety. They will only be liable for injuries where they or their agents, such as a teacher or coach, fail to meet the required duty.

Do students have a duty to protect themselves? Students have a duty to exercise reasonable care for their own protection and safety. They will assume the risks and dangers ordinarily inherent in a game or sport including a risk of injury from an unforseeable accident for which no amount of precaution, except elimination of the activity, could prevent injury.

FACTS: Mitch failed to complete a simple exercise, a jumping jack, and was injured. A baseball bat slipped from the coach's hands and injured Guy. Mary was hurt during a kickball game. The only explanation for this injury was the presence of many participants.

Sue was injured during basketball practice. It was later discovered that she had very weak ankles which could not support jumping. Could any of these participants recover from the coaches or schools for their injuries? **YOU'RE THE JUDGE!**

DECISION: All of the injuries were the result of unforseeable accidents. They all assumed the risk of such injuries.

Students may also be held to have assumed the risk of, or contributed to, their injury where they are aware of—and appreciate—the risk or danger, but choose to proceed anyway.

FACTS: Hank's nose was broken during a boxing match. Bill hurt his back rebounding during a rough, but fair, basketball game. Judy, with a qualified spotter, was injured attempting a difficult gymnastics maneuver which she had done before. Could any of these student-athletes recover for their injuries against the school? **YOU'RE THE JUDGE!**

RESPONDEAT SUPERIOR?

BEE
HIGH SCHOOL
COACH

DECISION: Hank, Bill and Judy had consented to subject themselves to the known dangers and risks. Therefore, they contributed to, and assumed the risk of, injury from their participation.

Should consideration be given to: the type or manner of consent given, the nature of the activity, and the age and experience of the student?

FACTS: Jeff, 16, in his first try-out for the school's football team, was instructed, "In this drill, you must attempt, without blockers, to run through five tacklers."
Susan, 15, in her first try-out for the school gymnastics team, was instructed, "You have to execute five consecutive tuck-and-rolls." Both were then injured. Was either's consent informed? Was it voluntary? Were they pressured? Who was liable?

DECISION: **YOU'RE THE JUDGE!**

Respondeat Superior!

In states which have waived sovereign immunity, schools may—under the rule of **respondeat superior**—be held liable for the negligent acts of their teachers and coaches.

This rule provides, "A school is liable for injury caused by employees of the school, acting within their duties, if such conduct would allow a complaint against the employee, as an individual, apart from the school."

FACTS: Junior, a coach at Emerald High, negligently instructed football players during tackling drills. When several of the players were injured while using the improper tackling techniques, they sued the school. Was the school liable for the acts of their coach? **YOU'RE THE JUDGE!**

DECISION: The school was held liable under the rule of respondeat superior.

A SCHOOL'S DUTY MAY EXTEND TO THESE OBLIGATIONS:

> Greater New England High School Athletic Association
> 4141 Fairfax Ave.
> Greendale, MA 34341
>
> ☐ Equipment ☐ Instructions
> ☐ Training ☐ Supervision
> ☐ Facilities ☐ Coach Or Instructor
> ☐ Medical Attention ☐ Discipline & Rules
> ☐ Competition ☐ Transportation
> ☐ Physical Condition of Participants

Equipment — Was the equipment suitable, in proper condition and provided, where necessary, to ensure the safety of participants?

FACTS: During a floor hockey game, Warren was struck in the head by the puck. "He wasn't wearing a helmet," said the coach.

Another player, Evan, was seriously injured when a hockey puck hit between gaps in the helmet he was wearing. Was the school liable for the injuries? **YOU'RE THE JUDGE!**

DECISION: The court found that requiring the students to play without proper protective equipment was negligent.

Any equipment furnished must be proper. Another high school athlete, Wilfred, participating in the high jump, was injured when he fell in a landing pit consisting of vinyl bags filled with foam rubber. The school was found negligent for supplying improper equipment and facilities.

But where a pole-vaulter, Walt, fell backwards into the wooden boxes used to support the vaulting bar, recovery for his injuries was denied. The court commented that "the usefulness of the boxes outweighed the risk of injury."

Can a violation of safety standards that results in injury, lead to liability for negligence?

FACTS: Howard, 15, was injured while participating in a high school summer football practice. The practice was supervised by two coaches. The team, without protective equipment, was engaged in a game of "jungle football." Howard was struck in the eye, resulting in blindness. He sued the school for providing neither proper equipment nor supervision. Was the school liable? **YOU'RE THE JUDGE!**

DECISION: Yes. The practice sessions were in violation of safety standards, which required both proper equipment and proper supervision.

Courts have found other school districts liable for carelessly and negligently allowing players to wear ill-fitting, inadequate equipment (cracked helmet) and, furthermore, for refusing to furnish proper equipment upon request.

Instructions — Were instructions given adequately and propely, including any warnings necessary to ensure the safety of participants?

FACTS: Gardner, 11, injured his shoulder. He said, "I was attempting to perform a headstand. There were no instructions."
   Felicia, a 17 year-old high school student, broke her wrist when she was instructed to try an exercise known as "jumping the buck." She told the instructor, "I don't want to, I have weak wrists." But nevertheless, she was instructed to try the exercise.
   Landers injured his back attempting a backward somersault during gym class. The teacher was aware that Landers was overweight, untrained and fearful, but instructed him to "work on the maneuver on your own." He collided with another student who was also instructed to do the same exercise on the same mat.
   Another student, James, was instructed to execute a somersault. In so doing, he was injured. He had done them many times before without injury. Were the schools negligent for not providing proper instructions? **YOU'RE THE JUDGE!**

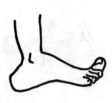

DECISION: James assumed the risk of, and contributed to, his injury. The courts found the other schools negligent and liable for the injuries. They either gave improper instructions or no instructions where they were required.

Negligence has also been found where inadequate instructions on using the trampoline, rings and springboard all resulted in injuries to students.
   Similarly, negligence for improper instructions was found where students were injured after being instructed to try tumbling exercises in stocking feet and slipped, or where students were instructed to

play in bare feet, and their bare feet stuck to the floor, causing them to fall.

Participants will assume the risk of injury from an unforseeable accident, where there is no negligence in instructions or in providing equipment or supervision. Can participants also be guilty of contributory negligence?

> FACTS: Ed Sowers ran into a javelin during an outdoor physical education class. He had been ordered, "Stay on the track!" but forgot and was running on the grass when the accident happened. Should the school have taken other precautions? **YOU'RE THE JUDGE!**

> DECISION: No. The instructions were adequate. Sowers, not wearing his glasses, was unable to see the javelin. His own negligence was the cause of his injury.

Can participants be guilty of assuming the risk of, or contributing to, their injuries where they are not aware of the dangers that face them?

> FACTS: "We started to box. We wanted to see who would get the best of it, so we went right at it as hard as we could. In the second round we started just as bad as ever and I got hit in the temple. I became dizzy and staggered." testified Hector.
> Neither Hector nor his opponent had received proper training. Hector received serious injuries to his head, which required draining hemorrhaging blood. The supervising teacher sat in the bleachers, watching and gave no instructions or warning.
> Darrow, 10, suffered injuries when he ran into another player while playing line soccer at school. He had never received instructions on what to do if two players arrived at the ball simultaneously, and was never warned of the dangers of the game. Did Hector and Darrow assume the risks of such injuries? **YOU'RE THE JUDGE!**

> DECISION: No. Teachers must exercise reasonable care to prevent injuries, including giving warnings and instructions, before allowing participation in a dangerous activity. The plaintiffs could not assume risks that they were not aware of.

A similar result was reached where students, trying out for their high school football team, were urged to lift weights by the coach. They were not given proper instructions, nor were they warned of the risk of injury. Varon, 15, fell while lifting a 250-pound weight, resulting in paraplegia.

In baseball, are proper instructions and a warning necessary when teaching participants how to slide?

FACTS: During a "suicide squeeze" attempt, Sanders—using his head as a battering ram—bowled over the catcher when the batter missed the sign and did not bunt the ball. When Sanders was injured, he sued the school for "giving me improper instructions."

In a previous incident, Sanders had used his body in a slide into third base. The coach shouted, "Nice play!" Did such a statement mean that the coach approved of the head first slide? Was there negligence in not providing proper instructions or a warning of the risk of injury from such a slide?

DECISION: **YOU'RE THE JUDGE!**

Are instructions and a warning of the risk of injury always required? What if a participant was experienced and already knew, or should have known of the dangers of that sport?

FACTS: Handel, a high school freshman football player weighing 140 pounds, said, "I broke my neck carrying the ball." He sued the school district for not providing proper or sufficient instructions and warning and for furnishing him with defective equipment.

Handel described what happened, "I saw the Hale players in front of me and I knew I couldn't go any farther so I put my head down and just ran into 'em. That's when I heard my neck snap."

Handel had received instruction in carrying the ball, but alleged that the hazards and risks of the game had never been explained. Was the school liable? **YOU'RE THE JUDGE!**

DECISION: No. Handel had played football for the two previous years; he was not inexperienced. The coaches gave adequate, standard instructions; practices were held without negligently omitting any details. Handel assumed the risk of, and, by playing, contributed to, such an injury.

But where it is found that coaches either did not give proper instructions and warnings, or gave instructions that were either incomplete or for improper techniques—such as by suggesting or condoning fighting—then liability may be found where injury results.

Training — Was training adequate, proper and of the amount necessary to ensure the safety of participants?

FACTS: A 200-pound student, Govel, 18, was injured while performing an exercise called the "elephant." The exercise consisted of executing a somersault in midair from a springboard over parallel bars. While in the air, his foot struck the bars and he fell to the bare floor. Was the instructor negligent for instructing an untrained student to try such an exercise? **YOU'RE THE JUDGE!**

DECISION: The instructor was negligent. The exercise should only have been attempted by highly skilled pupils. Furthermore, the instructor was negligent for failing to have mats in the proper places.

What if a training program is too rigorous and an injury results?

FACTS: Sampson was injured during weight training. Although 6'2" and 250 pounds, he had never lifted weights before. He was instructed to perform numerous exercises and was injured after one hour of lifting. Sampson alleged that the injury occurred because of physical fatigue, brought about by too rigorous a training program for a beginner. Who was liable for the injury?

DECISION: **YOU'RE THE JUDGE!**

Another student was injured while voluntarily umpiring a baseball game. Instead of wearing the usual umpire equipment, he stood behind a portable backstop. A foul ball came back against the netting, striking him in the eye. He couldn't recover for his injury. The court found, "He was aware of the danger and risk of such an injury."

Supervision — Was proper supervision provided to prevent participants from confronting unreasonable risks of injury? Was consideration given to the size and strength of the participants?

FACTS: Morry, 15, was participating in wrestling for the first time. He practiced with the wrestling team for about six weeks. Then, during a wrestling match, broke his neck and severed his spinal cord.

The coach, a former wrestler, had only one season of previous coaching experience. Morry was required to wrestle two matches with boys heavier than he was.

Was the school liable for negligent instruction and supervision?
YOU'RE THE JUDGE!

DECISION: Morry did not receive proper instruction or supervision. He was not taught the proper way to escape from the hold responsible for the injury. The coach was also negligent for improperly delegating "the important function of refereeing" to another student.

While the referee (an agent working for one of the schools) had his attention diverted from the wrestling match as he was fixing the mats, Stephens' spinal cord was severed by his opponent's illegal full-nelson.

After a suit by Stephens, the court found that the school, by failing to adequately supervise the contestants, breached its duty to provide proper supervision. Stephens could not assume the risk of injury from such incompetence and negligence.

What if there are too many participants to supervise, or too small a playing area and injury results? In these cases, similar decisions were reached where injuries resulted.

> FACTS: Many basketball players were allowed to participate in a gym class. One student, Richy, was struck by a player on an opposing team when a third player on an adjacent court ran onto the court where Richy was playing, pushing the opposing player into him. Was this proper supervision? **YOU'RE THE JUDGE!**

> DECISION: The court held that there was a failure to provide sufficient supervision. With proper supervision, the injury would not have occurred.

Negligence may also be found where a supervisor fails to provide an experienced and competent person to supervise.

> FACTS: Kirk, a school football player, tore a ligament in his knee while being tested for leg strength by an untrained student. Was the school liable for the injury? **YOU'RE THE JUDGE!**

> DECISION: The school was held liable for providing improper supervision.

Another school district was found liable for the death of a student who was accidently struck in the head by a golf club.

The court reasoned, "Death would not have occurred had the supervisor not rearranged the mats so that the golfers were in violation of the teaching procedure."

The student wasn't familiar with the game, hadn't attended the class where instruction was provided, and none was provided prior to the accident.

But where Judy, 18, and Henrietta, 17, were injured "fooling around" on the trampoline and horizontal bars after class, and the teacher had warned the students, "Do not use the equipment!" the students' education and prior experience in using the equipment was considered. The court found that the participants were aware of, and appreciated, the risk involved. They were liable for their injuries.

Who would be liable for an injury where no amount of supervision could have prevented it?

> FACTS: Karl died from a head injury he received when he bumped heads with another player. He was trying for a rebound in

a basketball game at the school gym. His family sued the school, alleging, "Improper supervision caused the injury."

Wright was hit in the eye and injured by a tennis ball thrown by one student for another to hit. The coach was in his office. Were the schools liable? **YOU'RE THE JUDGE!**

DECISION: The bumping of heads during a basketball game, or being hit by an unintentionally thrown ball, are hazards of those games which participants assume. The accidents were unforseeable. Even if supervision had been present, the likelihood of the accident occurring would have been the same.

Would fault be found if unsupervised games were often rough and had resulted in previous injuries?

FACTS: Red was injured while being blocked during a school touch football game.

Vinnie was injured when, during a high school football practice, "An opponent tackled me, using his arm as a battering ram."

Dirk was injured when "the players started horsing around and playing very rough." These practice games were all unsupervised. Did the schools exercise reasonable care for the players' protection and safety? **YOU'RE THE JUDGE!**

DECISION: If proper supervision would not have prevented an injury, then there will be no liability. Red was blocked in the proper manner. The lack of supervision was not the cause of the injury.

As to Vinnie's injury, the presence of proper supervision may have prevented the injury. If the coach knew, or should have known, that any improper technique might be used in playing the game when he wasn't present—then the school could be guilty of negligence for not providing proper supervision.

As to Dirk's injury, the coach was negligent. It could be expected that proper supervision would have prevented such an injury.

Similarly, a lack of supervision was found where a 16-year-old student fell and died from a fractured skull after "slap boxing" outside the school gym during gym class.

The teacher responsible for supervision was "sitting with his back to the office window." Testimony showed the teacher would have stopped the fight had he seen it, and that the students would not have been fighting had he been present.

Can a school be held responsible for not supervising spectators?

FACTS: During a high school softball game, spectators moved toward the field and took over the players' benches. A third baseman, Domino, while attempting to catch a foul ball, tripped over a spectator, fell over a bench, and broke his leg. Was the school negligent for not providing proper supervision? **YOU'RE THE JUDGE!**

DECISION: School supervisors were held liable for the injury. Negligence was for allowing the spectators to congregate close to the base line, where they pushed the bench into a dangerous position obscuring it from the view of any player.

Physical Condition Of Participants — Was there proper concern for the physical condition of the participants?

Reasonable steps must be taken to minimize the possibility of injury, particularly where any participant may not be physically able to perform, either due to an injury or otherwise generally unfit.

One student, Lowe, was required to participate in gym exercises over her protest, "I don't want to, I'm hurt." When she was injured, the school was found negligent for improperly requiring her participation.

FACTS: A student, Ann, was injured after she was instructed, "Work on your own." She was attempting a backward somersault during physical education class. The teacher was aware that Ann was overweight, untrained and fearful. Did the teacher have the proper concern for Ann's safety? **YOU'RE THE JUDGE!**

DECISION: No. The injury was the result of negligence in instructing Ann to work on the maneuver on her own. She was unfit to participate.

Similar decisions have been reached where students were too weak to perform and injury resulted when they were forced to attempt an exercise.

FACTS: Chris, 17, was injured attempting a diving somersault over two persons kneeling on the floor. The instructor was watching. Proper performance of this feat depends upon a participant's agility and strength. This was not tested. Did Chris assume the risk of such an injury? **YOU'RE THE JUDGE!**

DECISION: The court ruled, "The school was negligent for improper supervision. The instructor should have had knowledge of Chris' capabilities prior to allowing her to attempt such a feat."

Would it be proper concern for a participant's safety where the participant is "persuaded" to play while injured?

FACTS: Lowell, 17, a high school football player, charged, "I was injured during practice. Two weeks later I was persuaded by the coach to play. He knew that I hadn't recovered from my injury." Lowell was injured further, necessitating a back operation. Was the coach negligent? YOU'RE THE JUDGE!

DECISION: The court held that the coach knew or should have known that Lowell had not recovered from his previous injury and that further serious injury was likely to result. The coach persuaded Lowell to play while injured. That was a violation of the coach's duty to exercise reasonable care for the safety of the player.

However, where an exercise such as a sit-up did not require any more than a minimum of strength, and a student—appearing able to perform—willingly attempted it and was injured, the student was held to have contributed to his injury by attempting the exercise.

Facilities — Did the school fulfill its duty to provide safe, suitable and adequate facilities in the proper condition?

Where a student was tackled and had his face pushed into unslaked lime used to mark the sidelines, or; where a school knew or should have known of holes in the field, or; where sharp metal sideline markers were used, or; where a barrier surrounding a field was falling down; (and players' injuries resulted from all of these conditions) negligence by the schools may be found for their not maintaining the facilities in the conditions necessary for the protection and safety of the participants.

Numerous other situations have been found to be violations of the duty to provide safe facilities.

FACTS: Students were forced to play on a street marked off next to their school. One student was struck by a car.

Other students were injured when forced to play on an outdoor court where there were holes, slick spots and broken glass.

Also, where a school was aware, or should have been aware, that glass in a door adjacent to the gym was not safety glass and that a wall was too close to the basket, participants—not aware of these safety hazards—were injured. Were the schools negligent in not providing proper facilities? YOU'RE THE JUDGE!

DECISION: The court found the schools negligent for "not providing proper and suitable facilities" and, for, violating their duty to exercise due care for the students' protection and safety.

Schools have also been found negligent, where injuries resulted, in maintaining facilities when: there was no proper padding of poles

or supports, floors were too slippery, or mats did not stay in place.

If an injury was caused by an open and obvious condition, or one not dangerous, will an injured participant assume such risks as part of the game?

FACTS: In a softball game during gym class, Walter fell into a ditch while chasing a foul fly quite a distance from the field. "I saw the ditch while warming up, but forgot about it." he grumbled. Did Walter assume the risk of such an injury? **YOU'RE THE JUDGE!**

DECISION: The facility was not inherently dangerous. Walter assumed the risk of such an injury.

FACTS: Martin sustained a back injury when he slipped and fell going in for a lay-up during a basketball game. Water had condensed on the floor and had been mopped up prior to the game. Fans helped, and heaters were used in an attempt to dry it. Did the school breach its duty to take reasonable care to protect the players? **YOU'RE THE JUDGE!**

DECISION: No. Since none of the coaches or referees responsible for approving the playing conditions considered the floor's condition serious enough to even discuss canceling the game, the school did not act unreasonably.

Coach Or Instructor — Did the school fulfill its duty to exercise due care in the selection of coaches and instructors, considering their qualifications and ability, especially where the activity was a potentially dangerous one?

FACTS: Bill Rosel drowned during a required swimming class. He had remained unnoticed on the bottom of the pool for five or six minutes.

The complaint filed by Rosel's parents charged, "The school was negligent in allowing student assistants to supervise a beginners class without having experience and training sufficient to protect the swimmers." The assistants had certification for lifesaving, but not for water safety instruction. Was the school liable for the injury? **YOU'RE THE JUDGE!**

DECISION: Yes. The court held that the school was negligent in the selection of the instructors.

An activity, otherwise safe, may become potentially dangerous because of the nature of the activity or due to large numbers of participants where there is unqualified supervision.

FACTS: A school placed a janitor in charge of a gym class during lunch hour. Alex, 12, was injured during a tumbling maneuver in which the janitor participated.

Another school, after dismissing the football coach, temporarily placed a teacher in charge of practices. A player was injured while performing improper tackling and blocking drills. Did either school breach its duty to provide qualified coaching? **YOU'RE THE JUDGE!**

DECISION: The courts held that the schools were negligent and had breached their duty to carefully select and obtain suitable coaching for students, especially where safety was involved.

What if the instructions were improper, but the player knew the proper technique?

Where a coach gives improper instructions, a player may be held to have assumed the risk of, or contributed to, any injury if he knew that following the improper instructions might result in injury. This would be especially so where a participant was not forced into using such improper instructions.

Furthermore, if an injury is the result of an accident, an accepted risk of the game and no one's fault, such as where a bat slipped from a coach's hands, there will be no liability. Assumption of the risk will apply.

Medical Attention — Did the school fulfill its duty to provide proper medical attention to ensure the protection and safety of the participants?

This duty may include providing medical assistance where immediate attention is necessary (such as in lifesaving techniques) or may require that a player be monitored while awaiting trained medical assistance better able to handle more difficult situations

Where a coach or assistant attempts to provide medical assistance, it should be provided with the care required to prevent further injury. Furthermore, it should only be given within their training and experience in handling such emergencies.

FACTS: Walsh was injured during a high school football scrimmage. When he couldn't get up, the coach suspected a neck injury. After finding that the player could still move his fingers and toes, the coach allowed Walsh to be taken from the field without the aid of a stretcher. When Walsh reached the sidelines, he had no movement in his hands or feet.

Undisputed expert testimony indicated that additional spinal damage took place after the tackle, due to his being moved. Was this proper medical attention? **YOU'RE THE JUDGE!**

DECISION: No. The coach was negligent for not only removing Walsh from the field, but for not waiting for a doctor.

The death of another high school football player resulted from heatstroke suffered during football practice. He was placed in a shower of room temperature water, covered with a blanket and given an ammonia capsule.

Expert testimony indicated, "Every effort should have been made to stop the player's accumulation of heat. Room temperature water and a blanket increased his accumulation of heat." The coaches "were negligent in denying the boy medical assistance and in applying an ill-chosen first aid."

A school will assume liability where it allows a student to participate, knowing that further injury is more likely. It will not be liable where an injury is due to a previous or hidden injury (unknown to the school) or properly not thought serious enough to limit or prohibit participation.

Discipline & Rules — Did the school fulfill its duty to make and establish rules for the maintenance of discipline?

This may be especially important in physical education classes where large numbers of students may be present.

May an instructor discipline students? An instructor may discipline a student as long as it is not excessive or too physically punishing.

Punishment drills or other excessive forms of discipline may be negligent where they exceed that discipline reasonably expected as part of the game, or where the discipline breaches the duty to exercise reasonable care for the player's protection and safety.

FACTS: Robert was put through a series of punishment drills for damaging a door in the dorm.

The punishment came after a two-hour football practice and lasted for 90 minutes. Robert became completely disoriented. He was found dead in his room, the cause of death acute dehydration. His family sued, alleging improper training and discipline. Was the school negligent? **YOU'RE THE JUDGE!**

DECISION: The suit was settled for the family. Reportedly, one of the terms of the settlement was an agreement that the school would not subject players to such drills in the future.

Another coach, displeased with a seventh grader's blocking, grabbed him by the face mask and knocked him to the ground. The player received a severely sprained neck. When a suit by the player against the school followed, the court held that the coach was negligent. He could use reasonable force necessary for discipline, but could not use physical violence.

As long as rules are reasonable, are known by the players, and have as their purpose the aiding in and providing for orderly and safe play, they will be upheld. However, where they are not enforced (or improperly enforced), liability for negligence may attach where such a violation of a rule was the cause of an injury.

Competition — Did the school use reasonable care in selecting competition, taking into consideration the nature of the sport and the age and experience of the participants?

> FACTS: During a high school football game, Barret, 17, was killed in a collision with a twenty-year-old player. A rule prohibited players over nineteen from playing. The deceased player's family sued the school for negligence for allowing improper competition. Was this negligence? **YOU'RE THE JUDGE!**

> DECISION: The court held that the rule was not for the safety of the players, but to encourage students desiring to compete to complete their education before reaching the age of twenty. Therefore, the violation of the rule was not the cause of the injury. Recovery was denied.

If the reason for the rule was to prevent older and potentially more experienced and bigger players from playing, would the result have been different?

Where participants are engaged in a contact sport, size and experience should be a concern.

> FACTS: Jackson High started a new football program. They scheduled the state's top-rated team, the Worcester Maulers.
>
> Many of the players were doubtful of their ability to compete. "That team is so much more experienced, bigger and physical!" the players complained.
>
> The coach replied, "It'll be rough, but you need the experience." When several of the much smaller and less experienced Jackson High players were injured, they sued the school. The players asked, "Did the school use due care in selecting our competition?" Was the school liable for the injuries?

> DECISION: **YOU'RE THE JUDGE!**

Where an injury is the result of unforseeable contact, or an accident, there may no liability. Therefore, where a student in a gym class was injured when run into by an older, much heavier student in a game of tag, there could be no recovery of damages.

Transportation — Did the school provide safe and timely transportation, exercising the highest degree of care for the protection and safety of the students?

There may be no duty where either sovereign immunity exists (unless the driver may be sued individually) or where the school has properly delegated its duty to transport the students to an independent contractor (such as a local bus company).

The transportation of student-athletes involves a greater than normal incidence of hazardous situations. Negligence may arise where the school employs an improper driver and injury results.

FACTS: A high school football coach directed one of his players, "Speedy," to drive the others home after practice, knowing that he was reckless and that he had an unsafe vehicle. After Speedy crashed, while driving too fast, the injured students sued the school for not providing safe transportation. Was the school liable for the injuries? **YOU'RE THE JUDGE!**

DECISION: Directing an unqualified, unauthorized or unsafe driver to transport students or allowing their transport in a known unsafe vehicle is negligence, even if the coach drives (unless qualified or authorized to do so).

Similarly, recovery was allowed where one vehicle was overloaded and injury resulted when the vehicle couldn't stop due to the overloading. It was also allowed where a passenger fell out of an overloaded vehicle.

Liability may also attach where a vehicle transporting student-athletes starts moving before all students are either in (or have exited from) or have gotten out of the vehicle's path, and injury results.

Other potential negligence may involve a violation of laws (i.e. speeding and allowing underage or non-licensed people to drive). Neglecting dangerous driving conditions or for allowing passengers to distract and affect the driver's ability to safely transport them are a few more examples.

FACTS: While on the team bus, headed for an away football game, several players, as usual, got very boisterous and began roughhousing. One player was knocked into the driver, who then crashed the bus into a pole. Several players received minor injuries. They sued the school for not providing safe transportation. Was the school liable for providing safe transportation? Did the players contribute to their injuries? May any of them recover damages for their injuries?

DECISION: **YOU'RE THE JUDGE!**

ODDS & ENDS....

FACTS: John, Ray, Charles and Edward were playing golf at the municipal golf course. They teed up their balls for the 18th hole in complete darkness.

After "teeing off," John and Ray began running down the fairway, golf bags over their shoulders, in a hurry to see where their drives ended up.

John fell in a fairway trap; Ray ran into a stalled electric golf cart. Charles and Edward drove into a hole dug to repair the watering and electrical systems. Edward, in his attempt to get out touched a "live" wire.

All were injured and sued the city. "The city maintained the golf course in a faulty condition. It neglected its duty to exercise reasonable care for our protection and safety." they alleged.

The city claimed that the golfers assumed the risk of, and contributed to, their injuries by playing in the dark. Could any of the golfers recover for their injuries? **YOU'RE THE JUDGE!**

DECISION: John could not recover. He assumed the risk of falling into the trap, a normal hazard of the sport.

Ray could recover, although his recovery might be eliminated or reduced for comparative negligence. The city was negligent in allowing the "dead" cart to remain on the course. But Ray was partially guilty of contributing to his injury by running in the dark, knowing that there may be hazards or other dangers.

Charles and Edward could recover if it could be shown that there were no warning signs, ropes or other evidence of an open and obvious danger.

Even if Edward and Charles assume the risk of falling into the hole, the city was found negligent for leaving a live wire exposed.

"The King can do no wrong" is not the prevailing belief that it once was. Nowadays, schools and municipalities are much more diligent in their duty to exercise reasonable care for the safety of those either using their facilities or under their control.

For activities taking place at, or under the control of, a school, a participant may assume that proper instruction, supervision, equipment and facilities will be given.

However, for sports activities taking place at a municipal facility, most of the activities (with the exception of swimming pools and mu-

nicipally run park's programs—which demand the same duty as that expected of a school) will not be supervised.

In these instances, will participants have a duty to protect themselves?

Where there is no required supervision, participants have more of a duty to exercise ordinary and reasonable care for their own protection and safety than do those participating in a supervised activity.

Participants assume all of the ordinary and common risks in a sport. A school or municipality does not insure a participant's safety. They may only be held liable for their own negligent acts, or for those committed by one for whom they are responsible, such as a teacher, coach or instructor.

8

PRODUCTS GUARANTEED SAFE

WHAT'S IT ABOUT?

Products Guaranteed Safe delves into **product liability**—the liability of a manufacturer or seller of a product (such as a football helmet) for an injury caused by their product.

Can a participant who is injured by a product be prevented from recovering damages where the advice "Buyer beware!" was not heeded?

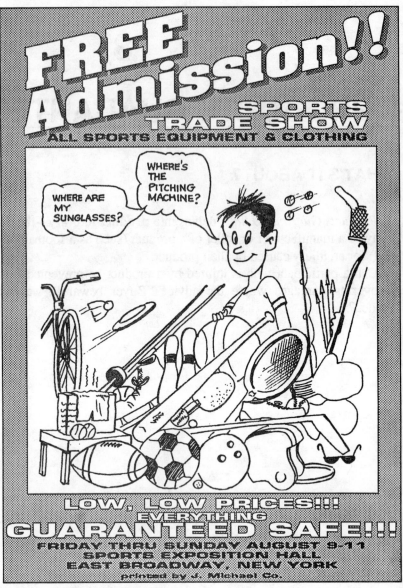

PRODUCT LIABILITY

FACTS: The TELEGRAM, a local newspaper, reported, "Last month, the following players were injured while participating in sports in the Stowe area: Johnson, when his football helmet cracked; James, when he caught and broke several fingers in a metal basketball net; Anders, when he tripped over and was stabbed by the football side-line marker; Turner, when he crashed through a shatterproof glass partition; Hanks, when Bob's new golf club came apart and struck him, and; 'Killer', when—during a boxing match,—the ropes gave way and he fell out of the ring."

Were the manufacturers of any of these products liable for defects in designing or manufacturing them? Did any of the participants assume the risk of, or contribute to, their injuries? **YOU'RE THE JUDGE!**

DECISION: Your answer will depend upon several factors: Did the players know of the defects? Were the dangers hidden? Was a warning necessary? The answers to these questions and other factors (such as age, experience, coaching and instruction) will help decide who was liable.

Product liability—the liability of a manufacturer or seller of a product for injury caused by a defect in that product—has undergone considerable change.

In early times, when **caveat emptor**—buyer beware—applied, a buyer was held to have assumed all risks of injury for any defects in a product!

FACTS: Mr. and Mrs. Johnson bought a new sportscar. While out for a ride, "The brakes failed and we crashed into Mason's barn. We hurt our backs," complained Mrs. Johnson.

Tommy got a new toy racing car for his birthday. When he accidentally dropped it, the glass window broke and cut him. Were the manufacturers of the sportscar and toy liable for the injuries? **YOU'RE THE JUDGE!**

DECISION: Caveat emptor prevented any recovery. Mr. and Mrs. Johnson and Tommy assumed all risks of such injuries!

Because, in many cases, caveat emptor treated consumers unfairly, it was replaced by shifting to the manufacturer and seller of a product the burden to use reasonable care to make certain that the products they made and sold did not harm purchasers.

In addition, manufacturers and sellers are now required to test for and warn against any hidden dangers. However, the manufacturer or seller does not insure the purchaser's safety.

What if the purchaser doesn't take care of the product he buys, or doesn't follow instructions and is then injured? Will the manufacturer be liable?

A manufacturer will not be held liable for injuries caused by improper use of any of its products as a result of failure to follow properly given instructions. Product tampering, improper maintenance or the predictable deterioration of a product at the end of its useful life are also valid defenses for a manufacturer in cases of product liability.

FACTS: John was using his new shovel to dig out rocks for his backyard putting green. "The handle splintered and gashed my arm!" he complained.

David got a new chemistry set for making the all-star softball team. He failed to follow instructions. "I mixed the wrong chemicals and was burned," he confessed

Rusty altered the engine on his new dirt bike and was injured when he crashed it. "The throttle stuck and I couldn't stop," he said.

Sarah never maintained the filter on her sport-fishing tank, causing the pump to malfunction, thereby killing her fish.

Jake was injured when his three year-old baseball bat splintered and cut his hand and arm. Were the manufacturers of any of these products liable for any of the injuries?

DECISION: **YOU'RE THE JUDGE!**

MANUFACTURER'S LIABILITY

Negligence

A manufacturer has a duty to use reasonable care, including inspections and warnings, to ensure the safety of those who may use their products. The breach of that duty, which results in an injury and damages, is **negligence.**

FACTS: Jackson broke his hand when, "My new bike rack snapped shut on my hand!"

The manufacturer used a clip which hadn't been tested properly; it couldn't hold back the spring.

Sandy, after being warned by Jackson, was injured while putting her books in the same rack. Was the manufacturer negligent? **YOU'RE THE JUDGE!**

DECISION: As to Jackson, the manufacturer was negligent for not using reasonable care in manufacturing or testing the rack.

Sandy was guilty of **contributory negligence** and assumption of the risk. Her lack of care for her own protection and safety contributed to the injury. Furthermore, having actual knowledge and appreciation of a danger—and then voluntarily assuming that danger—is **assumption of the risk.**

Strict Liability

Strict Liability—absolute liability regardless of any fault or improper care by the user—will apply if a potentially dangerous, defectively manufactured product causes an injury. Because of the unreasonably dangerous nature of such a product, there is an absolute duty to make it safe.

FACTS: Tommie, 14, and Susan, 7, were killed when they crashed their three-wheeled, all-terrain vehicles. Their families sued the manufacturer under strict liability, alleging, "The design was defective and they didn't test it right. Also, they didn't give proper safety instructions and warnings." The vehicles went out of control during, as the families described, "normal use." Was the manufacturer liable under strict liability?

DECISION: **YOU'RE THE JUDGE!**

Sales of three-wheeled, all-terrain vehicles are now banned. Unsold three-wheelers were removed from stores. Consumers were given free training and warned of the risks of using them.

Similarly, the sale of lawn darts was also banned because of their unreasonably dangerous nature and for the numerous, serious injuries they inflicted. Lawn darts—similar in shape to board darts, only longer and much heavier—were made to be used in the yard.

How may a manufacturer avoid strict liability? A seller may avoid strict liability by giving proper instructions and warnings which, if followed, will make a product safe.

FACTS: Go Easy Co. manufactured powered bicycles that could go 10-15 m.p.h.

Frank was instructed how to ride the bike and warned, "Do not pedal while the motor is on. That will break the chain and cause a sudden forward lurch. When he did so anyway, he fell and broke his foot."

Wally was neither warned of this danger, nor received or read any written warnings on his bike (as were printed on Frank's). He pedaled while the motor was on and was injured. "Can we recover damages for our injuries?" they asked. **YOU'RE THE JUDGE!**

DECISION: Frank was given instructions and warned of the danger. He assumed the risk of his injury.

Wally did not know of the danger; he did not assume the risk. Contributory negligence will not apply as a defense in strict liability. Therefore, Wally may recover for his injury.

Were There Any Warnings?

An otherwise unreasonably dangerous product, such as a rifle, may be rendered safe by the use of adequate warnings.

Likewise, a reasonably safe product, such as a motorized bicycle, may be rendered dangerous without adequate warnings.

Does a manufacturer or seller having a duty to warn of a product's dangers, also have a duty to warn of obvious dangers? There is no duty to warn of obvious dangers or those entirely under the control of the buyer.

FACTS: Allen was injured when his snowmobile skidded off an icy road.

Vic shot himself in the foot. "I knew that there was a safety on the gun, but I didn't have it on," he acknowledged. Could either recover for their injuries from the manufacturer on the theory that they should have been better forewarned of the risks? **YOU'RE THE JUDGE!**

DECISION: No. Neither Allen nor Vic could recover for their injuries from such obvious dangers which were entirely within their control. They assumed the risk of, and contributed to, their injuries.

Express Warranty

Express warranty—the written guarantee given to purchasers of a product, clearly indicating that the manufacturer or seller will replace or repair a defective product free of charge for a certain period of time. It arises where the manufacturer or seller makes a direct, positive representation concerning any product sold.

FACTS: "That skateboard will easily hold your 200-pound son." Based on that statement by a store owner, Mrs. Lucas bought a skateboard for her son, Tony. The first time Tony got on it, two of the wheels collapsed and he broke his leg. Did the store owner make an express warranty? Was he liable for Tony's injury? **YOU'RE THE JUDGE!**

DECISION: The store owner was liable for Tony's injury. Tony need only prove a breach of the express warranty.

Warranty Of Merchantability

For a product under an **implied warranty of merchantability,** the manufacturer or seller warrants or promises that its products are fit for the ordinary purposes for which they are used.

FACTS: Judy was injured when, "I sat at that new picnic table at the park and it collapsed."

Al was replacing a light bulb by standing on his golf bag. He fell and sprained an ankle. Could either recover from the manufacturer for their injuries? **YOU'RE THE JUDGE!**

DECISION: Judy could recover for her injury. The table was not fit for its intended use.

Standing on the golf bag was not an ordinary purpose of the bag. Al could not recover.

Warranty Of Fitness For A Particular Purpose

An implied **warranty of fitness for a particular purpose** is a promise that exists where the manufacturer or seller has reason to know the purpose for which a product will be used. Here, a purchaser relies on the seller's skill and judgment.

FACTS: To help stabilize his racing car, Rick ordered custom-made wind skirts. When they failed, his car became airborne and crashed into a retaining wall. Rick broke his collarbone and bruised his ribs. Did Rick assume the risk of such injuries?

DECISION: **YOU'RE THE JUDGE!**

Do these warranties have to be expressly given to any purchaser of a product by the manufacturer or seller? Both implied warranties arise by law. Words or actions are not necessary to prove a breach. They may only be excluded by conspicuous language, if at all.

Was The Design Defective?

A product's design is defective if, when used as intended or foreseeable, it fails to perform as safely as expected. A design is also defective if it causes an injury and the manufacturer can't show that the benefits of the design outweigh the risk or danger from it.

FACTS: Judy bought a bow. It snapped, injuring her shoulder.
Guy was injured riding his new bike down a bumpy, dirt road. "The rear tire just fell off!" he said in disbelief.
When his bike fell over, Jean cut his leg on his new motorcycle's mudguard.
Each of them sued the manufacturer, alleging defective products. Could they recover? **YOU'RE THE JUDGE!**

DECISION: Judy and Guy may recover. Their injuries resulted from intended or reasonably foreseeable uses. Jean may not recover. The benefits of the mudguard, to prevent objects from being thrown up at the driver or a passenger, outweighed the risk of the injury that it caused.

Ace Co. would like to avoid lawsuits regarding the manufacture of football helmets. Should they consider how rough the sport is, or the misuse that the helmets might get? If so, what other considerations should this manufacturer take into account in designing and making helmets?
In designing any product, a manufacturer must consider the amount of contact involved, the types of injuries in the sport, any

necessary warnings for the product's use, the product's durability (considering misuse and wear and tear), and whether the risk of injury will be increased due to the way the product is manufactured.

Baseball Pitching Machine

FACTS: While sweeping the gym floor, Sherwood, 16, was seriously injured by the sudden descent of the pitching arm of an automatic baseball pitching machine. "It hit me in the face. I've got these permanent scars," sobbed Sherwood.

Although the throwing arm could be unintentionally released while unplugged as a result of even a slight vibration, no operating instructions were provided. The only warning referred to the non-existent instructions. Was the manufacturer negligent? **YOU'RE THE JUDGE!**

DECISION: Yes. The hidden danger could only be understood by someone with knowledge not ordinarily possessed by a 16 year-old. The manufacturer was guilty of negligence in the design, manufacture and sale of the machine, and for not giving adequate warning.

Without a safety guard or shield, the machine was "a hazard likely to occur at any moment," commented the court.

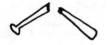

Baseball Bat

Will a manufacturer of baseball bats be liable where a broken bat made of defective wood breaks and injures a player?

FACTS: Shawn, the pitcher, was struck by a piece of a baseball bat which broke off when the batter hit a pitch. Shawn sued the bat's manufacturer, claiming, "The bat wasn't safe, and they didn't warn me that it could break." Did Shawn assume the risk of such an injury? **YOU'RE THE JUDGE!**

DECISION: Yes. The court noted, "It is common knowledge that bats frequently break, and immaterial that a properly made bat ordinarily will splinter with the grain while one made of defective wood may break across the grain. The risk of injury is not materially altered."

Swimming Pools

Product liability may arise out of a number of hazards from the use of swimming pools.

FACTS: Abe and Ben were injured when they dove into the swimming pools at their schools and struck their heads on the bottom.

The pool at Abe's school was marked 6'. Unknown to Abe, the water was only 5' deep. Expert testimony was given that, "Had the water been 6' deep, Abe would not have been injured."

Ben dove into his school's pool from the diving board, assuming that the water would be deep enough, although there were no depth markings.

When Judy began thrashing about in the deep end of a pool, a non-swimmer attempted to reach her with the safety hook, but it broke. She drowned.

Bob was injured when he slipped while running on the pool-side deck. Who was liable for these injuries?

DECISION: **YOU'RE THE JUDGE!**

Could the operator of the swimming pool be jointly liable with a manufacturer where they contributed to an injury, such as by not checking the depth of the water, or by not inspecting safety equipment?

Football Equipment

FACTS: A high school football player, Vincent, used a helmet and shoulder pads that he knew were "just a bit loose." When injured, he brought suit claiming that the equipment was defective. "Did I assume the risk of injury?" asked Vincent. **YOU'RE THE JUDGE!**

DECISION: Vincent had the opportunity to return any of the equipment if it was unfit, which was not shown. He voluntarily decided to use it and, therefore, assumed the risk of injury.

Similar results have been reached where injuries resulted when participants failed to wear prescribed protective equipment. Will liability result where defective equipment, or no required equipment, is provided?

FACTS: Fisher, a 17 year-old defensive back for his high school football team, was paralyzed after breaking his neck tackling an opponent. The tackle causing the injury was said to be a "spear" tackle. Such tackles were judged improper and are now banned.

Fisher sued the helmet manufacturer for negligent design, strict liability, and breach of warranty in that the helmet didn't protect him. Was the manufacturer liable for the injury? **YOU'RE THE JUDGE!**

DECISION: The helmet was defective in design, unreasonably dangerous, and did not perform as expected. Comparative negligence—where the negligence or fault of the injured player may reduce any recovery—reduced Fisher's recovery.

Another high school football player, Daniels, received permanent brain damage when his helmet caved in during a collision with a teammate. In deciding a suit against the manufacturer, the court commented that "the failure to warn that the helmet would not protect against head and brain injuries exposed the player to an unreasonable risk of harm."

Where a manufacturer fails to warn of such potentially serious injuries, may a court award punitive damages to punish the wrongdoer?

Punitive damages were awarded for gross negligence. The court described the conduct of the defendant as "knowingly indifferent to the player's rights, welfare and safety."

Hockey helmets have also been the subject of product liability litigation.

FACTS: Evan, 17, fractured his skull playing hockey. "I fell down to block the puck. It went through the gap in the helmet that I was given to wear." He sued the manufacturer, alleging a negligent design. Was the manufacturer negligent? **YOU'RE THE JUDGE!**

DECISION: The court found the manufacturer, "Guilty for the negligent manufacture of the helmet." The defense of assumption of the risk was denied as Evan was not aware of the danger involved. The gaps were not open and obvious.

In another case, an experienced hockey player, Manny, was injured when a puck struck him on the plastic chin strap of a helmet that he had purchased. He sued the helmet manufacturer.

The court found that, "The player, aware of the obvious danger, assumed the risk. There was no duty to warn, as that would not have discouraged him from playing a sport so fraught with risk of injury."

Gym Equipment

Injuries arising out of the use of gymnastic equipment have also lead to numerous product liability suits.

FACTS: Andrea was injured while using the uneven parallel bars. For no apparent reason, "They separated and I fell, landing on my back." she testified. Was the manufacturer liable under strict liability? **YOU'RE THE JUDGE!**

DECISION: The apparatus was inherently dangerous and defective when it left the manufacturer's plant, thus subjecting the manufacturer to strict liability (liability without regard to fault).

What duty do manufacturers of gym equipment owe to users? Manufacturers and sellers of gym equipment have a duty to use ordinary, reasonable care, to warn of any hidden dangers and risks, and to give any necessary instructions.

However, a manufacturer or seller does not insure a user's safety. There is no duty to warn of obvious dangers.

FACTS: Susan was injured attempting to vault over a horse. Judy was injured during her approach to the spring board. Both were given proper instructions and warned of the dangers of using the equipment. Did Susan and Judy contribute to their injuries? **YOU'RE THE JUDGE!**

DECISION: Yes. The defenses of assumption of the risk and contributory negligence prevented recovery. Susan and Judy were aware of and appreciated the risks, and, in addition, contributed to their injuries by using the equipment improperly.

Negligence has been found for injuries resulting from the use of defectively designed or manufactured trampolines (i.e. open space in the frame, weak seams, defective springs or supporting frame), or inadequate or non-existent warnings or instructions.

Other gym equipment also has been responsible for injuries.

FACTS: Lenny injured his back attempting to do a flip. "The gym mat wasn't supposed to slip." moaned Lenny.

Dominique injured her hip when a weight pulley collapsed and she fell to the floor. Did Lenny and Dominique assume the risk of such injuries? **YOU'RE THE JUDGE!**

DECISION: No. Both products were improperly designed or manufactured and unable to withstand the expected use. Strict liability applied. The manufacturers were liable for the injuries.

One court stated that, "Some manufacturers, fully aware of the dangers of a product and of past injuries, would rather risk liability than provide a warning which might reduce sales. Therefore, in addition to compensatory damages, they should be liable for punitive damages—to punish them in an effort to prevent further selling of such equipment without proper warnings and instruction."

FACTS: Wally Palmer, an 18 year-old university student, struck and injured his head against a gym wall while attempting a maneuver on a horizontal bar. He sued the manufacturer, alleging that for an inherently dangerous product, adequate warnings and instructions must be provided. The manufacturer felt that any dangers were open and obvious. "Weren't they liable?" he asked. **YOU'RE THE JUDGE!**

DECISION: The company had conducted tests which showed that the bar should be placed thirty inches from the wall, not eighteen inches as was the bar when Palmer was injured. Failing to warn of this hazard or to include instructions as to the proper use of the equipment made the company liable for punitive as well as compensatory damages.

How may a manufacturer avoid liability? A manufacturer may avoid liability where, after giving proper instructions, the equipment then was improperly installed or supervised.

The age and experience of participants, and the type of equipment in use may be factors in determining any liability.

FACTS: Hank, 12, was injured when, "One of the uneven parallel bars broke. I never used them before."

Jane, 18, was injured when she fell while doing a flip on a mat. She had performed the exercise successfully many times before. Would their different ages and experience help determine liability?

DECISION: **YOU'RE THE JUDGE!**

Golf, Equipment & Wheels

Product liability in golf may arise out of products used to maintain a course.

FACTS: Greg grabbed his clubs and headed for the golf course. Although in tip-top shape, on arriving home after playing, he felt sick.

His wife, in shock, cried, "A rash developed into blisters. His skin began peeling off. Then his internal organs failed and he died after two weeks."

An investigation revealed, "Greg's shoes, clubs and golf balls and the golf course were covered with a chemical sprayed on the course to remove brown spots." Testimony was that the chemical caused Greg's death. Was the golf course operator or the manufacturer of the chemical liable for Greg's death?

DECISION: **YOU'RE THE JUDGE!**

Product liability may also attach for injuries arising out of the use of golf equipment.

FACTS: Fred, 13, received permanent brain damage when a golf ball, attached to a training device, struck him.

"Golfing Gizmo" was designed to aid unskilled golfers improve their games. The labels on the carton and the instruction booklet read, COMPLETELY SAFE BALL WILL NOT HIT PLAYER.

Fred took his normal swing with and was struck by the ball, attached to a cord, as it rebounded.

An expert testified, "Fred caught the cord on his upward swing, thus drawing the cord and ball toward him on his follow-through." Was the manufacturer liable? **YOU'RE THE JUDGE!**

DECISION: The warranties that the product would perform in a safe manner and could be used safely was breached. Strict liability attached because of the defective and dangerous product. Also, the manufacturer was found guilty of fraudulent misrepresentation for the statement, COMPLETELY SAFE BALL WILL NOT HIT PLAYER.

Numerous cases have involved allegations of defective brakes or steering on golf carts.

FACTS: "The brakes just locked and the steering came loose on the new golf cart that we rented," explained John and Bob. "We got hurt when the cart overturned and we were thrown out." They sued the manufacturer for a breach of the warranty of fitness for a particular purpose.

Andy was injured when the golf cart that he rented hit a wall. He admitted, "I knew that the steering was getting loose, but I wanted to finish." Could John, Bob or Andy recover for their injuries? **YOU'RE THE JUDGE!**

DECISION: John and Bob had no knowledge of any defect. The manufacturer was liable for a breach of a warranty. The cart should have performed as required for its intended use.

Andy voluntarily assumed a known risk. Therefore, the manufacturer was not liable. If the golf course operator knew, or should have known, of the problem, he could share in the liability.

Strict liability has been found where a golf cart was inherently dangerous and defective as designed. The manufacturer could have used four wheels, for instance (instead of three), to increase the stability of the cart. Strict liability may also apply to snowmobiles, motorcycles, boats, and off-road vehicles.

Liability also attached to a manufacturer where defective tires were found responsible for a race-car driver's death.

Ski Equipment

FACTS: Ken Sanders purchased new skis. When the bindings failed to release during a fall, he broke his leg. He sued the manufacturer, alleging a breach of the warranty that the skis would perform as expected, and strict liability for not giving a warning.

One ad stated that, "The binding releases when it's supposed to."

"Was the manufacturer liable?" asked Sanders. **YOU'RE THE JUDGE!**

DECISION: No. The ad did not create an express warranty that the binding would release in every situation. The bindings could not be set to release during a slow fall and still keep the skier on his skis during normal skiing. The failure of the bindings to release was not the cause of the injury.

Other cases have denied liability where skis were used improperly, or where free lessons were refused and injury then followed.

Who might be liable where injuries result from ski lift accidents?

FACTS: Robinson and Jones, avid skiers, were "clowning around" when the ski lift started to move. They fell out and were injured. They sued the operator, alleging that the safety bar was not secured properly.

Several other skiers were injured when the ski lift they were riding "stopped suddenly and began to fall." There was no apparent defect.

Molly was injured when she fell off a ski lift after receiving improper instructions on how to secure the safety bar. Could any of these skiers recover for their injuries? If so, against whom? **YOU'RE THE JUDGE!**

DECISION: By clowning around, Robinson and Jones, experienced skiers, assumed the risk of their injuries.

With no apparent defect that the operator could have corrected, the manufacturer may be found liable for a negligently designed or manufactured ski lift.

The operator of the premises was liable for Molly's injuries.

Sunglasses, Pole Vaults &....

Who might be liable for injuries resulting from the use of sunglasses, a pole vault, a chin-up bar or pogo stick?

FACTS: Although he flipped down his "Baseball Sunglasses" which would give "instant eye protection," Palmer lost a fly ball in the sun. The ball struck and shattered the sunglasses, blinding Palmer in the right eye. Was the manufacturer liable? **YOU'RE THE JUDGE!**

DECISION: Yes. Since the sunglasses lacked the necessary safety features, they were not fit for baseball—the very purpose for which they had been sold. That was a breach of an implied warranty of fitness for a particular purpose.

Strict liability—liability without regard to fault—may be applied where a manufacturer is negligent in the design or manufacture of a product, or where there is a risk of injury from a hidden defect.

It applied where a pogo stick, a chin-up bar and a pole-vaulter's pole all broke, causing injuries. Users of these and similar products only assume the ordinary and apparent risks from such products, not the risk of injury from a hidden defect.

Were The Products Maintained?

There is ad uty to maintain equipment, either by checking it before use or by proper maintenance. Any failure of this duty may result in liability, either for the manufacturer, seller or lessor, or, for the user under assumption of the rusk or contributory negligince.

FACTS: Mark, a scuba diver, rented a tank from Jake's Scuba Shop. He said, "The tank's air supply line didn't work right. While I was diving, I couldn't get any air. When I began thrashing about trying to get Bill's attention, I accidentally knocked him unconscious." Bill was rescued, but suffered permanent brain damage.

Wally, also an experienced diver, rented a tank. In trying to reach the top after running out of air, he received a concussion from hitting the bottom of his boat.

Jan said, "I rented a spear gun and threw it in the boat. Later, it misfired and gashed me after bouncing off a rock." Was Jake's liable for any of these injuries? **YOU'RE THE JUDGE!**

DECISION: Jake's was liable for Mark's injury. Jake had a duty to exercise reasonable care to make the scuba tank safe for use. This could have been done by a reasonable inspection.

Wally, by not checking his capacity gauge, contributed to, and assumed, the risk of injury from such an obvious oversight.

Jan also contributed to and assumed the risk of his injury by throwing the spear gun in the boat, thus damaging it.

Dive Tables

A diving instructional agency prepared and distributed a diver's manual for beginners. It had Dive Tables in it giving divers the ranges they should stay within while diving to prevent injury.

One diver, within the ranges of the tables, got the "bends" (bubbles in the bloodstream), causing paralysis. He sued the agency, alleging the tables did not adequately warn beginning divers of the number of injuries from the bends.

The agency defended that the manual warned divers to stay well within the tables' ranges, a hole in some diver's hearts makes them more susceptible to injury, and it was the diver's duty to ascertain if they had such a defect. Did the diver assume the risk of such an injury or was the instructional agency guilty of negligence?

ODDS & ENDS....

An ad in a local newspaper read:

GO-CARTS
for sale
GUARANTEED SAFE!
Brand New
Call Ace at 415-2916

FACTS: Relying on this ad, several young children bought the go-carts from Ace and set up a racecourse in a nearby field.

Ace had purchased the go-carts with instructions and warnings that they be "used only on flat surfaces." But Ace didn't pass these warnings on, only telling the boys that the carts should "probably be used in a parking lot." Ace put a metal shield on the bottom for protection from sharp objects, "souped" them up and then resold them.

Several accidents occurred while the children were racing on the rough terrain in the field. Tommy's cart suddenly shot forward when a branch stuck the accelerator open. He crashed through a fence.

Dennis' brakes failed and he crashed when the brake line was punctured by a rock.

All of the children sued Ace, charging, "He didn't give us proper instructions and warnings." Was Ace liable for the injuries? **YOU'RE THE JUDGE!**

DECISION: The children were young and inexperienced. Ace misrepresented the carts as being GUARANTEED SAFE and altered them against their intended use. And, although the children may have assumed the normal risks of using the go-carts, they did not assume the risk of injury from defective and improper alterations.

An express warranty, or warranties of merchantability or fitness for a particular purpose, may apply equally to other than sports products, such as appliances or a television.

9

PREMISES - CLEAR & SAFE

WHAT'S IT ABOUT?

Premises—Clear & Safe spells out and illustrates the duty of the owner or operator of a sports facility, such as a football stadium or bowling alley, to exercise reasonable care for the protection and safety of those using their facilities.

This duty may be somewhat greater where it concerns young children. Do you know what an attractive nuisance is?

PREMISE LIABILITY

The owner or operator of a sports facility or a place or facility of public amusement or entertainment is bound to exercise reasonable care for the safety and protection of patrons (that is, the care which an ordinarily reasonable and cautious person would exercise under the same or similar circumstances).

Although a participant may be prevented from recovering if he contributed to any injury, or assumed the risk of an open and obvious danger, a participant will not assume the risk of injury resulting from the negligence of the owner or operator of the premises used.

FACTS: A plaintiff explained how he was injured. "I was shagging fly balls when it began to rain. I ran toward the dugout, but stopped. The underground, automatic tarp, making no noise, came up and rolled over my leg, breaking my ankle. I never saw it."

"Was I liable because I failed to make sure no one was near the tarp before it was activated?" asked the ballpark operator.

DECISION: **YOU'RE THE JUDGE!**

The owner or operator is not, however, the insurer of a participant's safety. Although he must be able to anticipate the normal actions of the sport or activity, he cannot be required to foresee every possible accident. Participants have a duty to use reasonable care for their own protection and safety.

FACTS: Even though ditches were being dug for new watering pipes, several high school athletes decided to use the local college's baseball field. Signs warned, FIELD CLOSED DUE TO REPAIRS. One of the players, Vinnie, was injured when he fell into a ditch while chasing a foul ball. Did he assume the risk of his injury?

DECISION: **YOU'RE THE JUDGE!**

The ordinary dangers of a particular sport may include the dangers common to a particular premises. However, such dangers must be obvious for a valid defense of assumption of the risk or contributory negligence.

FACTS: A baseball player ran into a clearly visible steel cable, constructed around the baseball field to restrain spectators from coming onto the field. He was injured and sued. He asked, "Did I assume the risk of such an injury?" **YOU'RE THE JUDGE!**

DECISION: Yes. The danger was obvious. Although the cable was not a risk normally inherent in a game of baseball, it became so where the player was aware of its existence and of the possibility of running into it.

A basketball player who had observed the first half of a basketball game, was judged to have assumed the risk of injury when he fell on the bleachers next to the court during the second half. He encountered a known and obvious danger.

The court indicated, "The duty to give attention to one's safety in a position of obvious danger is imposed because the ordinary man gives that attention. It is not careful conduct to pay no heed to the demands of safety."

An operator must provide facilities or premises properly designed and safely constructed for the use for which they are intended, and they must be maintained in a reasonably safe condition to avoid potential danger to users.

Will a participant assume the risk of a hidden danger or defect? A participant may assume the risk of injury from a danger or defect that is obvious, but not from a defect that is hidden.

FACTS: Albert, 19, was injured while playing basketball when he collided with a door jamb in a brick wall two feet from the basket. "I couldn't stop." explained Albert. He sued the gym operator for negligence for putting the basket too close to the wall.

Stevens, 17, was injured during a basketball practice for his high school team when his momentum carried him past the end line and into a glass window, which shattered.

In both cases, the players had played there before, and were aware of the hazards involved. Did they assume the risk of injury from such hazards? **YOU'RE THE JUDGE!**

DECISION: Albert had run into the wall numerous times before. He assumed the risk of his injury.

Stevens had also faced that risk before. However, he did not assume the risk that the panel would be of ordinary glass. He could have reasonably assumed that because of the closeness of the glass to the basket, it would be resistant to impact.

DEFENSE! DEFENSE!

The owner or operator of premises used for sports may rely on the defenses of assumption of the risk and contributory negligence.

Assumption of the risk requires that the participant have actual knowledge of the defect, a reasonable appreciation and awareness of all the dangers produced by the defect, and that the participant then voluntarily assumes such dangers.

FACTS: Ashcroft, an experienced jockey, suffered catastrophic injuries when, "My horse veered across the race track through an open exit gap." He sued the track, alleging that the accident resulted from the negligent placement of the exit gap which, in turn, resulted in the horse's behavior. Who was liable for the injury? **YOU'RE THE JUDGE!**

DECISION: Although Ashcroft was familiar with the horse, the track and the location of the exit gap, and was an experienced jockey, he did not assume the risk of such an injury from an open exit gate. He was not aware of that danger. The track was held liable.

Contributory negligence is a lack of proper care by an injured person for his own protection and safety which contributes to an injury.

Will contributory negligence apply if an injury would have occurred despite any reasonable action by an injured person?

FACTS: A number of participants were injured where the management of horse and auto racetracks allowed: horses to run in the opposite direction; restraining barriers not properly secured; exit gates, through which a horse could run during a race, left open; "dead" cars and other debris and equipment left on the track; and improper or no barriers for an auto race.

Would contributory negligence prevent recovery of damages for those injured in these situations? **YOU'RE THE JUDGE!**

DECISION: Where management improperly maintained or constructed the premises, negligence would be found. However, there would be contributory negligence by the participants where they failed to exercise reasonable care for their own protection and safety.

Participants may assume the risk of injury from ordinary dangers. But, will they assume that risk from an extraordinary danger?

A jockey was killed when he was thrown from his horse and struck his head on the concrete footing of a post supporting the track railing. The elevated footing was non-existent at any other race track. The court found that, although the jockey may have assumed the risk of being thrown from his mount, he did not assume the risk of injury from an extraordinary danger or negligent design.

The duty owed by an owner or operator of premises or facilities will apply to many different sports or activities.

BOWLING ALLEY

The proprietor of a bowling alley owes a duty to patrons to exercise ordinary and reasonable care to keep the premises in a safe condition. If he fails to discover or correct a problem which might place patrons in danger, there may be liability.

FACTS: One proprietor failed to inspect for, or clean up, drinks and gum on the floor and approaches of his bowling alley.

Herb, an unsuspecting bowler, groaned, "The approach was wet. I slipped and wrenched my back."

When another proprietor failed to fix an approach after it became worn and splintered, a bowler, Jerry, was injured when his foot stuck. Were the proprietors liable for these injuries?

DECISION: **YOU'RE THE JUDGE!**

However, a proprietor is not an insurer of a patron's safety. Where a danger was not obvious and the owner either didn't know it existed, or a reasonable inspection would not have revealed the danger, the owner will not be charged with a breach of his duty to provide a safe place.

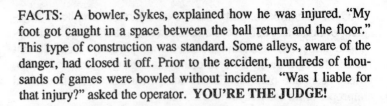

FACTS: A bowler, Sykes, explained how he was injured. "My foot got caught in a space between the ball return and the floor." This type of construction was standard. Some alleys, aware of the danger, had closed it off. Prior to the accident, hundreds of thousands of games were bowled without incident. "Was I liable for that injury?" asked the operator. **YOU'RE THE JUDGE!**

DECISION: No. Neither the danger, nor the risk was obvious. Sykes assumed the risk of such an injury.

SKATING RINKS

Proprietors of ice and roller skating rinks have a duty to exercise reasonable care in maintaining their premises in a reasonably safe condition to guard patrons from unreasonable risks. Some specific steps to be taken include the elimination of overcrowding, keeping the skating surface clear of debris, and posting or repairing holes or soft spots in the rink as well as all approaches or aisles.

Do patrons have the right to assume that the premises they are using are reasonably safe?

FACTS: An iceskater was injured when, "I tripped when my skate struck a wooden ledge. I was reaching for the handrail."

An expert testified, "The handrail should have been moved to the very edge of the skating area."

A rollerskater was injured when he slipped and fell through a window. There were two windows adjacent to the rink. One was protected by an iron grating. The other had a bench placed under it in an attempt to protect the skaters. Were the operators of these premises negligent? **YOU'RE THE JUDGE!**

DECISION: Yes. The defects created obvious and unnecessary risks to the skaters who had a right to expect premises safe for their intended use (skating). The rink operators were liable for not using reasonable care in protecting the skaters.

An operator cannot be required to foresee every possible accident. Where a skater left the skating area and tripped and fell through a window in the spectator area, the proprietor was found not liable.

SWIMMING POOLS

The proprietor of a swimming facility must exercise ordinary or reasonable care to maintain the premises in a reasonably safe condition. This includes all swimming pools, deck areas, rescue and other equipment, fences and bathhouses.

FACTS: At one swimming pool, there was broken glass both in and next to the pool. Another pool was closed because of the condition of the water. A warning sign was posted, but there were no depth markers. At still another pool, there was one lifeguard on duty for more than fifty kids.

If an injury resulted from any of these situations, could the proprietor be found liable for improperly maintaining or supervising such premises?

DECISION: **YOU'RE THE JUDGE!**

A patron has a right to assume that the operator has provided a place that is reasonably safe for its intended use.

FACTS: Two children, ages 6 and 13, were trying to reach an errant ball knocked into a closed public pool.

The pool's walls and floor were slimy and slippery. The children waded into seven feet of dirty water at the deep end where they drowned after trying in vain to climb out.

"The entire pool was dry except for the deep end. There's a great drop-off, slanting down at an angle." said a policeman.

A neighborhood boy had warned them not to climb the chain link fence to the pool. A similar accident had happened two years earlier when two brothers, who had climbed the fence, drowned.

Did the children assume the risk of, or contribute to, their deaths? Was a greater duty of care owed to protect the children? Was the city liable?

DECISION: **YOU'RE THE JUDGE!**

AMUSEMENT RIDES

Will certain potentially dangerous activities require more care? Certain types of rides, such as amusement park rides and go-carts, because of their potential danger, may require a higher degree of care beyond reasonable and ordinary care.

FACTS: Minnie, confined to a wheelchair, was put aboard the merry-go-round at an amusement park. After about two revolutions, she and her wheelchair—with the brakes locked—were thrown from the ride. Minnie died from head injuries. Was the operator liable for her death?

DECISION: **YOU'RE THE JUDGE!**

The more dangerous the ride, the more care that is required to see that the ride is properly constructed, inspected, operated and maintained.

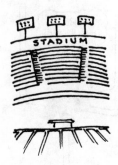

FACTS: Eight youths were trapped inside the Haunted Castle, a ride at the Great Adventure Amusement Park, when a fire broke out. They all died. Was the operator liable?

DECISION: **YOU'RE THE JUDGE!**

SEATS & BLEACHERS

An operator of premises used for sports and other activities is also under a duty to exercise reasonable care for the safety and protection of patrons with regard to seats, chairs or benches.

If they are known to be defective, or if defects should have been known by a timely and reasonable inspection, liability may attach.

FACTS: A wooden soccer grandstand caught fire, killing many soccer fans. The club had been warned that the grandstand was a fire risk.

One witness testified, "Under the seats there were holes in the floorboards. You could see loads of litter which built up over the years."

When the fire broke out, probably under one of the wooden seats, the fans couldn't get out. The gates had been padlocked to keep out those who had not paid for admission. Was the operator negligent?

DECISION: **YOU'RE THE JUDGE!**

SKI LIFTS & SLOPES

The operator of premises used for skiing has a duty to exercise reasonable and ordinary care to maintain the premises, including slopes and equipment, such as lifts, in a reasonably safe condition.

FACTS: A lift operator failed to warn Ann Forman, 16, that the lift was closing down for the night. She was stranded when the chair stopped moving. Becoming hysterical at the prospect of being stranded overnight, "I jumped 25 feet to the ground and shattered my hip," she testified.

At another ski lift, an operator failed to lock the safety bar for Sally, 9, causing her injury from a fall. And Bob's injury was the result of a failure to inspect the lift, which needed repair.

Johnson was injured when he was unable to get onto a moving chairlift. There were no instructions. Were any of the operators liable for any of these injuries? **YOU'RE THE JUDGE!**

DECISION: "Operators owe the highest degree of care to invitees," commented one court.

The lift operators were held liable for failing to warn Forman that the lift was closing; for not locking Sally's safety bar; for not properly inspecting the lift Bob was using, and; for not giving Johnson proper instructions.

What if the skiers were aware of the dangers? Where skiers are aware of, and appreciate, the dangers involved and fail to act for their own safety and protection, they may not recover.

FACTS: When a ski lift operator failed to lock a safety bar, Ray, an experienced skier, fell and injured his neck.

Hank was injured when the ski lift he was riding on collapsed. It could not be foreseen that the bolt would fracture.

An inattentive skier, Paul, was injured when he was unable to get on a moving chairlift. Were the proprietors liable for any of these injuries? **YOU'RE THE JUDGE!**

DECISION: Ray assumed the risk of his injury. Although the manufacturer may be, the operator was not liable for Hank's injury. And there was no negligence by the operator where inattention caused Paul's injury.

MAINTENANCE OF SLOPES

FACTS: White, an experienced skier, said, "While coming down an intermediate trail, I hit a stump which was covered with snow, fell, and fractured my leg." White sued the ski resort for improperly maintaining the skiing premises. "Did I assume the risk of injury?" asked White. **YOU'RE THE JUDGE!**

DECISION: The court found that White assumed the risk of encountering such a hazard and being injured.

Another court sustained an award for a 25-year-old novice skier whose skis became entangled in a clump of brush encroaching three to four feet in from the edge of a novice trail. The court pointed out that, "The risk of encountering brush or other such hazards on the trail was not an inherent and assumed danger or risk of the sport."

However, a ski operator does not guarantee the safety of all its patrons. Skiers still assume the risk of injury from open and obvious dangers.

Will an operator be liable where a skier is confronted with an extraordinary risk or danger?

FACTS: An expert skier and racer, Philips, told how he was injured. "I was in a tuck position skiing down the lower half of an intermediate run, when I collided with a snow-cat which was traveling up the slope. I tore ligaments in my knee and cut my face."

Philips sued the operator, who defended, "He was out of control when he made a sweeping turn into the equipment."

Another skier, Thompson, was injured when he ran into a chairlift tower. The tower was obstructing a passage down a slope and was not padded. Were the operators liable for not exercising reasonable care for the skier's safety? **YOU'RE THE JUDGE!**

DECISION: Philips had skied that run many times before without seeing a snow-cat at that place. He could not foresee it being there and, therefore, did not assume the risk of such an injury. The operator was negligent in allowing the snow-cat on the ski slope while skiers were in the area.

The operator was liable for Thompson's injury. Skiing should have been prohibited in that area.

Negligence was also found where a novice skier was injured when struck from behind by a sled coming down a run next to the ski slope. The runs were separated for the first forty feet, after which there was no barrier to keep the sledders and skiers apart. The court stated, "Allowing skiing and sledding next to each other created added dangers which were not inherent in each sport individually."

BASKETBALL

FACTS: Dawson, a pro basketball player for the Magicians, slipped on a puddle of water while playing in a game. The puddle was the result of leaks in the roof. Dawson sued for career ending injuries, alleging negligence against the operator of the auditorium for not fixing the leak. Was the operator liable? **YOU'RE THE JUDGE!**

DECISION: The roof was known to be riddled with leaks. The owner, aware of the defects, owed a duty of reasonable care to the player, but failed to exercise that duty.

An operator may be found negligent for failing to correct a known problem, but not where the problem did not create an unreasonably dangerous condition.

FACTS: Walter, a pro basketball player, slipped and injured his knee when condensation formed on a newly waxed floor due to the combination of heat in the building and the ice (for hockey games) under the portable basketball floor.

Elliot and Rupert, pro baseball players, were injured when one crashed into an unpadded outfield wall and the other tripped on an uneven outfield surface.

Should professional players be required to assume greater risks than an average participant would assume? What if they were aware of the defects? Did they play there voluntarily? Should the owner be liable for not correcting the defects?

DECISION: **YOU'RE THE JUDGE!**

BALLFIELDS

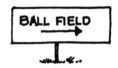

Players have a right to assume that a field will be safe for its intended or anticipated use. But what if the danger is obvious?

FACTS: A player, Sal Luckman, in a softball game, tripped over a hole and suffered a broken leg. "The hole was clearly visible," he admitted. "Didn't he assume the risk of the injury?" questioned the operator of the field. **YOU'RE THE JUDGE!**

DECISION: Yes. While the field was poorly designed, the condition was unmistakably evident and the danger obvious. Luckman had a duty to use reasonable care for his own protection and safety.

Neither could another baseball player recover damages when he was injured in a game after tripping on a cement curbing around the field. He had played there many times before.

In holding that momentary forgetfulness of the certain dangers was one of the risks that a player assumes, the court noted, "One who takes part in a sport accepts the inherent dangers in so far as they are obvious and necessary, just as a fencer accepts the risk of a thrust by his opponent."

BOWLING

A risk which might ordinarily be assumed, may not be assumed under certain circumstances, such as in the excitement of the sport.

FACTS: Murphy, a bowler, was assigned the last alley in a bowling house. Parallel to and lower than the alley was a walkway to the rear of the lanes. "After delivering my ball, I turned and walked back looking over my shoulder at the pins. I stepped off the edge of the alley and fell, hurting my leg and hip," swore Murphy. Did Murphy assume the risk of such an injury? **YOU'RE THE JUDGE!**

DECISION: No. What may have been perfectly obvious to a person walking normally is likely to be forgotten by a bowler in the excitement of a game. The design presented an obvious danger. "An owner must be able to anticipate the normal actions of a participant of a sport," remarked the court.

WHAT A RACKET!

Participants using tennis facilities may be held to have assumed the risk of, or contributed to, an injury where a danger was open and obvious. In the case of hidden dangers, they will not. Negligence against a proprietor of a tennis facility has been found for not keeping the court in a reasonably safe condition (clear of leaves, pine needles, and the like).

Should a professional be more aware of the dangers of a sport than the average player?

FACTS: Jane Heldman, a pro tennis player, severely injured her knee. She alleged that her injury was caused by a defect in the tennis floor. The tape used to hold the "Roll A Way" tennis floor down was not sticking, thus creating gaps or spaces in the court. Also, there were air pockets and a few problems with water drainage. Did Heldman assume the risk of injury? **YOU'RE THE JUDGE!**

DECISION: The court held that a pro should have a higher degree of knowledge and awareness of such dangers than would the average player. After appeal, the case was settled in favor Heldman.

Another player, Joe Smith, was guilty of contributory negligence even though he was not aware that a tennis court was constructed too close to a wall which he ran into.

The court commented, "It is needless to say that there are many cases holding that one is charged with the duty of seeing that which he ought to have seen, had he looked."

In a similar case involving a ping pong game, it was held that a player observed or should have observed that the table was too close to a window, through which he put his arm. He was guilty of contributory negligence. But what if the danger was not so obvious?

FACTS: Courts for handball, where players batted the ball with their hands, were now being used for racketball. Cheney was injured when one of his opponents' rackets rebounded off the wall and struck Cheney in the head. He sued, arguing, "I was not aware that the courts were too small for players with rackets." Was the operator liable?

DECISION: **YOU'RE THE JUDGE!**

GOLF COURSES

Proprietors or operators of golf courses have a duty to exercise reasonable care for the safety and protection of patrons. This includes the duty to make reasonable and timely inspections, and to correct any defects.

> FACTS: Brian was hit by a following player's golf ball. Joe— believing the yardage on the par 4 to be correct—hit away. "I knew that I couldn't hit it that far," said Joe. The yardage given was much more than the actual distance. Was the operator liable? **YOU'RE THE JUDGE!**

> DECISION: The operator, aware of the incorrect yardage, was grossly negligent in maintaining the premises. Punitive damages were awarded "to punish the wrongdoer."

Where a bridge collapsed, sending a golfcart and players into a canal, the operator was found liable for not maintaining the premises. The patrons had a right to expect reasonably safe premises.

Does the operator's duty to exercise reasonable care extend to those who are not patrons?

> FACTS: When the water sprinklers on a golf course were turned on, a startled passerby on an adjacent public way was hit by the water, crashed his car, and broke his leg. Was the operator of the golf course liable?

> DECISION: **YOU'RE THE JUDGE!**

Where a golfer slipped and fell on his way to the locker room, the operator was found negligent for not, at least, putting a strip of non-slip material on which the golfers could walk to enter the locker area.

However, an operator was found not liable for injuries received outside the locker room, such as where a golfer slipped on a walk-way. The golfer had no right to expect such an area to be non-slip. Should a cart path be non-slip?

> FACTS: Steve said, "I slipped on a cart path, shattering my right elbow. The path was worn and slippery. No one warned me, and I didn't see it." Was the proprietor negligent in failing to correct any defect, or did the golfer assume such a risk?

> DECISION: **YOU'RE THE JUDGE!**

Whether or not an operator may be liable for injury from a defect in premises will depend upon the awareness of the patron, whether the operator knew or should have known of the condition, and either corrected or warned patrons of the danger, or knowingly left it un-safe.

Even if an operator was negligent, any injured patron must still

show that a hazard was the cause of the injury, not his own contributory negligence. Furthermore, if the patron knew of the condition, he may be held to have assumed the risk.

> FACTS: Willy and Ernie were injured when they rode into protruding branches on a cart path and then hit a rock, crashing the cart. The dangers were open and obvious.
> Richard was injured when his golf cart overturned in a sand trap. Did these golfers contribute to or assume the risk of injury? Was the operator liable?
>
> DECISION: **YOU'RE THE JUDGE!**

GOLF COURSE DESIGN

A golf course owner or operator may be liable for failing to exercise reasonable care for the protection and safety of patrons, such as where adjacent holes or other areas of a golf course endanger players there.

Golfers assume the normal and inherent risks in the game, but do they assume extraordinary ones?

> FACTS: Golfers were allowed to use woods on the driving range. Hank belted a drive out of the range, striking and injuring a golfer on the third hole.
> Paul "duck hooked" one off the range, striking and injuring a golfer on the second hole. Did the golfers assume the risk of such injuries? Was the proprietor liable?
>
> DECISION: **YOU'RE THE JUDGE!**

A golf course owner or operator also has a duty to exercise reasonable care in the use of powered carts. Liability may even attach if negligence is shown for giving the cart to someone who uses it improperly.

> FACTS: Mildred suffered multiple leg fractures from a runaway golfcart. Her husband told what happened. "Another cart hit the one that she was riding in, causing it to hit and pin her against a restroom wall." Was the owner of the golf cart liable for Mildred's injuries? **YOU'RE THE JUDGE!**
>
> DECISION: The court held that even if the owner exercised due care, he could still be liable. The court decided, "A golf cart, when negligently operated, has the same ability to cause serious injury as does any motor vehicle. The golf cart is a 'dangerous instrumentality' which imposes liability upon the owner when he entrusts it to someone who negligently operates it."

WAS IT AN ATTRACTIVE NUISANCE?

An **attractive nuisance** is a condition, device, machine or other agency, which is dangerous to young children (generally those under the age of 12) because of their inability to appreciate danger, and which may reasonably be expected to attract them to the premises.

A possessor of land owes a duty to exercise reasonable care to protect children from such dangers. He may be liable for any injury to a child trespassing where:

- the place or its condition is one which the landowner knows or should know that children are likely to trespass on—such as a swimming hole;
- the condition is one which the landowner knows or should know involves an unreasonable risk of death or serious injury to children—such as hidden obstacles or protruding objects;
- the children, because of their youth, either do not realize, or fail to discover the danger;
- the risk and danger to the children outweighs the usefulness of the condition, and;
- the landowner fails to exercise reasonable care to eliminate the danger or otherwise protect the safety of the children.

FACTS: Howie, 13, and other youths, were using the swimming hole on Mr. Jensen's land. Although it was dangerous, they had used the pond in past summers. Mr. Jensen knew that the kids were there. Howie was swimming when Hank fell out of a dead tree and landed on him. Howie drowned.

Bobbie, 12, was sledding down Mrs. Magruder's hill. "I hit an old car fender buried under the snow and broke my collarbone!" he cried. Mrs. Magruder knew that the kids sledded there.

Jane Sweeney, 9, skating on Grady's pond near her house, moaned, "I hit a tree stump and fell through the ice. I broke my arm."

Witkowski's farm was next to the park's picnic area. A container of fertilizer had been left near the fence. Kim, 5, reached through the open fence and drank some. She became violently ill.

Did the landowners know or should they have known of the youths' presence? Did these conditions create attractive nuisances?

DECISION: **YOU'RE THE JUDGE!**

What if the danger or hazard was obvious and the children were older? The age of a child and the obvious nature of the risk or hazard could prevent the use of the attractive nuisance doctrine.

FACTS: Kirk, 17, was hit by a golf ball while practicing soccer on a golf course. There was no fence or sign prohibiting Kirk from entering the course. Did Kirk assume the risk of and contribute to his injury?

DECISION: **YOU'RE THE JUDGE!**

ODDS & ENDS....

FACTS: Dick and Joe were at an annual golf outing. "We were having a great time drinking a few beers and trying to play," muttered Dick.

In attempting to cross a narrow bridge on the way to the 10th tee, they crashed their cart. Joe broke his ankle and Tom gashed his arm and leg.

They both sued the operator of the golf course for negligently maintaining the premises. They alleged, "The bridge was too narrow and unsafe, the boards old and decayed from years of use and harsh winters, and there was no railing."

The operator countered, "Dick and Joe were aware of the dangers. Furthermore, they contributed to their injuries by drinking and by 'swerving to and fro,' as one witness put it." Was the operator liable for the injuries? **YOU'RE THE JUDGE!**

DECISION: Yes. The golfers had the right to assume that the premises would be in a safe condition for their expected use. And, although they contributed to their injuries by their condition, the accident may have occurred anyway, even had they not been drinking. Had they noticed the condition of the bridge before attempting to cross, they would have assumed the risk of their injuries.

To prevent attractive nuisances, property owners should be keenly aware of their responsibility and duty for the protection of children.

10

MEDICAL TREATMENT

WHAT'S IT ABOUT?

Medical Treatment defines and outlines the duty owed by schools, doctors, medical personnel and others, such as coaches or park supervisors, to provide proper medical assistance to injured participants or others.

Do people who are injured have to give their consent to be treated for an injury?

Medical Providers Group A
4530 West Park Ave.
Worcester, MA 01201

Dear Athletes and Others:

We, the schools, team owners, doctors and others, who may be called upon to render medical assistance to you, recognize our duty to render such assistance in a proper and timely manner in order to ensure your protection and safety.

However, there will be injuries that are the result of the negligence of a small number of our members. We will be negligent where we have breached our duty to use the care and skill rightfully expected and necessary for your protection and safety, and that breach results in an injury and damages.

Not to minimize the seriousness of any injuries, but they are few in number. However, they are the ones that receive the attention of the courts.

Yours truly,

Medical Providers Group

WHAT DUTY IS OWED?

Medical treatment, or the lack of it, which results in an injury or the further aggravation of one, may result in liability.

FACTS: While watching a baseball game, Allen, 15, was struck above the left ear by a hard-hit foul ball. At first, he slumped forward in his seat, "out like a light." Then, he came, groggy and stuttering.

He staggered to the ballpark's first aid station where he was examined by a doctor. The doctor advised him that he had a bump on the head, but that he appeared to be all right and could resume his activities. The doctor did not take his blood pressure nor did he inquire as to Allen's reaction after being hit.

After the game, Allen began stuttering again, crying and shaking. After he was refused admittance at two hospitals, he was admitted at a third.

He was examined by a neurosurgeon and given medication for cerebral hemorrhaging. His condition deteriorated. A test revealed a mass in the brain. Nine hours later, Alan suffered a convulsion which made his condition terminal. When he died three days later, his parents sued the team, the park's doctor and the hospital for providing negligent emergency medical services.

An autopsy revealed that Allen had suffered a fracture when he was hit by the baseball. Bleeding from the time of the accident had resulted in the hemorrhage and his death.

Expert testimony was, "If Allen had been put at rest after arriving at the first aid station, instead of being allowed to move about freely, it was more likely than not that the bleeding would have stopped. He'd be alive today."

Other testimony was that the hospital had opportunities to perform surgery to prevent Allen's death. Was either the team or the park's doctor negligent? Was the hospital negligent?

DECISION: **YOU'RE THE JUDGE!**

Even if the hospital breached its duty to use that degree of care and skill expected, its failure did not relieve the doctor or team of liability for any negligence on their part. Were they both negligent?

LIABILITY OF SCHOOLS & OTHERS

What is the duty of those who conduct sports activities? Their duty is to provide reasonable medical assistance to injured participants or spectators as soon as possible under the circumstances. This includes providing safe facilities and equipment, and persons with the necessary skill and experience. However, they are not insurers of a participant's or others safety.

FACTS: Matt, participating in a bobsled run, failed to negotiate a curve. He received severe fractures of his left leg, a collapsed lung and some bruises.

Following the accident, Matt was transported down the slope on a stretcher and then to the nearest hospital eight miles away. The leg was placed in a cast. However, normal circulation did not return. When gangrene set in, the leg had to be amputated.

Matt sued, alleging negligence in the state's failure to provide sufficiently prompt medical assistance after the accident. He claimed, "I suffered undue exposure through an unreasonable delay in removing me from the snow and cold."

Was the state liable? **YOU'RE THE JUDGE!**

DECISION: No. The court held that the state had adequately discharged its duty after the accident. They promptly produced blankets, a stretcher and a doctor, and promptly transferred Matt to the hospital. Matt assumed the risk of the original injury, as well as the complications.

What if prompt assistance is not rendered? Even in such a case, there may be no liability where the delay does not cause or aggravate an injury.

For example, a football player, who had injured his ankle, was told to "wait on the sidelines until practice is over," before being given medical attention. There was no liability because the delay in receiving medical assistance did not aggravate the injury.

Where there is an injury, must those in control always first summon assistance?

Where a football player, Jim Duda, knocked his shoulder out of place during practice and the coach snapped it back, and sent him to the doctor, there was no liability for failing to obtain medical assistance. The injury did not appear serious and the court felt that there was no need to first summon assistance.

The duty of care, to provide or render assistance in a timely manner in order to insure a participant's protection and safety, will also require that any injured party be properly cared for until medical attention can be obtained.

FACTS: A football player, Scott, suffered a neck injury. Testimony indicated, "The player had been able to move his hands and feet before the coach ordered players to carry him from the field without a stretcher, but not after." Was the coach negligent for improperly rendered medical assistance? **YOU'RE THE JUDGE!**

DECISION: The court found that such conduct on the part of the coach was negligent, not only for allowing the player to be moved, but for failing to wait for a doctor.

Transportation to a hospital may be preferable to summoning a doctor to the scene, particularly where an injury, such as an ankle injury, would not be aggravated and time could be saved.

Liability may attach for negligent or unnecessary medical assistance that is rendered in a non-emergency situation.

FACTS: A high school football player's death resulted after a heat stroke, suffered during practice. Instead of cooling the player's body, an assistant coach placed him in a shower with room temperature water and then wrapped him in a blanket. This increased his accumulation of heat and caused his death. Was the school negligent? **YOU'RE THE JUDGE!**

DECISION: The court held, "The duty to secure reasonable medical assistance was breached. The school was negligent in not providing medical assistance, and in plying ill-chosen, improper first aid."

Similarly, where a teacher immersed an athlete's infected finger in a pan of boiling water, causing permanent disfigurement, liability for negligence was found for rendering unnecessary, forced medical care in a non-emergency situation. Trained medical assistance should have been summoned.

"A school should not assume the role of the physician," noted a court. Thus, liability was found where a physical education teacher overruled a doctor's opinion and note, and forced a student to participate in a broad jump class. The student was then injured.

Similarly, a coach was negligent where he determined—without a release from the doctor for a previous injury—that a boy was fit to play, and then re-injury resulted.

What if an injured athlete does not want medical assistance from non-medical personnel, but it is given anyway?

FACTS: A baseball player injured his leg during practice. "I do not want assistance from anyone except a doctor," he insisted.

An assistant then rendered medical assistance which aggravated the injury. Was this negligence? **YOU'RE THE JUDGE!**

DECISION: Yes. Where non-medical personnel is requested by an injured athlete not to give non-emergency medical assistance and gives it anyway, liability may then apply. The assistant was liable for the aggravation of the injury.

If a physical problem is not known of or could not be discovered by a reasonable person, then there may be no liability.

FACTS: Winthrop had a defect in his circulatory system. An examination did not reveal the problem and Winthrop did not divulge it. He was then struck in the head by a basketball and died, the result of participating in such condition. His family sued the school. Was the school liable for allowing Winthrop to play? **YOU'RE THE JUDGE!**

DECISION: The injury was not the responsibility of either the school or its personnel.

Liability may attach where a required examination of participants is either done improperly or not at all and such an examination would have revealed a problem which caused an injury.

Furthermore, it may be a school's duty to ensure that students not physically or mentally mature enough to participate for a particular sport or activity do not participate where injury might result.

If the sport or activity does not warrant an examination, then the failure to do so may not result in liability.

FACTS: A physical exam was neither required nor warranted for a try-out for the golf team. Had Jones been given one, it would have discovered a spinal problem. When he injured his spine while playing for the team, he sued the school for not examining him and discovering the problem. Was the school liable?

DECISION: **YOU'RE THE JUDGE!**

LIABILITY OF DOCTORS & OTHERS

What is the duty of a doctor who is rendering medical assistance?

A doctor is under a duty to use that degree of care and skill expected of a reasonably competent doctor in the same class of the medical profession to which he belongs, acting in the same or similar circumstances.

A doctor who holds himself out as an expert, will be held to a higher degree of care, as utilized by experts in that field.

Will it make a difference if a doctor provides medical assistance for a fee or for free?

FACTS: Dr. Adams was the school's football doctor. He was paid a fee for his services.

Dr. Bellows volunteered his services at a free medical clinic.

Dr. Charles, on his way home, stopped to help a jogger who had been hit by a car. Will the degree of care required by each doctor be different depending on the circumstances under which it was rendered? **YOU'RE THE JUDGE!**

DECISION: Legally, with few exceptions, it makes no difference whether the doctor undertakes the care for a fee, honorarium, or out of the kindness of his heart.

A doctor does not insure the success of all treatments, and will not be responsible for honest mistakes of judgment where the proper treatment is open to reasonable doubt. Liability will only occur where there has been negligence in following the standard and established procedures for treatment of an injury.

What must one injured show in order to recover for an injury alleged to be the fault of a doctor?

It must be shown that the doctor breached his duty to provide competent care, which resulted in an injury and damages.

FACTS: Johnson, a former football player and now coach, complained of back spasms. The doctor gave him an injection just below the left shoulder blade. It punctured one of his lungs.

"Yes, I did it," the doctor admitted. "I guess I misjudged the thickness of his chest wall. Usually, athletes have a lot thicker wall. I guess coaches aren't as thick as quarterbacks."

Was this competent care, an honest mistake of judgment for which the doctor was not liable?

DECISION: **YOU'RE THE JUDGE!**

Failure To Recognize An Injury

Does a doctor have a duty to determine the nature of an injury before further injury results?

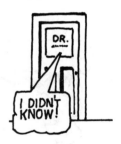

FACTS: A high school football player, Martin, while attempting a quarterback sneak, was tackled and slammed to the ground. He didn't move. Since he could still move his hands and feet, his spinal cord was not severed.

A doctor then allowed Martin to be carried from the field without a stretcher. It was then discovered that the spinal cord was severed. Was the doctor negligent? **YOU'RE THE JUDGE!**

DECISION: Yes. Severance could only have happened when Martin was carried from the field. The court found, "A doctor of reasonable skill and knowledge would have treated the athlete immediately to determine the nature of the injury and would have instructed that he be removed in a manner that would not cause further injury."

Physical Examinations

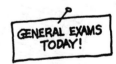

The type and extent of any physical examination required will depend in part on the reason for which it is given.

FACTS: Incoming school athletes were given a general exam. The next day a football player, Ed Wardell, was injured when his left

knee gave way. The exam had not revealed any problem with the knee.

A boxer, Juan Mendolina, died from a blow received during a prize fight. The doctor who had examined the fighter after two previous losses by technical knockouts failed to discover a pre-existing brain injury.

Were the exams extensive enough? Was either doctor liable for the injury? **YOU'RE THE JUDGE!**

DECISION: A general examination given to all incoming school athletes would not be required to be as extensive as one required of boxers who had been knocked out and needed clearance before being allowed to fight again.

Where Wardell was injured the day after an examination which should have revealed the defect which caused the injury, then liability could attach to the doctor.

However, if the injury would have occurred even where the doctor treated Wardell, there can be no liability.

In a questionable decision, the doctor who examined Mendolina was found not liable for an honest error of judgment.

Another's Conduct

It might also be shown that another's conduct was a "substantial factor" in bringing about an injury.

FACTS: An athlete died from a severe concussion received in basketball practice the day after an examination should have revealed the concussion. The coach had allowed the boy to play after he complained of severe headaches. Who was liable? The doctor, the coach or both? **YOU'RE THE JUDGE!**

DECISION: The coach may be equally as liable as the doctor who failed to diagnose the concussion. The coach's conduct was a "substantial factor" in bringing about the death.

Do I Have Your Consent?

Usually, a doctor must obtain the consent of an adult patient before medical treatment can be given.

Must a doctor obtain the consent of a minor before giving medical treatment?

The general rule for minors is that since minors are deemed to be incapable of giving valid consent, consent for their treatment must be obtained from a minors' parents or guardians.

FACTS: John, 15, broke his ankle. He was sent to the hospital for medical treatment. Frances, 16, had a stroke while playing field hockey and needed immediate medical attention. Was parental consent needed in either situation? **YOU'RE THE JUDGE!**

DECISION: Parental consent was needed for John, but not for Frances. The general rule is subject to the following exceptions which allow a minor to give valid consent where: an emergency exists, a parent or guardian is inaccessible, or the minor is near majority and able to give a knowingly informed consent.

For consent to be valid, it must be the **informed consent** of the patient. A patient will be informed after a reasonable disclosure of any available alternative procedures and all dangers, advantages and disadvantages are made known to the patient.

Must consent be obtained in an emergency situation?

FACTS: While returning from a soccer game, Hans was injured and rendered unconscious in an auto accident. There was no time to reach his parents. Therefore, a doctor gave necessary emergency medical attention. Hans later sued the doctor for acting without his permission. Was the doctor negligent? **YOU'RE THE JUDGE!**

DECISION: No. If consent cannot be obtained, it may be implied from the circumstances in which treatment is given. This is especially true in emergency situations.

Disclosure of Medical Information

In order to make decisions concerning their bodies, athletes have a constitutional right to be informed of their medical condition.

Informed consent requires a doctor or others to inform an athlete of his condition or be liable for any subsequent injury resulting from an undisclosed risk.

What if the interests of a team conflict with an athlete's right to be informed of his physical condition?

FACTS: The Whalers football coach ordered the doctor, "Don't tell Killer what's wrong with him. I need him for Sunday's game. If you tell him, he might not play hurt."

Killer played and, due to his condition, aggravated the injury to his shoulder. He sued the team and the doctor. Were they liable for the additional injury? **YOU'RE THE JUDGE!**

DECISION: Both the doctor and the team were found liable. Although Killer may have decided to play while hurt, there still was a duty to inform him of his condition.

Similarly, another pro football player recovered damages against his team and the team's doctor for their "fraudulent" concealment of the severity of an injury to the player's knees. They prescribed a diet of pain killers and steroids so that the player could continue playing. The court commented, "The team and its doctor had a duty to inform the player of everything about his injury and they did not."

Where a doctor claims, "It won't get any worse," or "You're OK, no injury," or words to that effect, or nothing at all (where there is an injury), liability may attach.

FACTS: Edwards injured his knee during a pro football game. The team doctor recommended treatment. Edwards sat out the season, but returned the next pre-season. After being released, he underwent surgery to the knee. The surgeon found that he had sustained extensive damage to the knee, which was aggravated by his continuing to play football, and that surgery should have been performed at the time of the original injury. Was the team's doctor liable? **YOU'RE THE JUDGE!**

DECISION: The court awarded Edwards a judgment against the team's orthopedic surgeon for medical malpractice. Upon appeal, the case was settled.

Similar actions, alleging a conflict of interest, between a doctor's duty to a team and his duty to inform a player of his condition, have been brought.

FACTS: Jim Cranston, a baseball player, alleged that a team physician examined him before spring practice and discovered a symptomatic blood condition, but failed to treat it or report the condition to him. Soon after Cranston was released from the team the following year, he was hospitalized with a kidney disorder and died. If the disorder resulted from the blood condition, was the doctor liable?

DECISION: **YOU'RE THE JUDGE!**

Confidential Information

A doctor may be held liable for the disclosure of confidential information relating to a patient.

What if such an opinion is rendered in good faith or gratuitously? This is so even though it is rendered in good faith, and even if gratuitously.

Where the disclosure of confidential information about a patient is given with knowledge that another will rely upon it, the doctor may be responsible for damages incurred because of any innaccuracies of the opinion.

What if a doctor intentionally gives a false statement concerning a patient's condition, which leads to further suffering?

FACTS: After Davis had recovered from a blood clot, the team doctor was alleged to have announced, "Davis is suffering from a rare blood disease which will prevent him from playing pro football again."

This was printed in the newspapers. Davis read the article and became panic-stricken. He suffered from extreme emotional distress and torment. He sued the team and its doctor for the false statement. Was the doctor liable for causing Davis' further injuries? **YOU'RE THE JUDGE!**

DECISION: The court held that there was evidence to find that the doctor intentionally or recklessly inflicted mental stress by a false statement concerning the supposedly fatal disease.

Permission To Play

Liability may also attach where a doctor grants permission to an injured athlete to participate when his condition does not warrant it, or where there is a premature termination of treatment.

FACTS: Homer had suffered several concussions. He was warned by the team doctor, "Don't play tackle football." Nevertheless, his parents gave their signed permission. The doctor certified Homer's participation.

When Homer received another concussion, resulting in part from his previous condition, he sued the school. They defended, "The parents signed a letter of consent." Who was liable—the doctor or Homer and his parents?

Rusty suffered permanent brain damage as a result of a head injury received during a high school football game. His parents sued his doctor, alleging that he had been "improperly allowed to return to contact sports after an initial treatment for a related head injury."

The doctor had recommended that he could return, but to "take it easy." Was the doctor liable? **YOU'RE THE JUDGE!**

DECISION: Both doctors were negligent for allowing Homer and Rusty to return to play. If the doctors thought that they had not sufficiently recovered, it should have been evident that returning to a contact sport would only place them in an unreasonably dangerous situation, with the possibility for further injury more likely.

Liability was also found where a high school football player was allowed to play a few days after his release from a hospital after suffering fainting spells. The negligence consisted of: the premature termination of treatment, a failure to advise the player that he was unfit to play, and allowing his return where his condition did not warrant it.

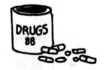

DRUGS

FACTS: Several athletes charged that owners, trainers and physicians negligently administered illegal and harmful drugs so that the athletes would perform while hurt and play more violently.

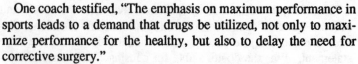

One coach testified, "The emphasis on maximum performance in sports leads to a demand that drugs be utilized, not only to maximize performance for the healthy, but also to delay the need for corrective surgery."

Another doctor testified, "While a painkiller may serve to inhibit pain, such a practice may cause or worsen an existing injury by inhibiting the natural warning system of the body, thereby increasing the risk of further injury."

Would such practices constitute negligence by those administering the drugs? Will your decision depend upon whether or not the players had informed consent?

DECISION: **YOU'RE THE JUDGE!**

Where there is an absence of a clear disclosure to an athlete of the dangers that drugs might pose, the athlete cannot validly consent to such prescription. This would be negligence by whomever administers the drugs.

What if a drug given to one participant causes injury to another?

FACTS: A jockey, Mario, was killed when a horse (not the one ridden by Mario), broke down during a race, causing a pile-up. The jockey's estate sued the owner and trainer of the horse that broke down for improperly administering drugs to the horse. They alleged, "The horse was given a large dosage of an anesthetizing drug to numb pain so that he would continue running until he broke down."

Would such a practice, if it was the cause of the pile-up, be negligence?

DECISION: **YOU'RE THE JUDGE!**

"Blood doping" and the use of steroids to enhance the performance of athletes, with the alleged aid or approval of coaches, trainers and doctors may be negligence. Furthermore, steroids are included in a list of substances that are banned by both the NCAA, the Olympics and professional sports. Using any of these substances may lead to a suspension of the player from participation in school athletics, the Olympics or professional sports.

FACTS: A football team's trainer recommended that certain team members, in order to maximize their performance, use steroids. He obtained their consent. Later, when the athletes developed health problems, they sued the trainer and school for medical malpractice. They alleged that it was negligence to recommend such a practice to them. They further alleged, "Future health consequences were not explained—such as heart and liver problems."

The trainer defended by testifying as to the alleged "consent." Was the consent informed? Was the trainer negligent?

DECISION: **YOU'RE THE JUDGE!**

WARRANTY

FACTS: A doctor promised Seve that surgery on his injured knee would make it "as good as new." The surgery, although performed with all the care and skill expected of the doctor, with results as good as could be hoped for, left Seve with a bum knee. His career was over.

Seve sued the doctor for a breach of warranty —the doctor's promise, guarantee or assurance—to make his knee "as good as new." Seve relied upon this promise in consenting to the operation. Was the doctor liable for his failure to bring about the expected result?

DECISION: **YOU'RE THE JUDGE!**

There must be promissory language by the doctor. This language may be implied. And there must not only be a promise, but some reliance by the athlete upon that promise.

FACTS: Hugo needed surgery on his knee to have any chance of continuing to play pro football. He asked his doctor, "Will I be able to play after the surgery and rehabilitation?" The doctor didn't answer; he just smiled and nodded his head. When after the surgery, Hugo had to retire, he sued the doctor, alleging, "I relied on the doctor's warranty to correct my knee." Was the doctor liable? **YOU'RE THE JUDGE!**

DECISION: Yes. The doctor, by saying nothing, but implying by his actions that the surgery would allow Hugo to play, was liable. Hugo relied on that promise.

What if a doctor guarantees a certain result? What if he only predicts what the result may be?

Generally, a doctor does not warrant certain results. However, where a doctor does guarantee certain results, there may be liability for non-performance. However, liability will not attach for mere predictions of outcomes.

FACTS: Jack's doctor told him, "Surgery could correct your knee." And later added, "I think that everything will be okay, but if you would like, I can do the procedure again."

Another doctor told an athlete, "Don't worry about the stitches coming undone." Did the doctors promise certain results, or were these statements just opinions of the outcome? **YOU'RE THE JUDGE!**

DECISION: Courts are reluctant to hold that everytime a doctor tells the patient that a certain treatment will fix the patient up fine, or not to worry about it, that the doctor has warranted his curing the patient.

The courts found that such language implied uncertainty. They were mere opinions, not promises.

Doctors have to be allowed to calm or help patients without fear of warranting results. However, there is a limit as to what type of re-assurance a doctor can give without warranting his work.

FACTS: "I guarantee that your leg will be fine after recovery from this surgery," and "I promise that there will be no complications." Did these statements, made to athletes by their doctors, warranty certain results? **YOU'RE THE JUDGE!**

DECISION: Yes. The statements go beyond normal assurances and may lead to liability where the results are not as warranted. A doctor must remember that what the patient may think of as suc-cess may be completely different from what the doctor thinks of as success.

Just as opinions and some assurances may not be promises, an of-fer of information to a patient is unlikely to be found as a guarantee of certain results.

FACTS: A star female athlete, desiring not to have children, had a tubal ligation (tubes tied). The doctor stated that this was perma-nent. When the athlete became pregnant, and thus unable to com-pete, she sued the doctor, alleging that his promise of permanency meant that she would never become pregnant. Did the doctor promise such a result? **YOU'RE THE JUDGE!**

DECISION: The doctor's statement was non-promissory. It was only intended to inform the patient that the operation was non-reversible.

There are no strict guidelines as to what constitutes a warranty or promise. The test appears to be: What did the patient think that the doctor was or was not promising?

Where doctors stated that: "Treatments would not leave a perma-nent scar," or "would make a patient's arm 100% perfect," or, "Treatments were perfectly safe," or, "Treatment would please the patient to her personal satisfaction," promises were found. Such statements contained less prediction and more warranty.

FACTS: A dentist assured a hockey player that his difficulty would be over. With his new dentures, he would be able to eat nor-mally—including corn on the cob. When the hockey player could not eat normally, he sued the doctor, alleging that the doctor breached "his promise to end my difficulty." The doctor felt that he "was only reassuring the patient." Was the doctor liable for damages for a breach of promise? **YOU'RE THE JUDGE!**

DECISION: Yes. The hockey player was not a worried patient facing a serious health situation where a reassurance might be needed. It was an elective treatment where no reassurance was needed. The language was a breach of warranty.

CONSENT FORMS

Is a doctor shielded from liability by a written disclaimer in a consent form which the patient signs?

FACTS: Les, injured in a football game, needed surgery. He signed a consent form stating, "No guarantee or assurance has been given by anyone as to the results that may be obtained."

Kirby, injured playing soccer, signed a consent form providing, in part, "No result has been guaranteed."

Both doctors, when asked about the potential results, said reassuringly, "Don't worry, everything will be just fine."

If the results obtained by Les and Kirby were not what they expected, and they sued, would the consent forms that they had signed release the doctors of any liability? **YOU'RE THE JUDGE!**

DECISION: Even though there were signed consent forms, the courts may look to see whether there was an oral guarantee. Therefore, a doctor is not shielded from liability by a written disclaimer, unless it is also coupled with an oral disclaimer.

A doctor's best defense in preventing liability would be by the use of statements such as, "Assuming no complications," or, "Except for the unlikely event of a complication," instead of "I promise!" or "I guarantee!"

ODDS & ENDS....

Weight Control

Attempts at weight control occur most frequently where an athlete either desires to lose weight to qualify for a team, or where a weight loss is necessary to compete at a desired level.

FACTS: Several athletes, in an attempt to make the wrestling, boxing and 150-pound football teams (only for players weighing

150 pounds or less), went on crash diets. They all became too weak to compete competitively and, as a result, were injured.

Testimony showed that, in some instances the school either participated in, directed, or condoned the crash dieting. In others, the school did not know of the dieting. When could a school be held responsible for an athlete's injury which was the result of dieting? **YOU'RE THE JUDGE!**

DECISION: Where crash dieting is directed, condoned, or participated in, by a school or doctor—negligence may be found where injury results. And this may be so even where the coach or other school personnel did not direct it, but knew of the attempt and did nothing to stop it.

When possible, anyone being treated for an injury, or seeking or needing medical care, should receive a reasonable disclosure of their medical condition and any available alternative procedures, including all dangers, advantages and disadvantages. Only then can an individual give an informed consent for themself or another.

11

CONTRACTS - PROMISES! PROMISES!

WHAT'S IT ABOUT?

An agreement to do or not to do a particular thing—that is a contract. *Contracts—Promises! Promises!* gives samples and interprets a professional athlete's player contract, including no-cut and guaranteed contracts and bonuses. It also discusses a player's duty to perform.

Can a team breach a player's guaranteed contract? What is misrepresentation? What is fraud?

CONTRACTS

FACTS:

CONTRACT

I, _____, agree to play basketball for the Boston   Blues. They agree to pay me $100,000 a year for 3 years.

_____   _____   _____
DATE   YOU the PLAYER   Boston Blues

Do you think that this **contract** —an agreement to do or not to do a particular thing—between YOU and the Boston Blues fulfills the legal requirements for: a valid and enforceable contract of an offer, an acceptance of that offer, and consideration (your services as a player for money)?

DECISION: **YOU'RE THE JUDGE!**

Does a contract have to be in writing? An **express contract** is one that may be formed by either written or oral language. Thus, had you and the Blues orally agreed to a contract, that may have been a valid contract.

The Blues have made YOU an **offer**—a promise to enter into a contract that is clear and that is communicated to YOU. YOU may accept their offer, reject it or make a counter-offer. Or, the Blues could withdraw their offer at any time before YOU accept it.

If YOU decide to accept their offer, the **acceptance** must comply with the Blues terms. If YOU add or omit any terms, such as by insisting, "I accept, but I want a bonus," then a **counter-offer** is created, which the Blues may then accept, reject or counter-offer.

Both you and the Blues must give **consideration**—something of legal value. The considerations are your services as a player and the Blues' payment of money.

Lastly, in order to have formed a valid and enforceable contract, no defenses must exist. These defenses may apply to not just a contract between an athlete and a professional team, but also in other contracts, such as between an agent and an athlete.

FACTS: You and the Blues signed the contract. What if there was an absence of consideration—you didn't play or they didn't pay?

What if there was: **fraud**—intentional deception or dishonesty; **misrepresentation**—false statements by YOU or the Blues; **duress**—high pressure or threats; **unconscionable conduct**—unreasonable, dishonest or conniving? May any of these defenses be used to void the contract? **YOU'RE THE JUDGE!**

DECISION: If any of these defenses are present, then the contract may be voided by the offended party.

Will this contract between YOU and the Boston Blues resolve questions, such as:

- "What if I report in bad shape?"
- "Will I get a bonus if I play well?"
- "What if the team doesn't pay me?"
- "What happens if I don't try or if I'm injured?"
- "What if I am fined, suspended, waived, traded or fired?"

Although a simple contract may fulfill the basic requirements of an offer, acceptance and consideration, it may not solve all of the problems that may arise. That is why professional sports teams and their players sign a uniform or standard player contract similar to this:

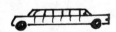

UBA PLAYER CONTRACT

THIS **CONTRACT** is between YOU, herein called the Player, and the Boston Blues, herein called the Club, a member of the UNITED BASKETBALL ASSOCIATION.

In consideration of the promises made to each other, Player and Club agree as follows:

TERM This contract is for one year, August 1 to July 31. The Club is entitled to a one-year renewal option under the same terms and conditions as the original contract.

COMPENSATION For Player's services and other promises, the Club will pay the Player $1,000,000, earned BONUSES, and expenses for traveling, meals and lodging.

SERVICES The Club employs Player as a skilled basketball player. Player agrees to give his best efforts, and to behave and abide by fair play and good sportsmanship.

OTHER SPORTS & SERVICES Player has exceptional and unique skill, and will not, without permission, play for any other team or participate in any dangerous activity, including wrestling, boxing, racing, hockey, sky diving, football, bullriding or mountain climbing.

PHYSICAL CONDITION Player represents that he has no physical or mental defects and that he will maintain himself in first-class physical condition.

PICTURES, PUBLICITY & PUBLIC APPEARANCES Player grants Club permission to use his picture for publicity and promotion. Player will make public appearances, cooperate with media and will make ads only with the Club's permission.

INJURY If Player is injured, he will receive medical care and pay, as long as unable to play, but only for the remainder of the season. If Player is dismissed while unable to play, see Collective Bargaining Agreement (CBA) for grievance procedure.

PERFORMANCE, CONDUCT & DISMISSAL If Player's performance is unsatisfactory, or his conduct adversely reflects on the Club or the integrity of the League, then Club may fine, suspend or dismiss Player. CBA grievance procedure will govern.

RULES & DISPUTES Player will abide by all rules. Any disputes will be submitted to arbitration under the CBA, except that the commissioner shall have sole authority with regard to conduct involving the integrity of the game.

ASSIGNMENT Unless otherwise agreed, Club may assign this contract and Player's services to any other Club in the League.

APPROVAL The commissioner shall have the right to approve or disapprove this contract on reasonable grounds.

OTHER AGREEMENTS This contract and any attachments contain all that the parties have agreed to, and along with the Collective Bargaining Agreement, League Constitution and Rules, will govern the relationship between the Player and the Club.

SPECIAL PROVISIONS

A. Player's compensation is guaranteed. He may not be cut or traded during this contract.

B. Player will receive a signing bonus of $50,000, and an interest-free loan of $250,000.

C. Player will receive bonuses for the following: games played, points scored, rebounds, victories, awards and home attendance.
Player will have free use of a chauffeured limo and a house for one year and of the arena for one night. A buy-out provision will be in effect for the option year of this contract. The Club will grant a scholarship to the Player for further study.

_____   _____   _____

PLAYER—YOU   CLUB—Boston Blues by   Date

This contract—a product of the collective bargaining process between a league and its players—plays the predominant role in defining the rights and responsibilities of the professional team athlete.

FACTS: After signing this contract, you were injured during preseason. The team doctor said, "You will be out for the year." Will you receive your pay?

The Club argued, "You were injured playing checkers during the off-season." They decided to waive you. Can they waive you while you are injured?

DECISION: **YOU'RE THE JUDGE!**

General rules concerning contracts in professional team sports may also apply to contracts in other employment situations (such as individual sports, agent representation, endorsements and public appearances).

What are the rights and responsibilities of the parties to a contract?

A contract involving an athlete is sometimes called a **personal service contract**—agreement exchanging an act (personal performance) for a promise (to pay).

FACTS: Marilyn (a pro ping pong player), John (a pro basketball player), and Sid (a pro football coach), all signed personal service contracts.

Marilyn couldn't make a match. She asked, "Can my husband take my place?"

John had an endorsement appearance to attend, but wanted to play golf instead. He wanted a teammate to take his place.

Sid needed a vacation. He asked his assistant, "Will you take my place for a week?" May any of these pros assign their duties to others?

The Club would like to assign John's contract to another team. Can they? **YOU'RE THE JUDGE!**

DECISION: Personal service contracts call for the performance of services and the exercise of skill and judgment that may only be performed by the person with whom made. The athlete or coach may not assign (transfer to another) his or her duties to be performed.

However, unless the player has a no-trade provision in his contract, a team has the right to assign a player's contract to any other team in the league.

Other Agreements?

Will a court, in interpreting a contract between a professional player and his team, allow oral evidence as to what the parties agreed to?

In interpreting contracts where the parties have different views, the **Parol Evidence Rule** may come into play. It reads: "If the parties intended the contract—and any attached or referred to documents—to be their whole agreement, then the court will not allow any evidence of other agreements."

FACTS: In negotiating his contract, Pedro, a major league baseball player, was promised, "We'll give you a bonus!" However, when the season ended, he discovered that the bonus was not in his contract. In attempting to collect the bonus, may Pedro introduce evidence of the oral promise? **YOU'RE THE JUDGE!**

DECISION: No. Pedro should have made sure that the bonus was in the contract before he signed.

There are exceptions. Prior agreements, such as last year's contract between the parties, may sometimes be used—not to change the agreement—but to explain or define any unclear terms.

Approval

Approval of a contract by the commissioner or president of a league is generally required. This power is given to ensure that the interests of the player and the league are protected, such as to prevent improper bonuses.

FACTS: Max, a pro football player, signed a three year contract to play for the Rams. The contract required the commissioner's approval. When, after one year, Max declared, "I want to play elsewhere!" the team sought to enjoin him from doing so. The commissioner had given his approval only for the first of the three years on the contract. "Can I play somewhere else?" asked Max. **YOU'RE THE JUDGE!**

DECISION: Yes. Max could play elsewhere. There was no contract as commissioner approval was not obtained for the last two years of the contract.

Today, although commisssioner approval is still necessary, it is not required to complete a contract. The contract is binding when both the player and the club have signed it.

Term

FACTS: Marcel, a pro football player, wanted to play tennis during the off-season. His contract prohibited tennis. Did the contract cover the off-season? **YOU'RE THE JUDGE!**

DECISION: The term of the contract was for one year. This prevents Marcel from participating in prohibited conduct during the off-season.

When a contract does not prohibit a specific activity, a player may participate—such as a talented professional athlete participating in pro football and baseball in the same season.

Some professional sports leagues, such as major league baseball, limit the length of contracts between teams and their players.

Compensation

Contracts specify that players have a right to a definite salary. However, any action by the player's club to fine or discipline a player for his conduct may reduce that salary.

This may be so even where the player has a no-cut contract.

FACTS: Tom, a pro hockey player, got into a fight and was injured. The team stopped his pay, fined and suspended him. His contract did not cover this situation. Tom sued for his salary and asked, "Can I recover?" **YOU'RE THE JUDGE!**

DECISION: The general rule is that where a player's salary has been terminated for an injury which occurred while playing for the team, the player may recover for the remainder of that year.

Players will not be paid when they are on strike. Also, they may not be paid if an owner locks out his players when, through their representatives, they can't agree on a new Collective Bargaining Agreement. Some player contracts may allow for payment during a strike or lockout.

Bonuses

A player's right to receive any bonus will depend upon whether the bonus is awarded for signing or for performance, and whether the player has performed, if required.

May a player keep a signing bonus if he is cut from the team without performing?

Signing bonuses, offered as inducements to get players to sign, generally only require that players sign the contract and be "ready,

willing and able to perform." If cut, a player may retain the bonus. If not ready, willing and able to perform or, if required to perform and the player does not, then the player may have to return part or all of the bonus.

> FACTS: Two pro football players, Brown and Sable, signed to play in a new football league starting the next year. The team had financial difficulties and, as the players never played, there was a dispute as to their bonuses. The team sought to recover the bonuses, claiming, "The players didn't even attend camp, let alone play in any games!" Could Brown and Sable keep the bonuses? **YOU'RE THE JUDGE!**

> DECISION: Yes. The players were prohibited from signing with any other team (for play during the contract), and furthermore, the players' names were used for publicity purposes (selling tickets). This was of benefit to the team and was consideration by the players for the bonuses.

However, a player may forfeit a bonus if he fails to fulfill an obligation of his contract—such as when his contract calls for the player to report at a certain weight and he reports overweight.

Power To Terminate

Can a player terminate his contract if his team doesn't pay him? A player's ability to terminate a contract generally involves disputes concerning salary or medical care.

> FACTS: Dan, the quarterback for the Marlins, injured his knee. The team decided not to pay his salary or medical expenses. His contract had a payment of salary clause. Could he terminate the contract for non-payment of his salary? **YOU'RE THE JUDGE!**

> DECISION: The most widely used payment of salary clause reads: "If the team fails to pay the player or otherwise fails to perform a material obligation (provide for required and necessary medical care), then, under arbitration, if the decision is for the player, the team shall have the opportunity to make the payment before the player can terminate the contract."

Renegotiate

What if a player feels that, because he performed beyond that expected of him, he deserves to have his contract renegotiated? May he?

FACTS: Tony, a late-round draft choice, was offered a long term "take-it-or-leave-it" contract for a minimum salary. By the end of his first season, he was a star running back for the Indians. He walked out of training camp when the team wouldn't renegotiate his contract. The Indians first fined, and then threatened to release him. Could they do so? **YOU'RE THE JUDGE!**

DECISION: By not playing, Tony was in violation of his contract. Tony should have attempted to negotiate a clause into his contract calling for renegotiation if a certain level of performance was reached. Also, he could have negotiated an incentive or performance bonus to be based upon his play.

No-Cut, No-Trade & Guarantee?

Under a **no-cut contract,** will a player be paid even if he is in poor physical condition and cut from the team?

A no-cut provision ensures that a player's salary will not be affected by his performance, even if he is cut from the roster. And, absent a more specific agreement (denying salary for injury due to certain defects), a no-cut clause would entitle a player to his salary even if he were in poor physical condition or even if he were injured during the off-season.

FACTS: A clause in your contract read, "This is a no-cut contract. Player shall not be traded without his permission. Player's salary is guaranteed."

What if your performance was poor or you were subject to disciplinary action (suspension)? The team would like to terminate your contract, without pay, by cutting or trading you. Could they do so?

DECISION: **YOU'RE THE JUDGE!**

May players be fined? Although a team is entitled to a player's best efforts, poor performance, due solely to attitude, would be very difficult to prove. As to discipline which is necessary in maintaining control of players, it is doubtful that a team would restrict a coach's authority by giving a player a clause prohibiting discipline. Therefore, players may be fined.

FACTS: Harry signed a guaranteed contract with the Bulldogs. After violating curfew for the third time, the team suspended him without pay. Could he recover the salary provided for in his contract? Could he be fined? **YOU'RE THE JUDGE!**

DECISION: As with a no-cut contract, Harry must make a good faith effort to perform. He is subject to discipline, which may include a fine or suspension (with loss of pay).

May a player with a no-cut contract be traded? Absent a more specific agreement, a player with a **no-trade provision** may not be traded without his consent. If he is, then he may void the trade. Major league baseball players with ten years in the majors and five years for their present team may veto any trade involving them.

A **salary guarantee** may provide, "The player's salary will not be affected by his performance or by his physical condition, even if due to an off-season injury." A majority of professional athletes in team sports (except most NFL players) have contracts guaranteeing pay in the event of their being cut or injured. In the NHL, teams may buy out a player's contract.

> FACTS: "Mad Mike" signed a contract with the Steamrollers pro football team. He was cut after the last exhibition game. Could he recover his salary? **YOU'RE THE JUDGE!**

> DECISION: Mad Mike's contract was not guaranteed. When he did not make the team, the contract was voided; no further salary had to be paid.

And, if a player moves to another team or retires, it is doubtful that the parties intended that the player receive his salary.

A more standard form no-cut provision may provide that inadequate physical condition, whether due to improper conditioning or an off-season injury, may be grounds for terminating a contract. A player's salary would not be affected by performance, as long as the performance was a good faith effort.

What is arbitration? Disputes concerning injuries and salary may be settled by **arbitration**—a process whereby owners and players submit their dispute to an impartial third party or parties for resolution.

> FACTS: Tom, a pro football player, had a no-cut contract which could only be terminated for off-season injuries which hampered his play. Tom reported to training camp unable to play, asserting, "The injury that I received at the end of last year still bothers me."
> The team refused to pay his salary, arguing, "He injured himself in the off-season playing basketball."
> How will this dispute be resolved? **YOU'RE THE JUDGE!**

> DECISION: The matter will go to arbitration to determine whether Tom's off-season activity created a new injury or whether last year's injury was responsible for Tom's inability to play. Doctors will provide the necessary information for arbiters to make a decision.

Injury & Physical Condition

A professional athlete's ability to perform is the basis of his liveli-hood and of the contract with his team. Therefore, his physical condi-tion and the risk of injury are primary concerns.

Upon signing a contract a player, in effect, warrants, "I have unique skill and ability. I am in, and will stay in, good physical con-dition. If I am injured and cannot perform due to a violation of any of these promises, or if I fail the pre-season physical exam, the team may have the right to terminate my contract."

If a player is injured while performing for the team, how long will the team pay him?

> FACTS: Al, a pro football player, was injured in a game. John, a teammate, was hurt during the off-season working on his house. Hank, another teammate, was injured when he fell off a stage dur-ing a required public appearance. They all failed pre-season physi-cal exams and were forced to retire.
>
> What type of injuries will the team cover or pay for? For how long will the team pay for these injuries? **YOU'RE THE JUDGE!**

> DECISION: Generally, a team will accept liability for injuries to players sustained in performance of their contract. That would in-clude all games. Thus, Al could recover his salary for that season.
>
> Activities unrelated to the contract, such as John's, are not cov-ered, even if the injury had happened during the season.
>
> However, a contract may provide that a player is covered in oth-er situations where he is "carrying out an obligation of his con-tract" (making a required public appearance or speech). Hank could recover his salary.
>
> For injuries covered, the team will generally pay medical ex-penses and salary for the remainder of that season only. A multi-year contract with a no-cut provision may guarantee payment for the remainder of the contract.

What if a player was injured trying to stay in shape during the off-season?

> FACTS: An NBA player, Gene, was told by his team that he did not work out enough in the off-season. So Gene decided to join a summer basketball league. When he was injured while playing in the league, his team refused to pay his guaranteed salary, saying, "You played without our consent." Should the team have had to pay Gene?

DECISION: **YOU'RE THE JUDGE!**

Often, an injury may be the result of the combined effects of several blows, and then may not appear until some later time.

FACTS: Gabe, a pro football player, passed his team's pre-season physical exam, but then he was injured. The team terminated his contract, claiming, "The injury was the result of Gabe's debilitating back injury from a previous year, and for which we are not responsible." Gabe sued for his salary. Was the team liable? **YOU'RE THE JUDGE!**

DECISION: Gabe had reported to camp in good condition and the team physician certified this condition, noting that Gabe did not suffer from any symptoms of his previous injury. The team was liable.

A player who fails a pre-season exam may face termination or suspension without pay. A player will be examined after an injury to determine his ability to play and, if he is found unable to play due to the injury, the team physician will determine when he is fit to return to play.

FACTS: Kevin, a pro baseball player, was injured. After missing three months, he was declared fit to play by the team physician. His ability and skill in playing had been lessened by the injury and he was cut from the team. He sued for his salary, alleging, "I should have been paid throughout the period of my rehabilitation." Should he have? **YOU'RE THE JUDGE!**

DECISION: If Kevin, after rehabilitation, was still unable to perform at the level required of him, he could be terminated without pay. If, however, his ability to perform was still subject to improvement from an injury as a result of his playing for the team, then he would be entitled to his salary throughout his rehabilitation, but only for the remainder of the season, unless he had a guaranteed contract.

Any dispute regarding a player's physical fitness may be submitted to arbitration, where an independent medical review will determine the player's fitness.

Conduct & Rules

Who may discipline a player? The player's team? The commissioner? A player, in signing a contract—and subject to fine, suspension or dismissal—in effect agrees, "I will abide by rules intended to govern my conduct and to discourage activities, such as fighting, abusing officials or gambling." Any fine will be determined by the amount thought necessary to punish and to deter others from similar conduct. A commissioner or president may review a team's discipline and meet out any additional discipline thought to be necessary.

Is the player being disciplined entitled to due process? A player's contract or league rules may provide for arbitration, or **due process**—the right to notice and a fair and impartial hearing with representation.

Who will determine if any discipline is fair and reasonable? An independent arbitrator may ensure that any disciplinary rule is related to the league's interest in protecting the integrity of the sport, that the rule is fair and reasonable, and that it is exercised in good faith, not due to a vindictive motive or other personal reason.

FACTS: Jack, a pro basketball player, admitted, "I gambled on my team's games."

Without notice and a hearing, the team suspended him. Jack's contract provided for a hearing before any disciplinary action. Should Jack's suspension have been lifted and Jack given a hearing?

Paul, a pro baseball player, was fined and suspended for fighting during a game. He was given a hearing with the commissioner, who upheld the fine and suspension. Paul asked for "review by either the court or an independent arbitrator." Should Paul have been given a second hearing? **YOU'RE THE JUDGE!**

DECISION: Jack's suspension was upheld. The court applied the **"unclean hands" doctrine,** which holds that "one doing something wrong (having dirty hands) cannot ask for relief."

Jack had caused irreparable harm to the players, team, league, fans and youth. Therefore, because Jack had bet on the games in which he played, he was denied the due process procedures provided for in his contract. However, Jack should have been given an opportunity to mitigate the seriousness of the offense.

Paul, as provided by his contract, had the right to the grievance procedure, which entitled him to a hearing and review by an independent arbitrator.

You're Fired!

Tenure (permanent employment) rarely applies to a professional athlete. "Survival of the fittest" does.

It is in an owner's or promoter's interests to have only the very best players performing for them, but with no more security than is necessary. What are a team's or player's rights and duties regarding termination?

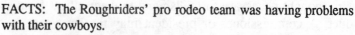

FACTS: The Roughriders' pro rodeo team was having problems with their cowboys.

Bronco Billy reported for the season "out of shape"; Randy could no longer stay on the bull; Bill continued to violate curfew; Larry intentionally missed the bus for the regional championship, and; Swen didn't show up for a public appearance. "Can we terminate any of the cowboys' contracts?" asked the Roughriders' owner. **YOU'RE THE JUDGE!**

DECISION: The team retained the right to terminate the cowboys' contracts for failing to: "maintain good physical condition, exhibit sufficient skill and ability and observe disciplinary rules, or for otherwise materially breaching their contracts."

Refusing to participate in scheduled competition may be material, but failure to show up for one public appearance probably would not be a material breach. Only Swen's contract wasn't terminated.

A player may be given the right to terminate a contract, especially where his team fails to pay his salary. And if a team discharges a player without good cause, then the player will be excused from performance, while still having a proper demand for his salary.

A team terminating a player's contract for good cause will be under no further obligation to employ or pay the player, except if the termination was for an injury occurring during play or in fulfilling other duties, or where the player had a no-cut contract guaranteeing his salary. Will a no-cut contract save a player from being terminated for disciplinary reasons?

FACTS: Due to continual disciplinary problems, Speedy, a star running back for the Tigers, was unable to perform to the satisfaction of the team. The Tigers considered terminating his contract, but the contract had a no-cut clause. "Can we terminate Speedy's contract? Should we?" asked the Tigers. **YOU'RE THE JUDGE!**

DECISION: Although the Tigers could terminate Speedy's contract, it is doubtful that they would let a player with marketable skill go. Generally, a team will attempt to sell the player's contract, trade him, or at least place him on waivers for a stated price to other interested teams.

Ability To Perform?

Who determines a player's ability to perform? Discretion to determine a player's skill or ability to play is given to a team through their head coach, manager or the team physician.

A player may be concerned that a coach's or doctor's loyalty to the team may influence any decision, thus negating "good faith" in determining the player's ability to perform. Therefore, where physical condition is at issue, a player's contract may provide for an independent exam and arbitration.

The **"good faith test"**—where "as long as the team acted in good faith and with honesty, its discretion will be upheld"—is generally used where a team has discretion as to whether or not it is "satisfied" with a player's ability.

FACTS: Pro football players, Tillman and Gambrell, after recovering from knee injuries, were pronounced fit to play by their team physicians. After failures to perform satisfactorily, they were dismissed. "Can we recover our salaries?" they asked. **YOU'RE THE JUDGE!**

DECISION: The court held, "The players were properly dismissed under a clause in their contracts permitting the clubs to dismiss them if they were not in proper physical condition." They had recovered as fully as possible, but not enough to satisfactorily play. The physicians had exercised good faith in examining the players.

A second test used to determine if a team's decision concerning a player's ability to perform is reasonable is the **"reasonable man standard."** It states, "If a reasonable man would have been dissatisfied with a player's ability, then his club's discretion in dismissing the player will be honored"—unless the player's ability was hampered by an injury received while playing for the team.

FACTS: Floyd, a pro football player, was placed on the injured reserve list. He was later ordered back to duty and promptly cut from the team, allegedly due to his inability to perform sufficiently. He sued for his salary, contending, "I should be paid while I'm still recovering from that injury." Was he awarded his back pay? **YOU'RE THE JUDGE!**

DECISION: Yes. The evidence did not establish if the team doctor had stated that Floyd was physically able to perform. Floyd was advised by the trainer that he had been placed on the active or ready to play list on the advice from "higher up." Although a reasonable man may have been dissatisfied with Floyd's ability, it was due to an injury previously incurred while playing for his team.

Option & Reserve

FACTS: Dave's contract to play for the Orioles contained an option clause allowing the team to renew his contract for one year without his consent.

Ed's contract with the Blue Sox had a reserve clause allowing the team to renew Ed's contract without his consent for as many years as he played. Could the teams use such clauses to prevent Dave and Ed from playing for other teams? **YOU'RE THE JUDGE!**

DECISION: Under the typical **option clause,** a club may renew an exclusive right to a player's services without his consent for one year after the expiration of the present contract. Although certain veterans may be exempt, the option clause is a part of every contract and may not be stricken through private negotiation.

Provisions that give a team rights to a player's services for an indefinite period are referred to as **reserve clauses.** Unless a player and his team contract for the player's services for an indefinite period of time (life contract), reserve clauses are no longer allowed.

If a player signs a new contract, then the option year will extend to the year after the contract expires.

What should a player do if he intends to "play out" his option so that he may negotiate with other teams?

If a player intends to play out his option, he should leave the new contract unsigned, thereby forcing the club to exercise it's option if it intends to keep the player for another year.

In some sports (NBA), the option clause has been replaced with a right of first refusal clause giving a club the right to match any salary offered to one of their players by another team. This applies unless the player is a five-year veteran. There, a player automatically becomes a free agent with no right of first refusal clause in his contract. If a player is not a five-year veteran, any new contract must include a twenty-five percent pay raise for his team to retain the right of first refusal.

Was There A Breach Of Contract?

FACTS: D.J. and Tommy Lee sued their team, the Blues, charging, "We weren't paid our salaries."

Due to a pre-season injury, D.J. wasn't able to play. Tommy Lee was ready, willing and able to perform for the team. Could they recover their salaries? **YOU'RE THE JUDGE!**

DECISION: Yes. Both contracts were breached. D.J. was unable to play due to an injury received while fulfilling duties under his contract. Tommy Lee was ready, willing and able to perform his duties.

Can a player be "forced" to perform? **Specific performance** requires a party to perform. But, as a general rule, this is inappropriate as it violates the Thirteenth Amendment to the Constitution which prohibits involuntary service. It is difficult to force compliance, and furthermore there is the undesirability of forcing two opposing parties to work together.

FACTS: Although the Whales were ready, willing and able to pay "Shark," he wanted to play water polo elsewhere. He asserted, "I won't play until they agree to trade me." Could the Whales force Shark to play for them? If not, could they prevent him from playing for another team in their league? **YOU'RE THE JUDGE!**

DECISION: The Whales could not force Shark to play for them.

A pro sports team enforces its contracts by an **injunction**—order of a court preventing a party (player) from doing or continuing an act (playing for another team), done in order to prevent injury (to the team). The injunction may be temporary until a trial can be had to determine the rights of the player and the team.

A court may issue a permanent injunction preventing a player from playing for another team. The team seeking an injunction must show that money damages are inadequate and that irreparable harm is likely if the injunction is not granted. The difficulty in replacing a player after rosters have been filled and the season has begun provides substantial proof of irreparable harm.

What if a contract is too one-sided or harsh? Enforcement may be denied where a contract is too one-sided or harsh, or where an injunction would seriously inhibit a player's opportunity to realize the fair value of his services.

FACTS: A pro basketball player, Randy Heyman, entered into a contract to play semi-pro ball for a minimum salary. After a successful season, he signed a contract with the ABA, a new pro league, with a substantial increase in salary. Could his former team get an injunction to prevent him from playing for the ABA? **YOU'RE THE JUDGE!**

DECISION: The former team might be entitled to damages for breach of contract, but not to an injunction. The old contract was too harsh and one-sided to permit enforcement. Any restraining order would seriously inhibit Heyman's opportunity to realize the fair value of his services in the "big" league.

Equity is justice administered by the court according to what is fair. "He who comes into equity must have clean hands." Thus, where a party seeking an injunction comes into court with unclean hands (has done something wrong), the court may then deny relief.

FACTS: Jack, a pro football player under contract to the Cougars, "jumped" to the Whalers, but then attempted to return to the Cou-

gars. Could the Whalers enjoin Jack from going back to the Cougars?

The Cougars asserted the defense of unclean hands. "The Whalers interfered with our original contract with Jack, and because of this, they should not be able to enforce any contract with him." **YOU'RE THE JUDGE!**

DECISION: The Whalers, who enticed Jack to abandon an existing commitment to the Cougars, could not complain when Jack decided not to honor the improperly secured contract with the Whalers. The Whalers came into equity with unclean hands.

May this defense be used where a party seeking an injunction has deceived a player into signing a contract?

FACTS: Jack, a pro basketball player under contract to the Hoopsters wanted to play for the Dribblers. The Hoopsters, who had signed Jack to a contract in violation of NCAA rules, sought to enjoin Jack from leaving. The Dribblers asserted, "The Hoopster's had unclean hands in signing Jack while he still had college eligibility left." Were the Hoopsters granted an injunction? **YOU'RE THE JUDGE!**

DECISION: No. The court refused to grant injunctive relief to the Hoopsters, ruling that their action was intended to deceive others. Jack could play for the Dribblers.

If another team or league signs or seeks to sign a player already under contract for services to begin after his present contract expires, this may be interference. Can it be enjoined?

FACTS: Ken, a star quarterback for the Bulls, signed to play for the Fumblers in a new football league. His services were to begin after his contract with the Bulls expired. The Fumblers announced the signing and had Ken begin promoting Fumblers' season tickets. Although Ken would not play for the Fumblers until his present contract expired, could the Bulls enjoin Ken from such publicity for the Fumblers? **YOU'RE THE JUDGE!**

DECISION: Ken's primary duty was to the Bulls until his contract expired. The promotional work interfered with the Bull's right to his services. An injunction was granted.

However, where there has not been any publicity which unreasonably interfered with a player's present duties, then no injunction would be issued for a contract which was to take effect after a player's present contract expired.

AGENTS

SECTION C   **Worcester Times**   SPORTS

SPORTS AGENTS

In the early days of sports, players did not need representation in negotiating contracts with their teams. The reserve clause bound the players to one team for as long as that team desired. Players were given a "take-it-or-leave-it" offer. The players were happy to do what they did best and get paid for it, with free travel, publicity and short work hours.

Then, sports exploded. Enormous revenues from attendance and T.V. helped professional leagues to expand. Along with new teams came new stadiums.

The demand for players became greater than the supply. Salaries rose. Teams fought for players' services. Along with the rise in salaries came other benefits, such as "no-trade" and "no-cut" clauses. Unions were formed and players sought "free agency." They challenged the clubs for more freedom to choose for whom they would play. They now had bargaining power.

And, thus was born the **sports agent**—one who, with consent, represents an athlete in negotiating a contract for the player's services. And, although most dealings between players and agents have been proper and to the benefit of the players, not all have.

HAVE I GOT A DEAL FOR YOU!

Rights & Duties Of Agent & Player

What are the rights and duties of players and the agents who represent them in negotiations with their teams?

I WON'T PAY!

FACTS: John and Billie Joe, pro basketball players, hired agents to represent them in negotiations with the Knickerbockers.

John's agent, Cal, negotiated a substantial pay raise and incentives. But John fumed, "I'm not the highest paid forward, so I'm not paying him."

Billie Joe's agreement with his agent, Al, called for Al to manage Billie Joe's money. When it was found out that Al had used the money for his own private investments, Billie Joe sued. Al had made a substantial profit. What were Cal's and Billie Joe's remedies? **YOU'RE THE JUDGE!**

DECISION: Cal may sue for the agreed upon fee. Unless the agreement called for the agent to obtain the highest paid contract, he had fulfilled his duties to John.

Billie Joe was discharged from the obligation to pay his agent. He could rescind the contract, recover the ill-gotten profits made by Al and recover any other damages that he suffered.

An agent is required to use reasonable care and skill, to act in good faith and with loyalty, and to disclose all relevant information to the player. The player is under a duty to pay the agent, as agreed, for his services.

FACTS: Sidney, an agent, agreed to represent Paul and Bob in contract negotiations with pro hockey clubs. Without the player's knowing, Sid agreed to give the Slashers "first crack" at his clients in return for a fee. Paul and Bob then signed with the Slashers.

Paul and Bob found out about Sid's deal with the Slashers and also that his fee was too high."Can we rescind our contract with Sid and recover wages lost due to Sid not dealing with any other teams?" asked Paul and Bob.

In addition, Sid encouraged Dave to break his contract with his agent and let Sid represent him. Could Dave's agent recover damages from Sid? **YOU'RE THE JUDGE!**

DECISION: Paul and Bob should have agreed that they, and not the team, would pay the fee, and then, only as the players received their salary. The team should not have paid Sid's fee as this would suggest a conflict of interest—was the agent working for the team or the players?

Paul and Bob could rescind their agreements with Sid and receive any lost pay. Giving a team "first crack" at the player's services was a breach of the duties of reasonable care, good faith and loyalty. Sid failed to disclose information that the players should have had in negotiating their contracts.

If Paul and Bob can prove that had it not been for Sid's actions, they could have received higher wages and benefits, then Sid will be liable.

Furthermore, if Dave, at Sid's encouragement, broke his present contract with his agent and signed with Sid, Sid may be liable for any damages the other agent may have suffered in lost fees. This was contractual interference.

May an agent recover money that he gave a player while the player still had college eligibility remaining? An arbitrator ruled that the player did not have to repay the agent. The arbitrator voided the contract between the player and the agent because the agent violated regulations regarding agents soliciting collegiate players.

NCAA Rules

NCAA rules and regulations forbid an athlete from agreeing to be represented by an agent until his collegiate eligibility has expired.

> FACTS: Frank orally agreed to have an agent represent him. "You can represent me after the college season is over," he said.
>
> Bob signed an "offer sheet," offering to allow an agent to represent him in negotiations for a pro contract. To prevent Bob from violating NCAA rules, the agent didn't sign the agreement until Bob had completed his amateur eligibility. Did either of these athletes violate the rule prohibiting representation before their eligibility has expired? **YOU'RE THE JUDGE!**

> DECISION: Yes. Representation, whether written or oral, is prohibited. This prohibition includes entering into agreements (offer sheets) not effective until eligibility is up Both athletes violated the rule which is rationally related to the NCAA's objective of preserving amateurism in collegiate athletics.

All participants in Division I, NCAA basketball tournaments are now required to sign an affidavit stating that they have not signed with an agent (nor will they), during the tournament.

This action allows the NCAA to not just penalize the athlete's school, but to pursue the player and his agent for any damages which the school might suffer (loss of revenue from television coverage).

If, when signing an offer sheet, an athlete ceases to perform for his school, would the offer sheet would be enforceable by either the athlete or agent against the other?

> FACTS: An offer sheet between a college star, Rudy, and an agent was not disclosed. Rudy continued to play. Upon completing his amateur eligibility, Rudy signed with another agent. The first agent sued Rudy for breach of contract. Could the first agent recover the fees that he would have earned as Rudy's agent? **YOU'RE THE JUDGE!**

> DECISION: The defense of unclean hands was used in denying enforcement of the contract. The agent was wrong in signing Rudy before his eligibility was up, and, therefore, he should not benefit from his wrong.

NCAA rules also prohibit an athlete from: negotiating or signing a contract in a sport in which he intends to compete; asking to be placed on a draft list; accepting expenses or gifts from an agent; or receiving preferential treatment or benefits because of outstanding athletic ability.

FACTS: A college player, Frank, who had signed with an agent after his junior year, confessed, "I accepted cash and other favors. Can I still play for my college?" **YOU'RE THE JUDGE!**

DECISION: Frank was in violation of NCAA rules prohibiting him from signing with, or accepting anything of value from, an agent. He forfeited his remaining eligibility. Furthermore, the school could be required to forfeit games in which Frank had played.

However, recent rulings may alter these rules.

FACTS: Chris and Eddy, college football players, admitted, "We took money from agents." They both were declared ineligible to compete further for their college.

Chris petitioned the NFL for entry. NFL rules prohibit eligibility before an athlete's college class has graduated or before four years from when the athlete entered college.

Eddy wanted to have his college eligibility restored. Was either player successful? **YOU'RE THE JUDGE!**

DECISION: Previously, the NFL allowed the drafting of underclassmen who were either kicked out of school or off their team for infractions.

Here, the NFL agreed to draft Chris, made ineligible because of dealings with an agent.

Eddy was permitted to pay back the agent and—by becoming free of any contractual obligations—resumed his collegiate career.

To avoid prosecution, the players agreed to pay back part of their scholarships.

Does this mean that a college athlete can now violate the NFL draft eligibility rules and then, without any consequences, determine whether he wants to remain an amateur or turn pro?

An athlete may compete as a pro in any sport in which he does not participate as an amateur. But he is no longer eligible for any athletic scholarship. He may retain or talk to an agent for that sport only, provided he does not agree to be represented or does not accept anything of value. And an athlete may ask a pro league about his eligibility to be drafted.

FACTS: Tommy, a pro basketball player represented by an agent, John, signed a contract to play in a new league for a team partly owned by John. John had also represented Tommy in attempting to sign with his old team, the Dunkers.

Tommy protested, "John didn't represent me properly. He withheld information which would have affected my decision. I didn't know that he owned the new team." Tommy signed with the new league. Could Tommy rescind his contract with John and play for the Dunkers? **YOU'RE THE JUDGE!**

DECISION: Yes. "No man can faithfully serve two masters" whose interests are in conflict, noted one court. John had a duty to provide Tommy with the best representation. He also had a duty to provide his own team with the best players. These duties conflicted. John may be more interested in Tommy as a player than as a client. The failure to inform Tommy of every material fact that might have influenced his decision, was a breach of duty.

This duty may also be violated where an agent, who represents several players competing for positions on the same team, fails to inform the players of his competing representation.

Misrepresentation & Fraud

An agent may be guilty of **misrepresentation** if he intentionally makes a known and false misrepresentation of an important fact to the player which the player then relies on to his detriment.

FACTS: An agent represented his services to players as one of "total services." The agent said, "I will negotiate your contracts, take your paychecks and bonuses, pay your bills, make investments and put the remainder in trust for you."
   The agent signed players and then lost their money through gambling and bad investments. Was this fraud and misrepresentation? **YOU'RE THE JUDGE!**

DECISION: The agent, who deceived players into signing such agreements and misrepresented facts, was convicted of grand larceny. The players received judgments for the lost money, but never collected.

There have also been numerous cases where agents were able to recover commissions earned after the players they represented refused to pay for proper services.

Tampering

An agent who makes improper payments to an athlete may be charged with **tampering**—improperly interfering with another's rights (such as the rights of a school or of those presenting a game).

FACTS: Murray played college football for the Winitoka Tigers. While Murray had college eligibility remaining, an agent, Jansen, gave him money in hopes of representing him in the pros.

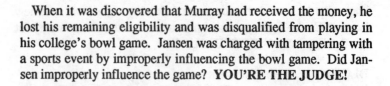

When it was discovered that Murray had received the money, he lost his remaining eligibility and was disqualified from playing in his college's bowl game. Jansen was charged with tampering with a sports event by improperly influencing the bowl game. Did Jansen improperly influence the game? **YOU'RE THE JUDGE!**

DECISION: Yes. Jansen was sentenced to one year in jail. He appealed. To avoid prosecution, Murray agreed to pay back part of his scholarship.

ODDS & ENDS....

Bye-Bye!

Unless otherwise agreed, a player is bound by the contract that grants his team the right to assign the player's contract to any other team in the league. However, as it is an individual performance that is bargained for, an athlete may not assign his duties to another.

FACTS: Dink, a pro basketball player for the Hoopsters, objected to being traded to the Ice Breakers. "The trade will disrupt my family and business. And, as my style of play will not fit in with the Ice Breakers, my ability to improve and my pay will suffer." Could Dink prevent the trade? **YOU'RE THE JUDGE!**

DECISION: Unless Dink had a no-trade provision in his contract, his consent to assignment in his contract and promise to "perform for his new team" will generally preclude any objections, including having to move, disruption of family, social and business ties, new climate or city or new teammates or management.

In order to be able to improve, a team needs this right to trade a player. Therefore, a team has broad discretion as to when and whether or not to assign a player's contract.

Regulation

The NCAA has adopted a registration program intended to help athletes select honest and competent representation.

FACTS: Jack, an agent, signed Dana to a contract representing her in negotiations for the Women's Pro Basketball League. Dana signed a contract before her college eligibility had expired. When she graduated, the agent began negotiations, but Dana had decided on another agent. Was the contract enforceable? **YOU'RE THE JUDGE!**

DECISION: No. An agent must register with the school of any player he seeks to represent and state on the contract, "Amateur athletes may jeopardize their athletic eligibility by signing this contract." And, to prevent early, undisclosed signings, an agent must, within five days, file any contract with an athlete with the school, or else it is void and unenforceable.

The NFL now requires all agents, seeking to represent players, to be certified. The maximum fees that may be charged for representation are set by the NFL. Arbitration may be used to settle any dispute.

Other sports provide some protection by requiring signed agreements between a player and an agent be filed. The NBA prevents any team from contacting players until their collegiate eligibility has expired.

In several states, agents must register and are subject to an investigation. Upon proper notice and hearing, their license or registration may be denied, revoked or suspended. This law does not cover agents for athletes in individual sports, such as golf or tennis.

In other states, agents who contact college athletes must obtain a license or face criminal charges.

The same basic principles for the formation of a contract—offer, acceptance and consideration—involving professional athletes applies to everyday agreements, such as those used to buy a home or car.

12

WE'RE IN LABOR

WHAT'S IT ABOUT?

A **union**—called a player's association in professional sports—represents players in bargaining with team owners concerning the player's wages, discipline, safety and other conditions of work in hopes of reaching a Collective Bargaining Agreement. *We're In Labor* explains this process and discusses unfair labor practices, arbitration and strikes.

Can a team renew a player's contract indefinitely? Do you know how players finally became "free agents?"

LET'S ORGANIZE!

The right to form a **union**—a group of people, organized to bargain with their employer concerning wages, hours, grievances, and other terms and conditions of employment—is given by the National Labor Relations Act (NLRA) of 1935.

FACTS: You played pro volleyball for the Spikers in the newly formed American Volleyball League (AVL). You and the other players were concerned about wages, hours, bonuses, job security, rules, safety, equipment and discipline. Several of the players announced, "We'll form a union to help us negotiate an agreement with the owners!" Could you do so?

DECISION: **YOU'RE THE JUDGE!**

This NLRA grew out of the decades of labor strife between labor and management, beginning in the late 1800's and early 1900's when workers attempted to organize the steel mills in Pittsburgh, railroad yards in Chicago and auto manufacturing plants in the Midwest.

Prior to the NLRA, there was no such requirement that employers bargain. Such refusals to bargain led to strikes which, in turn, led to violence as workers set up picket lines in an attempt to keep out non-union workers. Management "blacklisted" the strike leaders, hired non-union labor and employed strike breakers. Often, the purpose of these actions was to create violence rather than prevent it.

Labor disputes also began in sports at this time. The first baseball player's union, The Brotherhood, was formed to deal with owners of baseball teams in the National League over such issues as the reserve clause and salaries. When an agreement couldn't be reached, the players formed their own league. But when the new league failed, the players were offered higher salaries by the National League.

The **National Labor Relations Act (NLRA)** gave employees, "The right to form a union, to bargain collectively, and to engage in other activities necessary for their aid and protection."

> FACTS: A majority of the players in the American Volleyball League (AVL) formed a union and elected you president. Must the owners bargain with you over wages and other concerns? **YOU'RE THE JUDGE!**

> DECISION: If a majority of the workers (players) in a bargaining unit wish to be represented by a union, then the employers (league and clubs) are required to bargain with the union.

Enforcement?

The NLRA established a **National Labor Relations Board (Board)** to hear charges of, and to prevent, unfair labor practices, as well as to monitor elections to determine if a majority of employees (players) desire union representation. Must the two sides bargain in good faith?

> FACTS: One AVL owner admitted, "We cut that player because of his union involvement." The owners also refused to bargain in good faith (make an honest effort to resolve differences and reach an agreement) with the player's union. "What can we do?" you asked. **YOU'RE THE JUDGE!**

> DECISION: You would file an unfair labor practice charge. The employers may be guilty of not bargaining with you and for cutting a player due to his union activity. Both of those practices are prohibited.

PLAYER'S ASSOCIATIONS

How does a union become the representative of a group of players?

In professional sports, a player's union is called an association. At a secret election, if a **player's association**—such as all of the players in the AVL—receives a majority vote, then bargaining with the league may begin. If an agreement (Collective Bargaining Agreement) can't be reached—settling disputes between the players and the owners—a strike is likely to follow.

Disputes in professional sports grew out of player demands for more freedom and higher salaries. Babe Ruth was supposedly asked in the midst of the great depression if he felt badly asking for a larger salary than that of the President. "No," replied Ruth, "I had a better year than he did."

Were baseball owners required to bargain with any union representing their players?

FACTS: In 1946, the modern era of sports labor history began. Newspapers reported, BASEBALL PLAYERS ORGANIZE THE AMERICAN BASEBALL GUILD!

When the owners refused to bargain, the Baseball Guild went to the Board. Should the owners, subject to a strike, fine and injunction, be forced to bargain with the Guild? **YOU'RE THE JUDGE!**

DECISION: For the NLRA to apply, labor practices had to involve **interstate commerce**—play or trade among more than one state. Although baseball was played among the states, the Supreme Court held, "Baseball was not interstate commerce!"

Therefore, the Act did not apply. Owners could not be forced to bargain.

However, baseball then changed some league practices, instituting a pension plan, minimum salary, player representation system and a spring training allowance (called "Murphy Money" after the man who organized the Guild).

Player reps took requests and suggestions to the owners, but the owners were not required to bargain. Although a long way from being a union, this system was the forerunner to present day players' associations.

Professional sports leagues have been around for many years, The National League of baseball goes back to 1876. The National Hockey League (NHL) began in 1917. The National Football League (NFL)—first the American Professional Football Association—began in 1920. And the National Basketball Association (NBA) dates to 1946. However, unions representing professional athletes only date back to the 1950's and 1960's.

"How can we get more money and other benefits out of the own-ers?" asked the players.

FACTS: The key is to become a free agent—able to negotiate with any team—and thus have teams bid up your salary.

Owners fought to prevent free agency. "Through the draft and reserve clause, where the player was reserved to play for only that team holding his contract, his bargaining power was limited. He couldn't sell his services to any other team." How could the players become free agents? **YOU'RE THE JUDGE!**

DECISION: There were two ways a player might accomplish this. One was an antitrust suit, alleging that the player was being pre-vented from selling his service to the highest bidder. Second was a collective bargaining approach, in which the players would bargain with the owners in hopes of reaching an agreement that would give them free agency status.

It was not until the 1960's that the first collective bargaining agreements in sports were signed. But, it was still unclear whether the Board would hear disputes in pro sports.

The players' union in baseball asked the Board, "Will you please take jurisdiction and hear our cases?"

FACTS: In two cases, one involving the hiring of a union band at an Athletics' baseball game and the other involving major league umpires who wanted an election for union representation, the Board was again asked to hear the cases. Would the Board order an election to allow the umpires to bargain collectively with the owners? **YOU'RE THE JUDGE!**

DECISION: Yes. The Board indicated, "We find that professional baseball (as other pro sports) is an industry affecting commerce, and is subject to our jurisdiction." The Board ordered an election among the umpires, and in so doing markedly altered the future of player-league relations.

Players in all professional sports were now entitled to all of the rights and protection of the National Labor Relations Act (NLRA)—the right to: organize, designate a representative (Player's Associa-tion), and bargain collectively with the owners and the league.

NEGOTIATING AN AGREEMENT

Collective bargaining is the process of negotiations between la-bor (the league) and a union (the players) concerning the mandatory subjects of wages, hours, and other terms and conditions of employ-ment with the goal of arriving at an agreement or settling a dispute.

Any agreement between owners and a player's association covering wages, hours, and other terms and conditions of employment is called a **Collective Bargaining Agreement (CBA).**

Will any agreement reached bind all of the players, even those who are unhappy with it?

FACTS: The players of the AVL now had a player's association. In bargaining with the Owner's Council (representing the owners) a CBA was reached. Tony and several other players asked, "We're unhappy with the agreement. Is it binding on us? Can we negotiate for ourselves?" **YOU'RE THE JUDGE!**

DECISION: If the bargaining process produced an agreement, reached by good faith bargaining over mandatory subjects, in representations of the majority of the players, then the agreement will be binding upon all players, whether or not individual players are satisfied with all of the terms of the agreement.

UNFAIR LABOR PRACTICE?

The NLRA makes it an **unfair labor practice** for an employer (owner) to "interfere with employees (players) in the exercise of the players' rights to organize, to discourage membership or to refuse to bargain collectively." If an owner does so, will they be required to take whatever action is necessary to remedy the unfair labor practice?

FACTS: Several players testified, "The owners, in trying to break our union, cut players during a strike, disciplined others for taking part in union activities, interfered with our activities by trading and eliminating player reps, and advised players that any discussion of strike-related issues would result in a fine, suspension, or other disciplinary action." Were any of these acts unfair labor practices? **YOU'RE THE JUDGE!**

DECISION: All of these acts were unfair labor practices. The teams and their owners were enjoined from such actions, and were also required to take back the players with reinstatement of back pay.

Is it also an unfair labor practice for an employer or employees to refuse to bargain over mandatory subjects?

FACTS: NBA owners, in collective bargaining with the NBA Player's Association, offered, "Let's discuss the college draft, the option clause and compensation for free agents signed by another team."

The player's association refused to bargain, contending, "These subjects are non-mandatory. They all restrain players from bargaining freely for the rendering of their services." Did the player's union have to bargain? **YOU'RE THE JUDGE!**

DECISION: The college draft, option clause, and free agent compensation, all have a direct and substantial impact upon employment, duration, salary, and the ability to transfer between teams, and thus fall within "hours, and other terms and conditions of employment." Therefore, the player's association was under a duty to bargain over these subjects. Their refusal to do so was an unfair labor practice.

WAS THERE GOOD FAITH BARGAINING?

Good faith bargaining is the mutual obligation to meet at reasonable times, to make "relevant and necessary" information available and to confer in "good faith" over mandatory subjects.

FACTS: In bargaining, neither the AVL Player's Association, nor the owners would make concessions, nor could they reach an agreement. In addition, the owners refuse to negotiate over the colors and logos of the league's teams. Was this good faith bargaining? **YOU'RE THE JUDGE!**

DECISION: The players' union and the league only have to bargain in good faith; they are not required to either make concessions or to reach an agreement. Both parties must bargain over mandatory subjects, but are not required to bargain over permissive subjects, such as team colors or logos.

MANDATORY BARGAINING SUBJECTS

Mandatory bargaining subjects, which have to be bargained over by the player's association and owners, are those subjects covered by "wages, hours, and other matters affecting the terms and conditions of employment."

FACTS: The NBA established a maximum salary cap—the maximum amount any NBA team could pay its players.

When the N.J. Nets reached their salary cap, they were only permitted to offer their number one draft pick a one-year contract for a much smaller amount than other similar draft picks were receiving.

The player sued, alleging, "The draft and the salary cap are illegal restraints of trade—preventing me from earning my full, free market value." Did the draft and salary cap illegally restrain trade? **YOU'RE THE JUDGE!**

DECISION: No. The draft and salary cap were mandatory subjects—requiring them to be bargained over. They were bargained

over in good faith between the league and the player's association. Therefore, they are protected by labor laws. They could not be challenged as being antitrust—restraints of trade.

Mandatory subjects may cover a very wide range of items, from artificial turf to certain league rules. An employer may institute unilateral changes concerning permissive subjects of bargaining. For example, if playing rules are permissive subjects of bargaining, sports leagues could change them without first bargaining with the player's union.

FACTS: Major league baseball team owners instituted random drug-testing clauses into players' contracts. The players contended, "This is a mandatory subject, requiring bargaining and an agreement before they may be inserted into our contracts." Did the owners have to negotiate over the testing clauses? **YOU'RE THE JUDGE!**

DECISION: An arbitrator ruled that teams violated the collective bargaining agreement by including the testing clauses without negotiation with the player's union. However, testing would still be allowed where there was probable cause to believe that a player was using drugs.

The problem is distinguishing between what is mandatory and what is not. A player's union may think that most matters bear some relationship to wages, hours, and other terms and conditions of employment. Owners objected to this view "We shouldn't have to bargain over every little thing," they contended.

FACTS: The first major sports cases concerning mandatory bargaining subjects involved an NFL rule which fined any player who left the bench while a fight was in progress on the field.

As to the use of artificial turf, the players felt it was responsible for a number of injuries. Were these mandatory subjects requiring bargaining in good faith before their implementation? **YOU'RE THE JUDGE!**

DECISION: Yes. The Board held, "The rule to fine players was unilaterally implemented by the owners. It was an unfair labor practice."

The Board further concluded, "Artificial turf was a condition of employment and, therefore, a mandatory bargaining subject, but that the council had met its obligation of good faith bargaining by discussing the matter with the union."

Several years later, the NFL implemented both "sudden death" (to eliminate ties), and a new punt rule. The NFL Player's Association felt, "Both rules subject the players to an undue risk of injury and are a change in work conditions which should have been discussed beforehand." Should they have?

It was decided, "The playing rules were mandatory subjects for bargaining, but that the owners' invitation for the association's views satisfied their duty to bargain in good faith."

FACTS: Which of the following are mandatory subjects: wages, hours and other terms and conditions of employment? Which will require bargaining between owners and players?
• Disciplinary and safety rules.
• Scheduling—game rules and season length.
• Arbitration—salary, grievance & injury.
• Reserve system-draft, option, trades & free agency.
• Contract negotiations—salary, bonuses, guaranteed, no-cut, no-trade. **YOU'RE THE JUDGE!**

DECISION: Except for individual contract negotiations, all of these subjects require mandatory bargaining before they may be included in a collective bargaining agreement between owners and a player's association.

ATHENS NEWS
SECTION B

RESERVED!

"Through collective bargaining, the reserve system was drastically changed. For the first time, players were given rights concerning the draft, option clauses, free agency and salary.

The option clause and salary issues became subject to arbitration with results that were to 'free' the players from the restrictive reserve system of the past. Thus was born the **'free agent'**—a player playing out his option and becoming eligible to negotiate and sign with any team."

Collective bargaining led to agreements between owners and players providing for much less compensation for free agents.

In the NBA and NFL, a team with a restricted free agent player who has signed with another team in the league, may have a **right of first refusal**—where the losing team has the option of signing the free agent for the amount agreed upon between the player and the other team. However, in the NBA, this right will not apply to five year veterans. They automatically become free agents with no compensation to the player's former team.

If the player is not re-signed in the NBA, there is no compensation. In the NFL, the team losing a restricted free agent receives draft choices from the signing team. Unrestricted free agents, those not on a protected list, may bargain freely with any team. If signed, the losing team receives no compensation.

In baseball and soccer, there is no compensation for a lost free agent. In the NHL, if the two teams can't agree on compensation, then an arbitrator decides.

Although some sports require more compensation than others, all have helped players to increase their value by making their services more readily available to other competing teams.

PROTECTION FOR AGREEMENTS?

Antitrust laws might make **restraints of trade**—restrictions on a player's ability to trade his services with other teams—illegal. However, the labor law exemption to the antitrust laws provides, "Any agreement between owners and a player's association over mandatory subjects, if negotiated in good faith, is protected from antitrust laws."

FACTS: Players in the AVL contended, "Restrictions on our mobility to move between teams were illegal restraints of trade."

The owners replied, "The restrictions were mandatory subjects of bargaining, were bargained for, and therefore are protected by the labor exemption." The owner's negotiations were "take-it-or-leave-it." Was any agreement reached protected? **YOU'RE THE JUDGE!**

DECISION: The courts found that negotiations were unilateral and not bargained for in good faith. Therefore, the reserve system, including draft and compensation rules, was illegal. The labor exemption would not protect them until they were negotiated over in good faith bargaining.

To encourage resolve of disputes between owners and players over terms and conditions of work or the players' right to organize, "No injunction shall be granted, except as necessary, to prevent an irreparable injury."

ARBITRATION & GRIEVANCES

What is arbitration? **Arbitration** is a method of resolving disputes between owners and players in which parties submit their dispute to an impartial third party (arbitrator) for resolution— a decision. Will a court enforce any decision?

FACTS: The owners and players in the AVL negotiated an agreement (CBA) which had an arbitration clause to resolve disputes concerning salaries, injury and discipline. When Jose, a star forward for the Rockets, was suspended for abusing an official, he snapped, "I'll sue in court for reinstatement!" Could he? **YOU'RE THE JUDGE!**

DECISION: No. Where the parties agree to arbitration, the player and club lose the right to go to court, with narrow exceptions. Only if the arbitration clause does not extend to a particular claim can an injured party use the courts. However, the courts can be used to enforce any arbitration award.

A court will seldom vacate an arbitration award, unless the arbitrator "exceeded his authority, did not have jurisdiction to hear the matter, or where there was fraud or misconduct." If no jurisdiction is found, then a court will resolve any dispute.

IMPARTIAL ARBITRATION?

FACTS: The players in the AVL maintained, "We were forced to settle for a grievance system which calls for arbitration before the commissioner of all disputes dealing with discipline, salary, performance and trades. The commissioner was selected and paid for by the owners." Was this impartial arbitration? **YOU'RE THE JUDGE!**

DECISION: No. The commissioner had acted without authority and was not fair and impartial.

Collective bargaining agreements had diminished the commissioner's or president's power to matters relating to player contracts, discipline and the integrity of the game. They were replaced by the impartial arbitrator. Baseball, in 1970, selected its first impartial arbitrator for handling disputes.

Player contracts now had salary, injury, performance, conduct, dismissal and dispute clauses calling for impartial grievance or arbitration procedures.

GIVE ME FREEDOM!

Disputes over the reserve system in baseball led to the beginning of "freedom" for all professional athletes in team sports.

Generally, teams released a player only when he was no longer of use to them or of value on the trading block. Such was not the case with Ken Harrelson, who got into a dispute with Mr. Finley, the owner of the A's, for whom he played. Harrelson was fired, thus becom-

ing a free agent. The bidding was fierce; he wound up signing with the Red Sox for a substantial salary increase.

A few years later, Catfish Hunter and Finley also had a disagreement.

FACTS: In 1974, Hunter negotiated a contract with the A's. Finley refused to make some of the payments. Hunter claimed, "Since Finley breached the contract, it was void." The dispute went to arbitration.

Finley argued, "The arbitrators should allow me to make the payments due, thereby forcing Hunter to continue to play for my team." Did Finley breach the contract, making Hunter a free agent, and consequently able to deal with any team? **YOU'RE THE JUDGE!**

DECISION: The independent arbitrator treated the contract as void and released Hunter from any services under the contract, thus making him a free agent.

Bidding for Hunter's services was also fierce. Finally, the Yankees won out, paying Catfish substantially more than what he had earned with the A's.

Players were now aware of the gains to be made as free agents. They began to bargain more vigorously. Several refused to sign new contracts, deciding instead to play out their option year. And, although most eventually signed, a few didn't.

NORTHEASTERN LAW REPORTER

The year was 1975. Andy Messersmith, a pitcher for the Dodgers, decided not to sign a contract, but instead to play out his option. The Dodgers exercised their option to renew the contract for 1975 and Messersmith played under those conditions. When the season ended, Messersmith declared, "I am now a free agent, free to negotiate with any team for my services!"

Dave McNally, a pitcher for Montreal, also refused to sign a contract for the 1975 season, thereby forcing Montreal to renew his contract under the option clause.

The player's association filed a grievance, asserting, "Both players should be declared free agents." And to prevent other clubs from blacklisting them, they argued, "The language in the Player's Contract, 'The Club shall have the right to renew this contract for the period of one year on the same terms,' gave the club the right to extend the contract for one year only, at which time the player's relationship with the club was terminated."

The Dodgers responded, "When we exercised our option to renew the contract, the renewal was of all the terms in the contract, including the term which gave us the right to renew again, thus we could renew perpetually. Furthermore, Messersmith was on our reserve list, thereby preventing other teams from negotiating with him."

Were Messersmith and McNally free agents, or could the teams renew their contracts again, and again, and again?

The Arbitrator ruled that Messersmith and McNally were indeed free agents, free to bargain with any club, and that they were no longer on any reserve list, as that list applied only to players under contract. "The clubs did not have the right to renew any contract beyond the renewal period of one year."

McNally had retired, but Messersmith, after spirited bidding for his services, signed with Atlanta for a substantial salary increase.

This decision ended the reserve system as it had existed. Many players began to play out their options and negotiate with other teams for increased salaries.

In order to promote competition, fan interest and team identity, the baseball owners and the player's association created a new reserve system. Thus, although the reserve system remained, protected by the labor exemption to the antitrust laws, it was less restrictive. It gave players much more freedom to bargain with other teams.

What if the baseball owners decided to "hold down" the free agency market by not signing them?

FACTS: Owners of major league baseball teams refused to offer contracts to free agents, thus forcing them to re-sign with their original teams for less money.

The owners were found guilty of collusion and conspiracy in holding down salaries by stifling the free agency market. But what damages would the players receive? Monetary damages? Free agency again? **YOU'RE THE JUDGE!**

DECISION: Those players who did not have the opportunity to become free agents were declared free. Any team signing them would not have to compensate the losing team. Any free agent not signed could remain with his present team. All affected players could file for money damages.

Arbitration was now used to resolve many disputes such as: free agency compensation, contract disputes, performance, salary, discipline, waivers, fines, and injury grievances.

FACTS: "Johnson, a pro basketball player, was acting defiant, uncooperative and peculiar," testified an official. He was given a disciplinary suspension for his conduct.

The player's association explained, "Medical testimony at an arbitration hearing will show that Johnson should have been placed on the disabled list because of an emotional illness." Should the team have been required to submit the dispute to arbitration? **YOU'RE THE JUDGE!**

DECISION: Yes. The matter was submitted to arbitration. It was concluded, "Johnson should have been placed on the disabled list, instead of given a disciplinary suspension for conduct resulting from emotional illness."

STRIKES & LOCKOUTS

A **strike** (the primary weapon of the players)—is the act of refusing to work—as a means of forcing owners or a league to give in to player demands.

The primary economic weapon of the owners is the **lockout**—locking the players out of work—as a means of forcing them to agree with the owners.

Unless otherwise agreed, a lockout clause in a professional athlete's contract would prevent the player from being paid in the event of a labor dispute.

Collective bargaining agreements typically include a "no strike-no lockout" provision in which the player's union agrees not to engage in any strike or other action interfering with the operation of the league, and the league or any of its clubs agree that they will not engage in any lockout of players. When may players strike or owners lockout the players?

FACTS: Players in the AVL were unhappy with their Collective Bargaining Agreement (CBA). The agreement contained a no strike-no lockout provision. "Can we strike? What will happen if we strike before the agreement expires?" they asked. **YOU'RE THE JUDGE!**

DECISION: Strikes and lockouts will generally occur after a collective bargaining agreement containing the no strike—no lockout provision has expired.

The NLRA guarantees players the right to engage in strikes. Generally, no restraining order or injunction prohibiting a strike or lockout will be issued unless the strike or lockout occurs while an agreement is in effect.

Without the ability to enjoin strikes or lockouts, the effectiveness of arbitration or collective bargaining agreements would be greatly reduced.

There have been numerous strikes and lockouts in professional sports, most of them leading to additional benefits and to more freedom for players from the reserve system.

ODDS & ENDS....

Arbitration

FACTS: Babe and Lou couldn't agree with their baseball teams on salaries. They asked for salary arbitration. How will an arbitrator decide the matter?

Speedy, a star running back for the Dolphins, had an injury grievance with his team. The team warned, "He's ready to play. If he doesn't, we'll cut him."

Speedy responded, "I haven't recovered from an injury that I got while playing, and therefore, I should still be paid." How will arbitration resolve this matter?

A number of players from all sports were found to be gambling and fighting. How would they be dealt with? **YOU'RE THE JUDGE!**

DECISION: Baseball salary arbitration uses a "high-low" system where qualified players and their teams submit their offers to the arbitrator. The arbitrator chooses one or the other, with no room for change.

For injury grievances in football, each party presents his own medical opinion to an arbitrator. If the opinions differ, an impartial physician renders an opinion. These three opinions are then given to the arbitrator for a decision.

Matters involving the integrity of the game or player discipline are under the sole authority of the commissioner or president, whose decision is final and binding. A player or team may appeal the decision only to the commissioner or president, who may then conduct a hearing, receiving evidence upon which he will base his final decision.

The rulings that made baseball players free agents have had a great effect not only on professional team players' and others' salaries, but also on the price that you pay to see professional team sports.

13

ANTITRUST - ANTIWHO?

WHAT'S IT ABOUT?

Antitrust—AntiWho? examines **antitrust** in sports—practices designed to illegally monopolize a sport by restraining or preventing players from competing or by stifling competition.

Do you know which major sport is exempt from antitrust laws, or how such laws affect other sports?

ANTITRUST

FACTS: The Spikers were part of the new National Volleyball League (NVL), which had franchises in most major markets. Attendance and TV ratings were booming and, with no competition or large salaries, ticket prices were kept up.

Along came the United Volleyball League (UVL), attempting to franchise teams into some of the remaining markets. One UVL owner grumbled, "We're having problems competing with the NVL. They've signed most of the quality players." Even so, NVL attendance and TV ratings began to fall.

The NVL owners suggested, "Let's expand into the markets where the UVL has teams."

The NVL "proposed" to its arenas and equipment dealers, "Only sell your products and rent space to the NVL. After the UVL is driven out of business, there will be no competition. We'll take care of you." They all agreed.

The UVL contended, "The NVL and its arenas and equipment dealers are attempting to monopolize pro volleyball by illegally conspiring to restrain trade (by not renting the arenas and selling equipment to the UVL at a fair price), and by expanding with the sole purpose of eliminating us from competition."

The players of the NVL wanted increased salaries, more freedom and other benefits. But, because of the draft and reserve clause, the players couldn't deal with anyone else. This kept salaries down. The NVL attempted to stop the players from forming a union by breaking up meetings and refusing to bargain with them.

In an attempt to end these problems, the NVL considered offering the UVL the chance to be taken over by, or to merge their most solvent teams into, the NVL, thus eliminating the need for high salaries. With no competition, the NVL could once again have a monopoly in pro volleyball.

Was this **antitrust**—practices designed to prevent full and free competition in an attempt to eliminate competition, illegally monopolize pro volleyball, restrain competitors from competing for players, arenas and fans, and restrain players from trading their services to other teams?

DECISION: **YOU'RE THE JUDGE!**

Professional sports leagues have used the draft and reserve clause to distribute superstars among teams and thus maintain interest, balance and competition. This attempt to monopolize players' services by restraining their mobility is opposite the players' interest in being free to sell their services to the highest bidder.

Furthermore, a league may also attempt to exclude or restrain weaker competitors from competition for fans and media support.

These competing interests between players, teams and competitors may involve activity that is contrary to fair competition.

What must be shown to prove that an activity is unlawful? In determining whether any activity is unlawful, it must be shown that the activity unreasonably restrained trade or commerce, and that it was not exempt from antitrust laws.

FAIR COMPETITION & MONOPOLY

The first known case dealing with antitrust was decided in 1414.

FACTS: Richard was sued for breaching an agreement to not "use his art of a cloth dyer's craft within the town for half a year." He had sold the business and agreed, "I will ply my trade elsewhere so as to not take customers away from the new owner." Did such an agreement restrain Richard from his trade? **YOU'RE THE JUDGE!**

DECISION: The court reasoned that this was an attempt at a restraint which was void as being against common law supporting fair competition and protection of a free market.

Now the year was 1602. You were a judge in the courts of England and were called upon to hear the following case.

FACTS: Allen made and sold playing cards. But Queen Elizabeth had granted Darcy "the sole right to sell playing cards in England."

Darcy took Allen to court, alleging, "Allen is infringing on my exclusive right to sell playing cards." He asked that you "restrain Allen from his trade."

Allen responded, "Darcy's grant from the Queen amounted to a **monopoly**—exclusive control of goods (cards) or services (advice on using goods). Darcy's grant limits and restricts my right to purchase, sell, or exchange cards or advice." Will you dismiss Darcy's suit? **YOU'RE THE JUDGE!**

DECISION: Yes. You applied the common law and decided, "Darcy was attempting to monopolize the business of selling playing cards. This practice infringed on Allen's right, privilege, freedom and opportunity to engage in a trade. Darcy's grant, if it were allowed to stand with no competition, might lead to higher priced and poorer quality cards."

Furthermore, it would harm not only Allen and any future competitors, but would deprive the public of a choice of playing cards. Darcy's suit was dismissed. Allen could make and sell playing cards.

This developing law and the Statute of Monopolies (making most monopolies void or voidable) was merged into the common law of the new colonies in America.

Dissatisfaction with the common law's protection and, with concern over the abusive practices by corporate giants in the mid to late 1800's, led to not only the Sherman Antitrust Act, but to other antitrust laws as well.

SHERMAN ANTITRUST ACT

John Sherman, a U.S. Senator, felt that "businesses must conform to rules" to prevent unfair competition and, thus, promote free and fair competition and protect the public. This would give the little man a chance to compete with the giants.

So that the public might have better prices, service, quality, choice and innovative products, Senator Sherman proposed a bill to deal with illegal **trusts**—business firms combined for the purpose of controlling prices or eliminating competition—and, **combinations**—groups of businesses—that prevent full and free competition and tend to increase the costs to the consumer.

The bill, passed in 1890, was known as the **Sherman Antitrust Act.** It was an act opposing and aimed against trusts—antitrust—that would protect trade and interstate commerce against unlawful restraints and monopolies.

FACTS: Testimony proved, "The World Croquet League (WCL) illegally monopolized that sport throughout the U.S., and; the Western Horseshoe League (WHL) illegally monopolized that sport in California." Would the Sherman Antitrust Act prevent these monopolies? **YOU'RE THE JUDGE!**

DECISION: The Sherman Antitrust Act is a federal antitrust law, concerned with the regulation of activity in **interstate commerce**—trade of goods or services among different states. This act would prevent the WCL's monopoly.

If a monopoly exists solely within one state—**intrastate**—such as by the WHL, enforcement would have to be by state antitrust acts.

Section 1 of the Sherman Antitrust Act provides that every contract, combination of companies (teams), or conspiracy, which restrains interstate trade or commerce is illegal. This section requires that there be an agreement by more than one person or team.

FACTS: Did the NVL violate this section by conspiring to control prices (to eliminate competition) by restraining interstate trade and commerce between the UVL and the arenas and equipment dealers, and by expansion, designed to eliminate competition? **YOU'RE THE JUDGE!**

DECISION: These were violations of section 1 of the Sherman Act. There was an agreement between the owners and teams in the NVL.

Section 2 of the Sherman Antitrust Act provides that every person or team who monopolizes, or attempts, or conspires to monopolize interstate commerce shall be found guilty. Here, one person or team may act alone.

FACTS: Did the NVL conspire in an attempt to monopolize interstate trade or commerce in the professional volleyball market? **YOU'RE THE JUDGE!**

DECISION: The NVL, equipment dealers and arenas all violated Section 2 of the Sherman Act prohibiting conspiracies to monopolize.

Furthermore, the NVL's draft may have violated the Sherman Act as an attempt to monopolize pro volleyball by restraining players from trading their services to other teams.

A court may issue an injunction prohibiting such conduct.

CLAYTON ANTITRUST ACT

This act supplements the Sherman Antitrust Act and other existing laws against unlawful restraints and monopolies.

Section 2 of the **Clayton Antitrust Act** (1914) prohibits **price discrimination**—where a different price is charged to similarly situated buyers.

> FACTS: The equipment dealers and arena operators announced to the UVL, "You can buy our equipment or rent our arenas, but at higher prices than we charge the NVL." Was this discrimination? **YOU'RE THE JUDGE!**

> DECISION: The equipment dealers and arenas were guilty of price discrimination.

Section 3 of the Clayton Antitrust Act makes it unlawful to sell, or offer to buy, goods or services on the condition that the buyer will not buy from a competitor of the seller, or that the seller will not sell to any other, where the effect is to lessen competition and create a monopoly.

> FACTS: Were the NVL, equipment dealers and arenas in violation of this section where the NVL offered to the arenas and equipment dealers, "We'll rent or buy from you, if you will refuse to deal with NVL competitors." Would such practices be illegal? **YOU'RE THE JUDGE!**

> DECISION: As these practices will lessen competition and promote a monopoly, they are violations and illegal.

This is called a **boycott**— an agreement refusing or refraining to deal—sometimes called a group boycott or blacklisting.

Are player's unions permitted to solicit members or to strike? Must a league bargain with them?

Section 6 of the Clayton Antitrust Act permits unions (player's associations) and its members to carry out legitimate objectives, such as bargaining, soliciting and striking. Furthermore, the Act prohibits any injunction involving a dispute over terms or conditions of employment. This allows bargaining, soliciting and strikes, free from restraint.

Thus, the NVL can't prevent players from attempting to unionize, and the NVL would be required to bargain in good faith with any elected player's union.

> FACTS: Were the attempts by the NVL to prevent players from soliciting for union members, and their refusal to bargain, in violation of this section?

DECISION: **YOU'RE THE JUDGE!**

Section 7 of the Clayton Antitrust Act prohibits **acquisitions** (acquiring) or **mergers** (joining together) of teams where the effect may be to substantially lessen competition and create a monopoly.

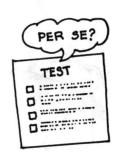

> FACTS: Will any acquisition by the NVL of any of the UVL teams, or any merger between the two leagues, be in violation of this section?

DECISION: **YOU'RE THE JUDGE!**

On a showing of irreparable harm, the Clayton Antitrust Act provides for an **injunction**—either a temporary or permanent restraining order prohibiting illegal activities.

> FACTS: May the NVL, dealers and the arenas be enjoined from any of their practices? **YOU'RE THE JUDGE!**

DECISION: If it is likely that the UVL will prevail, the court will issue a temporary restraining order, enjoining the NVL from illegal activities which may cause irreparable harm. If the UVL should win at trial on any of the above violations, the court would then issue a permanent injunction.

FEDERAL TRADE COMMISSION ACT

The Federal Trade Commission Act declares that unfair or deceptive practices in interstate commerce are unlawful. It established the **Federal Trade Commission** to aid in the enforcement of the Sherman and Clayton Antitrust Acts in protecting consumers as well as competitors.

THIS IS A TEST!

A court may use two tests in helping it determine if restraints on trade or commerce are unlawful.

The first is called the **per se** (by itself) **rule.** It holds that, "Certain agreements or practices, because of their deadly effect on competition and lack of any redeeming value, are unreasonable and illegal, without inquiry as to the harm they have caused or the reason for their use."

> FACTS: The NVL, in order to restrain trade (keep the UVL from competing), agreed to fix prices with the dealers and arenas, allocate territory and boycott the UVL. They also offered to acquire or merge with the UVL. Should these practices be governed by the per se rule? **YOU'RE THE JUDGE!**

DECISION: Agreements having no objective other than to restrain trade and whose principal effect is to govern prices or foreclose markets are undue restraints of trade and per se illegal.

The second test is called the **rule of reason.** It holds that, "The legality of restraints on trade is determined by weighing all factors, such as the effect of any restraints on competition, the power of the parties and the economic conditions or the evil believed to exist."

FACTS: Did the NVL, dealers and arenas, by their agreements and practices designed to close out the UVL, violate the rule of reason?

DECISION: **YOU'RE THE JUDGE!**

ANTITRUST EXEMPTIONS

There are exemptions to the antitrust laws, the most notable being baseball. All other sports fall under the umbrella of antitrust protection.

The effect of an exemption is to make "certain conduct free from the obligations of antitrust laws." These exemptions are permitted in the interest of promoting competition.

Baseball

When an arbitrator's ruling held that baseball's reserve clause only bound a player for a one-year option, the perpetual right to renew a player's contract after it expired (which the club owners had for ninety years) was eliminated.

In collective bargaining, a compromise was reached between the clubs and the players. The clubs retained exclusive rights to its players for a number of years, after which the players would become free agents. This allowed players greater mobility in selling their services to other teams.

Even though its reserve clause has been modified, baseball still enjoys its long-standing immunity from the antitrust laws.

FACTS: In 1922, the National League (NL) sought to monopolize baseball by buying some clubs and inducing the others in a rival league, except one, to join them. The one club left alleged, "This is a conspiracy to monopolize baseball by eliminating competition. Isn't it a violation of the Sherman Act?" **YOU'RE THE JUDGE!**

DECISION: The court held that baseball was purely a state affair. Any transportation across state lines was not the essential thing, that being the business of giving exhibitions of baseball.

The court reasoned, "Because the travel was incidental, it was not interstate travel and the exhibitions were personal effort and not trade or commerce." Therefore, the Sherman Act didn't apply!

Would the courts, in more modern times, do away with baseball's exemption to antitrust laws?

The Supreme Court affirmed baseball's exemption when Curt Flood, a major league baseball player, brought an action charging that the reserve clause in his contract significantly impaired his ability to sell his services. The Court applied the doctrine of **stare decisis**—a policy whereby the court does not disturb previous case rulings. And so, baseball remained an exception to the general rule applying antitrust laws to sports.

Would You Like To Merge?

FACTS: The Clayton Act prohibits mergers whose effect may be to lessen competition and create a monopoly. The American Football League (AFL) and the National Football League (NFL) wanted to merge, as did the American Basketball Association (ABA) and the National Basketball Association (NBA). Would such mergers lessen competition and create a monopoly? Should they have been allowed to merge? **YOU'RE THE JUDGE!**

DECISION: Congress approved the mergers, deciding, "Antitrust laws shall not apply to an agreement by which two leagues combine into an expanded league, if this would increase rather than decrease the number of professional clubs so operating." The assumption was that the other leagues would otherwise have folded.

Collective Bargaining Agreements

The Clayton Act provides, "Antitrust laws shall not forbid or restrain unions from carrying out their activities."

If a player's union and league undertake to settle player-related issues, and if they reach an agreement which is the result of good faith bargaining—**collective bargaining agreement (CBA)**,—will the labor exemption to antitrust laws prevent a court from reviewing the agreement?

FACTS: The players of the NVL organized a player's association and then began bargaining with the owners. After reaching agreement on a draft, the reserve system and other matters, the players—by majority vote—approved the agreement. The players, for these concessions to the league, received increased salaries, better retirement benefits, and less restrictive work conditions and rules.

Several players, unhappy with the agreement, sued, arguing, "The draft and reserve system are a violation of the antitrust laws

prohibiting the restraint of players from selling their services."
Was the Collective Bargaining Agreement (CBA) a violation of
antitrust laws? **YOU'RE THE JUDGE!**

DECISION: Although some issues, such as player-related rules
and movement of clubs are not protected by the labor exemption,
the players will have to abide by the agreement.

The judge noted, "The labor exemption reflects a policy strongly
favoring negotiation between clubs and players in order to resolve
disputes." The union's interest in insuring employment for the
players may require accepting restraints—such as a draft and option clause—on player mobility in return for the concessions of increased pay and other benefits.

Will any such agreement bind players who are not members of
the association (such as unsigned draft picks)?

Even though an amateur athlete is not part of the bargaining unit,
the courts have held that a player's association may bind these new
entrants to a league.

But, where leagues did not conduct good faith bargaining, the
courts rejected the league's right to protect its draft and reserve systems within the labor exemption. Proper bargaining then resulted in
exempt agreements.

What kind of approval is needed by a union? The labor exemption
will only be applied to those agreements which have been approved
by the union. Approval must be more than passive consent; it must
be the product of serious, good faith bargaining.

FACTS: Kapp, Smith, Mackey and other players alleged, "The
draft system, Rozelle Rule (which gave the commissioner authority
to determine compensation to a team for loss of a free agent), and
the standard player contract restrained our ability to market our services among competing teams." The player's union's approval of
these practices was not the product of good faith bargaining.
Would the labor exemption apply to these practices? **YOU'RE
THE JUDGE!**

DECISION: The court held, "These practices were not the product
of good faith, serious bargaining and therefore, not immune from
antitrust laws.

The annual player draft was a group boycott. The Rozelle rule was
a nonmandatory, illegal subject. The labor law exemption only applies to mandatory subjects of collective bargaining, wages, hours
and other terms and conditions of employment. "The league might
avoid further antitrust problems by entering into meaningful collective bargaining with the player's union," commented the court.

Sports Broadcasting Act

The **Sports Broadcasting Act of 1961** exempted professional sports leagues from antitrust attack for controlling the broadcasting rights to sporting events. This allowed each major pro sports league to pool and sell the rights of its clubs, as a package, to networks. Congress granted a limited antitrust exemption, but only to leagues.

FACTS: Several boxing promoters acquired all broadcasting and movie revenues from fights involving champions and contenders, and in all of the principal arenas where championships could be successfully held. They required each title contender to agree, as a condition to fighting for the championship, that if he won, he would only take part in title fights promoted by them. As a result, they had promoted 19 of the last 21 championship fights.

The Government charged, "The defendant promoters were engaged in interstate commerce because of their negotiations and ticket sales across state lines. By their acts and by eliminating the leading competing promoter, they restrained and monopolized trade." Did they? **YOU'RE THE JUDGE!**

DECISION: The defendants restrained trade (prevented other promoters from competing) and monopolized the promotion of championship fights, both in violation of the Sherman Act.

Blackouts

The Sports Broadcasting Act's exemption also covered television blackouts of NFL regular season and play-off games to protect ticket sales.

But this limited exemption is denied for any agreement prohibiting the televising of other games.

FACTS: NFL bylaws provided that no team would have their game broadcast by television or radio, within 75 miles of another team's home game or, away game broadcast at home without permission from the home team. The commissioner had an unlimited power to prevent any team from broadcasting any of its games.

The U.S. Government alleged, "This practice illegally restrains trade by restraining teams from the choice of where to broadcast their games." Was this practice illegal? **YOU'RE THE JUDGE!**

DECISION: The league's bylaws restrained the sale of broadcasting (trade) in interstate commerce, and were illegal. A new contract restricting the individual teams from determining where their games would be broadcast was also prohibited.

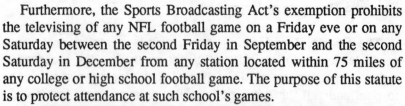

Furthermore, the Sports Broadcasting Act's exemption prohibits the televising of any NFL football game on a Friday eve or on any Saturday between the second Friday in September and the second Saturday in December from any station located within 75 miles of any college or high school football game. The purpose of this statute is to protect attendance at such school's games.

And pro football games not sold out 72 hours before the start of the game may be blacked out.

Can an NFL team prevent the televising of their games within their "home territory?"

FACTS: Two TV stations, one within 40 miles of Miami, and one not, wanted to televise Dolphins home games. Both signals reached into the 40 mile area. The NFL prohibited such televising.

The stations wanted to know, "Is such a prohibition an illegal restraint of trade—restraining us from carrying the games?" **YOU'RE THE JUDGE!**

DECISION: Agreements prohibiting the televising of an NFL home game, without permission, from within or without a team's home territory—40 miles in any direction—on the day when the team is playing at home are exempt from the antitrust laws. Teams needed this protection in order to protect gate sales.

Is baseball broadcasting also exempt from antitrust laws? Broadcasting of baseball does not fall within that sports exemption to the antitrust laws.

FACTS: An owner of a baseball team breached a contract with one radio station and then conspired with another to eliminate competition for the game's radio audience. Did baseball's exemption to the antitrust laws protect this conspiracy to restrain competition from broadcasting the games? **YOU'RE THE JUDGE!**

DECISION: Broadcasting, although related, is separate and distinct from baseball. It is not protected. The conspiracy could be enjoined or prohibited.

OTHER PROFESSIONAL SPORTS

Professional sports affect interstate trade by the sale of broadcast rights to games, and by employing and dealing with organizations, people and player's associations located throughout the country.

In cases involving the attempt to exclude or eliminate competition—monopoly (the refusal to deal with others)—group boycotts, and the use of a draft, courts have held that, except for baseball, all other sports are subject to antitrust laws.

Some cases have ruled on underlying issues in addition to holding that antitrust laws apply to that sport and therefore, the sport is not exempt from antitrust laws.

Auto Racing

FACTS: In an Indianapolis 500 race, the STP car completely out-ran the competition. Following that race, the United States Auto Club (USAC), sanctioning organization for professional championship auto races, changed its rules and required modification of the car's engines.

STP challenged the rule change as, "An unlawful exercise of monopolistic power in restraint of trade, in that it discriminated against us and is unreasonable." Would the court enjoin USAC from enforcing this rule? **YOU'RE THE JUDGE!**

DECISION: No. The court decided, "The rule change was a proper exercise of USAC's power to promote equal competition in auto racing." Furthermore, USAC did not have monopoly power as membership in USAC was not required and the rule change applied equally to all participants.

Bowling

FACTS: Several bowling centers brought an antitrust action against Brunswick, one of the two largest equipment manufacturers and the largest operator of bowling centers in the U.S.

They contended, "The defendant Brunswick, by acquiring competing bowling centers that could not pay for equipment bought from Brunswick, might lessen competition and create a monopoly." Was this a monopoly? **YOU'RE THE JUDGE!**

DECISION: No. Had the acquired centers secured financing elsewhere and remained open, the plaintiffs would have suffered the same loss. "Mere size, without unlawful intent or conduct, is not a violation of antitrust laws," noted the court.

Boxing

Several boxing promoters were found in violation of the Sherman Act for monopolizing the promotion of championship fights, and for restraining others from promoting such fights.

Football

FACTS: A pro football player broke the reserve clause of his contract and signed with a team in a rival league. When suspended from playing in the NFL, he brought an action arguing, "The NFL conspired to monopolize pro football by blacklisting me from playing."

The NFL countered, "Pro football was not meant to be included within the reach of the antitrust laws." Was pro football subject to the antitrust laws? **YOU'RE THE JUDGE!**

DECISION: Yes. The court held that pro football operated in interstate commerce and was not exempt from such laws.

Golf

The Professional Golfers Association (PGA), which sponsors professional golf tournaments, adopted eligibility rules limiting entry by excluding golfers who did not meet certain requirements. This was thought necessary because there was neither enough time nor space on the golf courses to accommodate a large field.

Art, a pro golfer, complained, "My contract to play on the tour was terminated because of my lousy play." He brought an action alleging, "The PGA conspired to monopolize professional golf tournaments. Furthermore, they restrained me from my trade—playing golf."

The court held, "The PGA is entitled to adopt reasonable measures to keep tournaments to a manageable number. In so doing, they treated all golfers alike." There was no attempt to restrain golf pros or to monopolize tournament golf.

Several other cases have dealt with golf equipment.

FACTS: Polara developed a golf ball that was said to limit hooking and slicing by self-correcting in flight.

The U.S. Golf Association (USGA) refused to approve the ball for its competitions, stating, "A legitimate goal of the USGA is to preserve the character and integrity of the game."

Polara sued, claiming the USGA conspired to restrain and restrict the sale of their ball. Was this an illegal restraint of trade? **YOU'RE THE JUDGE!**

DECISION: The court found no illegal restraint of trade. It held that the USGA acted "solely in accordance with its responsibilities to the game of golf" in refusing to approve the golf ball. The USGA felt that the ball would change the competitive nature of the game.

Polara appealed and the case was settled. The USGA will continue to make specifications for equipment.

In other cases involving golf equipment, the USGA has challenged putters and "square-grooved" golf clubs, which allegedly allow a player more control of the ball.

FACTS: The USGA adopted a new method of measuring the grooves and was considering outlawing clubs with such grooves in

USGA tournaments. The manufacturers contended that the USGA conspired to restrain and restrict the sale of their clubs. Was this an illegal restraint of trade?

DECISION: **YOU'RE THE JUDGE!**

Hockey

Peters wanted to enter a hockey team in the NHL. When denied, he brought an action alleging that the defendants, owners of three of the six teams in the only pro hockey league, conspired to restrain commerce and to establish a monopoly of pro hockey teams. Did they?

The action was barred by the **statute of limitations**—requiring that actions not brought within a specified time are to be dismissed.

Soccer

FACTS: The NFL, in the interest of protecting its clubs, sought a ban requiring NFL owners who also owned North American Soccer League (NASL) teams to sell their interests in the NASL clubs.

The NASL alleged that this would deprive them of owners and thus restrain the business of pro soccer. Would the ban violate the antitrust laws? **YOU'RE THE JUDGE!**

DECISION: Yes. The rule of reason test required the court to consider all factors of the case, such as: effect on competition, power of parties, whether the ban was reasonable, and its purpose. The ban might lessen competition if the NASL couldn't find acceptable new owners. The NFL was the more powerful of the two leagues. The ban was held anticompetitive, thus NFL team owners did not have to sell their interests in NASL teams.

Tennis

A manufacturer brought suit against the United States Tennis Association (USTA) for banning its "double-strung (spaghetti) racket." The USTA claimed, "The racket will significantly alter the flight of a tennis ball by imparting exaggerated topspin, thus defeating competitive goals of the game."

The court found no restraint of trade. It was a legitimate goal of the USTA to preserve the character and integrity of the game of tennis.

Wrestling

FACTS: Harold was a pro wrestler and a promoter. He was informed, "You have to pay a 'booking fee' to the Wrestling Alli-

ance before you can promote any matches in which you wrestle."

Harold alleged that this action prevented him in his business of promoting wrestling matches. "It damaged my ability to earn an income," he fumed. Was this a conspiracy to monopolize pro wrestling? **YOU'RE THE JUDGE!**

DECISION: No. The court found that the group did not have the power to remove or exclude Harold. It only received a small booking fee. In fact, Harold's income increased the year after the action was brought.

ACQUISITIONS & NATURAL MONOPOLIES

Before the American Football League (AFL) and the American Basketball Association (ABA) were absorbed into the NFL and the NBA respectively, there was litigation. Both AFL and ABA teams alleged that the older leagues were restraining trade by preventing them from flourishing, and that mergers might lessen competition and create a monopoly.

The court, in the AFL versus the NFL case, looked to see how many desirable, potential franchise areas were open to the newer AFL. They found that the NFL had not dominated the market. There were many desirable areas still open. The AFL's case was further weakened by its ability to obtain a television contract and to sign star college players. Thus, the NFL succeeded.

Do you know what a natural monopoly is?

FACTS: You owned the only sporting goods store in Worcester, a small rural town. You trained your employees to "properly fit and instruct customers."

A new sporting goods store, Mr. Compete, moved into town. When unsuccessful, Mr. Compete sued, alleging, "You monopolized the sporting goods business in Worcester, prevented us from competing, and restrained trade by hiring all of the competent employees." Did you restrain trade by creating a monopoly? **YOU'RE THE JUDGE!**

DECISION: Your sporting goods store may be what is called a "natural monopoly." It is in a town where only one store can survive. As long as you have done nothing to abuse this power that you have, there will be no antitrust problems.

Such may also be the case where a new professional sports league challenges the power of an older, more established league. There may not be enough interest to support two leagues and the fans will naturally want to see the best perform.

FACTS: The United States Football League (USFL) filed an anti-trust suit against the NFL, alleging that the NFL monopolized player and TV contracts and stadium leases, thus making successful entry into pro football impossible. They asked the court to break up this monopoly and permit the USFL to have access to stadiums. Did the NFL have a natural monopoly? **YOU'RE THE JUDGE!**

DECISION: The court found that the NFL had a "natural monopoly," which is permitted. Only one league could survive. The USFL, because of mismanagement, was responsible for its own downfall. The USFL was awarded $3 in damages!

The USFL then decided to suspend their football operations.

ODDS & ENDS....

Baseballs & Bubblegum

FACTS: Rawlings had a contract to manufacture all Major League Baseball (MLB) baseballs. MacGregor, who wanted to bid on the ball contract, alleged, "By only allowing one manufacturer of balls, MLB is restraining trade."
    For quality control reasons, MLB insisted on only one supplier. Was this a restraint of trade in denying others an opportunity to furnish the baseballs?

DECISION: **YOU'RE THE JUDGE!**

Selling baseball trading cards packaged with bubblegum has also brought charges of a restraint of trade.

FACTS: Fleer, a bubble gum manufacturer, sued another manufacturer, Topps, and MLB, contending that "Licensing agreements between Topps and MLB excluded Fleer from selling baseball trading cards."
    The agreement between Topps and MLB had no effect on the sale of trading cards with low-cost products other than bubblegum. Furthermore, Fleer could negotiate with minor league players, and could also attempt to persuade major league players from renewing their agreement with Topps. Was such an agreement a restraint of trade? **YOU'RE THE JUDGE!**

DECISION: The court found no unreasonable restraint of trade, nor any conspiracy to monopolize the trade of baseball cards.

Through negotiations, there are now several manufacturers selling packaged bubble gum and baseball cards.

The Sherman Antitrust Act—to promote free competition—was passed so that the public might have better prices, service, quality, choice and innovative products.

14

AM I ELIGIBLE?

WHAT'S IT ABOUT?

Am I Eligible? reveals attempts by professional athletes to become eligible to participate in individual sports, such as tennis and golf; or to participate, by way of a draft, in team sports, such as baseball. It also discusses "hardship," discipline and players' rights. Do you know what the hardship rule is?

BOYLSTON NEWS   JUNE 7, 1972

Jan cried, "I failed to qualify at qualifying school for the PGA pro golf tour!"

"I had my playing rights taken away because of poor play." said Ben sadly.

"I've always dreamed of playing pro football," Michael sighed, "but I wasn't drafted or given a try-out."

Johnson explained, "I wanted to play pro ball at home for the Cowboys, but was drafted by the Saints."

All of these players felt that the rules governing their eligibility and participation either boycotted them from participating at all or restrained them from playing for the team of their choice. Should the players have been allowed to participate, or to play or negotiate with any team?

ELIGIBILITY & THE DRAFT

Athletes participating in individual sports are limited by rules governing both admittance and the retention of any right to participate.

In team sports, athletes are limited both in their entrance to league and in their freedom to negotiate with teams in that league. And, they are required to participate in a player draft. This is a system where, generally, teams select players in the inverse order of how the teams finished in the previous year's standings.

Do you know how a professional sports team drafts its players?

FACTS: The Bucs finished with the worst record in pro football and the Cavaliers with the worst record in pro basketball. Who will receive the first draft pick in each sport? **YOU'RE THE JUDGE!**

DECISION: In football, the team with the worst record chooses first, and so on, with the championship team selecting last. However, any team may trade its draft choice. The team receiving it, even if the championship team, will then draft in that team's place.

In basketball, a lottery is used in which the bottom teams draw for the first several picks. The remaining teams then draft in inverse order of their finish, with the champs drafting last. Again, draft picks may be traded.

This procedure is continued throughout. However, many "rounds" are necessary. A round is completed when each team, or a team receiving that team's draft choice, has selected a player.

The team drafting a player has exclusive negotiating rights to that athlete. No other team in that league may negotiate with the player without the drafting team's permission. If there is a competing league, an athlete may be chosen and negotiate with either league. What if a drafted player won't sign?

FACTS: Holloway was drafted by the Celtics, but declared, "I won't sign!" How long would the Celtics hold their rights to sign him? Did Holloway become a free agent by not signing? **YOU'RE THE JUDGE!**

DECISION: A team's rights to a drafted player are no longer perpetual. If a team does not sign a drafted player within one year, the player could then be drafted by any team in the next draft. If, again, the player is not signed, he would become a **free agent**- able to negotiate and sign with any team.

Thus, eligibility rules may restrict an athlete in different ways. An athlete in an individual sport is restricted in his ability to enter a sport, while an athlete in a team sport may be restricted in his choice of a team.

TEAM SPORTS

Each professional team sport has its own eligibility rules concerning an athlete's ability to participate.

Baseball

Major league baseball holds two drafts a year, one for high school and four-year college players, the other for junior college players.

> FACTS: Abe went to high school, Ben to a four-year college and Charlie to a junior college. They all wanted to play pro baseball. "When will we be eligible to be drafted?" they all asked. **YOU'RE THE JUDGE!**

> DECISION: High school seniors or students whose eligibility has expired are eligible for the draft.
> Any draft choice who enters and remains in a four-year college without signing a contract cannot be drafted again until after his junior year or until he turns 21. A four-year college student may become eligible by quitting school or transferring to a junior college.
> A junior college player is eligible for the draft at any time, except during the school's baseball season.

If any one of them is drafted, but not signed, they are again eligible for the next draft.

Basketball

When does an athlete become eligible for the NBA draft? Generally, a player becomes eligible for the NBA draft when his college eligibility expires. However, any player, including a high school senior, may give up his remaining amateur eligibility to be drafted.

This is called the **hardship rule.** An athlete simply declares "hardship" and becomes eligible for the draft.

> FACTS: The NBA "Four Year Rule" provided, "No player is eligible to be drafted, or to play in the NBA until four years after his class has graduated from high school."
> Haywood signed a contract with an NBA team. The commissioner rejected the contract as Haywood had only been out of high school for 3 years. Haywood sued, arguing that the rule restrained trade "by denying me the opportunity to earn a living." Was the rule illegal? **YOU'RE THE JUDGE!**

> DECISION: Yes. The court held, "The rule preventing Haywood from being drafted or negotiating with any team was an unreasonable restraint of Haywood's right to earn a living by selling his services to play basketball." The rule was illegal.

For similar reasons, the court also found that the NBA draft violated antitrust laws. However, through collective bargaining, a modified draft was agreed to between the league and players.

If a player asks to be drafted, but isn't, is he still eligible to play in college?

A player asking to be placed on the league's draft list forfeits any remaining college eligibility, even if he withdraws his name from the draft or is not drafted.

Hockey

FACTS: An NHL rule prohibited a player with only one eye, Weldon, from playing professional hockey. Weldon sued, alleging a group boycott for restraining him from playing. Was the rule illegal? **YOU'RE THE JUDGE!**

DECISION: "No. It was a valid safety precaution," ruled the court.

Any amateur who turns 18 by September 15 is eligible for the NHL draft. If a drafted player enters college rather than sign a contract, he remains the property of the team that drafted him until six months after he graduates or leaves school. Unsigned players not entering college are subject to two more drafts, after which they become free agents, able to negotiate with any team.

The World Hockey Association (WHA) used to have a different age limit.

FACTS: Ken Linesman, 19, was prevented from playing in the WHA due to a rule prohibiting persons under the age of 20 from playing. He sued, arguing, "The rule denied me the opportunity to earn a living. It's a group boycott in that the NHL conspired to refuse to deal with athletes under the age of 20." Was the rule a boycott? **YOU'RE THE JUDGE!**

DECISION: Yes. This was a classic case of a **per se** illegal **group boycott**—the WHA and its teams refusing to deal with certain players. If an injunction was not granted, Linesman would have suffered irreparable harm in not being able to earn a livelihood.

Soccer

The Major Indoor Soccer League (MISL) holds its draft after the end of the college season. Any drafted, but unsigned player, is eligible for the next draft. A player then drafted, but unsigned until the next draft, becomes a free agent, able to negotiate with any team.

Football

The NFL's rules are the most restrictive. They hold that only players whose college eligibility is up or whose college class has graduated are eligible for their draft. Loss of eligibility (by dismissal, withdrawal or by signing with another league) generally does not qualify a player for the NFL draft, unless he otherwise meets their eligibility rules.

Several players have been admitted after petitioning the league for early eligibility. Would a challenge to the NFL's eligibility rules for preventing an athlete from earning a living be successful?

FACTS: Walt Glen, a star college player, said, "Players in other sports are allowed to play before their college eligibility is up. I want to play in the NFL after my junior year." He challenged the NFL's eligibility rule as being a group boycott for refusing to deal with him, alleging, "The rule is preventing me from earning a living." Was the eligibility rule a restraint of trade?

DECISION: **YOU'RE THE JUDGE!**

Any player eligible for the NFL draft, but not then chosen, immediately becomes a free agent able to negotiate with any team. However, this is generally because the player lacked sufficient skills. Therefore, the demand for his services may be minimal.

For a player who has been drafted, the original drafting team retains exclusive rights for two years, after which the player becomes a free agent, able to negotiate with any team. However, a player may be drafted and negotiate with a team in another league.

FACTS: Jim Cousins, who was drafted by the Bills, explained, "I signed with the Canadian Football League (CFL) for two years. After that contract expired, Houston, in the NFL, offered me a contract. Can I negotiate with them or any other team in the NFL?" asked Cousins. **YOU'RE THE JUDGE!**

DECISION: Cousins could negotiate with any team, subject to the original team's right to match any offer the player received. The Bills matched the offer and then traded Cousins.

The USFL, which suspended operations, had eligibility rules similar to those of the NFL, but their eligibility rule was challenged.

FACTS: Walker sought an exception to the USFL's eligibility rule prohibiting him from playing before his college eligibility was up.

He sued, arguing, "The USFL's rule prohibiting the signing of underclassmen is a group boycott—a refusal to deal—and illegally restrains the players' opportunity to earn a living." Was Walker allowed to play? **YOU'RE THE JUDGE!**

DECISION: Yes. The USFL's regulation barring the signing of underclassmen was declared an "illegal restraint of trade." The USFL allowed Walker to play after his junior year of college.

Will the draft deprive an athlete of being able to negotiate with any team to earn the best living possible?

FACTS: Smith was drafted by, and played for, the Redskins. After a career-ending neck injury, he filed an antitrust suit claiming, "If it had not been for the draft, I could have negotiated a contract containing injury protection provisions." Should Smith have recovered any damages for not being able to negotiate a better contract? **YOU'RE THE JUDGE!**

DECISION: Although the court found the draft to be an illegal group boycott and an unreasonable restraint of trade, it nevertheless ruled, "There was not enough evidence to show that had there been no draft, that Smith could have negotiated a better contract."

INDIVIDUAL SPORTS

Athletes in individual sports, such as bowling, golf and tennis, may also allege that eligibility rules improperly restrained or prevented them from the opportunity to earn a living by participating.

FACTS: The Women's Tennis Association (WTA) announced that, "Girls of any age are allowed to participate in professional tennis tournaments, but those under a certain age must take rest periods from the tour to pursue an education."

Christina, 16, didn't want to miss any tournaments, nor did she desire to continue with school. The state law where she lived allows the "discontinuance of school at age 16."

Christina challenged the WTA rule as being a boycott which denied her the right to earn a living. "Do I have to continue school?" she asked.

DECISION: **YOU'RE THE JUDGE!**

Operators of a bowling house and a billiards hall attempted to induce competitors to refuse to deal with other establishments. When the competitors competed at other establishments and then sought to enter the operators' tournaments, they were refused. The courts found these practices illegal boycotts.

Other players, deprived of their livelihood, have not been so successful in alleging that a rule excluding them from participation was an unreasonable refusal to deal with them.

FACTS: A U.S. Lawn Tennis Association (USLTA) rule threatened to bar any player from sanctioned tournaments if the player

signed to play in non-association sanctioned tournaments. Held-man felt that her threatened suspension would cause her a financial loss. Was the rule illegal? **YOU'RE THE JUDGE!**

DECISION: No. Uniformity in playing rules and competition of high caliber and ethical standards were proper concerns. Players were given **due process**—a fair and impartial hearing, with the right to be represented and the right to appeal.

In a similar case, U.S. Trotting Association (USTA) members were prohibited from racing horses in non-association sponsored meets. They alleged a group boycott—that they were being illegally prohibited from racing—but the court found the rule reasonable and necessary to ensure that races were free from illegal or improper conduct.

Can an athlete be suspended for having a "physical disability"?

FACTS: Juan had been a competent jockey for several years before it was discovered that he had only one eye. When suspended, he sued, alleging a group boycott for preventing his playing. Was the rule prohibiting him from competing a valid safety rule?

DECISION: **YOU'RE THE JUDGE!**

Pro golfers have also been denied eligibility for not meeting performance requirements. One court observed, "PGA rules are reasonable in attempting to keep the number of players at a manageable number so as to maintain a high level of competition, free from being bogged down by incompetent players."

Rules regarding racing cars have also been found to be reasonable.

FACTS: An STP car, which had outrun its competition in the Indy 500, was required to change engine specifications. The rule applied to all participants. Was the rule reasonable? **YOU'RE THE JUDGE!**

DECISION: The rule, adopted to achieve competitive races, was reasonable and not in restraint of trade.

HAVE YOU BEEN BEHAVING?

Disciplinary rules involving suspension from competition may be ruled an illegal boycott. Restraining an athlete from the right to play and earn a living is, in effect, refusing to deal with the athlete during the suspension.

FACTS: Lillian, a pro golfer, was suspended from the Ladies Professional Golf Association (LPGA) for allegedly cheating (moving her ball). Initially, a board comprised of fellow players heard Lillian during an investigation, then issued a fine and probation. Later, without a hearing, Lillian was suspended for one year. She sought an injunction preventing her suspension on the grounds that the LPGA's action illegally prevented her from earning a living. Did it? **YOU'RE THE JUDGE!**

DECISION: Yes. Suspending Lillian was a per se restraint of trade. There was no hearing or due process, and since members of the board were fellow competitors, they stood to gain financially from her suspension. The plaintiff was granted an injunction preventing the association from suspending her from play.

A league or association needs, however, to have self-regulation in order to insure that their competitions remain free of illegal and fraudulent activities which might erode fan support.

FACTS: A pro basketball player admitted placing bets on his team to win. He was suspended under a clause in his contract prohibiting gambling.

When he applied for reinstatement and was denied, he brought an action, charging, "The NBA conspired to restrain me from earning a living." Was the rule reasonable and necessary? **YOU'RE THE JUDGE!**

DECISION: The court found that the rule was reasonable and necessary for the survival of the league in avoiding even the slightest connection with gambling. There was no conspiracy in restraint of trade.

Must a player faced with suspension for an alleged violation be given a hearing?

A court must determine if the interest an authority seeks to protect is proper, if reasonable procedures were followed in determining whether a violation had occurred, and if the player was given due process—a fair and impartial hearing with representation.

FACTS: Bill Nance, a pro bowler, was suspended for knowingly bowling with another bowler who had changed his name in order to obtain a higher handicap, and for accepting ill-gotten prize money.

Nance sued for readmittance, charging, "The suspension is unfair. They're preventing me from earning a living." Were the restrictions an illegal restraint of trade? **YOU'RE THE JUDGE!**

DECISION: The court found no conspiracy, and furthermore, followed a general policy of the court not to review a suspension from voluntary associations unless there is bad faith, which was not found.

YOU'RE RESERVED!

An option clause generally gives a club in professional team sports the right to renew a player's contract for one additional year. And a club could renew a contract for as long as it chose to. Players had to sign the contracts containing this clause or not play.

FACTS: You were a pro baseball player and asked to sign a contract containing the following clause:

"The Player grants the Club a perpetual right to renew the Player's contract. If the Club renews the Player's contract, it will contain the same terms, except as to salary, which shall be determined by mutual agreement.

The Player agrees that the Club shall have the right to enjoin him by injunction from playing for any other team."

Was this an illegal restraint of trade, perpetually prohibiting you from dealing with any other team?

DECISION: **YOU'RE THE JUDGE!**

Reserve and option clauses have since been changed. Players now have more freedom to trade their services. But first, a bit of history leading up to the modern day "reserve system."

In the first reserve system in 1879, the National League baseball clubs adopted a secret agreement. Each owner could reserve or protect players who were placed on a reserved list, with other teams agreeing not to negotiate or attempt to hire another team's players unless given permission.

When this clause was inserted into players' contracts, the players objected.

They organized the first union, the National Brotherhood of Professional Players. The union demanded the end of the reserve clause. When the owners refused, the Player's League was formed.

FACTS: When two players, Ewing and Ward, sought to "jump" to the Player's League, their owners attempted to prevent them by pointing to the reserve clause in their contracts.

Ewing and Ward contended, "The agreement has nothing to do with the Player's League. Besides, the reserve clause is unfair." Would the court prevent Ewing and Ward from jumping leagues? **YOU'RE THE JUDGE!**

DECISION: The reserve clause could not prevent the players from playing for a team that was not part of that agreement. The teams in the Player's League had not agreed to reserve players.

The court also held that the right to reserve was perpetual and, therefore, "too unfair and vague to enforce."

The owners then changed the reserve clause to permit them to re-new the players' contracts. Later leagues in other pro sports adopted similar restraints on players' mobility.

How would the courts interpret this "right to renew" option? Was it too harsh or one-sided in favor of the owners?

FACTS: Heyman played semi-pro basketball for the Capitols. When he signed to play in the newly formed ABA, the Capitols sought an injunction to restrain him. Heyman had signed a contract giving the Capitols the option to renew the contract for a one-year period. Did the court grant the injunction? **YOU'RE THE JUDGE!**

DECISION: No. The contract provided that if the Capitols exercised their option and renewed the contract, Heyman's salary could be fixed by the club. And, while binding Heyman for one year, the Capitols could terminate the contract at will. The court found this to be too harsh and one-sided.

When several players in the NBA attempted to sign contracts with teams in the American Basketball League, NBA teams sued, alleging, "Under the players' contracts, the clubs have a 'right to renew' option, binding the players to play for them for the next season, whether or not they signed new contracts."

Could this option be perpetually renewed? When the players sued, the court held that the right to renew was valid, but only for one year.

FACTS: Harris had played football for the Cowboys in the NFL. In violation of the option clause in his contract, he signed and be-gan playing for the Dallas Texans of the AFL.

Peters, under contract to the Islanders, sought to jump to the newly formed World Hockey Association (WHA). Could Harris and Peters be enjoined from playing for the new leagues? **YOU'RE THE JUDGE!**

DECISION: The courts granted temporary injunctions, finding, "The clubs' exercise of their options granted them a right to renew the contracts for one year."

The players had voluntarily accepted employment. The "balance of hardship" was on the club's side as they would lose the money paid for the rights to the players' services if they never played for them.

Players are now prevented from jumping to new leagues, at least until their contracts have expired. Reserve, option clauses have also been enforced in cases between teams and players in the same league.

PLAYERS' RIGHTS ARE BORN!

When players began to successfully challenge draft and eligibility rules, their rights took a turn for the better.

Football

When NFL teams could not agree on compensation for a free agent, the "Rozelle Rule" was then used.

> FACTS: Kapp had come to the Patriots from the Vikings. When Kapp declared, "I refuse to sign a contract!" the commissioner ordered him to either sign or not play.
>
> If agreement as to compensation could not be reached between the teams, then the commissioner determined it. This practice was known as the "Rozelle Rule."
>
> Kapp didn't sign, but instead sued the NFL. He alleged that the Rozelle Rule was unreasonable and that the NFL was blacklisting players by refusing to deal with them. Did the rule unreasonably restrain a player's ability to seek work? **YOU'RE THE JUDGE!**
>
> DECISION: Yes. The Rozelle Rule was not the product of collective bargaining. It applied to players even if they had become free agents by playing out their contracts. And, as other teams could not deal with a player unless giving compensation, it restrained a player for an unlimited time. "This went far beyond any need for protection of a team's interests. Impartial arbitration to decide on compensation, if any, would be necessary."

The NFL owners were forced to bargain with the NFL Player's Association. The result was an agreement liberalizing the draft and changing the Rozelle Rule.

Now, if a player becomes a free agent and is given an "offer sheet" by another team, the team that may lose the player has a **"right of first refusal"** and may sign the player for the offered salary. If not done, the losing team is then compensated by future draft choice(s), depending upon the free agent's new salary. Very few "free agents" have been signed.

When the Collective Bargaining Agreement between the owners and players expired in 1987, without agreement on a new one, the players went out on strike.

They wanted "unrestricted free agency"—the ability to move to another team after their contract had expired without the new team having to compensate the player's old team for their loss. After several weeks, the striking players, without a new agreement, returned to work. Without an agreement, did the players become free agents?

The NFL instituted a new free agency plan. Each team would protect a certain number of its players. Those not on this restricted list became unrestricted free agents—able to sign with any team—with no compensation to their former team.

Basketball

FACTS: Several NBA players sought an injunction preventing the NBA from enforcing its draft and option clause.

They maintained, "The draft restrained us from bargaining freely for employment. The reserve or option clause could be renewed perpetually. If we played out our contracts and sought to play with other teams, we were blacklisted—no one would deal with us." Were these practices group boycotts by the NBA teams? **YOU'RE THE JUDGE!**

DECISION: The court found that these practices were, in effect, group boycotts by their refusal to deal with the players, except through these restrictive practices.

The NBA owners and the NBA Player's Association agreed to a Collective Bargaining Agreement (CBA). The draft remained, but if a team did not sign a drafted player before the next draft, the player would again be eligible to be drafted. If again, the athlete was not signed before the next draft, he became a free agent.

Would a team continue to have the right to renew a player's contract perpetually? No. At the end of a contract and one-year option, a player became a free agent. And, if an NBA player is a five-year veteran, he automatically becomes a free agent.

FACTS: Jake asserted, "I'm a free agent. I played out my contract and one-year option with the Bulls. I then received an offer from the Kings." Did the Bulls still have any rights to sign Jake? Did the Kings have to compensate the Bulls? **YOU'RE THE JUDGE!**

DECISION: If a team offered Jake a contract, the original team had a "right of first refusal." They could match any offer that Jake received. If the original team did not match that offer, the new team would no longer be required to compensate them.

The Bulls decided to match the Kings' offer, signed, and then traded Jake to the Kings.

Hockey

The NHL also replaced their perpetual reserve clause with a one-year option.

Collective bargaining produced a method whereby the team signing a free agent would make an "equalization payment" to the losing team. If the teams could not agree on a player(s), cash, or draft pick (s) (or any combination of these) for payment, then a neutral arbitrator would select, without change, one of the two teams' proposals.

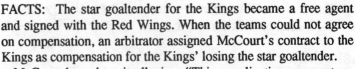

FACTS: The star goaltender for the Kings became a free agent and signed with the Red Wings. When the teams could not agree on compensation, an arbitrator assigned McCourt's contract to the Kings as compensation for the Kings' losing the star goaltender.

McCourt brought suit alleging, "This equalization payment restricted my ability to choose who I would play for." Would the court prohibit the compensation? **YOU'RE THE JUDGE!**

DECISION: No . The labor exemption holds that if the reserve clause was the product of bona fide, good faith bargaining, over a mandatory subject (employment), then it was exempt from the antitrust laws and could not be enjoined as a restraint of trade.

Baseball

Although baseball, with its perpetual reserve system was exempt from antitrust laws, collective bargaining and arbitration also came to the rescue of baseball players.

Finley, owner of the A's, fired one of his players, Harrelson. Later, an arbitrator released another A's player, Hunter, from his contract. They both became free agents, signed with other teams, and received substantial pay raises.

While this did not change the reserve clause, other players now demanded higher salaries. Several refused to sign their contracts. Most players eventually signed, but one did not.

FACTS: Messersmith, a pitcher for the Dodgers did not sign his 1975 contract, but instead played out his option. He challenged the team's right to perpetually renew his contract and the reserved list, prohibiting other teams from dealing with him. Was Messersmith a free agent? **YOU'RE THE JUDGE!**

DECISION: Yes. An impartial arbitrator ruled that by playing out his option, Messersmith had become a free agent. The team could not renew his contract beyond the option year. Furthermore, other teams could deal with him as the reserve list applied only to players under contract.

A new Collective Bargaining Agreement (CBA) allowed players who play out their option after six years of service to become free agents. Players now may, in certain instances, veto a trade involving them.

RULES! RULES!

Playing rules may have several objectives: to heighten fan interest; to promote fairness of competition and for the integrity of the game, and; to insure the safety of the players.

FACTS: The American League (AL) decided to do away with the designated hitter rule, thus several players who couldn't play in the field would be cut.

Football changed its tackling rules, creating the need for quicker defensive players.

New tennis rackets and golf balls were prohibited from being used in tournaments.

Those affected—players and manufacturers—sued, protesting that, "The rules' changes illegally restrained our ability to earn a living." Would the changes be permitted? **YOU'RE THE JUDGE!**

DECISION: Someone will be affected no matter what rules' changes are made. Uniformity in regulating and improving the games is essential to hold fan interest. And, as long as a league is not attempting to suppress competition by eliminating certain players or products, then restraints designed to promote the game and protect competitors will be justified.

SQUAD SIZE

Can professional sports teams limit the number of players on each team?

Restrictions on squad size, while limiting the employment of some players, are necessary for competitive balance. Otherwise, one owner might be forced to hire more players to compete with another owner who had the resources to increase his roster, and thus his ability to win.

FACTS: The NFL cut its roster limit to forty-three players. Basketball cut its squad size to eleven. Golf cut the entrants for any tournament to one hundred-twenty-five. Those participants who now didn't qualify sued, complaining, "The reduced limits prevented us from trading our services. The rules were illegal group boycotts." What limit should apply? **YOU'RE THE JUDGE!**

DECISION: If a league or association sets a limit in the interest of maximizing profits and competitive balance, and not solely to restrict competition for players, then there will be no restraint of trade.

TRADE DEADLINES

Can teams be prohibited from acquiring players after a certain point in the season?

Although trade or acquisition deadlines may restrict the movement of players, they also prevent teams in play-off or pennant contention from "buying up" stars to assure winning. These restraints are

are only for a limited time, as they disappear when the season is over. They are necessary for competitive balance.

What if a deadline is not for competitive balance, but to lock out certain players?

FACTS: The NFL sought to prevent WFL players from entering the NFL after the WFL had folded. The regular trading deadline date was October 28. The NFL set a date of October 22 as the deadline for acquiring WFL players. Did this improperly interfere with those WFL players' trying to sign with NFL teams? **YOU'RE THE JUDGE!**

DECISION: Yes. The players were granted an injunction preventing the NFL from interfering with their attempt to secure employment in the NFL. Had the NFL set the same acquisition date for WFL players as its regular trading deadline, then the injunction may not have been granted.

ODDS & ENDS....

Ticket Tying

A **tying** arrangement "ties" the purchase of one product to the required purchase of another. Is this legal?

FACTS: You wanted to buy season tickets to see the Bills. The team only sold a package including tickets for pre and regular-season home games. You sued the Bills, objecting, "This is illegal! I only want regular-season tickets." Should you be able to buy a season ticket for only regular-season games? **YOU'RE THE JUDGE!**

DECISION: The court held that teams may sell season ticket packages which include pre-season tickets.

The purchasers of season ticket packages received special privileges, such as preferred-location seats and parking. Individual game tickets were available, however, so fans were not compelled to buy something that they did not want.

Professional sports leagues and associations must balance their concern over eligibility rules, fairness of competition and player safety with an individual's right to earn a living.

15

MOVING ON

WHAT'S IT ABOUT?

Moving On tells how antitrust laws may affect attempts by professional sports' leagues to prevent their teams from moving from one city to another. Also discussed is **eminent domain**—a city's attempt to take private property (professional sports team) for public use.

May teams break their leases with stadiums in order to move? May leagues regulate who can own teams in their sport?

PRO TEAM GONE!

As one fan sighed, "It's like losing one of your kids to college ... it's hard to adjust to life without them. But at least your kid will come back for visits. When you've lost a team, they're gone for good." Fans everywhere have lost pro teams to other cities ... and to other fans.

Franchise free agency now allows teams to move... but it wasn't always that way.

OWNER

WE WANT TO MOVE!

CAN WE MOVE?

FACTS: The NHL's San Francisco Seals wanted to move to Vancouver. The St. Louis Blues wanted to move to Saskatchewan. There were no NHL teams in either place.

When the NHL denied permission for the teams to move, both teams sued, alleging, "The NHL is restraining trade by preventing

us from moving." Should the teams have been allowed to move?
YOU'RE THE JUDGE!

DECISION: The Sherman Antitrust Act provides that any agreement in restraint of trade is illegal. It prohibits competitors from restraining trade.

The courts held that the individual teams in the NHL were not competitors, but were acting together as one business enterprise. Therefore, there could be no agreement and, hence, no restraint. The teams could not move.

Furthermore, the teams could not successfully allege that the NHL was attempting to monopolize pro hockey. The teams were part of that monopoly and the law requires that one desiring to recover must be injured. The court pointed out, "The teams wished to continue to enjoy the protection of monopoly by the league, but wanted to enjoy it in different cities."

FACTS: What if the arena owners in Saskatchewan and Vancouver joined the teams in the antitrust suit as competitors to the arenas in St. Louis and San Francisco and as competitors to the NHL? Would there then be the necessary competition to show a restraint of trade?

DECISION: **YOU'RE THE JUDGE!**

Could other teams and arenas be more successful in showing that teams can be competitors and therefore, a league can restrain trade by preventing a team from moving to another city?

Rule 4.3 of the NFL Constitution required approval by three-fourths of the NFL clubs before another club could move within the home territory (within 75 miles) of any other NFL club.

The rule, similar to those used by other sports' leagues, was designed to keep owners from arbitrarily moving their teams to new locations, or to another team's home territory.

Such rules were subject to abuse by owners intent on denying an unpopular owner the necessary permission to move. Such was the case when Bill Veeck was denied permission by the AL to move his baseball team. Two days after Veeck sold the club, the new owner was given permission for the move.

In 1978, the L.A. Rams announced that they were leaving the Coliseum to play in nearby Anaheim. The Coliseum Commission then sought to have the Oakland Raiders move there. Were they successful?

FACTS: The commission and the Raiders sued the NFL, contending, "Rule 4.3 violates the antitrust law's prohibition against any agreement in restraint of trade."

The major issue was whether the NFL was a single business enterprise—which could not combine or agree with itself—or whether the NFL was comprised of 28 separate member clubs—who could combine, or agree, to restrain trade.

The NFL argued, "We are a single enterprise as evidenced by uniform playing rules, scheduling, the player draft, and sharing of television revenues and ticket receipts." Was the NFL a single business enterprise? **YOU'RE THE JUDGE!**

DECISION: No. The court found that the NFL was an association of 28 separate clubs. It further commented, "The clubs did not share all revenues, nor did they share their profits or losses. They were managed independently, each making its own decisions concerning ticket prices, player acquisitions and salaries, hiring of coaches and administrators and the terms of their stadium leases." The teams competed against each other for players, fans and the media.

The court, in mentioning a suit between the NFL and the NASL, noted, "The single entity defense fails where two teams compete in the same area for fans. League restraint of that competition often damages a stadium operator."

Now that the court held that the NFL could combine or agree to prevent a team from moving, the next question was, "Did they?"

FACTS: Did the NFL unlawfully combine or agree to restrain trade by denying the Raiders permission to play in the Coliseum and, thus, also restrain the Coliseum Commission from having another NFL team to replace the departed LA Rams? **YOU'RE THE JUDGE!**

DECISION: Yes. Rule 4.3, requiring clubs to approve any move, was arbitrary and unreasonable. It contained no considerations, such as the impact a team move would have on the new location or another NFL team, to guide owners in the approval process. It was subject to abuse, as owners could deny permission to move without using good faith.

The NFL and its members unreasonably restrained trade. They were permanently enjoined from interfering with the Raiders in their transfer to play in the L.A. Coliseum.

Other professional sports teams have moved or attempted to move. When the New York Nets desired to move to New Jersey, the New York Knicks objected. Because NBA rules required the consent of the team (Knicks) into whose territory a move is to be made, the Nets could not move. They sued. The suit was settled, and the Nets moved.

In a similar confrontation, the Colorado Rockies moved to New Jersey, with the Islanders, Rangers, and Flyers being paid indemnification fees for the profits that they would lose from having another team in their territory to draw away fans and TV revenues.

Would professional sports leagues now be prevented from restricting team movement?

The court in the Raiders case suggested that had there existed necessary, objective and reasonable restrictions on team movement, they would have been enforceable—whether in football or in any other league.

EMINENT DOMAIN?

In addition to leagues, cities have attempted to prevent teams from moving by using **eminent domain**—the power of a state or city to take private property for public use for fair compensation. It is commonly used to condemn land for public roads, bridges, railroads and airports. Land to build many sports stadiums was acquired by eminent domain.

CITY OF
OAKLAND

FACTS: The city of Oakland objected to the Raiders' moving and brought an action in eminent domain.

The city asserted, "We should be allowed to acquire the Raiders as property necessary for providing recreation and sports for our residents."

The city of Oakland felt that, "If acquiring, erecting, and operating a sports stadium was a permissible municipal function, then owning a sports franchise to play in the stadium should also be permitted." Was the city allowed to take the Raiders? **YOU'RE THE JUDGE!**

DECISION: No. Oakland's condemnation was "not for a valid public purpose." The court decided, "A pro football team was not what the Constitution intended as private property that may be taken by eminent domain for public use."

If the city of Oakland were allowed to do so, then every city might do the same. And every city could condemn any business that considered moving.

FACTS: Springfield attempted to condemn a theater group and its hit play, "The Babe," and prevent its going on tour.

Another city, Harrison, wanted to condemn a sporting goods manufacturer (who employed many of the town's people) and prevent its moving. Another city, Westfield, wanted to prevent you from moving your ticket and program print shop to another town. Should the cities be allowed to take these businesses by eminent domain?

DECISION: **YOU'RE THE JUDGE!**

LEASES

Most professional sports teams are tied to their stadiums and arenas by a long-term **lease**—an agreement for exclusive possession of property for a specific period of time.

Teams attempting to leave a city before their leases expired have been enjoined, as in the case of the San Francisco Giants, when they attempted to move to Toronto. Others have settled the matter as did: New York City and the Jets, San Diego and the NL, and the Braves and the city of Buffalo. When the Seattle Pilots became the Milwaukee Brewers, the city complained and was awarded a new franchise, the Seattle Mariners.

If a team left before their lease expired, could they be forced to return?

FACTS: The New Orleans Jazz moved to Utah before their lease was up. The stadium manager fumed, "I want an injunction preventing the move and forcing the Jazz to return to New Orleans, at least until their lease expires." Did the Jazz have to return? **YOU'RE THE JUDGE!**

DECISION: The stadium manager was denied an injunction as, by the time a petition was filed, the team had moved. They settled on the issue of damages for lost rent and profit.

With this new found freedom of movement, teams could now obtain more favorable lease concessions and lower rent in return for long-term leases of a stadium or arena. Such concessions even include allowing a team to break its lease where attendance does not reach a specified level.

One team was trying to enter a lease, not break one.

FACTS: Holden sought to lease RFK Stadium in Washington to use for an AFL pro football team. He contended, "The stadium is the only one in the area suitable for pro football." The operators of the stadium had signed a lease prohibiting use of the stadium by any pro football team other than the Redskins. Was this an attempt to monopolize pro football in that area? **YOU'RE THE JUDGE!**

DECISION: The Redskins combined with the operator of the stadium to improperly restrain trade, and to monopolize pro football in the Washington area by excluding competition from using the stadium.

"WE DON'T WANT YOU"

Professional sports leagues have rules regulating who may own a franchise in their leagues. Such rules may prohibit ownership by those involved with gambling or by those having an interest in another team.

> FACTS: Brown and Stone purchased the Celtics and then applied to the NBA for the transfer. When they were denied, they sued, alleging, "Our application was unreasonably denied."
> One owner said, "You're with Harry. He's been a crawl in the throat of these owners. He's a renegade and a troublemaker, and they are worried that you'll side with him on any matters before the NBA."
> The NBA contended, "We rejected the application because of business dealings between the three, practices which created potential conflicts of interest." Was this a restraint of trade for preventing the purchase? **YOU'RE THE JUDGE!**

> DECISION: The judge ruled that the antitrust laws were for the protection of competition, and the plaintiffs, Brown and Stone, wanted to join with the other owners, not compete with them. Therefore, the antitrust laws did not apply. Brown and Stone had to sell their interest in the Celtics.

In a similar ruling, another court found that the Mid-South Grizzlies were not competitors of the NFL. There was no anticompetitive behavior in rejecting their application for admission into the NFL.

These cases assumed that the league was a single entity, which could not combine or agree with itself to restrain or monopolize trade.

Would the decisions have been different had these cases been decided after the Raiders' case held that teams do compete with each other and, therefore, could agree to prevent approval?

> FACTS: Fisher reached an agreement to buy the NBA's Chicago Bulls. When agreement to lease Chicago Stadium (19,000 seats) for play could not be reached, Fisher arranged a lease to play in the Amphitheatre (10,500 seats).
> "Because I couldn't use the Stadium, the NBA rejected my application." Fisher said. The team was then purchased by the group who owned the Stadium.
> Fisher sued that group and the NBA for "restraining competition, conspiring to monopolize pro basketball, and for boycotting me to prevent approval of the sale." Should Fisher have been allowed to lease the Stadium? **YOU'RE THE JUDGE!**

> DECISION: "The Stadium is an essential and scarce facility." Far superior to the Amphitheatre, it could not (practically) be duplicated. Its owners must share its use on fair terms.

The court ruled, "The evidence of conspiracy was overwhelming and showed that the group intended to dictate who the next owner of the Bulls would be."

The defendants, in failing to outbid Fisher for the team, conspired to monopolize (with other owners) and to obtain a negative vote from the NBA, and thus restrained Fisher from his fairly won victory.

Damages, including punitive, were awarded. The NBA was a defendant until a settlement was reached.

STATE LAWS

May states use their antitrust laws in dealing with professional sports teams?

The potential burden on **interstate commerce**—trade between several states—by professional sports teams outweighs any one state's interest in regulating professional sports. Therefore, federal antitrust laws will apply.

When Wisconsin attempted to use state antitrust laws to prevent the Milwaukee Braves from moving, the court found that baseball was not only exempt from federal antitrust laws, but from any antitrust laws.

Where amateur sports do not deal in interstate commerce, state antitrust laws may apply.

FACTS: Grant, a high school student, attended a summer baseball camp for three weeks. His high school association had a rule providing that, "Any student attending a summer camp specializing in one sport for more than two weeks during the summer shall lose his eligibility for the following year."

When Grant lost his eligibility, he sued, alleging that the rule restrained him from developing his skills for college. Was the rule unreasonable? **YOU'RE THE JUDGE!**

DECISION: The court held that the rule was reasonable and did not violate state antitrust laws. It was necessary to prevent one student gaining an unfair advantage over others who could not attend, and to prevent their being "burned out" from exploitation and undue pressure.

THE NCAA & ANTITRUST

The majority of NCAA rules and regulations are for the protection of amateurism and education in college athletics. This pursuit may prevent the use of antitrust laws in any challenge to such rules.

FACTS: An NCAA rule limited the number of assistant coaches a school could employ in its football and basketball programs. This forced the firing of a number of assistant coaches. Did the rule un-reasonably restrain trade by preventing some coaches from work-ing? **YOU'RE THE JUDGE!**

DECISION: No. The court decided, "The NCAA's goal of pre-serving and fostering competition by preventing wealthy and pow-erful schools from having an unfair advantage over others—by hir-ing extra coaches—was a reasonable one."

The NCAA also attempted to limit squad sizes in those same sports, but after several suits, they voted to abandon those restric-tions.

Would the NCAA be subjected to the antitrust laws where its member schools established interstate commerce by: nationwide re-cruitment, team travel for games, and interstate TV broadcasting and sale of tickets?

FACTS: English played quarterback for Tulane. When the NCAA ruled him ineligible for not sitting out a year after his transfer from another college, English sued, alleging that the NCAA unfairly at-tempted to restrain him from playing. Did English have to sit out a year? **YOU'RE THE JUDGE!**

DECISION: English could not play. Antitrust laws did not apply to prevent the NCAA from enforcing its rules pertaining to recruit-ment, transfer and eligibility to preserve and foster competition in college sports.

The NCAA had limited its jurisdiction to men's athletics until 1981, when they voted to extend its activities into women's athletics.

FACTS: The Association for Intercollegiate Athletics for Women (AIAW), formed prior to 1981 to regulate women's athletics, sued the NCAA, alleging they expanded into women's athletics in order to monopolize and restrain trade in women's sports.

Many association members left and joined the NCAA. This loss of membership resulted in a substantial loss of revenue and pres-tige. Did the NCAA restrain the AIAW? Was this an illegal mon-opoly? **YOU'RE THE JUDGE!**

DECISION: The court found no antitrust violations. "The AIAW loss was the result of direct competition with the NCAA. The latter offered a superior product, management and promotional resourc-es, and uniform rules for both men and women."

The NCAA also sought to govern the televising of college foot-ball games by granting an exclusive right to networks to carry games live.

In the interest of protecting attendance, NCAA rules limited both the number of games to be broadcast each season, and also the number of times any school could appear.

Could NCAA schools make their own deals for televising their games?

FACTS: Most of the major football programs formed the College Football Association (CFA) and made their own deals for broadcasting games in which they played.

The NCAA announced disciplinary action for any member that complied with the CFA television contract. The schools could have withdrawn from the NCAA, but they were dependent upon the NCAA for administration in other sports.

Instead, they sued, alleging, "The NCAA limitations are illegal and restrain us from making our own deals." Were the NCAA limitations illegal? **YOU'RE THE JUDGE!**

DECISION: Yes. The court found that the NCAA plan was an illegal restraint of trade for: limiting the number of times a team could appear, fixing prices paid to the teams, and prohibiting members from selling TV rights on their own. The NCAA plan neither protected live, in-person attendance, nor equalized competition among its members.

In commenting on protecting the "small guy's" right to compete, one judge commented, "Where, by unfair and illegal practices—intent on monopolizing and restraining trade—the right to enter and compete is restricted, antitrust laws will be available to see that the 'small guy' gets an equal shot with the 'big guy' at selling his services or products."

ODDS & ENDS....

FACTS: You were the President of All-American U. Your football team had just completed an undefeated season.

You wanted to play in the Flower Bowl. However, because you were neither a member of the Big Eleven, nor of the Pac 9, you were not eligible to be selected.

You sued the Flower Bowl Committee, the NCAA and the Pac 9 and Big Eleven football conferences, arguing, "They restrained trade, conspired to monopolize the Flower Bowl game and boycotted us, all in violation of the antitrust laws."

The Flower Bowl defended, "You are eligible for other bowl games." Would a court enjoin the Flower Bowl's practice of only considering the Pac 9 and Big Eleven conferences in selecting schools to play in the Flower Bowl?

DECISION: **YOU'RE THE JUDGE!**

Although eminent domain may not be used by a city to take a professional sports team, it is used to take land for stadiums, roadways and airports.

16

SPORTSMANLIKE CONDUCT

WHAT'S IT ABOUT?

Sportsmanlike Conduct deals with the regulation of professional sports and their rules governing play, conduct and discipline, in order to protect the game and its participants.

Does the commissioner or president of a professional sports league or association have complete authority over the conduct and discipline of teams and players?

SPORTSMANLIKE CONDUCT

FACTS: Jimmy, a pro tennis player, was upset at a linesman's call. He screamed at the umpire, "If you don't overrule that call, I'll quit!"

When the umpire did not overrule the call, Jimmy walked off the court, defaulting the match. He was later fined and suspended from tournament play.

Johnnie, also a pro tennis player, was fined and suspended for abuse of officials and equipment.

Hank was banished from pro football for gambling on his team's games.

John and Mike were suspended from pro basketball and baseball for taking drugs. They were given sufficient warnings and rehabilitation.

Dale, a pro race car driver, and Jose, a jockey, were fined and placed on probation for improperly causing accidents by cutting off others.

Brad, Jan (pro hockey coaches), and numerous professional athletes, were fined and suspended for fighting or encouraging fighting. Were the fines, suspensions and probation proper and necessary? **YOU'RE THE JUDGE!**

DECISION: Yes. In order to protect the game's interest, its integrity, safety of participants, and to help promote and ensure orderly and fair play, discipline is necessary to regulate conduct which might be detrimental to a game and its participants. All pro sports will make, define and enforce such rules and regulations.

PUBLIC REGULATION

Public regulation by athletic commissions may be established to prevent abuses and promote and protect the public's interest in the legitimate and sportsmanlike conduct of certain sports. Those sports subject to such public control include: horse, dog and automobile racing, jai-alai, boxing and wrestling.

Licensing of all persons or organizations involved in a sport enables a commission to maintain proper control over that sport and its activities.

Athletic commissions issue licenses, provide reasonable rules governing the sport and enforce such rules by appropriate discipline.

The court remarked of the following case that the facts revealed a scenario "that might have been authored by Alfred Hitchcock."

FACTS: In a case referred to as the "Belmont Ringer Case," Matt, a veterinarian, arranged for the purchase of two horses from South America. One, Lebon, was worth very little; the other, Cinzano, was very valuable. Shortly after the horses were quartered at Matt's farm, an "accident" befell Cinzano. He was quickly destroyed.

Some time after, Lebon, who bore a striking resemblance to the deceased horse, went off in the ninth race at Belmont at odds of 57-1. He won by four lengths. Among the "lucky bettors" was Matt, who won $77,000. No one doubted that the "Lebon" who won the race was really Cinzano. Was this fraudulent? **YOU'RE THE JUDGE!**

DECISION: Yes. The court convicted Matt, sentencing him to a fine and imprisonment.

A commission may revoke, or suspend, a license previously issued, or impose other sanctions, such as fines.

Before the rights of those involved in a regulated sport are affected, is due process required? What if the loss is minimal?

FACTS: Tony, a promoter, was fined and his license suspended for allegedly fixing boxing matches. The Boxing Commission did

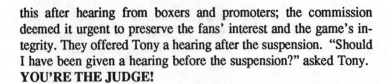

this after hearing from boxers and promoters; the commission deemed it urgent to preserve the fans' interest and the game's integrity. They offered Tony a hearing after the suspension. "Should I have been given a hearing before the suspension?" asked Tony. **YOU'RE THE JUDGE!**

DECISION: The court concluded, "The seriousness of the fine and suspension—jeopardizing Tony's ability to earn a living—required notice and the opportunity to a fair and impartial hearing with representation before the suspension."

PRIVATE REGULATION

The NCAA and college conferences govern most amateur collegiate sports. Each professional sport not subject to public regulation has its own rules governing eligibility, play, conduct, discipline and other matters. The goals of each are the same: the safety of the players and preserving the integrity of the game.

How may players or coaches who join a fight be disciplined?

FACTS: Ray and Matty, opponents in a college basketball game, got into a fight and were ejected from the game. Several players and one of the coaches came off the bench to join the melee. Could the players and coach be disciplined? **YOU'RE THE JUDGE!**

DECISION: Unsportsmanlike conduct results in an automatic one game suspension for the players and for any bench personnel—other than a head coach—who come onto the floor. For a second incident involving fighting, a player will be suspended for the next game; and for the third incident the player will sit out for the remainder of that year.

Will a court review a league or association's disciplinary rules?

Generally, rules defining conduct and disciplinary measures, as long as they are necessary to carry out the legitimate needs of a sport, will not be reviewed by courts if minimum due process is given (notice and a fair and impartial hearing with representation).

Any person affected by enforcement action may waive those safeguards by knowing and voluntary action.

FACTS: When Mike, a pro golfer, used clubs in competition that did not meet PGA specifications, of which he was aware, he was immediately suspended from further play without a hearing. The purpose of the rule was "to protect the integrity and fairness of the game."

"Why didn't I get a hearing?" asked Mike. **YOU'RE THE JUDGE!**

DECISION: Unlike Tony, the promoter, who was not scheduled to immediately promote another fight, Mike was in competition that would continue into the next day. The suspension was proper. A later hearing could be given to determine the validity of any violation.

COMMISSIONER & PRESIDENT

In 1920, baseball owners chose self-regulation by electing their first commissioner, Judge "Mountain" Landis. He was given broad and complete authority to investigate anything detrimental to the best interest of the sport, and to punish as he saw fit.

One court noted, "As long as a commissioner or president acts within his authority, and in the best interest of the sport, his decisions will not be overruled."

Will a voluntary and good faith agreement to arbitrate a controversy before a commissioner or president, with no access to the courts, be binding?

FACTS: A soccer play-off game was tied and went into overtime. The Sockers' coach, confused as to who had been declared eligible for the shoot-out, questioned the referees. They declared, "Jacques is eligible."

When the Sockers won, the Strikers protested that Jacques was ineligible. The referees were wrong; Jacques was not eligible to play in the shoot-out. Should the commissioner have awarded the game to the Strikers? Would a court decide the controversy? **YOU'RE THE JUDGE!**

DECISION: The Sockers had used an ineligible player. The commissioner awarded the game to the Strikers. This was not a judgment call (one that could be overturned), but a violation of procedures. The commissioner's decision was final; a court would not act.

All pro sports now have a commissioner or president who oversees the conduct of teams and players. Their authority includes the approval of contracts, resolution of disputes, discipline of teams and players for rules' violations and any other action deemed necessary for the best interests of the sport.

May players wear uniforms "different" from those approved by the league ?

FACTS: The NFL Cardinals decided to try to change their luck by wearing all maroon socks, instead of the usual maroon and white.

Tino, a soccer goalkeeper for the Strikers, painted his pants several different colors. He said, "I got tired of wearing black all the time." Another goalie wore polka dots and patches with his spon-

sor's logos on them. Could the commissioner ban such attire as "eyesores"? **YOU'RE THE JUDGE!**

DECISION: The Cardinal's socks violated the league's standard uniform code and the commissioner could ban them.

Goalkeepers are required to wear uniforms different from their teammates. Such uniforms were permitted.

Where the head of a league fails to respect the limits of his authority, courts will be available for a review of the controversy. Any authority must have a legitimate purpose, such as to protect the integrity of the game or sport.

FACTS: The commissioner of baseball warned all clubs to refrain from tampering with free agents prior to a special draft. One owner let it be known publicly that he intended to sign one of the free agents. After a hearing, the commissioner suspended the owner from baseball for one season and directed that his team forfeit their first-round amateur draft choice for the following year. The owner alleged, "The commissioner overstepped his authority in depriving me of the draft choice." Were the suspension and forfeiture upheld by the court? **YOU'RE THE JUDGE!**

DECISION: The court held that the suspension was within the commissioner's authority to invoke the no-tampering rule; the power to deprive the team of their draft choice was not within the commissioner's power.

Other owners have also been fined for tampering with players. One coach was fined for tampering with a game by allowing the opposing team to score so that one of the coach's players would have a chance to break a scoring record.

WILL I BE DISCIPLINED?

FACTS: James, a pro tennis player, was coached by Manny, who gave signals to James throughout his matches. Could either the player or the coach be disciplined for such conduct? **YOU'RE THE JUDGE!**

DECISION: Both were subject to discipline for violation of the rule which prohibited coaching during a professional tennis match.

A league in team sports, and an association in individual sports, establishes disciplinary rules governing conduct. These rules provide for specific sanctions—fines, suspension and termination—for violations and conduct detrimental to the integrity of the game.

FACTS: Kirk was fined and suspended from baseball by the commissioner for substance abuse. "The suspension was too harsh and the fine too much," he grumbled. He appealed. Who handled the appeal? **YOU'RE THE JUDGE!**

DECISION: Kirk's appeal was handled by the same commissioner. Any further appeal could be to an independent arbitrator.

If there was no provision in his contract providing for appeal to an independent arbitrator, appeal would be to a court. However, unless the rule was illegal or illegally applied, the commissioner's decision would be upheld.

Discipline may be used to discourage gambling, as in the case of an NBA player suspended for gambling on games. The court refused to enjoin the suspension for lack of a hearing, finding that the player was "morally dishonest. The appearance of players betting was enough to destroy public confidence in the integrity of the game." May discipline be used to discourage other activity as well?

FACTS: Ray, coach of the NBA Stingers, was irate over a referee's decision which cost him a game. He shrieked at the ref, "You blew the call! That cost me the game. Go read the rules book."

Pete, a baseball manager, irate over a call, bumped and pushed the umpire.

Rick, upset over a ref's call during a hockey game, yelled, "The ref is a no-good, vindictive - - who deliberately cheated us!" Could the commissioner fine or suspend the coaches for their conduct or comments? **YOU'RE THE JUDGE!**

DECISION: Yes. Coaches, owners and players have been fined and suspended for conduct not in the best interest of the game— where they have publicly criticized umpires and referees concerning a decision, or physically abused an official.

Players, managers and teams may also be fined or suspended for instigating brawls and riots.

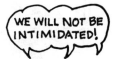

FACTS: In separate incidents involving fights by their teams, a baseball manager and a hockey coach both snarled, "We will not be intimidated!"

When brawls broke out, and spilled out into the stands, players, refs and fans were injured. Could the coaches be fined or suspended for instigating the fights?

DECISION: **YOU'RE THE JUDGE!**

Players are required to play within the rules. Conduct intended to injure an opposing player, or which reflects unfavorably on the game, is prohibited. As a result of flagrant, unsportsmanlike conduct

players in all major sports have been fined and suspended.

How is the type and amount or length of punishment determined?

Punishment is determined by the severity of any injury, the seriousness of the act, any defenses (self-defense), and any previous similar conduct. The more severe the act or injury, the more severe will be the penalty. In hockey, abuse of players is still permitted—although there now are more severe fines and suspensions for flagrant acts of violence or bench-clearing brawls (one player was even given a one day jail sentence for hitting another player with his hockey stick).

FACTS: At a soccer game, players assaulted each other and insulted the referees. Then the fans pelted each other with rocks and fought, causing the stands to collapse, killing and injuring spectators. Were the players and teams subject to fines and suspensions for their misconduct? **YOU'RE THE JUDGE!**

DECISION: Yes. Clubs, players and coaches have been fined and suspended for their own misconduct, as well as that of fans, which resulted in injury. In assaulting other players and insulting the referee, they incited the fans to act in a violent manner.

Another soccer player was fined and suspended for not wearing shin guards, as required to prevent the possible contraction of AIDS from an open wound.

A suspension is legal if it is intended to accomplish a legitimate goal, such as subjecting all players to the same rules. It must be reasonable, no more extensive than necessary, and follow procedural safeguards (including adequate notice and a fair and impartial hearing with the opportunity for representation).

FACTS: Dena was suspended from the LPGA for allegedly cheating by improperly marking her golf ball on the putting green. A group of her fellow players, in a closed hearing, suspended her. Could Dena have the suspension enjoined because she was not given a fair and impartial hearing? **YOU'RE THE JUDGE!**

DECISION: Yes. The members who suspended her were her own competitors and had a financial interest in whether or not she played. Such action was unfair and, therefore, prohibited.

Players must use their best efforts to observe the rules and conduct themselves in a professional manner which will reflect favorably on their sport. Were the following acts "good conduct"?

FACTS: John, a pro tennis player, was upset with an umpire's calls. He slammed his racket, hit balls into the stands and called the umpire a "jerk," his opponent a "cheat" and several people—

including the president of the tennis association—"idiots."

Evan was wearing a product endorsement patch, not approved of by the USTA, on his tennis shorts.

Rashina, an Olympic skier, wore an oversized logo on her headband. Red, a pro football player, wore a headband with a company's name on it.

Bull, a pro golfer, decided (after nine holes of a tournament) to change into shorts. Bob, not liking the course, called it an "overgrown parking lot" and also criticized the commissioner, calling him a "thief."

Gary, a pro bowler, drinking while bowling, kicked and broke the ball return during a tournament. Afterwards, he played cards in the locker room. Could any of these competitors be fined, disqualified or otherwise disciplined for their conduct? **YOU'RE THE JUDGE!**

DECISION: Yes, for: unsportsmanlike conduct; abuse of equipment, officials, players and fans; improper clothing; improper product endorsement or logo; improper comments; and drinking and card playing. Each of these competitors was subject to fines, suspension, disqualification or termination for his or her conduct, (which were all prohibited by the rules governing play in their respective sports). Such conduct was not in the best interests of their sports.

A commissioner or president in a team sport may also be given the authority to approve or disapprove player contracts, or other transactions between teams.

This is to insure that teams negotiate proper terms, that competitive balance between teams is maintained, and to preserve equal treatment of players. For example, a league may have an interest in insuring that players only receive proper bonuses, or that every player is subject to the same disciplinary rules and punishments as other players.

May a commissioner void the sale of baseball players from one team to another?

FACTS: Finley, owner of the A's, decided to sell three of his star players to the Red Sox for cash only; no players were to be exchanged between the clubs.

After conducting a hearing, the commissioner disapproved the deal. Finley went to court, asserting the commissioner had overstepped his authority by voiding the sale. Should Finley have been able to sell his players to the Red Sox? **YOU'RE THE JUDGE!**

DECISION: The court ruled, "The commissioner's decision to void the sale of the players was proper. The transaction was inconsistent with the best interests and integrity of the game." If ap-

proved, the sale would have lessened competitive balance between the A's and other teams by weakening the A's ability to perform. The sale would have contributed to destroying public confidence in a home team.

In resolving any disciplinary disputes, independent arbitration may be used to determine the fairness and reasonableness of any disciplinary action.

Review by a court will be limited to cases where the commissioner or president clearly overstepped their power or failed to give due process.

As one court noted, "It is intended that the commissioner or president will continue to wield strong authority, this necessary to protect the best interests of, and the public confidence in, professional sports."

ODDS & ENDS....

Gambling does not always have to result in a fine, at least not to the winner.

FACTS: Fred traveled from California to Pennsylvania for a friendly round of golf with Lloyd. The trip was worth his while because Fred won $24,000 on several bets concerning their skills. When Lloyd didn't pay, Fred sued.

Lloyd said, "Gambling is illegal. I don't have to pay." Did Lloyd have to pay? **YOU'RE THE JUDGE!**

DECISION: Yes. The court quoted from the state gambling statutes which defined gambling as including, "A sporting event, over which the person taking a risk has no control." Here, the court reasoned, "There was a golf match, where each player, by his playing, had control over the outcome. The wagering on this golf match did not constitute gambling." Lloyd was, in effect, fined $24,000.

Another golfer was charged with "hooliganism" and fined, after his drive hit a bird that then smashed into the windshield of a jet taking off from an air force base next to the golf course. The jet, in mid take-off, bounced off the runway and destroyed five planes.

Any enforcement of disciplinary rules by the heads of professional sports leagues and associations must have a legitimate purpose, such as to protect the integrity of the game.

17

WAR & PEACE!

WHAT'S IT ABOUT?

War & Peace! details "wars" between competing professional sports leagues for players, cities, stadiums, owners and TV coverage.

Are professional sports leagues allowed to merge in order to end a war?

Philadelphia News
August 10, 1976

SPORTS LEAGUES AT WAR!

There have been "wars" between professional sports leagues since 1871 when the National League began its "battles" with competing baseball leagues—with only the American League surviving.

The National Basketball Association (NBA) was formed in 1949 after a war between two competing leagues. Later, after a battle with the American Basketball League (ABA), the NBA admitted four ABA teams, thus ending the ABA.

And, in the face of litigation with the World Hockey Association (WHA), the NHL voted to admit four WHA teams.

What about the teams that weren't admitted—were they illegally banished from participating?

BATTLES FOR PLAYERS, CITIES.... & SURVIVAL

FACTS: The ABA and WHL teams that were not merged into the NBA and NHL complained, "By locking us out, the older leagues restrained trade and monopolized the sports." How could the older leagues attempt to prevent antitrust litigation? **YOU'RE THE JUDGE!**

DECISION: Teams left out of the mergers were compensated monetarily in hopes of preventing antitrust litigation for restraining trade and monopolizing the sport by eliminating some teams.

The National Football League (NFL), formed in 1920, had a monopoly in pro football until the American Football Conference (AFC) appeared. The two battled until, in 1950, the NFL absorbed three AFC teams, and thus resumed its monopoly ... that is, until the American Football League (AFL) appeared. Then, the NFL-AFL "war" lasted until 1966, when the two leagues were allowed to merge.

The NFL then engaged in a short-lived war with the World Football League (WFL)—which folded—before warring with the United States Football League (USFL).

The USFL began in 1983. They competed with the NFL for star players, not under contract, and for college stars.

When it became evident that spring football would not support the USFL, they challenged the NFL in the courts.

> FACTS: The USFL filed an antitrust suit against the NFL, alleging, "The NFL monopolized pro football by controlling stadiums and the major TV networks."
>
> A network broadcasting contract was necessary to stay afloat financially. They argued, "The NFL practices were an attempt to boycott us from competing in pro football." Did the NFL unreasonably restrain trade and attempt to monopolize pro football? **YOU'RE THE JUDGE!**
>
> DECISION: The court held that the NFL did not monopolize the networks. Furthermore, the NFL was a "natural monopoly"—only one league could survive. The USFL was awarded $3 in damages! They suspended operations in 1986.

Wars between competing leagues involved battles for players, interference with players' contracts and competition for cities, arenas, owners and TV contracts.

Players

How could these battles between warring sports leagues benefit players?

The battles provided players with an opportunity for increased salaries and benefits. Teams, in an attempt to lock up players, signed and paid them before their college eligibility was up—a violation of NCAA rules—and offered contracts and money (sometimes far different from that which appeared in the contract). Some players signed with more than one team or agent.

> FACTS: Tom signed to play for the Tigers in the new World Football League (WFL). He then received a better offer and re-signed with his old team, the Blitzers, in the NFL.

The Tigers contended that the contract they had with Tom was valid and that the Blitzers interferred with that contract.

Tom insisted, "I was persuaded by the Tigers to sign for a bonus which they didn't pay."

The Blitzers reasoned, "We knew nothing of Tom's dealing with the Tigers. Tom still had to fulfill his option year with us." Which team would Tom play for? **YOU'RE THE JUDGE!**

DECISION: The Blitzers had an existing contract with Tom. And even if they didn't, there would be no interference—as the Tigers came into court with "unclean hands." They were aware that Tom was under contract and should not have been negotiating with him for the current year. Tom would play for the Blitzers, at least until his new contract and any option ran out.

Stadiums

Teams cannot exist without stadiums and arenas that will seat large crowds. And, as these stadiums and arenas are expensive to build, most cities have only one. Thus, team owners in new sports leagues often have to settle for a lesser facility when a desired facility is under contract with an existing team in a competing league.

Despite head-to-head competition with established leagues, new leagues are attracted to the biggest cities. These large cities may be able to support more than one franchise and will already have existing stadiums and arenas.

Although it may be possible to share a stadium or arena with another team by juggling schedules, the existing league will often attempt to "tie up" a playing site by employing an "exclusive use" arrangement with the facility. Such arrangements have been found illegal.

An **"essential" facility**—one that could not practicably be duplicated—will not have to be shared if it would be impractical—as where a baseball team plays more games and more regularly than a football team, or where time may be needed to properly prepare the facility for the next game and another's use will not leave enough time. What if a stadium is privately owned? Must it still be shared?

Even where a stadium is privately owned, a duty exists to lease an "essential" facility where no other suitable facility exists for a pro sports team.

Cities

Success for a pro sports team will depend upon the support of fans. Experience has shown that the larger the city, the greater the likelihood for sufficient attendance.

As any existing league generally already has franchises in most large cities, a new league will have to fight with the existing league in order to locate franchises in these cities.

FACTS: The AFL tried to show that the NFL was monopolizing pro football by locating and expanding into all of the major cities, thus preventing the AFL from competing for fans in the largest cities. "Was this an illegal monopoly?" asked the AFL. **YOU'RE THE JUDGE!**

DECISION: The court decided, "There were still cities available with enough fans to potentially support teams. And those cities where the NFL already had teams might support a second pro football team. The NFL did not have monopoly power and, furthermore, had not undertaken expansion into new cities with the intent to destroy the AFL as a competitor."

The AFL could not prevent the NFL from expanding into new cities or from expanding its television coverage in order to protect part of the market for themselves.

FACTS: Did the USFL, in its battle with the NFL, have a similar problem in trying to show that the NFL had monopolized pro football by locating teams in all of the major cities? **YOU'RE THE JUDGE!**

DECISION: The USFL had franchises in, or near, the major cities, but several of them failed economically, then folded or were moved.

Owners

Professional sports leagues have attempted to "protect" themselves. Such a case was when the NFL attempted to ban ownership of teams by its club owners of teams in any competing sports league.

The court found that the ban unreasonably restrained trade, thus making it difficult for other leagues to find potential owners, thereby subjecting them to potential failure for lack of financial support.

Media

Sports are played at different levels: from sandlot or pick-up games, to collegiate sports, and ultimately to the highest level of ability and success—professional sports. Different leagues may vie, but eventually the fans will support the best league.

FACTS: A new volleyball league challenged the established United Volleyball League (UVL). As the fans preferred to see the

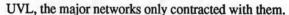

UVL, the major networks only contracted with them.

The new league claimed, "The networks locked us out. We won't be able to continue." Must the networks contract with the new league to cover their games? **YOU'RE THE JUDGE!**

DECISION: The media, to exist, will follow the fan's preference in deciding which games to broadcast. Leagues with lesser fan appeal will not be able to contract for television coverage as extensive as the desired league, or maybe not at all. As long as the networks did not conspire among themselves—or with the UVL—to lock out the new league, there will be no restraint of trade.

What will happen to the unwanted league? The ultimate outcome will likely be that one league will predominate while the other will disappear (or be merged or absorbed by the dominant league).

Merger

Merger or acquisition has settled several wars between competing leagues in pro sports.

Congress gave the NFL and AFL immunity from the antitrust laws prohibiting monopoly, thus clearing the way for them to end their war, declare a truce, and merge on the condition that the new league would have more teams than the two separate leagues. What if the players who were left out objected?

FACTS: After a long war, the ABA agreed to merge four ABA teams into the NBA.

Some ABA players objected, "The merger and the NBA's draft and reserve system monopolized pro basketball and prevented us from selling our services." They obtained an injunction preventing the two leagues from merging. Could the leagues still merge? **YOU'RE THE JUDGE!**

DECISION: After collective bargaining between the NBA and its player's association gave the players free agent status—with no unilateral right to renew by the losing team—the leagues were allowed to merge.

ODDS & ENDS....

FACTS: Before rumors of a new volleyball league, the UVL considered expanding. Could any new volleyball league successfully allege that any UVL expansion would prevent the new league from becoming established? Should the UVL have to forego expansion? **YOU'RE THE JUDGE!**

DECISION: Unless expansion was directly aimed at locking out a competing league, it is doubtful that such expansion could be enjoined.

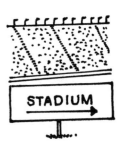

The effect of a league passing up expansion opportunities would be to deny fans in potential expansion cities the right to enjoy live pro sports, to deny qualified athletes and others the opportunity to earn a living, and to deny itself the opportunity to increase revenue. This could lessen the quality of the league.

18

OFFICIALS, REFEREES & UMPIRES

WHAT'S IT ABOUT?

All sports officials have a duty to provide fair and safe sporting events. *Officials, Referees & Umpires* considers who may be liable where an injury results to either a participant or an official during a sporting event.

Can an official's decision made during a sporting event be changed after the event is over?

Officials, Referees & Umpires' Union
5647 Fair Place, Plantation, FL 33324

Dear players, coaches, managers, fans and others:

This is our **OFFICIALS' CHECKLIST.** In the interest of providing a contest that (regardless of the result) will be: enjoyed by all, fair and safe, and leave you saying, "The ref did a great job!"—we will do our best to abide by it. We promise to:

BE SMART & WORK HARD

We will know the rules of the sport and give our best effort to keep ourselves and the contest under control with proper calls.

NOT BE "TOUGH" GUYS

If a coach, manager or player is on our back, but not enough to warrant a penalty, we won't be threatening or irritating by standing nearby just to "show 'em."

GET INTO THE "FLOW"

We will concentrate on players' reactions and the tempo of the game to prevent a "smooth" game from turning into a "ragged or rough" one.

LISTEN

We won't yell, but will treat everyone politely, answering all sensible questions. We will be firm, but relaxed, and accept some criticism. But we won't be "told off."

FORGET THE FANS

We will ignore the fans unless they interrupt the contest or our job. They may not know the rules, may be emotional and partisan, or merely delight in antagonizing us.

BE COOL & CONFIDENT

We will establish a calm atmosphere for the game by remaining "cool" under pressure. We will exude confidence and command respect. But we will not be cocky.

Officials, Referees & Umpires' Union

WAS THE OFFICIAL LIABLE?

FACTS: Two basketball referees worked hard to control a game. But then, a scuffle broke out. An injury resulted when a player was elbowed in the face. Were the officials liable?

DECISION: **YOU'RE THE JUDGE!**

What must an injured participant prove in order to recover damages against an official? What is an official's duty?

In order to recover damages from an official for an injury, an injured participant must prove **negligence.** That is, the participant must show that the official owed a duty to exercise due and proper care for a player's safety, that the official breached that duty, and that an injury and damages would not have occurred "but for" the action or inaction of the official.

However, officials do not insure participant's safety. Participants have a duty for their own protection and safety.

An official's **defenses** may be that any injured player assumes the risk of injury as one ordinary or common to the contest or sport, or that the player contributed to his injury by taking part in the contest.

> FACTS: Cater, a pro boxer, died several days after being knocked out in a fight. Many observers felt, "The referee should have stopped the fight. Cater was so dazed that he remained seated on his stool after the bell rang for his last round."
>
> During an investigation, a neurologist testified that "fight officials displayed gross malpractice of their official duties" by allowing Cater to continue.
>
> Cater's widow sued for "negligent supervision in failing to stop the fight." The referee and others defended by contending, "The boxer assumed the risk of injury by knowing, being aware of, and appreciating the risk." Was Cater aware in his condition? Was the referee liable?

DECISION: **YOU'RE THE JUDGE!**

After a high school wrestling match, the referee was sued for a failure of adequate supervision and control. The referee allegedly allowed a wrestler to continue with an illegal hold. As a result, the opponent was rendered a quadraplegic. The referee and other defendants settled out of court.

> FACTS: While another wrestling referee's attention was distracted by a yelling fan, one of the wrestlers applied an illegal hold, resulting in a severe injury to his opponent, Guererro. "Was the referee liable?" asked Guererro. **YOU'RE THE JUDGE!**

DECISION: A referee may be liable, not because of a failure to act in a proper manner, but rather because of a failure to act at all. The referee should not have allowed the fan to distract him.

A referee's job is to ensure that a game is played within the rules. If he allows a game to get out of control, or to be played in violation of rules, a new peril arises—injury to a player due to a lack of control or to rules violations.

May participants assume the risk of, or contribute to, any injury by participating?

FACTS: The Colts were playing the Steelers. Jones was running full speed as a play reached the sideline. He claimed, "I struck the aluminum down marker which was still stuck in the ground. The collision ruined my knee and cut short my career. The referees should have known that the equipment was dangerous and moved it out of the way. They didn't properly supervise and control their duties to protect the players." Were the referees liable for Jones' injuries? **YOU'RE THE JUDGE!**

DECISION: Apparently the jury was not convinced by Jones' allegations. They returned a verdict in favor of the referees. Jones—in playing football—had contributed to and assumed the risk of such an injury.

The care officials owe to a participant depends upon how apparent any risk is and their ability to prevent it.

FACTS: During a hockey game, a referee observed extremely rough play, but failed to sufficiently supervise it. He also failed to enforce rules designed to protect players from injuries from high sticking and slashing. Injuries resulted.

During a football game, a quarterback was injured by an intentional punch after throwing the ball.

Were either of these risks of harm apparent? Could the referees have prevented the injuries? **YOU'RE THE JUDGE!**

DECISION: The first risk was apparent and the injury could have been prevented. The risk of injury to the quarterback was not apparent.

What was the referee's ability to prevent injury? In certain sports, such as boxing and wrestling, a referee has a greater capacity for control than in others. In team contact sports, such as football or hockey, control is more difficult.

In team sports, only a referee's continual failure to control player misconduct should be declared a breach of his duty to care for a player's safety.

FACTS: The Bruisers and the Bumpers, in their quest for the Hockey Championship Cup, met in a play-off game. The referees were kept busy breaking up minor scuffles. When another scuffle broke out at one point, the referees decided not to interfere.

One of them thought, "Maybe if we let these two players go at it and get it out of their systems, everyone will calm down and the game will go on smoothly."

One of the players fighting was severely injured. Were the referees liable for letting the fight go on? Did they have control?

DECISION: **YOU'RE THE JUDGE!**

Officials do not insure a sports participant's safety. Where certain hazards and unavoidable accidents occur, against which a referee may not guard by the greatest degree of caution, liability may not attach.

FACTS: Karby, 16, died from a head injury received during a basketball game. He was hurt when a ball, thrown by a fellow player, hit him in the head. Did Karby assume the risk of injury? **YOU'RE THE JUDGE!**

DECISION: Yes. There was no liability by the referee for what was an unavoidable accident.

Will a participant assume the risk of injury from an unknown danger? A participant never assumes the risk from unknown danger. The fact that a participant is aware of one danger (player irresponsibility) cannot serve to extend assumption of the risk to another danger—a negligent referee.

FACTS: Ed received a severe injury during a scrimmage football game when Peter, who had been playing recklessly for some time, improperly ran into him. There were referees at the scrimmage. "Did I assume the risk of injury?" asked Ed. **YOU'RE THE JUDGE!**

DECISION: No. A player will not assume the risk of a referee's careless supervision. The injury would not have resulted had the referee's supervision been adequate. The referee's negligent supervision resulted in a foreseeable type of injury from an out of control situation.

However, if a participant, such as a professional, has skill, knowledge and training—beyond that of the average participant—assumption of the risk will be easier to prove.

INJURY TO AN OFFICIAL

Stiffer penalties, including suspension, have been used in an attempt to prevent attacks on, and abuse of, officials.

FACTS: A fan leaving a baseball game explained what happened. "The home plate umpire was in the parking lot after the game. The losing team's coach was yelling at the umpire and then hit him in the face." Was this contact part of the game, or was it an intentional assault? **YOU'RE THE JUDGE!**

DECISION: The coach was convicted of assault on a sports official and fined under a law intended to protect officials of sports contests.

An official only consents to, and assumes the risk of injury from, acts that are "part of the game" (such as where he is unintentionally run into). But where an official is shoved or struck, in an action clearly apart from the game, recovery of damages for injury may be possible.

FACTS: Toone, an umpire, ruled that a Cap outfielder had trapped a flyball. The opposing manager charged onto the field vehemently protesting. "If there is another bad call, I'll incite the crowd!" he warned.

In the ninth inning, the manager and his players charged onto the field after a close play. The manager refused to control his players and refused to help after several fans challenged Toone.

One fan injured Toone, who then sued the fan, the team, and the manager, claiming, "They owed me a duty to conduct themselves so as not to incite the crowd against me, and also to provide me with safe passage after the game." Who was liable for Toone's injury? **YOU'RE THE JUDGE!**

DECISION: Although the court held against the fan, it found that the assault was not the result of the manager's unsportsmanlike conduct. "It would be an intolerable burden on the club to hold it responsible for the actions of any emotionally unstable persons who might attend the game. The injury may have occurred even without the manager's conduct," commented the court.

Officials will be charged with knowledge of the danger involved in officiating sports, such as where athletes will cut back and forth. One court stated, "Referees who voluntarily participate must accept the risks to which their roles expose them."

Such was the case where football and baseball officials were "run over," and hockey and baseball officials were injured by pucks and balls. They assumed the risks of injury, having knowledge, awareness and appreciation of the risk involved.

FACTS: Umpire Dillard was standing behind the plate in a Little League baseball game when a ball bounced past the catcher and went out of play. Dillard yelled, "Time out!"

While time was called, the pitcher threw another pitch which struck the plate and then Dillard, who was not wearing shin guards or a groin protector.

Dillard sued the league for failing to provide him with adequate equipment, and he sued the pitcher for failing to heed the time out. "Who was liable?" asked Dillard. **YOU'RE THE JUDGE!**

DECISION: The risk of being struck by a baseball while umpiring was reasonably foreseeable, as was errant play from players so young. It was not the practice of the league to supply umpires with equipment. He assumed the risk of such an injury.

These players were young and inexperienced. Where such a situation involves an older, more experienced player, will an official still be held to assume the risk of injury?

FACTS: A volunteer track official was struck in the head by the shot put at the state championships. He stammered, "I was facing the track, standing in my assigned spot while officiating a race. The events were staged together in a small area. I never saw the shotput." Did the official assume the risk of such an injury?

DECISION: **YOU'RE THE JUDGE!**

WORKMEN'S COMPENSATION

State **workmen's compensation** laws compensate employees for injuries incident to their employment, without regard to the neglect or fault of their employer. An employee need only show that his injury arose from, and in the course of, his employment.

FACTS: An umpire, Clark, injured by an irate player, applied for workmen's compensation benefits. He explained, "I wasn't an employee of the Umpire Association or a school, but was an independent contractor. I worked for myself and could accept or refuse any assignment. The association or school had no control in directing my work or how it was done." Could Clark receive benefits? **YOU'RE THE JUDGE!**

DECISION: No. Clark was not an employee of the association or school. He could sue the player, the player's coach or parents, or the school.

However, where an official, such as an official for professional sports, is employed by an association or league and cannot refuse to officiate a certain game without jeopardizing his job, workmen's compensation may be available.

BAD FAITH

The general rule that officials' decisions will not be disturbed will not apply where a decision involves corruption or bad faith.

> FACTS: A horse won a close race. But before the winner was announced, one of three judges separately told each of the others that he and the third judge had agreed that another horse had won. Since each of the other judges believed that a majority of the judges was in favor of the second horse, they agreed. The second horse was declared the winner. Could the court overturn such a decision? **YOU'RE THE JUDGE!**

> DECISION: The court concluded, "Such conduct was fraudulent. The decision cannot stand. The power to correct corrupt or fraudulent decisions is necessary to insure public confidence in the honest and competent officiating of athletic games and contests."

ODDS & ENDS....

"We Contest The Decision"

The desire to win may provide the motivation to challenge an official's decision thought to be wrong. Generally, such challenges will amount to little more than verbal protestations.

> FACTS: Officials erred in not giving an automatic first down after the punter was "roughed" during a high school football game.
> The losing team protested, "That error led to our defeat. The last seven minutes, which determined qualification for the state playoffs, should be played over." Would the game, in part, be replayed? **YOU'RE THE JUDGE!**

> DECISION: No. The court ruled, "Football games are meant to be played on the gridiron and not in the courts. Players have no property right in the playing of the game by the rules. Decisions of officials do not present a controversy that can be heard by the courts."

Suits involving officials' errors in professional sports have also been denied.

The general rule is, "In the absence of bad faith or corruption, the decisions of sports officials will be final." That is so because of an official's experience, fairness and closeness to the action. However, there have been exceptions.

FACTS: In a high school basketball tournament, St. Michaels thought it beat Walther 67-66. St. Michaels scored at the first half buzzer, but Walther maintained that the buzzer went off several seconds after the clock had run out. The referees said the basket counted, but—after the game—reversed their decision, giving Walther the victory.

St. Michaels went to court seeking a ruling that the second half should be replayed. They asserted, "We certainly would have played differently had we known that the basket would not be counted." Should a court refuse to hear such a case, opening itself to appeal for every loss where an official's decision may be wrong? **YOU'RE THE JUDGE!**

DECISION: The second half was replayed, with St. Michaels again on the short end, 64-63.

Now matter how well officials perform their job in officiating sports events, they are sure to be booed.

19

DISHES, SATELLITES & PIRATES

WHAT'S IT ABOUT?

Dishes, Satellites & Pirates traces the history of television and cable in sports, explains who owns the TV and radio rights to sports broadcasts and discusses royalties and "piracy" of broadcast signals.
Do you know how the first "blackout" practice came about?

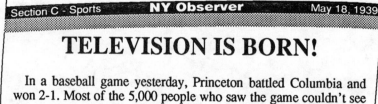

Section C - Sports   **NY Observer**   May 18, 1939

TELEVISION IS BORN!

In a baseball game yesterday, Princeton battled Columbia and won 2-1. Most of the 5,000 people who saw the game couldn't see the green grass, nor did they have to "dodge" foul balls. They didn't see the game in person, but watched it as the first sports event ever shown on TV!

TELEVISION SIGNALS

How would people receive a television signal? In the beginning, the only way a television signal could be received was by over-the-air transmission. The TV broadcasting station sent out a signal by antenna, which was received by another antenna—usually on the roof of a house—within range of the station. This is still the most common way by which most people receive television signals and programs.

But, with the advent of cable TV (CATV), television and sports became almost one. How did CATV begin?

CABLE TV

In the late 1940's, John Walson, an appliance salesman in Pennsylvania, realized that before he could sell new-fangled TV's to customers deep in mountain country—cut off from the broadcast signals in Philadelphia and Pittsburgh—he would have to guarantee reception. "How could I do that?" he asked.

Walson ran a wire to an antenna atop a nearby mountain, hooked his customers to it, and thus was born CATV!

That worked fine then, but how are CATV signals now brought into people's homes?

A cable station, such as ESPN or USA, after negotiating for broadcasting rights to a sporting event, sends the game's signal over Western Union land lines to the nearest city with the necessary transmitting microwave dish antenna (or directly from the game site if a dish is present).

From there, the signal is passed through the dish up to a satellite. At ESPN or USA, the signal is received back by another dish. The commercials, promos, and special effects are added, and then the complete show is beamed back up through the antenna of the dish to the satellite. Antennae at earth stations, set up by local cable companies that subscribe to the cable stations, then pull back down the completed signal and the picture is fed through cables to subscribers' living rooms.

These over-the-air and national cable broadcasts are supplemented by other forms of distributing signals for sports events. What are some of these other ways to distribute sports events?

"Superstations," like WTBS, WGN and WOR (which are local TV stations owning broadcast rights to local professional teams' games), beam signals by satellite to other cable operators. Thus, the Braves, Cubs and Mets can be seen coast to coast.

There also are: local cable companies; per-channel pay cable—such as HBO, subscription TV (where a decoder is needed to unscramble a signal), per-program home pay cable, and closed circuit for arenas and theatres—such as for a boxing match or other special event.

FACTS: People would now pay to watch sports at home, thus increasing the TV stations' revenue from commercials. TV began to dictate not only when games would be shown, but even when timeouts would be called during a game.

But what stations would be allowed to broadcast what games? And did the teams or the league own the rights to broadcast games?

DECISION: **YOU'RE THE JUDGE!**

TV & RADIO RIGHTS

"This telecast is presented by authority of the National Football League. It is intended solely for the private use of our audience, and any rebroadcast or other use of this telecast without the express written consent of the National Football League is prohibited."

This announcement is virtually identical to those used in other professional sports. Major League Baseball (MLB), in an effort to prevent unauthorized broadcasts, began making such a statement in connection with radio broadcasts of their games even before TV was in widespread use.

The first incident involving the unauthorized broadcast of a sporting event happened at the 1934 World Series—between the Cardinals and Tigers.

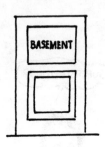

FACTS: Newton operated a radio station, WOCL, from the basement of his home. He would listen to the authorized radio broadcasts of games and, by using the information that he heard, give his audience a "play-by-play." His license renewal was challenged on the claim that he had improperly presented an unauthorized broadcast. "Can I still get my radio station license renewed?" asked Newton. **YOU'RE THE JUDGE!**

DECISION: Major League Baseball (MLB) had authorized the broadcast of World Series games by various radio stations, but not by Newton. Newton's conduct violated the Communications Act, which prohibits rebroadcasting, without consent, another station's programming. Newton's conduct was found to be a "dishonest, unfair utilization of another's labor and deceptive to the public." However, because the unauthorized broadcast had occurred only once, Newton's license was renewed.

Some early decisions denied the right of sports teams to control the broadcast of their games. Those decisions were few and not later followed.

FACTS: In 1938, radio station KQV stationed observers who watched baseball games over the fences at the Pirate's Forbes Field. These observers then relayed the information to KQV announcers, who then broadcast play-by-play descriptions of the games. The Pirates sued to enjoin KQV from the unauthorized broadcasts. KQV argued that the accounts of sports events constituted news and that any person had the right to disseminate the news. Was KQV enjoined from broadcasting the games? **YOU'RE THE JUDGE!**

DECISION: Yes. The court enjoined KQV from broadcasting the games without permission, commenting, "The Pirates—by going to great expense in creating the game, maintaining the baseball park and paying the players—had a **property right** in the news of the games. They could sell that right to others to broadcast the games, and could also restrict others from disseminating news of the game. KQV was guilty of unfair competition, unjust enrichment of another's property rights and of a fraud on the public."

Now teams could sell or license this right and prevent others from unauthorized live broadcasts of their games.

FACTS: Martin explained how he helped rebroadcast Giants baseball games. "I teletyped authorized reports of the games to radio stations across the country for immediate rebroadcast. The stations would pick up these broadcasts without paying the team and then insert their own play-by-play, complete with background sound effects of crowds, ball on bat and made up reasons for crowd noise." Was this legal? **YOU'RE THE JUDGE!**

DECISION: No. The court concluded, "Although some of these re-creations were more exciting than the game itself, they were unauthorized and illegal as a misappropriation of the Giants' property rights to control the broadcast of its baseball games. Martin was enjoined from sending the reports.

Teams could now control the broadcast of their games. But could they control any rebroadcast made after a game?

The right of teams to control the broadcast of their games extended not only to the live broadcast of the game but, also, for a reasonable time following the game or event, to any rebroadcast. Practices, other than reporting the game as part of a news broadcast, were prohibited. Incorporating film of games into movies or highlight films and supplying "up to the minute, ringside descriptions" of boxing matches were also prohibited.

To help protect this right to control an event's broadcast, sports teams began printing on the back of tickets:

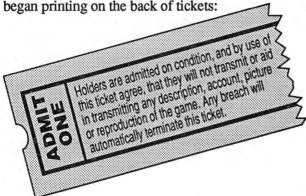

This sports property right concept was strengthened by a case concerning the celebrated "Flying" Zacchini's human cannon ball performance.

FACTS: On a nightly news show, a TV station broadcasted Zacchini's entire performance without his permission. The performer sued the station for "stealing my right to control who would see my performance." The station felt that it was only showing the news, a right given by the First Amendment. "Did the station misappropriate Zacchini's property right? **YOU'RE THE JUDGE!**

DECISION: Yes. Zacchini had the right to control the publicizing of his performance. The court found the station guilty of misappropriation and awarded damages to Zacchini.

What if the station had only broadcast part of the performance on its sports show?

The court explained, "Had the station only broadcast part of the performance, its right to do so would have been protected by the right to free speech and the right to disseminate the news."

Broadcasters, with the aid of satellite dishes (earth stations), have a wide variety of sports highlights to chose from in their daily sports shows. To what extent can a TV station rebroadcast highlights of a sporting event without the consent of the clubs or the clubs' licensees?

FACTS: Without consent, ESPN taped WSBK-TV telecasts of Red Sox and Bruins games. They excerpted highlights for their "Sportscenter" show, which was delivered via satellite to cable systems throughout the country—including those in the Boston area where WSBK had been selling their highlights to local TV stations. Was this practice an infringement on the team's right to control the broadcast of their own games? **YOU'RE THE JUDGE!**

DECISION: ESPN's action was an infringement of WSBK's property right (copyright) to control the broadcast of the highlights. The case was settled, with ESPN agreeing to pay a fee for its use of the highlights.

To prevent the selling of "Highlights and Bloopers" shows of its copyrighted games, Major League Baseball limits news shows to showing highlights no older than thirty-six hours. And total highlights can't exceed five minutes, with no more than two minutes from any one game.

What if a station also showed an awards ceremony after a sports event? Would that be allowed?

FACTS: Mason, president of WXXZ-TV, said, "Filming of the entire championship boxing match was sold for a delayed broadcast. But critical footage was excerpted without permission, showing highlights before the delayed broadcast. Also, the awards ceremony after the match was shown." Could either of these practices be enjoined? **YOU'RE THE JUDGE!**

DECISION: Yes. Both practices were enjoined. The right to a delayed broadcast may also extend to any highlights or awards ceremony taking place after the event.

WILL WE SEE THE GAME?

Increasingly, professional sports leagues and other professional sports have been selling their broadcast rights to pay cable TV.

The typical home viewer is being asked to pay for what was always free television.

Leagues and other sports asserted, "The broadcasts are our property to sell as we please." Should the sports and leagues have to provide free TV coverage of games and other sports events to the public, without whom the leagues and other sports could not survive?

EXCLUSIVE RIGHT TO PERFORM!

The **Copyright Act of 1976** gave professional sports leagues copyright protection—the exclusive right to "perform publicly" live sports events and control all broadcasts of their games.

FACTS: Superstation WZEZ simultaneously rebroadcasted a local station's coverage of the home baseball team without altering the programming or advertising. WZEZ had no control over the content or selection of the broadcast. They solely provided communication channels for the use of others. Was this a copyright infringement of the local station's right to control the broadcast? **YOU'RE THE JUDGE!**

DECISION: No. The Copyright Act allowed cable systems to convey such "secondary" broadcasts of copyrighted works. This is called "passive" broadcasting and is not copyright infringement. In return, each cable system must pay a fee which is distributed to the copyright owners.

Cable systems—the only media permitted to retransmit professional sports games without negotiating for the rights to do so—now negotiate for game broadcasting rights. Because of this "compulsory" license, a team's only right of control (other than scrambling signals) over cable's rebroadcast, comes from Federal Communications Commission (FCC) rules restricting some cable sports telecasts.

Baseball now scrambles some signals. Stations desiring to televise such games must obtain permission from the commissioner and pay a rights' fee. Those granted permission then buy a decoder.

RULES! RULES!

As cable systems had the right to carry an almost unlimited number of sporting events, teams and cable systems became concerned that the availability of too many games would hurt gate receipts and broadcast revenues. But how could the teams control the broadcasts of their games?

In addition to scrambling signals, two rules provide clubs with some control over the numbers and kinds of games that cable systems may carry.

> FACTS: The Celtics, playing at home against the 76er's, were not televising the game in Boston. They requested that cable systems in the Boston area delete the telecast of the game by the 76er's. One cable station decided to carry the game locally. Could the Celtics enjoin the station from carrying the game? **YOU'RE THE JUDGE!**

> DECISION: Yes. The "Sports" or "Same Game" Rule requires cable systems within 35 miles to delete the distant signal telecast of that club's home game—provided that the home game is not televised locally.

This rule protects a club's decision not to televise a particular home game, at the same time protecting the home gate and club's pay cable or subscription TV contracts.

> FACTS: The Red Sox wanted to establish a network of local stations in New England to carry its games through its flagship station—the one carrying its home games. These local stations wanted to prevent local cable stations from duplicating their telecast of games. Could they prevent the cable stations from carrying Red Sox games? **YOU'RE THE JUDGE!**

> DECISION: The second rule allows local stations to prevent local cable systems from duplicating a local station's broadcast.

The Atlanta Braves' flagship superstation, WTBS, sought to distribute play-off games nationwide by satellite. ABC, which held the exclusive nationwide broadcast rights, sued to prevent WTBS from carrying the games. WTBS was enjoined. Only local outlets of the participating teams were permitted to carry the games.

WHO GETS THE ROYALTIES?

As copyright owners of their games' telecasts, sports teams are entitled to all of the **royalties** or revenues from the telecasts. Although broadcasters have an interest in the commentary of the announcers, the public tunes into sports broadcasts mainly to see the event and the athletes.

FACTS: Many pro athletes asserted, "We are the show. Without our performance, there would be no game, no broadcast and no royalties. We should get a share of the royalties." Should the players share in the royalties? **YOU'RE THE JUDGE!**

DECISION: No. The "works made for hire" rule in the Copyright Act provides that a player's contribution to a copyrighted work (the games) becomes the property of the team. Furthermore, the players, in their contracts, agreed that all rights pertaining to pictures of the players are the property of the team.

Players, through bargaining with their team owners, could attempt to negotiate for broadcast revenues in addition to those already contributed to the players' retirement fund.

SCHOOLS & BROADCASTING RIGHTS

If schools competing in sports cannot resolve the distribution of any broadcast rights to their games, the home team will have exclusive rights in its home territory, and the visiting team in its home territory.

FACTS: The Holy Cross Crusaders played at home against the Boston College Eagles in the schools' annual fall football classic.

TV and radio stations approached both schools for the broadcast rights to the game—both locally, in Worcester, and back to the Boston area. Which school owned the rights to distribute the accounts and descriptions of the game locally? **YOU'RE THE JUDGE!**

DECISION: Holy Cross had the broadcast rights in the Worcester area; Boston College had the broadcast rights in the Boston area. If either sold its rights to a station which broadcasted to the other's area, the home school's rights would prevail.

Which school would own the rights to a national broadcast of the game? Neither school, alone, has the right to control the broadcasting rights in the other's area. Regional or national coverage supersedes local coverage and will only be carried upon agreement between both schools and the network or cable station seeking to purchase those rights.

SUPERSTATIONS

What is a "superstation"? A superstation is a local TV station whose signal is picked up by distant cable systems throughout the country and beyond. Stations such as WTBS (Atlanta), WGN (Chicago), and WOR (NJ) are superstations.

These stations show sports programming, which they and distant cable systems may carry without the consent of clubs or other copyright owners.

> FACTS: The Mets brought suit against WOR for carrying Mets games, which were then picked up by distant cable systems without consent or compensation to the club. Would WOR be allowed to continue this practice? **YOU'RE THE JUDGE!**
>
> DECISION: Yes. The court found this practice to be permitted under the "passive carrier" rule, and ruled, "Where WOR had no control over the content or selection of the broadcast, or the cable systems picking up its signal, and whose activity was solely to provide the channel for the use of others, then WOR could carry and make available the Mets' games without violating the law."

This made programing available to the public, which might otherwise not be available. Now, however, superstations and the teams whose games they carry have agreed to compensate other teams for lost attendance and TV revenues brought about by the intrusion of TV coverage into the other teams' home markets. In addition, baseball teams may now scramble their games. To obtain a decoder, stations must receive permission from the commissioner and pay a rights' fee.

PIRACY!

Teams, leagues and their licensed broadcasters use satellites to relay telecasts of games from the home site to the visiting club's home market or to network control points. Anyone having a satellite dish might intercept these telecasts.

However, the **Communications Act of 1934** prohibits the "interception and retransmission of broadcasts not intended for the use of the general public."

Later, in 1984, the U.S. Congress enacted the **Cable Communications Policy Act.** This act prohibits satellite transmissions except when they are made public or where the viewing is private. Home private viewing directly via satellite dish, without authorization from the cable programmer is permitted.

What is private viewing? Private viewing means viewing for private use in an individual home by means of equipment owned, or operated, by such individual.

Is public viewing by motel, bar, hotel and restaurant owners for the enjoyment of their customers permitted without the authorization of satellite programmers?

FACTS: The Miami Dolphins sued bars for intercepting and showing blacked-out telecasts of Dolphin home games, in violation of the NFL rule banning the broadcast of blacked-out games within 75 miles of the stadium where the home team is playing. The bars picked up the "clean feed" (without commercials) from a satellite to get around the ban.

The Dolphins argued, "This practice lessened game attendance and ticket sales. The game was our product and property. We don't like anyone stealing our property!"

The bars answered, "The games were news events that we could show. Nothing in the laws banned the use of satellite dishes." Could the bars continue to intercept the blacked-out games and broadcast them within the Dolphins home territory? **YOU'RE THE JUDGE!**

DECISION: No. The game telecast was the Dolphins' property and could be protected by copyright. The bars were enjoined from carrying any future games by such a practice. Now, some broadcasters scramble signals, reception for which requires permission, a rights' fee, and a fee for a decoder to unscramble the signals.

"POOLING" OF TV RIGHTS

The **Sports Broadcasting Act** allows certain professional sports leagues to pool all of the broadcast rights to their games.

By pooling rights, the NFL could prevent the networks from not televising games of "weaker" clubs. The act allows the networks to determine where the broadcasts will be seen.

Before this Act, pooling broadcast rights was illegal. By preventing networks from dealing only with successful clubs, it restrained trade.

Did the Sports Broadcasting Act offer any protection for high school and college football games?

FACTS: What if the NFL decided to begin Friday Night Football? Games would be carried nationwide every Friday during the season, with occasional Saturday games. Would this be allowed? **YOU'RE THE JUDGE!**

DECISION: No. The Sports Broadcasting Act protects high school and college football games by preventing any NFL telecasts on Friday evenings and Saturdays, from the second Friday in September to the second Saturday in December, from any station within 75 miles of the game site of a high school or college game.

The Sports Broadcasting Act only allows professional leagues, excepting soccer, to pool their broadcast rights. Colleges are not permitted such an arrangement.

FACTS: The NCAA restricted its member schools from negotiating on their own, prohibited them from televising games (except through the NCAA), and fixed prices of televised college football games. Was this an illegal monopoly of the televising of college football games? **YOU'RE THE JUDGE!**

DECISION: Yes. The court called the NCAA action a "commandeering" of schools' property rights in football games.
The court held, "The NCAA monopolized the market of televised college football games; it restrained trade by limiting schools' freedom to negotiate their own TV deals for coverage of their games."

The NCAA was still permitted to restrict Friday night games, impose TV sanctions against schools violating NCAA rules, and have its own TV plan, in which any school might participate.

BLACKOUTS!

In the 1930's, Judge "Mountain" Landis, the first baseball commissioner, prohibited radio broadcasts of major league games into minor league towns where the local team objected.

This rule was later expanded to prohibit radio or TV broadcasts into home territories of other teams, without permission, but "only when the other team was playing at home or telecasting an away game back to its home territory."

This, the first actual **blackout,** was repealed, but later followed by a similar NFL rule.

FACTS: The NFL rule prohibited a team from broadcasting its games into another team's home territory when the other team was either playing at home or broadcasting its away game back to its home territory. Could the NFL enforce such a rule? **YOU'RE THE JUDGE!**

DECISION: No. The Sports Broadcasting Act provided for a home territory blackout on a day when a team is playing at home, but not when the home team is playing away. For example, if the Dolphins were playing at home and chose to blackout a game not sold out, then a network could not televise the game in Miami's home territory, but could televise it elsewhere. They could televise other games into the Dolphins' home territory.

The act applies equally as well to blackouts in other major sports, and to play-off or championship games, as well as regular season games.

Another case helped to further define the 75 mile "home territory."

FACTS: A TV station, WTWV, sought to televise the Dolphins' home games which weren't sold out. The Sport's Broadcasting Act prohibited non-sold out games from being televised within the Dolphins' home territory, 75 miles in all directions from the game site, the Orange Bowl.

WTWV claimed, "The rule does not apply to us. Our transmitter is located 90 miles from the Orange Bowl, and, therefore, we should be allowed to broadcast the games."

"Can we blackout WTWV's signal?" asked the Dolphins. **YOU'RE THE JUDGE!**

DECISION: Yes. The 75 mile home territory protected the Dolphins from any television signal that reached into that protected area. It did not matter that the TV station was outside the 75 mile territory.

Blackout Lifting

In 1973, professional sports leagues were required to lift a local blackout of any pooled telecast of a game if all of the tickets available for purchase five days before the game were sold 72 hours or more in advance (unless the broadcast conflicted with a protected high school or college game). This law expired, but the NFL continues to follow it. And cable stations agreed to blackout hockey games in the participating team's home markets.

Owners have, on occasion, lifted a blackout although a game was not sold out within the required time.

ODDS & ENDS....

FACTS: Universal Studios sued Sony, alleging that Sony's videotape recorder (VCR) was being used to "copy Universal's copyrighted materials (movies)." Universal challenged the practice of home taping of TV programming."

Tom had a satellite dish in his backyard with which he picked up numerous sporting events. He paid for the dish, but paid no other fees. It, like the VCR, was for his private use, not for presenting a public performance of the game. Were these practices illegal? **YOU'RE THE JUDGE!**

DECISION: The court, noting that sports interests did not object to home recording, held that home taping for private, non-commercial use is permitted.

Although satellite dish reception for "private viewing" is legal, broadcasters are now scrambling their signals. In these cases, reception requires a fee for a decoder to unscramble the signals.

Many of us, with our VCRs, are virtual "pirates."

20

ENDORSEMENTS & TRADEMARKS

WHAT'S IT ABOUT?

Endorsements & Trademarks is an in-depth look at the marketing of sports products, trademarks, endorsements in advertising by "experts," and misrepresentations of products.

Can teams or players prevent the use of their nicknames or logos in selling products, such as T-shirts or hats?

DO PROS USE THE SAME PRODUCTS AS YOU?

Can you match pro athletes with the products they endorse in advertisements on TV and in newspapers, magazines and elsewhere? Do pros have to use the products that they endorse in commercials?

ENDORSEMENTS

Endorsements are advertising messages (statements, demonstrations, or the use of a name, likeness or nickname) which consumers are likely to believe reflect the beliefs of the endorser.

Endorsements appear in advertising—a description of a product or service to induce the public to buy or use it.

Sports figures are used to endorse products because of the public's infatuation with them and with sports. Companies hope that fans will then buy their products for identity, image and to show allegiance for a team, player or sport.

As the public may place great faith and belief in sports stars, care must be taken to ensure that any product or service they promote is promoted properly, and that it performs as advertised.

Many of the products and services endorsed by athletes are not superior to a competitor's, but are endorsed and used by athletes because of the compensation paid.

Does an athlete have to talk about a product in order for there to be an endorsement?

FACTS: A manufacturer of tennis racquets employed a pro tennis player to praise the ability of their racket to produce overspin and keep the ball in play.

An ad for golf balls had a pro hitting a manufacturer's golf balls, but saying nothing. Were these endorsements? **YOU'RE THE JUDGE!**

DECISION: Yes. If consumers think the advertising message reflects the tennis player's or golfer's personal views and those of the sponsoring advertiser, then even if no verbal statements are made, it is an endorsement.

The importance of this is that, to protect the public, endorsements are governed by strict rules.

FACTS: Ken and Tony, NBA stars, were asked, "Will you endorse our beer, chewing tobacco and whiskey?" Were the athletes permitted to appear in such ads? **YOU'RE THE JUDGE!**

DECISION: No. Most sports prohibit active athletes from being involved in any endorsement of alcoholic beverages or tobacco products. Such endorsements would convey the wrong impression that use of such products is conducive to the development of athletic skill or physical prowess.

Also, to protect the public, the Federal Trade Commission (FTC) established restrictions on the use of celebrity endorsements.

The FTC has the power over "unfair or deceptive acts or practices." They investigate any celebrity representations in endorsements that are false, misleading or deceptive.

What if a company uses an athlete's likeness for an endorsement—is this permitted?

Using a sports figure's name or likeness for commercials, without consent, may create liability.

FACTS: Frux Co., a manufacturer of tennis racquets, hired an endorser and made him up to look, act and talk like Rob, the number one ranked tennis pro. Was this an invasion of Rob's right to privacy? **YOU'RE THE JUDGE!**

DECISION: Yes. Rob had a valuable "right to publicity," earned by years of experience, which may be protected, contracted away or "left alone." The ad was an invasion of Rob's privacy. It was enjoined and Rob was awarded damages.

An advertiser must also refrain from falsely stating or implying that a celebrity endorser uses a product when he does not.

FACTS: A pro golfer, "Crunch," appeared in ads urging, "I recommend golf ball A. I use it." Later, he switched to promoting golf ball B, made by another company. Could the ads in which Crunch endorsed golf ball A still be shown? **YOU'RE THE JUDGE!**

DECISION: Ads in which Crunch endorsed golf ball A would be false. They can no longer be shown. The endorser, in any ad representing that he uses a product, must be a **bona fide user** —one who uses a product because he likes and approves of it at the time the endorsement is given.

A golfer could endorse two different golf balls, but it is unlikely that a company would allow the golfer to simultaneously endorse a competitor's product while endorsing the company's.

It should be determined at reasonable intervals whether the endorser still endorses the product. This is especially so where an athlete or sports celebrity endorses a product because of certain reasons and the product is later changed. If not determined, the endorsement may no longer be used.

FACTS: Slasher, a pro hockey player, presented his views in a "blind comparison test" of a soft drink. This was not designed to represent Slasher as a bona fide user. Must Slasher use the product? "Must we periodically check to see if Slasher still uses the drink?" asked the company. **YOU'RE THE JUDGE!**

DECISION: It is only when an endorser is held out as a bona fide user that tests for use requirements and checks on the endorser's views at "reasonable intervals" are required.

An endorsement used only once will not require further approval or use inquiry. However, a longer endorsement contract will require questioning at reasonable intervals.

What if the advertising message is by an announcer who is unfamiliar to the general public, except as a spokesman for a company's product? Are the rules then different?

FACTS: Dirk, unfamiliar to the public, endorsed a product, "Our whiffle balls can be thrown faster and they break more than any other." The ad ran for three years. Was this an endorsement? Must the company periodically check to see if Dirk still holds the same opinion of the whiffle ball? **YOU'RE THE JUDGE!**

DECISION: The ad was not represented as, or likely to be believed by consumers as, reflecting the opinion and beliefs of Dirk, but was represented as the opinion of the company. It was not an endorsement. Therefore, the company could continue to use the ad without checking Dirk's present opinion.

MISREPRESENTATION

Must an endorsement contain the exact words of an endorser? Endorsements may not contain deceptive representations. An ad that represents that the message is phrased in the exact words of the endorser must contain the precise language of the endorser.

FACTS: An advertiser for golf balls quoted an endorser, a pro golfer, as saying, "This ball won me the U.S. Open." What the golfer actually said was, "I used this ball when I won the U.S. Open." Was this a deceptive ad? **YOU'RE THE JUDGE!**

DECISION: Yes. The representation may deceive the public. It is not permitted.

An endorsement may be permitted even if not factually true in all respects. Allowing only partially true endorsements enables advertisers and endorsers to proclaim, for example, "This drink will make you a winner!"

This may be acceptable for some products, but not for those involving health, safety or children. There, the strictest standards apply, to ensure that there are no misrepresentations of any kind—no matter how slight.

Endorsers are generally free to comment on taste without requiring any substantiation, as by tests.

"I'M AN EXPERT!"

What is an expert? An **expert** is one who, because of education, training, knowledge or experience, has acquired special skills.

FACTS: The following, represented as experts in their fields, endorsed certain products: a race car driver for car performance products; a golfer for golf clubs and a tennis racquet; a tennis pro for golf balls; and, a basketball player for tennis shoes. Could these experts endorse those products? **YOU'RE THE JUDGE!**

DECISION: "Whenever an endorser is represented as an expert in an ad, then the expert must have such expertise." The golfer and tennis player cannot endorse each other's products.

If an organization endorses a product, then the endorsement must reflect the collective judgment of the group. And, an expert must judge the merits of any product endorsed.

FACTS: The Major Volleyball League (MVL) selected Juice-Aid as its "Official Drink." In ads promoting the drink, the MVL endorsed the product. "What must we do before we endorse the product?" asked the MVL. **YOU'RE THE JUDGE!**

DECISION: If a consumer is left with the impression that the product has nutritional value because of the connection between performance and diet, then the MVL must employ and rely on an expert in the field of nutrition before endorsing the product.
   Furthermore, use of the words "selects" and "official" imply that the endorsement was based on a comparison against competing brands. Therefore, to avoid an assertion of a deceptive ad, side-by-side comparisons must have concluded that the product was at least equal to its competitor's. If a product is represented as being superior to other products, then scientific testing must substantiate that.

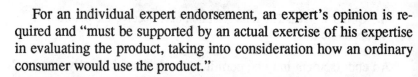

For an individual expert endorsement, an expert's opinion is required and "must be supported by an actual exercise of his expertise in evaluating the product, taking into consideration how an ordinary consumer would use the product."

FACTS: A novice skier endorsed skis, "These skis give you the feel and ease of movement needed in championship racing." Would this require an expert? Was this misleading? **YOU'RE THE JUDGE!**

DECISION: Yes. The ad required an expert who had used and examined the skis. The statements by the novice were false representations which may mislead the public.

"I'M A NON-EXPERT!"

A non-expert endorser and an advertiser must make "reasonable inquiry into the truthfulness of any endorsement." Reasonable inquiry means having information evaluated by competent, reliable and independent sources. This may lead to less confusion and deception.

However, as this will increase the time needed to respond to a competitor's endorsements, experts may be used where a quick reply to the competition is desired.

Is an expert opinion needed in advertising health or safety products?

Endorsing a product related to health or safety without proper reliance upon an expert evaluation may lead to a false and deceptive ad. Whereas, if an expert opinion is not needed, the endorser may rely upon personal experience.

> FACTS: Bruno, a pro boxer, endorsed an acne medicine, saying, "This made my skin clear up." Sly, a pro wrestler, also endorsed the medicine, "The medicine's ingredients reacted with my skin to clear it up almost immediately."
>
> Christine, a pro tennis player, endorsed a new car, "It runs great!" she said. "Hooker," a pro golfer, also endorsed the car, "It's the safest car there is."
>
> Must any of these endorsers rely upon expert advice? **YOU'RE THE JUDGE!**

> DECISION: Bruno's endorsement will not require expert advice, while Sly's endorsement of the acne medication will require the evaluation of an expert for Sly to rely upon.
>
> Christine's endorsement of the car only required her personal evaluation, while expert advice must be relied upon by Hooker.

Sports celebrities or athletes who endorse a product relating to health or safety without relying upon expert opinion may subject themselves to personal liability.

Payment to an expert or well-known endorser need not be disclosed as long as the advertiser does not represent that the endorsement was given without compensation, or as long as there is no other financial interest in the sale of the product or service used in the endorsement.

> FACTS: Mike Eagle, a pro golfer, was also the president of Par Busters, Inc., makers and promoters of Wind Breaker golf balls—guaranteed to fly lower and straighter in wind. Mike endorsed the golf balls in advertisements and received a share of the product's sales. Should Mike have been required to disclose his relationship with Par Busters in any ads that he appeared in? **YOU'RE THE JUDGE!**

> DECISION: Yes. Any relationship which might "materially affect the credibility of the endorsement" must be disclosed. If the public were aware that the endorser had a financial interest, other than a payment not dependent upon the success of sales of the product, it might conclude that the endorser would "puff" his endorsement to increase his financial gain from the sale of the product.

What if the endorser, an athlete, also agrees to use the product? Such might be the case where a tennis or golf pro, as part of an endorsement contract, agrees to wear certain clothing or logos or to use the advertiser's equipment.

FACTS: Gary, a pro basketball player, in violation of an agreement to use certain tennis shoes, wore a competitor's. What could the advertiser do?

Larry complained, "The shoe didn't perform as it was supposed to. It fell apart!" What could Larry do? **YOU'RE THE JUDGE!**

DECISION: If Gary broke his endorsement contract, then there may be a separate action to either enforce the contract or sue for damages for the breach.

If the shoes fell apart, Larry could break the contract, but without any damages.

TRADEMARKS

Professional teams, associations and athletes, in order to satisfy the public's desire to identify with them, expend money and effort to develop goodwill and a favorable reputation. This goodwill and reputation is then marketed by attaching their logos and names to merchandise which the public will buy.

To protect these names, logos, and other identifying marks, they are registered as **trademarks**—any word, name, symbol, or other mark or any combination, used to identify one's goods and distinguish them from another's.

FACTS: Big Mike owned a sporting goods store in Falmouth. He admitted, "I created consumer demand by 'copying' and then attaching pro and college logos, names, and pictures of pro sports teams and players to many items. Then I sold them, without permission, for a lower price than 'official' items were sold for." Was Big Mike guilty of **trademark infringement**? **YOU'RE THE JUDGE!**

DECISION: Yes. Big Mike would be guilty of trademark infringement if a federal trademark had been registered and he had used a copy or duplication of the trademark—without consent—in interstate commerce, in connection with the sale (or offer for sale, distribution or advertisement of goods), and that such use was likely to cause confusion with the public.

This practice tarnishes the image of the trademark owner and confuses the consumer, who relies on quality goods bearing the official trademarks of their favorite athletes and teams.

FACTS: A manufacturer's umbrella, the "Capabrella," looked like an oversized baseball cap. Another manufacturer, Ace Co., made a similar-looking umbrella. The similarity between these trademarks and products created confusion. Could Ace Co. be enjoined from making such an umbrella? **YOU'RE THE JUDGE!**

DECISION: Yes. This was an infringement of the Capabrella trademark. Ace Co. could be enjoined from manufacturing a similar looking umbrella, one which would confuse the public as to whose it was.

Trademark infringement is just one type of unfair competition. If the mark has acquired a secondary meaning, then the test becomes whether the activities of the infringer have created a likelihood of confusion. What is a secondary meaning?

FACTS: Georgia University sued a manufacturer for selling products which had on them a picture of a "Battlin' Bulldog." It was strikingly similar to the picture of Ulga, the "Georgia Bulldog," the university's mascot. Would the picture of the school's mascot, which was recognized as such without the words, or vice versa, be confused with the picture and words of "Battlin' Bulldog?" **YOU'RE THE JUDGE!**

DECISION: Yes. The school's mascot and his name had each acquired a secondary meaning as being the mark of the school. The manufacturer's picture and name would confuse the public. The manufacturer was enjoined from using the name or the picture.

An often used defense to a trademark infringement charge is the contention, "The mark is functional and, therefore, can't be protected." Any feature of a product which is essential to the usefulness of the product is **functional**—necessary for the product's use.

FACTS: Ace Golf Co. designed two golf carts. One had a regular looking steering wheel. The other, designed like a bent golf club, was very distinctive. Were these steering wheels functional?
The Tucci Tennis Shoe Co. used velcro instead of shoelaces to secure its tennis shoes. Was this functional? **YOU'RE THE JUDGE!**

DECISION: The regular steering wheel was essential to the use of the cart; it was functional and could not be protected as a trademark. The other steering wheel was very distinctive; its design could be protected.
The use of velcro was functional and essential to the use of the shoes. It could not be protected by a trademark.

Any feature that is not related to identification or individuality is functional.

FACTS: The Bombers hockey team wore all white uniforms. Could they obtain a trademark on the uniform and then prevent anyone from selling such uniforms?
The Slashers used a unique combination of several colors for their uniforms.

The Trippers used another identifying mark with their colors—an emblem of a hockey player being tripped. Were these marks functional, or could they be protected by trademarks? **YOU'RE THE JUDGE!**

DECISION: The Bombers' uniform is not related to identification or individuality and, thus, may not be protected.

The Slashers' and Trippers' uniforms may be protected. They have certain color combinations and other identifying marks which are not functional.

If a product would be desired, regardless of the feature, then the feature is functional and cannot be protected by a trademark. For example, an article of clothing, such as a football jersey, or an emblem shaped as a football or baseball, with no logo or team colors, may not be protected. These are functional items.

INSIGNIAS, SYMBOLS & EMBLEMS

Trademark infringement may also involve a name, word, or phrase, either alone or in combination with goods or services.

FACTS: Dallas Emblem Co. duplicated and sold NHL team symbols on patches. The NHL sued for trademark infringement, claiming, "This was done without our consent. There would have been no market for a patch without the NHL's symbols. This use would confuse or deceive the public."

Dallas argued, "The insignia was an aesthetically pleasing feature of the patch, essential to its usefulness, and therefore could not be protected by a trademark." Should the NHL, or any other league, team, or other association be able to protect their insignias for their own use? **YOU'RE THE JUDGE!**

DECISION: Yes. "Dallas misappropriated a valuable right belonging to the NHL." They were enjoined from any further manufacture and sale of such emblems, without consent. The bare patch, without the NHL team symbols, would have no market.

For deliberate and fraudulent infringement, a court may, in addition to granting an injunction, award punitive damages. Such marks—as NFL, NBA, PGA and others—took substantial amounts of money and time to establish. To allow someone else to improperly use such marks is a serious misappropriation of a valuable and protected right to publicity in the mark. Can such a mark be functional, as well as a trademark?

Such marks acquired a strong secondary meaning of identification of the teams. A patch, without such an insignia, is of little, if any, value. Thus, the symbols have aesthetic value as well as indicating their source or origin. The marks are a functional component of the product as well as a trademark.

UNIFORMS

FACTS: A clothing manufacturer sold "replicas" of NFL jerseys—football shirts with large numerals, NFL team colors and either the name of an NFL city, team or player. The NFL contended, "Such jerseys, sold without our consent, confused the public since they desired and purchased the jersey believing that it was an 'official' NFL jersey—one made or authorized by the NFL."

Would the public be likely to buy the jerseys without the official NFL team colors, numerals, design, and city or player's name? Was this trademark infringement? **YOU'RE THE JUDGE!**

DECISION: The public purchased the jerseys because of the NFL colors, design, and name, and because they thought that they were purchasing "Official" NFL jerseys. The manufacturer confused and deceived the public. A functional feature, such as a fanciful nickname or design, can also serve as a trademark. The manufacturer was enjoined from the manufacturing and sale of the jerseys.

A cinema showed a movie in which uniforms strikingly similar to those worn by the Dallas Cowboy Cheerleaders, were worn.

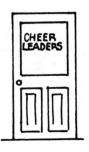

The cinema argued that the uniform was purely functional as an article of clothing. The court held that the uniform had taken on a secondary meaning as that of the Cowboy Cheerleaders and, as such, could be protected from unconsented use. The improper use confused and deceived the public into believing that the Cowboy Cheerleaders were taking part in the movie.

In general, a uniform or color is not capable of becoming a trademark. But a certain combination of colors, as in team insignias, can become a trademark when recognized by the public as that of a certain team or group. Therefore, trademark rights are recognized for pro sports teams' uniforms.

Colleges may similarly protect their name and identifying marks.

FACTS: The University of Pittsburgh sued a manufacturer for selling clothing and other items with the school's colors and name on those products. Could the manufacturers be enjoined from selling such clothing or other items? **YOU'RE THE JUDGE!**

DECISION: The court enjoined the manufacturer. It found that the demand for a product with Pitt's name on it resulted from the efforts of PItt, not the manufacturer. The public wanted a Pitt T-shirt or other item, not the manufacturer's.

Infringement involving other products has also been found. Thus, manufacturers of tennis racquets were enjoined from using the name Seiko. Dad's Root Beer Co. was enjoined from using Cincinnati Reds trademarks on placemats. Another manufacturer was enjoined from using Titleist trademarks on golf balls and other equipment.

One court commented, "Fair competition requires that those developing goodwill and a recognizable name, symbol, or insignia be allowed to protect those marks. The public desires products authorized by their favorite teams, league, players or others, not those of an infringer. Infringement of a trademark tarnishes the owner's reputation and confuses and deceives the public."

WORDS, NAMES & PHRASES

FACTS: The state of Delaware devised a football lottery called "Scoreboard," which included different games based on picking winners of NFL games, some against the spread.

The NFL sued, charging, "The lottery misappropriated the name of the NFL (unfairly capitalizing on our success and popularity), infringed on our trademark in that name, was unfair competition, and harmed us by forced association with gambling." Was Delaware enjoined from running the lottery? **YOU'RE THE JUDGE!**

DECISION: Since gambling in the state of Nevada existed without harm to the NFL's reputation, there was no misappropriation. Confusion existed among the public as to whether the NFL was directly associated with the lottery, therefore the court ruled that the lottery tickets must explicitly declare that the NFL was in no way connected with the lottery.

The game, where fixed payoffs were paid dependent upon the number of games bet, was to be discontinued. This was similar to the "card," which is illegally wagered upon during college and pro football seasons.

Others have been more successful in preventing the use of their name, nickname or identifying phrase.

Wilson, holder of a trademark for "Advantage" tennis racquets, balls and golf equipment, could not enjoin Arthur Ashe from endorsing "Advantage Ashe" sunglasses. The products were not similar, and the public would not be confused or misled as to the origination of either product. Ashe had developed considerable goodwill in the term "Advantage Ashe," which was also the title of his autobiography.

FACTS: Drew "Bundini" Brown registered a trademark on the phrase, "Float like a butterfly, sting like a bee," a reference to the boxing abilities of Muhammad Ali.

When Kawasaki Motors began using the phrase in its ads,

Brown sued for an infringement of his trademark. Could Kawasaki be enjoined from use of the phrase?

DECISION: **YOU'RE THE JUDGE!**

In addition to teams, players and organizations may also claim trademark protection of their names or nicknames with which they have come to be identified with. Elroy "Crazylegs" Hirsch was thus able to prevent the use of that nickname, and the Olympic Committee could prevent the use of the word Olympics as an infringement on their trademark of the name.

ODDS & ENDS....

Who Dat doesn't own that which it thought it owned, a judge ruled. Own what?

FACTS: Who Dat Inc. claimed that it owned the football cheer: "Who dat say dey gonna beat dem Saints? Who dat?"

Who Dat sued a company that sold T-shirts imprinted with the cheer. Who Dat owned the rights to a recording, popular in New Orleans, in which some NFL's Saints sang the cheer between verses of "When The Saints Go Marching In." Could Who Dat enjoin the making of the T-shirts? **YOU'RE THE JUDGE!**

DECISION: The court ruled that the "Who Dat" cheer had been around for many years and was now in the public domain— anyone could use the phrase.

Sneakers & Patches

FACTS: Nell, an NBA coach, wore socks and sneakers which had the manufacturers' logos on them. Bert, a pro quarterback, had a logo patch on his jersey. Ernie, a pro tennis player, had a large logo patch on his shirt. Dunk, an NBA player, had logo patches on his uniform and wrist and head bands. Could any of these players be prohibited from such product endorsements? **YOU'RE THE JUDGE!**

DECISION: Although product endorsements may, in certain sports and in a specified manner, be permitted, rules prohibited Nell and Dunk from wearing such logos. Although the coach

couldn't, some players could endorse such products during a game. Rules also prohibited Bert from displaying any patch and Ernie from wearing a patch of that size.

Professional athletes, by their product endorsements, play a major role in the buying attitudes of the public.

21

PRIVACY

WHAT'S IT ABOUT?

Privacy tells how the **right of privacy**—the right to be left alone—came about and developed.

Can a fan's picture, without the fan's permission, be published or used in a magazine, newspaper or other media?

Worcester News
Section A

June 22, 1905

Yellow Journalism!

The late 1800's was an era of vicious newspaper circulation battles and sensational, but often deceptive, press coverage in an attempt to win readership.

One such newspaper wrote of the private social affairs of a prominent attorney, thus prompting an article arguing for a **right of privacy** –"the right to be left alone, free from intrusion or invasion of one's private rights"–except as could be justified by freedom of the press and speech–guaranteed by the First amendment to the Constitution.

RIGHT OF PRIVACY

The first case testing this theory of a right of privacy involved a flour mill.

FACTS: The mill ordered, without consent, a woman's portrait lithographed on its boxes. The woman, Roberson, complained, "I didn't like being referred to as the 'Flour of the Family,' so I sued."

"Was the use of the picture without my permission an invasion of my right to privacy?" she asked the court. **YOU'RE THE JUDGE!**

DECISION: No. The court held that no right of privacy existed.

The following year, the first right of privacy law made it "wrong to use the name or likeness of any person for trade purposes (publishing or making public)" without that person's consent.

"Any person who unreasonably interferes with any others' interests in not having their affairs known, or their picture or likeness exhibited to the public, is liable to the others." The first case recognizing this new **right of privacy,** came in 1905.

FACTS: A newspaper ad for an insurance company contained a photograph of Pavesich. It quoted him as saying, "Buy James Company's life insurance."

Pavesich had not consented to either the picture or the quote and sued. Was this an invasion of Pavesich's right of privacy? **YOU'RE THE JUDGE!**

DECISION: Yes. The court found an invasion of Pavesich's right of privacy and awarded him damages.

A right of privacy must be balanced against freedom of the press and the public's right to know anything of "legitimate news value," especially if it concerns a **"public figure"**—any person who has achieved fame or notoriety, and who commands substantial public interest, such as an athlete.

However, where published matter deals with one's private life or is malicious and without consent, recovery for invasion of privacy may be had even if the story is true.

The right of privacy is divided into four separate branches:

Intrusion

Was there an unreasonable **intrusion** upon one's privacy or individual life?

If so, this may be a violation of the right to privacy.

FACTS: Two newspaper reporters went to the home of Jack, "The Mad Healer," a famous wrestler who practiced healing. By lying, they gained admittance to Jack's home, where one of them complained of "tennis elbow."

While examining the elbow with an assortment of gadgets, Jack

was secretly photographed and the conversation was recorded by a hidden microphone.

When the photos and tape recording were published as part of a story on Jack's practice, and also used to charge Jack with quackery, Jack sued the newspaper for an "invasion of my privacy." The newspaper asked, "Were we guilty of an unreasonable intrusion into Jack's private life?" **YOU'RE THE JUDGE!**

DECISION: Yes. The court reasoned, "A privilege might exist for the publication of the pictures and story as news of a public figure, but it does not extend to the intrusion." The newspaper was liable to Jack for damages.

Often an intrusion is not physical, but consists of eavesdropping in private areas, such as a home or maybe a locker room. When an athlete is in a public area or a private area (locker room) opened to the public (reporters), only a reasonable photo or recording may be taken.

Would it be an intrusion if such a photo or recording was not published?

The invasion of privacy is the intrusion itself. Thus, taking pictures or recording statements of athletes at a private party or in a closed locker room, without permission, would be an intrusion into the private affairs of the athlete, and this would be so even if the pictures or story were not published.

May a newspaper publish a photo or recording gathered by an invasion of privacy by another?

FACTS: Hank admitted, "Without permission, and by using a telescopic lens, I took pictures of athletes and their guests at a private pool party. Also, I used a sensitive recorder hidden in the sauna to record players talking about officials and other matters. I then sold the material to a local newspaper. They printed it." Was the newspaper or Hank guilty of an invasion of privacy? **YOU'RE THE JUDGE!**

DECISION: The media simply published the work of another's intrusion. The courts usually will not hold the newspaper liable, although Hank may be.

What if the newspaper were aware of the intrusion? Even if the media was aware of the intrusion, the courts generally will not hold them liable. The reasoning is that the news gathering process would be severely hampered if the media were required to consider how independent sources obtained the news.

What if the media encouraged or aided an illegal invasion of privacy?

FACTS: A local newspaper drove Hank, not an employee, to an athlete's home where, with the camera that the newspaper had given him, Hank took pictures of the athlete through the window. Was the newspaper guilty of an unreasonable intrusion into the athlete's private life? **YOU'RE THE JUDGE!**

DECISION: The newspaper encouraged and aided Hank in acts of an unreasonable intrusion. They were liable to Hank for damages.

If the media is on private property, its license to report "newsworthy" items is limited to engaging in directly related activities, not to unrelated business.

FACTS: A reporter, Sandra, was invited to a team owner's office for a private celebration. While there, she took pictures. Could her newspaper print the pictures without an invasion of the privacy of those at the private party? **YOU'RE THE JUDGE!**

DECISION: Any printing of the pictures taken at the party would be an invasion of privacy. The pictures were of an unrelated, private nature. That is not permitted.

Public Disclosure

Was there an unreasonable **public disclosure** of embarrassing private facts?
If so, and even if true, this may violate the right to privacy.

It may be difficult to determine when publicity is unreasonable, when facts are private, or when private facts are offensive and objectionable. Truth is not a defense from liability since it is the publication of private facts that creates the liability.

FACTS: Tom, 16, a child prodigy in mathematics and golf, amid considerable public attention, gave up both and attempted to live down his fame and success. He succeeded in concealing his identity until a magazine published a story under the title: WHERE ARE THEY NOW. The article recounted Tom's unusual background, traced his attempts to hide his identity, described his menial employment and detailed certain conduct, such as his collecting old beer cans. Was Tom's privacy invaded? **YOU'RE THE JUDGE!**

DECISION: The court held, "The facts disclosed were not offensive or objectionable to reasonable persons."

However, there are limits to what a court will allow in balancing the public's interest in publicity against an individual's right to privacy.

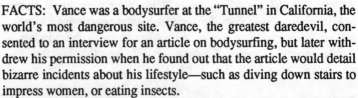

FACTS: Vance was a bodysurfer at the "Tunnel" in California, the world's most dangerous site. Vance, the greatest daredevil, consented to an interview for an article on bodysurfing, but later withdrew his permission when he found out that the article would detail bizarre incidents about his lifestyle—such as diving down stairs to impress women, or eating insects.

The magazine, referring to Vance as abnormal, claimed, "The story was newsworthy."

Vance sued, arguing, "The article, which I didn't consent to, was an unreasonable public disclosure of embarrassing private facts. My right to privacy was invaded?" Was it? **YOU'RE THE JUDGE!**

DECISION: Yes. The court decided, "The magazine pried into the strictly private affairs of Vance's private life, reporting details that were not news. Truth was no defense."

However, the media may be protected in publishing almost anything true about individuals which has any "legitimate news value."

The limitation on what the media may publish may depend upon whether an area is private or open to the public.

FACTS: The Times newspaper published a picture of Bubby, star football player for the Hamilton Bears, while he was undressing in the locker room. The press had not been admitted, but the door was ajar. Bubby sued the Times for making an unreasonable and embarrassing public disclosure.

The newspaper claimed, "The picture was publicity that was public. The door was open." Could Bubby recover for an invasion of his right to privacy? **YOU'RE THE JUDGE!**

DECISION: Yes. Ordinarily, publicity of what is already public, and what anyone present would be free to see, is not an invasion of privacy. However, the press had not yet been admitted and there was nothing of legitimate news value. Caution and discretion should be used with "good taste."

False Light

Was there publicity or a publication of facts—by words or photos—which placed one in a **"false light"**?

If so, this may violate the right to privacy. False light exists where views not held, or actions not taken by a person, are attributed to that person.

FACTS: A magazine depicted a nude black man seated in the corner of a boxing ring. Ali, the former heavyweight boxing champ, sued the magazine, alleging that the depiction, without permission, was a picture of him which placed him in a false light. Was this a newsworthy item which the magazine could publish without permission? Did it place Ali in a false light? **YOU'RE THE JUDGE!**

DECISION: The court found that the depiction was a portrait or picture of Ali. Moreover, "There was no newsworthy dimension to this unauthorized use of such likeness. It placed the boxer in a 'false light' by attributing to him actions which he had not taken."

Would the intentional fictionalization of activities involving identifiable persons or places create liability?

FACTS: Notre Dame sought to enjoin the release of a book and movie involving the school's name and symbols, alleging that the movie and book placed the school in a "false light" by attributing to it views not held, and actions not taken, by the school.

The story was of a fictional female player who ran for the winning touchdown when Notre Dame players would not tackle her. Could the school prevent the release of the book and movie? **YOU'RE THE JUDGE!**

DECISION: No. The court decided, "The work was a form of expression of social and literary criticism, protected by the freedom of the press to disseminate 'newsworthy news' to the waiting public."

One may not fictionalize dialogues by attributing to another words not spoken.

FACTS: A book fictionalized the great baseball pitcher, Warren Spahn, and his relationships with others. The author invented dialogues involving, not only Spahn's life in baseball (in which Spahn was deemed a "public personality," and of which there was a legitimate public interest), but also fictionalized Spahn's personal and private life. Could Spahn recover damages for an invasion of privacy? **YOU'RE THE JUDGE!**

DECISION: Yes. Spahn's life could not be fictionalized. Nor could he be placed in a false light in the public's eyes by attributing to him innacurate, distorted, and fanciful words and acts. This is not protected by the freedoms of speech and the press. It was an invasion of Spahn's right to privacy.

A publication placing one in a false light, which is not an intentional or reckless falsification, but an innocent mistake or negligent act, may not be actionable. Such would be the case where a picture was accidentally published or views were attributed by mistake, and then retracted.

Appropriation

Was there an **appropriation**—unauthorized use of a name, picture or likeness of another for profit?

If so, this may violate the right to privacy—sometimes called the **right of publicity.**

The media are seldom sued for appropriation in reporting the news to the public. Invasion of privacy suits for misappropriation of one's name or likeness are usually connected with ads or promotions for products or services.

> FACTS: "Big Mike," a former football star, consented to allow his picture and name to be used in connection with honoring outstanding college football players and in promoting college football. When his name and likeness appeared without his consent in an ad for a soft drink, Big Mike sued. Was this an appropriation of Big Mike's right to publicity? **YOU'RE THE JUDGE!**

> DECISION: The court ruled, "The privacy of a public figure may not be lawfully invaded by the use of his name or picture for commercial purposes without his consent, unless it is of legitimate news value, which here it was not."

Similar decisions were reached where other manufacturers attempted to enhance the sale of games by using pro golfers' and baseball players' pictures and accomplishments without permission.

Although an athlete's right to privacy is more limited than that of the average person, athletes are entitled to relief where their names and pictures are used improperly. Athletes have invested years of practice and competition to build a recognizable and marketable personality—a valuable **right of publicity.**

> FACTS: Elroy "Crazylegs" Hirsch sued Johnson for marketing a shaving gel for women named "Crazylegs." Hirsch alleged, "The company appropriated a nickname that I made famous for my own use. I had a property right in the publicity value of my nickname, which was my identity." Did Hirsch have a property right in his nickname? **YOU'RE THE JUDGE!**

> DECISION: Yes. The court found that the publicity value in Hirsch's name gave him interest in controlling commercial uses of his name and the prevention of others from profiting from the use of his name without his consent. Any improper use would confuse the public as to whether Hirsch had approved the product.

What if an athlete's name or likeness is used, but is reasonably related to a matter of legitimate public interest? Then, unless the matter is an ad, it's use is not actionable.

Such was the case where a book included on the cover, without his permission, the likeness of former football great, Johnny Unitas. Unitas sued, but was unsuccessful. The court found that, "The subject matter of the book was of legitimate public interest and reasonably related to the use of Unitas' picture."

FACTS: Sports Illustrated used Namath's name and picture in ads designed to sell subscriptions. The ads read, "How to get Close to Joe Namath" and, "The man you love loves Joe Namath." Namath sued, alleging a wrongful use of his photograph without his consent, which deprived him of income from a right to publicity in his name and picture. Was this an invasion of privacy? **YOU'RE THE JUDGE!**

DECISION: No—as long as the picture was only used to illustrate the quality and content of the magazine in which it originally appeared many times, and where the use of Namath's picture was merely "incidental" to advertising of the magazine. He must also have been fairly depicted, and the language of the ads could not indicate an endorsement of the magazine.

Where athletes gave unrestricted permission to have their photos taken and distributed to the public, generally, actions for invasion of privacy were dismissed when their photos appeared on a calendar distributed by a beer wholesaler. An example of which had a player posed only in a bowling shirt and holding a bowling ball. A beer bottle was later engraved onto the photo for an ad campaign.

FACTS: Cepeda, a pro baseball star, gave Wilson Sporting Goods an exclusive right to use his photo to sell baseballs and gloves, and to license others to sell the same. When Wilson contracted with Swift to sell Cepeda baseballs for $1.00 off when customers sent in a label from a hot dog package, Cepeda sued Swift for invasion of privacy for using his name without his permission. Did Swift invade Cepeda's right to privacy? **YOU'RE THE JUDGE!**

DECISION: The court dismissed the suit, noting that Cepeda had given his permission to Wilson to license others to sell baseballs. Swift had not attempted to indicate that Cepeda either used or endorsed its products.

Where the use of an athlete's picture exceeds the consent granted, or an athlete's or performer's entire act, is published, recovery for an invasion of privacy may be awarded.

Such was the case where Ettore fought Joe Louis in 1936 and consented to motion pictures of the fight. In 1950, when NBC broadcast that fight as one of the "Greatest Fights of The Century," Ettore sued for an invasion of privacy.

The court held, "The consent given by Ettore could not be used for a later TV show not contemplated at the time of the fight." The court did note, "Ettore only got upset when the third round, his best, was cut from the show."

> FACTS: Morrison performed his diving act at a circus. A TV station, against Morrison's wishes, filmed and showed the entire act on a news program. Morrison sued for an invasion of privacy—the publicity right to the value of his performance.
>
> Could Morrison recover for the right of publicity value in his performance? **YOU'RE THE JUDGE!**
>
> DECISION: Yes. Although the press may have a right to freely cover newsworthy events which the public has an interest in, it is not permitted to carry a performer's entire act, no matter how short.

Athletes in professional team sports sign a contract which grants to their teams the right to use players' pictures or likenesses for promotional and publicity purposes.

A professional athlete also has a right to publicity in his name and picture or likeness, which the athlete may sell.

After one baseball player sold the right to use his picture to Topp's baseball cards, a competing company attempted to use the player's picture. Topps successfully sued, preventing the competing company from using the player's picture.

SURVIVAL, JOKES & IMPERSONATIONS

Does the right to publicity survive an athlete's death?

> FACTS: After Jesse, a well-known track star, passed away, a book on his life was published. His estate sued, alleging that the book was an invasion of Jesse's right to publicity which now belonged to the estate. Could any sale of the book be enjoined? **YOU'RE THE JUDGE!**
>
> DECISION: No. The right of publicity does not survive an athlete's death. Cases involving the right of privacy can only be asserted by the person whose privacy is involved.

What if an alleged invasion of privacy occurred as an obvious joke?

Recovery was also denied where "Groucho" Marx, in one of his comedy routines, joked, "I once managed a prizefighter, Canvasback Cohen. I brought him out here, he got knocked out, and I made him walk back to Cleveland."

The comment was limited to public facts. Cohen, by entering the

The comment was limited to public facts. Cohen, by entering the ring, sought publicity, became known by his nickname and lost his right to privacy in that respect.

Is a voice impersonation an invasion of the right to publicity?

FACTS: A former pro athlete, Babe, waged a satirical campaign for political office. Without his permission, a company sold posters and a factual biography of Babe. In commercials promoting a product, another company used a voice impersonation of Babe. Was Babe's right of publicity invaded or misappropriated? **YOU'RE THE JUDGE!**

DECISION: Babe was a newsworthy public figure, and, therefore, did not possess a right of publicity. He could not enjoin the posters, a factual or truthful biography or commercials which did not use a name or likeness. Use of the voice in impersonation could be enjoined.

ODDS & ENDS....

The back of most tickets to sporting events grants permission for the use of a fan's image or likeness in any display of the game to which the ticket admits the fan. But, as a spectator is not a public figure, use of such a photo without consent will be limited to situations deemed "newsworthy" and in the interest of the public.

FACTS: A photo of a spectator at a football game, "hammimg it up" with his fly unzipped, was shown in a national sports magazine article on football fans entitled, "A Strange Kind of Love." The article implied that the spectator was a "crazy, drunken slob."

The spectator sued for, "An invasion of my right to privacy. The photo, an appropriation of my picture, subjected me to ridicule, placed me in a false light and embarrassed me." Was the photo newsworthy? **YOU'RE THE JUDGE!**

DECISION: Yes. The publication of the spectator's photo, taken with his encouragement and participation, even though taken without the spectator's express consent, was protected by the First Amendment freedom of the press to publish news of legitimate public interest. The spectator was in full view of the fans, drinking beer, waving a banner, and after being told who the photographer was, began to scream and holler. imploring the photographer to take more pictures. There was no invasion of privacy.

The different branches of invasion of privacy often overlap one another. For instance, the appropriation of an athlete's name or pic-

ture for an ad endorsing an alcoholic beverage may also place the athlete in a false light as a serious drinker. And, an act of intrusion into the private affairs of an athlete may be followed by the publication of private facts which may embarrass the athlete.

The right to privacy—the right to be left alone, free from intrusion of one's private rights—applies equally to all.

22

INSULTS & LIES

WHAT'S IT ABOUT?

Insults & Lies explains defamation and how it can injure others, whether done in writing or speaking by attacking another's reputation.

Do you know the difference between a public and a private figure?

Superior Court of New York

COMPLAINT

JJ Jock, plaintiff

v

NY Telegram, TV Sports Channel (TVSC),
Larry Libel and Sam Slander, defendants

Here comes the plaintiff, JJ Jock, who states as follows:

1. This is an action for **defamation** —a statement that injures the reputation and diminishes the esteem and respect in which the plaintiff is held by exposing him to public hatred or disgrace; or that excites adverse, derogatory or evil feelings or opinions against him.

2. JJ plays professional kickball for the NY Playgrounders. Larry Libel and Sam Slander are reporters for the NY Telegram and TVSC.

3. JJ alleges that the defendants made defamatory, unwarranted and untruthful attacks on his character by the following:

a. a defamatory statement made in writing—**libel**. A story in the Telegram reported by Larry Libel, "JJ couldn't kick a ball as well as minor leaguers. He's a second rate reserve who couldn't fight his way out of a paper bag. And he bet on his team to lose."

b. a defamatory statement made in speaking—**slander**. TVSC repeated a statement made by Sam Slander, "JJ couldn't beat my 10-year-old kid in kickball. He's on drugs. His performance wasn't even up to his usual standard—lousy."

4. These statements were communicated to other persons by publishing and broadcasting them in the Telegram and over TVSC.

5. JJ's good reputation is essential to his ability to make a living. These accusations will diminish that ability, thereby causing injury to his reputation, subjecting him to hatred and disgrace, and to unpleasant comments and opinions.

Wherefore, JJ, asks this court to award damages for injury to his reputation and character in an amount that the court deems necessary and proper.

FACTS: JJ Jock filed the above complaint for defamation against Larry Libel and Sam Slander, and the newspaper and TV station that they worked for.

Did the statements by Larry Libel and Sam Slander defame JJ?

DECISION: **YOU'RE THE JUDGE!**

IS AN ATHLETE A PUBLIC FIGURE?

A **public figure** is one who commands a substantial amount of public interest, has achieved widespread fame or notoriety, or has searched for public adulation and acclaim.

To recover for defamation, a public figure must prove that a defendant's statements were made with **malice**—knowledge that they were false, or made with reckless disregard for the truth.

> FACTS: Cepeda, a star baseball player with the Giants, sued a magazine for an article which portrayed him as an ineffective and unpopular team player.
>
> Chuy, a football player with the Eagles, claimed, "A false statement to a sportswriter, stating that I was suffering from a rare blood disease, injured my reputation." Were Cepeda and Chuy public figures? **YOU'RE THE JUDGE!**
>
> DECISION: Regarding one's playing career, an athlete is a public figure and, therefore, must prove malice to recover for defamation. "An athlete's choice to engage in a profession which attracts wide public attention, and where the athlete invites such attention and seeks public acclaim, makes the athlete a public figure."

Chuy was denied recovery for defamation because of the court's misinterpretation of the law. Cepeda lost because he could not prove malice; that is, that the article was false or made with a reckless disregard for the truth.

Also, a coach portrayed in an article as one who "incited crowds to such a point of hysteria as to result in physical abuse of the referees," was unable to recover as he too, was unable to prove that the statements were published maliciously.

Another coach was more successful in his defamation suit.

> FACTS: In an article, Butts, the athletic director at Georgia, was accused of conspiring to rig or fix a football game. The article was entitled: THE STORY OF A COLLEGE FOOTBALL FIX, and it accused Butts of giving "Bear" Bryant, the coach of Alabama, Georgia's plays.
>
> The article revealed that an insurance salesman had accidentally overheard a telephone conversation between Butts and Bryant, in which (according to the article), "The Georgia players, their moves

analyzed like those of rats in a maze, took a frightful physical beating."

Butts sued, charging, "The truth of the article was a serious departure from good investigative standards and the accuracy of its charges amounted to reckless and wanton conduct." Was Butts defamed? **YOU'RE THE JUDGE!**

DECISION: Yes. The magazine assigned the story to a writer who was not a football expert. He made no attempt to have such an expert check the story. Interested in cultivating an image "designed to provoke people, make them mad," the magazine ignored precautions to insure publication of the truth. The magazine's "highly unreasonable conduct" established that it had acted in reckless disregard in determining whether the article was false or not, thus proving malice. Punitive damages were awarded "to deter the wrong-doer from repeating the trespass."

Others may also be public figures where they are drawn into a public controversy, such as an agent in negotiations for a player, especially where contact with the media was sought out. Is a coach a public figure?

FACTS: "Sam is a despicable human being. He's a fat liar!" This statement was screamed at an owner's meeting by an opposing owner of another pro basketball team. The statement could not be supported. Was the coach a public figure? Was the statement defamatory? **YOU'RE THE JUDGE!**

DECISION: The coach was a public figure. The remarks were not privileged and were defamatory.

A member of a team may also be defamed. True magazine published a story entitled: THE PILL THAT KILLED SPORTS, which discussed the taking of drugs by athletes. Evidence showed that the substance given to the football players was "spirits of peppermint," a harmless substance used for the relief of dryness of the mouth. The article exposed the entire football team to public hatred and contempt.

What if a statement made about a public figure is deemed to be "fair comment"?

FACTS: A boxer's reputation as a "canvasback," unable to fight, was the subject of a comedy routine. Was the athlete defamed? **YOU'RE THE JUDGE!**

DECISION: No. Recovery was denied where malice could not be proved. The comments were limited to public facts and were "fair comment" about matters of legitimate public interest concerning a public figure.

Is name calling of those, considered public figures, defamation? Although it may be, it is not always.

FACTS: A sports agent, Harris, sued a former NFL football coach, Damon, for slander, alleging, "He called me a 'sleezebag' who 'slimed up from the bayou.'" Was this slander or constitutionally protected speech? **YOU'RE THE JUDGE!**

DECISION: The judge commented, "While it may not be a compliment to be called a sleezebag, the mere absence of complimentary effect does not make a statement defamatory." The judge added, "It is all too rare today to hear the clear, clean ring of a really original insult."

PRIVATE FIGURES

The public may have a legal right to information about public figures, but not as to private figures, or as to the private and personal life of a public figure.

This may be partly true because private figures rarely have access to the media as do public figures; they cannot fight back.

Athletes found to be private figures, as regarding their private and personal lives, need only show mere negligence or fault to prove defamation.

In a case involving a fictitious biography about the famed baseball pitcher, Warren Spahn, the court held that he was a public figure only in his professional career, thus upholding a verdict for "unauthorized exploitation" of his private and personal life.

How is it determined if one is a public or private figure? One's exposure to the public may determine whether he is a public or private figure.

FACTS: A high school wrestling coach sued a newspaper for libel. The newspaper had written that the coach lied in court when testifying about his part in a fight at a wrestling match. Was the coach a public figure? **YOU'RE THE JUDGE!**

DECISION: The court ruled that the coach was not a public figure. His exposure as a high school wrestling coach was not enough to make him a public figure.

DEFENSE! DEFENSE!

Although a statement may be defamatory, if the defamed party gave **consent** to the statement, or if the statement was truthful, recovery may be denied.

What if a truthful statement is used to hurt another? An exception exists where truthful information is used to hurt another.

FACTS: Bruiser, a pro football player, had a mental illness. A reporter, to whom Bruiser would not grant an interview, wrote, " Bruiser suffers from a mental illness, the possible side effects of which are physical outbursts. I'd stay away from Bruiser!" Was the statement, although true, defamatory? **YOU'RE THE JUDGE!**

DECISION: Truthful information, used for the sole purpose of hurting the defamed party, would be malicious and defamatory. Bruiser could recover damages.

To protect the public's interest, judicial and administrative proceedings are given absolute immunity from liability. Thus, where a report concerning gambling in professional sports was posted on a bulletin board, it was immune from liability for defamation.

And a statement made in a kidding manner, intended as a joke, such as, "Heck, Joe would never have to throw a game, but just pitch normal," may not be with malice. An athlete or other public figure must accept a harsher degree of criticism about their performance than would a private person.

For how long after an athlete's career will "fair comment" be allowed?

FACTS: Dempsey, a former boxing champ, sued a magazine for libel for the cover headline, "Dempsey's Gloves Were Loaded" and the inside story entitled, "He Didn't Know the Gloves Were Loaded." The story suggested that Dempsey won his championship by using "loaded gloves."

Allegedly, Dempsey's manager put plaster of paris mixed with water on Dempsey's bandaged hands. Did the privilege of fair comment about athletes protect the magazine from liability for defamation? **YOU'RE THE JUDGE!**

DECISION: No. Unless malice can be proven, fair comment, even about an athlete's pro activity after he had retired, will be allowed so long as it is newsworthy and of public interest. However, reaching back forty-five years was too great a period of time. Such statements were not fair comment.

Lies in a newspaper article which are stated as facts are libelous. How about lies in cartoons?

Lies which are stated as such by the use of cartoons, satire or parody are considered "kidding." Such statements are protected by the First Amendment's freedom of speech and are not libelous.

FACTS: A sports magazine had an ad parody purportedly quoting well-known Coach Pete discussing a fictitious beating of his mother by him, and a habit of "getting drunk" before games. Should the courts find a way to balance free speech rights with legal protection against offensive attacks or insults which "go too far"? **YOU'RE THE JUDGE!**

DECISION: The court ruled, "The ad was not libelous," and did not award damages for emotional distress. The ad was protected by the First Amendment's right to free speech.

Although not defenses, if an alleged defamatory statement is retracted, or if the anger of the speaker was—in part—due to provocation by the alleged defamed party, such factors could lessen any damages.

MALICIOUS PROSECUTION

Malicious prosecution is the misuse of the law or courts with the desire to inflict injury on another.

FACTS: Dave and Guy, owners of opposing NBA teams, were bitter rivals. Dave, in a suit against the league to move his team, named Guy personally as a defendant.   Guy charged that by naming him personally as a defendant, Dave was guilty of malicious prosecution. "That was a malicious, spiteful and vindictive abuse of process. I suffered a heart attack because of it." The jury agreed that Dave's actions were indeed malicious.   Could Guy recover damages for his heart attack? **YOU'RE THE JUDGE!**

DECISION: Guy had a right to freedom from the deliberate misuse of the law or the courts. He should not have been named a defendant in Dave's suit. Dave was found responsible for Guy's heart attack and had to pay damages, including punitive damages—to deter future wrongdoing.

ODDS & ENDS....

Statements made on TV or radio may be **slander** because they are spoken, or **libel** because, as with printed statements, they may be recorded.

Do any of the following allegations fall within the definition of **defamation**—a statement that injures the reputation and diminishes the esteem and respect in which the plaintiff is held by exposing him to public hatred or disgrace, or that excites adverse, derogatory or evil feelings or opinions against him?

FACTS: Michaels, a star professional soccer goaltender for the Sockers, sued several writers, sportscasters and others for defamation of his reputation and character for their statements and actions following the World Soccer Bowl. Michaels had allowed all eight goals in a 8-3 loss.

Michaels, in a complaint, alleged the following as being defamatory:

• Statements made at a post-game gathering and on TV that Michaels "choked" and appeared to be throwing the game;

• A picture in the paper showing Michaels lying on the ground with a following story entitled: MICHAELS LYING DOWN ON THE JOB!;

• A drawing of Michaels walking off the field, showing fans making indecent gestures and the choke sign while others pointed towards him;

• Cartoons showing Michaels giving the choke sign, accepting cash from a shady looking character and leaning on the side of the net as soccer balls whizzed by;

• The placing of a statue of his likeness in front of the stadium with his hands around his neck, in a choking position; and,

• The burning in effigy of a likeness similar to Michaels at a public meeting called by the team's booster club.

Which of these acts could be considered slander (spoken), libel (written), both, or neither? **YOU'RE THE JUDGE!**

DECISION: Pictures, cartoons, drawings, statues or other likenesses—where either reference (by use of writing), is made to a picture or there is no accompanying writing—may be considered libel as it is the publication or printing that creates potential liability for defamation.

The picture, drawing and statue are considered statements or writings; the words are inferred by what one might think when seeing them.

Only the statements at the post-game gathering and the cartoon showing him accepting money were found to be actionable libel for which Michaels could recover damages if the statements were proved false.

Cartoons, satires, parodies and jokes, such as you might find on the sports, comic or editorial pages, are considered "kidding." Such statements are protected by the First Amendment's freedom of speech.

23

YOUR TICKET PLEASE

WHAT'S IT ABOUT?

May spectators be denied admission to sports events? *Your Ticket Please* discusses this, ticket prices, seating and "scalping."

If you lose your ticket to a sports event, will you still be admitted?

Section C   **WORLD NEWSPAPER**   July 10, 1978

SPECTATOR VIOLENCE!!

Spectator violence is hardly new. As far back as 70 A.D., spectators at the games in Pompeii broke into wild sword fights, resulting in many deaths. Gladiator events were banned for a decade. Centuries later, thousands of people were killed when rival chariot-racing groups set off a series of riots that nearly destroyed Constantinople.

In more recent times at soccer games, referees' calls resulting in a home team's loss, and a late goal by a home team (after which the departing fans rushed back, while others tried to leave), resulted in hundreds of deaths. Other injuries and deaths were caused by fans pelting each other with rocks. Moats and fences had to be built to separate the fans from players, referees and the field.

And at hockey and baseball games promoting "Disco Night" and 10¢ beer, spectator violence also led to injuries.

These and many more incidents like them, most less severe, involving fans intent on interfering with the orderly and safe procession of a sports event, have brought about a need for increased security and stricter enforcement of admittance and expulsion procedures regarding spectators.

YOU CAN'T COME IN!

May spectators be denied admission to sports events? Operators of athletic facilities and other places of public amusement may, in the absence of law, admit or exclude persons at their pleasure, and also make such rules and regulations as they see fit to govern the admission of persons to their premises.

FACTS: When you go to most any sporting event, the back of the ticket will generally have a provision—in small type—to the effect that:

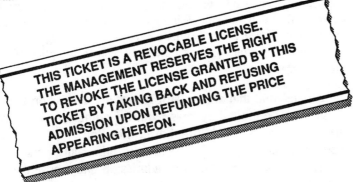

THIS TICKET IS A REVOCABLE LICENSE. THE MANAGEMENT RESERVES THE RIGHT TO REVOKE THE LICENSE GRANTED BY THIS TICKET BY TAKING BACK AND REFUSING ADMISSION UPON REFUNDING THE PRICE APPEARING HEREON.

What would your rights be if you were excluded from a sporting event by such a provision? **YOU'RE THE JUDGE!**

DECISION: The ticket does not give the right to enter or remain in the facility. It is a mere license, revocable at the will of the operator, who may decline to permit the holder to enter, or remove him after he has taken his seat. And, unless the denial of admittance or expulsion is accompanied by insult or more force than is reasonably necessary, a spectator's only recourse would be to recover the price of admission on the ticket.

Thus, spectators have been refused admittance or ejected from sports events for any conduct which interferes with the event or other patrons' enjoyment of it, or is in violation of the law. Such exclusion promotes the protection of other spectators and the participants in the sporting event.

FACTS: "I was kicked out of the racetrack" Jake explained, "for trying to fix races and for illegal betting."

Paddy growled, "I was ejected from a hockey game for throwing bottles!"

Grady was kicked out of a baseball game for being "objectionable" to other fans, for paying players and for buying tickets from scalpers.

Stan was ejected from a basketball arena for swearing. Striker was banned from the bowling alley after admitting, "I beat up another bowler."

Streaker was asked to leave a soccer game for going onto the field during play.

Killer snarled, "I was kicked out of the football stadium and charged with rioting for encouraging the crowd to tear down the goalposts!" Were these expulsions proper? Could those expelled recover damages? **YOU'RE THE JUDGE!**

DECISION: Persons admitted to sporting events are required to conduct themselves in an orderly and proper manner. A proprietor may use reasonable steps to end any improper conduct or disturbance, as by requesting the offending person to stop, or by ejecting a disorderly fan within the limits of good order, without insult, abuse, or defamation. Only such force as may be necessary for removal may be used, and only after a request to leave is ignored

The ejected patron could, at best, only recover the price of admission.

The general rule that an operator may deny admission to anyone he pleases may be limited by laws requiring admission, or by constitutional requirements which forbid discrimination.

Such laws may require the operator to admit any person over a given age who presents a ticket of admission and whose conduct is not offensive.

TICKET PRICE

FACTS: A local theatre was charging $500 for a ticket to the closed circuit viewing of a heavyweight championship boxing match. Another theatre was charging $10, but only allowing 25 people to attend. Theatre held 200. Could you do anything about such an outrageous price, or the few number of people allowed in? **YOU'RE THE JUDGE!**

DECISION: Proprietors may charge what they choose for admission, limit the number admitted and, generally, regulate the terms and conditions of admission in any reasonable way. As one proprietor remarked, "If the terms of admission are unsatisfactory, no one is obliged to buy a ticket."

WHERE'S MY SEAT?

The right to a seat by a spectator depends upon the ticket that he holds. If the ticket is not for a reserved seat, he may take any unoccupied seat which has not been previously sold to another. But he cannot, after being notified by the proprietor to vacate it, continue to occupy a specially located seat for which an extra charge is made.

FACTS: Joey bought a reserved seat for a basketball game, but the proprietor failed to give him his seat. Joey's conduct was in no way offensive and the proprietor gave no reason for denying him the seat. Could Joey recover damages in excess of the ticket price?

DECISION: **YOU'RE THE JUDGE!**

Generally, a spectator ejected from a sport's facility will be unable to recover damages in excess of the ticket price.

However, an action may be maintained against a proprietor or security for a breach of the duty to give proper treatment and protection to patrons not guilty of any misconduct, or for any improper ejectment.

Due process—a fair and impartial hearing with representation—may be required to determine whether there was a reasonable basis for excluding any person from a public facility. Such a hearing may not be required for exclusion from a private facility.

HANDS UP!

May fans entering a sporting event be searched?

FACTS: Fans attending a sporting event were subjected to warrantless, pat-down searches by police officers. Upon entering another stadium, other patrons were warned by a tape recording, "A search for drugs, alcohol, weapons and other contraband will be made of fans and their belongings."

Not everyone was searched, just those suspected of carrying prohibited materials. When these fans were confronted by the police, they gave their "consent" to be searched. Were these pat-down searches legal? **YOU'RE THE JUDGE!**

DECISION: No. The pat-down searches were unconstitutional, a violation of the Fourth Amendment's protection from unreasonable search and seizure. Searches could not be made on mere hunches. Probable cause to believe that an unlawful act was being committed was necessary. An injunction stopping the searches was granted.

WE WERE SCALPED!

Generally, **scalping** is selling an admission ticket for a price higher than the original price of the ticket.

A scalper acquires tickets and holds them until other buyers have exhausted the box office supply. Then the scalper offers to resell his tickets at a price higher than the original price. Those wishing to attend the event are compelled to either pay the scalper or not attend.

FACTS: John was arrested for scalping admission tickets to the finals of an NCAA basketball tournament. The back of John's ticket read: THIS TICKET IS NOT TRANSFERABLE. RESALE PROHIBITED. The law under which he was prosecuted read, in part:

> IT IS UNLAWFUL FOR ANY PERSON TO SCALP AN ADMISSION TICKET TO ANY AUDITORIUM, STADIUM, RINK, ATHLETIC FIELD OR ANY OTHER PLACE TO WHICH TICKETS ARE REQUIRED FOR ADMITTANCE.
> TO SCALP ADMISSION TICKETS MEANS TO SELL ANY TICKET AT A PRICE ABOVE THE PRICE PRINTED THEREON OR AT A PRICE HIGHER THAN THE STANDARD RETAIL PRICE FOR WHICH SUCH TICKET WAS ISSUED OR OFFERED FOR SALE.

John purchased tickets and then offered them for sale at inflated prices. He alleged that the law unreasonably interfered with his right to conduct a legitimate private business for profit. Was John guilty of scalping tickets? **YOU'RE THE JUDGE!**

DECISION: John was convicted of "scalping" tickets. The court commented, "There is a legitimate public interest in the regulation of such events and in enabling all of the members of the public desiring to attend such events to have an equal and fair opportunity to obtain admission tickets for the proper price. Such laws protect the general public from the abuses of ticket speculators, and the evils, fraud and theft that generally go with scalping."

Do states regulate the selling of tickets to sporting events? Yes. Several states have laws regulating the resale price of tickets to these events. These statutes either prohibit a resale price in excess of the original box office price, or establish a maximum profit for resales.

FACTS: Guy bought tickets for a football game for $10 and sold them at the stadium for $15. Helga, a travel agent, bought tickets for $20 and sold them for $40. In another state, Frances bought tickets for $10 and sold them for $12.

John and his family were attending a game. John said, "Our son couldn't make it, so we sold his $22 ticket for $25. Jimmy was offered $50 for his $25 play-off ticket. He accepted. Were any of these people guilty of scalping? **YOU'RE THE JUDGE!**

DECISION: Guy was guilty; his state prohibited the resale of tickets for any price in excess of the face value. Helga was not guilty. Travel agents are not covered by the law.

Frances was not guilty. Her state allowed resale not exceeding two dollars over the face value of the ticket. Neither was John guilty. He was not familiar with the law. His was an isolated incident, not one by a regular scalper. And, neither was Jimmy guilty. He didn't offer to sell the ticket.

Generally, any anti-scalping law is enforceable. Some may allow scalping anywhere in the state, or from outside the state, except at the game site on the day of the game. Other states may only make selling (not offering to sell) tickets at a profit, a violation.

TICKET TYING!

FACTS: Fans brought suits against NFL teams, claiming that, "Ticket selling practices illegally 'tied' the purchase of one product (the season ticket) to the purchase of another product (exhibition game tickets)." The teams only sold season tickets to purchasers who also bought tickets to all pre-season exhibition games. Was this a permitted practice? **YOU'RE THE JUDGE!**

DECISION: Yes. There were individual tickets available to each regular season game and, therefore, fans were not compelled to buy an exhibition game ticket to get a regular season game ticket.

Professional teams have a "legitimate monopoly" over the presentation of regular season and exhibition games. Such teams could not be found guilty of restraining free competition for exhibition games as no one else presented them.

LOST TICKETS!

What happens if you lose your ticket? Will you still be admitted?

FACTS: Sloan had a season ticket for the Rangers' hockey games. Upon purchase of the season ticket, Sloan signed a form which provided, in part:

> ### SEASON TICKET FORM
>
> UPON RECEIPT OF TICKETS PURCHASED, RISK OF LOSS OR THEFT OF TICKETS SHALL PASS TO THE SUBSCRIBER. MADISON SQUARE GARDEN SHALL NOT BE OBLIGATED TO ADMIT THE SUBSCRIBER TO GAMES UNLESS TICKETS ARE PRESENTED.

Sloan, having either misplaced or lost his ticket to a game, was denied entry. The Garden offered, "We'll sell him a ticket to the same seat and refund the admission price if the ticket is later found."

Sloan sued the Garden, protesting, "The demand of two payments for the same seat unfairly benefits the Garden. Should I have had to pay for the same seat twice?" **YOU'RE THE JUDGE!**

DECISION: Sloan failed to produce his ticket, as agreed. He must pay twice for the same seat (if he wants to attend), unless he is able to later produce the ticket.

The fact that the seat might be empty is no assurance that the ticket has not been used. "It is likely that if someone had the ticket, they would hide amongst the crowd of some 20,000 and not sit in the proper seat!" commented the judge.

CROWD CONTROL

What would happen if fans deliberately delayed a game by throwing debris onto the court?

FACTS: Central New England College was playing a basketball game against Eastern U. Eastern's fans, excited over their team's comeback from a large deficit, threw toilet paper and other debris onto the court. The game was delayed. Could the officials penalize Eastern for their fans' behavior? **YOU'RE THE JUDGE!**

DECISION: Under NCAA rules, Eastern was assessed a technical foul. Central was awarded two free throws and control of the ball. Central won the game, 80-79.

Similarly, another college team, Vanderbilt, lost a game when, with one second remaining in the game and a two point lead, its fans threw tennis balls onto the court. Vanderbilt was assessed a technical foul. The opposing team, Florida, made the two free throws and then won the game in overtime!

FOUL BALL!

If you were at a Major League Baseball game and caught a foul ball, would you have to return it to the field?

No, you wouldn't … but it wasn't always that way.

At a game back in 1925, Reuben—a spectator— caught a foul ball. When he wouldn't return it, a court was called upon to settle the dispute.

The judge, in holding that spectators now could keep foul balls, reasoned that the "safety of the spectators and the disturbance to the game caused by the continued stoppage to retrieve the balls" called for such a ruling. "Besides, teams would not want to risk the loss of fans if the disputes continued."

A DAY IN COURT

Numerous fans have had their day in court concerning incidents involving sports contests.

One case in a Georgia traffic court involved a baseball fan ticketed for ignoring a DO NOT ENTER sign.

FACTS: Barry and several of his friends testified, "Whenever we went to Braves' games, about thirty-five a year, we didn't notice the sign." Did Barry have to pay the fine? **YOU'RE THE JUDGE!**

DECISION: The judge asked if the fans, by claiming to see so many games, were using this as an insanity defense. He dismissed the charges, figuring that Barry had suffered enough.

Two men cracked the formula for a promotional contest which called for finding matching numbers on cards. The men rounded up about 4,000 winning tickets, claimed more than $20 million in winnings and free trips to the Super Bowl. The sponsoring company cancelled the football-theme contest after learning of the winning tickets. Did the company have to pay?

A number of baseball fans, angry over a strike, filed suit when games for which they had purchased tickets were cancelled.

The fans listed damages as: "Interference with personal and vacation plans; mental anguish and tension, and; our safety is now jeopardized by individuals who might react violently when now unable to rid themselves of their tensions and problems by attending baseball games." The suit was dismissed.

Other fans have had better success in courts.

FACTS: Jimmy, unhappy that the Dolphins were "trying to make me use my ticket to see NFL replacement games during the strike," sued the team for a refund.

The team argued that Jimmy was only entitled to half of his money back because he enjoyed other amenities besides his club-seat (such as air conditioning, a lounge and preferred parking). Was Jimmy entitled to a full refund? **YOU'RE THE JUDGE!**

DECISION: The judge agreed that replacement games did not constitute real NFL games, which Jimmy had paid to see. He ruled that, "The club violated its contract with the ticketholders by fielding the replacement team." Jimmy got a full refund.

ODDS & ENDS....

Fan Clubs

FACTS: Dana, with help from Jimmy (a pro tennis player), ran a fan club for the latter. For a minimal fee, she wrote a newsletter and distributed photos and souvenirs.

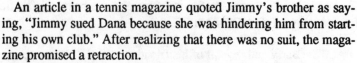

An article in a tennis magazine quoted Jimmy's brother as saying, "Jimmy sued Dana because she was hindering him from starting his own club." After realizing that there was no suit, the magazine promised a retraction.

Fan club members demanded money back, calling the club a fraud. Another pro became hesitant about having Terry start his fan club.

Dana charged Jimmy and his family with violating their agreement, interfering with her club members and damaging her reputation. Could she recover damages?

DECISION: **YOU'RE THE JUDGE!**

Dwarf Tossing?

Dwarf tossing is a contest where—nowadays—the "tossed" wear helmets when hurled down a padded sidewalk. This sport originated in England where it is now banned.

The city of Chicago would not issue a permit to have such a contest at a local bar. The bar was offering prizes for the longest toss over the thirty foot record. And they would furnish a "house dwarf" for any contestants without a dwarf!

Tortillas! Peanuts!

FACTS: Fans at sporting events hurled tortillas, beach balls, fireworks, stink bombs and other objects into the crowd. Vendors hurled peanuts and other products. Could these activities be prohibited? **YOU'RE THE JUDGE!**

DECISION: After complaints from fans who said that they were hit by tortillas and peanuts, one city—for safety reasons—enacted an ordinance banning the throwing of any objects at sporting events. Vendors were exempted from the ban.

Other fans complained about beer drinking which they alleged caused fights and other "rowdyism." Some professional sports teams now offer seating in sections where alcoholic beverages are prohibited, or prohibit the sale of alcohol during the later part of the sports contests.

A crowd at a sports event may play an essential role in determining the outcome—from cheering for their favorite team or athlete to more directly affecting the outcome by disturbing play.

24

FANS & INJURIES

WHAT'S IT ABOUT?

You were a spectator at a sports event and were injured. Who was liable for the injury—a player, the player's team, the operator of the facility, or another spectator? Did you assume the risk of your injury or contribute to it? *Fans & Injuries* discusses injuries to spectators and who may be liable.

Should a spectator at a baseball game assume the risk of injury from a ball that may be traveling in excess of 100 m.p.h.?

Chicago Gazette
Section C - Sports

FANS INJURED - WHO'S LIABLE?

The danger that a sports activity will cause injury to spectators has existed from the time of the gladiators. As one court commented:

"A defect inherent in the nature of man is that perversity of spirit which attracts us to spectacles of danger in which the participants risk injury and death for our amusement. As far back as the events in the coliseums of ancient Rome, spectators were subject to risks for there must have been occasions when a lion escaped the arena to prowl amongst the patrons, or a gladiator lost control of his weapon to the detriment of a front row observer."

The dangers have changed, but so too have the rights of spectators. In the days of gladiators, an injured spectator had no rights. The spectator of today may seek recovery for an injury by proving that the injury was due to the negligence of another and not the result of a known and appreciated danger (thus not one that they assumed the risk of injury from).

An owner or operator of a sports facility, a player or participant or another spectator may be liable where they breach their duty to care for the protection and safety of spectators. What are the duties of an operator of a sports facility or a participant?

WHO'S LIABLE?

Except for injuries due to another's negligence, spectators will assume the risk of most injuries.

In the eyes of the court, the spectator "is a hearty and ruddy-complexioned Greek god, with a spirit that sets him apart from mere mortal men. He is deemed to foresee a ball, puck or other object that comes speeding in an unfamiliar orbit towards him. And, he is expected to be patient and forebearing—slightly ruffled, but unconcerned by the freshly imprinted baseball seams on his forehead."

FACTS: Fans at baseball and hockey games and at a golf tournament were struck by errantly thrown or hit balls or pucks. Other fans were injured when bats, sticks or clubs "slipped" from players' hands. Still others were injured when a racing car went out of control, and also, when players left the field in pursuit of another player or a ball. Will fans assume the risk of such injuries?

DECISION: **YOU'RE THE JUDGE!**

The owner or operator of a sports facility is bound to exercise ordinary or reasonable care for the protection and safety of spectators at a sporting event.

FACTS: Frank, an usher at the town hall, explained what happened on roller derby night, "The place was packed with 3,000 screaming, rowdy fans. But the security was minimal. Some fans were hurt when, because of the lack of security to break up several scuffles, a big fight broke out!" Was this reasonable care? **YOU'RE THE JUDGE!**

DECISION: No. Such security was not that care which could reasonably be expected. Operators must employ a sufficient number of qualified personnel to maintain their premises in a reasonably safe condition.

However, as long as he acts reasonably, the owner or operator is not an insurer of a spectator's safety. Spectators will assume the ordinary risks of the sport or from attendance at a sports facility.

If the crowds at the roller derby games had been pretty quiet, and then suddenly, without warning, a fight broke out, and several fans sitting nearby, but not involved, were injured—and no amount of care would have prevented the injuries—would the spectators then be held to have assumed the risk of such injury? Yes. A proprietor will not be liable even though security may have been inadequate.

FACTS: Phillips was injured during a fight in the stadium parking lot following a baseball game. When he saw two drunks sitting on

his car, he yelled at them. "One of them hit me," he complained. Phillips sued the Dodgers for not having proper security to protect him. There had been other fights and related mischief in the parking area during preceding games. Was the team liable for Phillips' injury? **YOU'RE THE JUDGE!**

DECISION: No. The court found Phillips primarily responsible for his own injury. The security was adequate. The court observed, "It's an easy matter to know whether a stairway is defective and what repairs will put it in order, but how can one know what measures will protect against the thug, the addict, the degenerate, the psychopath and the psychotic?"

NEGLIGENCE

What are the elements of negligence? To find an owner or operator of a sports facility or another guilty and liable for a **tort**—civil wrong committed against an individual—an injured spectator must prove **negligence**—that is, that the defendant owner, operator or another had a duty of care for the protection and safety of the spectator, that there was a breach of that duty which caused an injury, and that the injury and damages would not have occurred but for the acts or conduct of the defendant.

DEFENSE! DEFENSE!

The owner or operator of sports facilities, or another, may allege the defenses that: the spectator was guilty of **assumption of the risk**—the spectator assumed the risk of injury—having had actual knowledge and appreciation of the ordinary and inherent dangers of the sport, but chose to face them anyway; was guilty of **contributory negligence**—the spectator acted in a way that contributed to the injury (as by remaining when in danger) or took part in the activity which resulted in injury. Does a spectator have a duty to protect himself, such as by leaving when injury is imminent?

FACTS: Jan, a spectator at a football game, groaned, "I was injured when another spectator taking part in a fight fell on me." The crowd had been unruly for the whole game. Did Jan assume the risk of such an injury? **YOU'RE THE JUDGE!**

DECISION: Jan had the last clear chance to avoid the injury. He knew that the crowd was getting rowdy. He assumed the risk of, and contributed to, the injury by remaining. Security had kept the unruliness to mostly shouting until the injury.

Furthermore, if an injury was the result of an unavoidable accident, as where a spectator unintentionally bumped into another causing an injury, there would be no liability by the operator of the facility.

Can injured spectators recover even if they were party at fault for their injuries?

Comparative negligence compares the negligence of the spectator with that of the defendant, and allows the spectator to still recover, although his recovery may be reduced by his own negligence.

FACTS: Junior said, "I was injured at a football game, when I slipped in the aisle." Junior was found to be 60% at fault—he knew the liquid had been spilled—a common occurrence at such a game. The operator was found to be 40% at fault—he could have cleared the mess away. Could Junior recover for his injury? What if Junior were only 40% at fault? **YOU'RE THE JUDGE!**

DECISION: In some states, a spectator's recovery is denied where he is found to be more than 50% at fault. In others, irregardless of Junior's fault, he could recover 40% of the total recovery awarded by the court.

Still, in others, if Junior were 40% at fault, he would only recover 20% of the total award. In this case, the court compares the two, subtracting Junior's 40% fault from the operator's 60% fault.

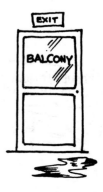

SAFE FLOORS & AISLES?

The owner or operator of a sports facility represents that, except for unknown defects not discoverable by reasonable means, his facility is reasonably safe. Is he relieved of liability merely because he had no precise knowledge of a defective condition?

FACTS: Several spectators at a basketball game were injured when they slipped on a spilled liquid or on a worn and loose carpet in an entranceway. Spectators at a football game were injured by splinters in the bleachers and by loose nails. Did these spectators assume the risk of such injuries? Were the operators liable for the injuries? **YOU'RE THE JUDGE!**

DECISION: As to the spill and the carpet, the operator either knew or should have known of the defective condition. He was liable. Likewise, the operator of the football stadium should have attended to the loose nails.

However, the spectators assumed the risk of injury from splinters, common in wooden bleachers. The condition was not bad enough to require immediate attention.

However, where something not connected with the operation of a facility and not placed there by an operator, makes the premises unsafe, an operator is not under a continuing duty of inspection. He is

not responsible unless he knew or should have known of the condition.

FACTS: Fran testified, "I was injured when I tripped on an umbrella in the aisle."

Hughey was injured when he tripped over cans in the aisle. Was the operator liable for such injuries? **YOU'RE THE JUDGE!**

DECISION: Fran assumed the risk of his injury. Hughey could recover for his. The operator should have corrected the condition. The condition was either known of, or should have been known of.

An operator must use reasonable care to ensure that aisles and floors are in a reasonably safe condition.

FACTS: A statute read, "No temporary seats or persons are allowed to remain in the aisles."

John was struck by a foul ball while walking up an aisle crowded by fans sitting in it. The accident had occurred in the split second when John saw the ball and turned up against the rail. "Can I recover for my injury?" he asked. **YOU'RE THE JUDGE!**

DECISION: No. John assumed the ordinary risks and hazards of the game. Even had there been no fans in the aisle, the accident could have occurred.

However, where a spectator was unable to move out of the way of a prohibited crowd in an aisle and was injured, an operator may be liable.

Has an operator exercised proper care for spectators' safety by merely posting warning signs?

FACTS: Warning signs at all entrances to an arena read, NO BOTTLES, CANS OR OTHER CONTAINERS ALLOWED. There was no security check at these entrances. A fan received a fractured skull when he was hit by a bottle. Was the operator of the arena liable for the injury? **YOU'RE THE JUDGE!**

DECISION: The operator should have provided at least a minimum check, which may have prevented such an injury. He was liable.

SAFE STAIRWAYS & RAILINGS?

Although there is no duty to warn of obvious dangers, an owner or operator of a sports facility has a duty to warn spectators of any known dangers, or those which could be discovered by inspection or supervision.

FACTS: Martin was injured when a broken railing at a hockey rink collapsed from the pressure of other spectators leaning on it. It was foreseeable that the spectators would act as such in an attempt to see the game. Another spectator broke his foot when he tripped over a step under repair. He could not see the AREA UNDER REPAIR sign, as the lighting was out in the walkway. Were the operators liable for these injuries? **YOU'RE THE JUDGE!**

DECISION: Yes. The operators violated their duty of care to the spectators by not taking the proper precautions necessary to alleviate the dangers.

SAFETY LAWS

If an injury to a spectator at a sports facility results from a defect, which violates a safety law designed to provide for the safety of premises used for sporting events, liability may be found against the owner or operator of the facility.

FACTS: A law made it UNLAWFUL TO PERMIT INTOXICATED, BOISTEROUS, OR DISORDERLY PERSONS TO ENTER OR REMAIN ON THE PREMISES. Another law required "handrails on all stairwells." Another required a "safe place" for spectators. If spectators were injured due to a violation of one of these laws, would the operator be liable?

DECISION: **YOU'RE THE JUDGE!**

ORDER!

The owner or operator of a sports facility has a duty to maintain order on his premises. If he does nothing to restrain or control improper conduct after he knows, or should have known of it, and injury results, he may be liable.

However, there will be no liability where the owner or operator could not have reasonably anticipated an assault.

FACTS: Roy, 17, attending a Harlem Globetrotters basketball game, was assaulted in a dimly-lit public restroom. It happened suddenly. There had not been any assaults during prior events on the premises. Was the operator liable? **YOU'RE THE JUDGE!**

DECISION: Roy was denied recovery where the defendant sports arena could not have reasonably anticipated the danger which caused the injury. The court noted, "Reasonable care requires intervention only when more than ordinary rudeness and jostling takes place."

An operator must provide adequate security or other protective measures to prevent harm to spectators.

Promoters of wrestling or boxing matches, or even operators of hockey arenas or football stadiums may anticipate more fan rowdiness than would be present at a basketball or baseball game. Therefore, proper security will be required to handle such conduct.

FACTS: Phillips cried, "I was struck by a broken bottle while at a baseball game!" It was not expected that the games would be rowdy.

Johnson, while trying to leave a wrestling match, was hit and injured by a soda-pop bottle that was thrown by a spectator. For several minutes, before Johnson was injured, a group of spectators were fighting and throwing bottles. Could either spectator recover for his injuries? **YOU'RE THE JUDGE!**

DECISION: Phillips could not recover. His injury was not foreseeable; there was neither prior notice nor ample time to prevent the occurrence. Johnson could recover; there was ample notice and time for the operator to prevent such conduct.

Another fan recovered damages when she was injured after falling on a broken bottle. Evidence showed that the bottle was "probably there before the crowd began leaving. Reasonable inspection would have discovered it or prevented fans from leaving with bottles."

But where proper supervision would not have detected the bottle, there would be no recovery. Could such a fan recover if bottles were prohibited from the sports facility?

Maintaining order may also require that an operator be aware of a fan's condition.

FACTS: A man rocking on an upper deck railing, while shouting obscenities at one of the teams, fell and plunged to his death before thousands of horrified fans. Another spectator was injured in the fall. It was reported that the decedent had been drinking heavily. Was there time to foresee the potential for injury and remove the fan? Was the operator liable for the death and the related injury?

DECISION: **YOU'RE THE JUDGE!**

STOP PUSHING!

The owner or operator of a sports facility has a duty to use reasonable care to keep the premises safe.

FACTS: The arena was overflowing—standing room only—for the state basketball play-offs. Mrs. Petry broke her elbow when she was pushed while trying to get through the crowd in the aisles to her seat. Were these reasonably safe premises?

DECISION: **YOU'RE THE JUDGE!**

Is an owner or operator of a sports facility liable for injuries produced by dangerous conditions which the operator knew or should have known of?

FACTS: Lee was injured when she was pushed off her chair and trampled on by other spectators who were attempting to recover a foul ball. An usher assigned to keep order wasn't there. Did Lee assume the risk of such an injury? **YOU'RE THE JUDGE!**

DECISION: The club was liable for the injury for not providing supervision and could have prevented it by warning spectators to keep their seats when foul balls came. The operator knew, or should have known, of the dangerous condition.

However, an owner or operator of a sports facility may not be liable for injuries resulting from a dangerous condition not known of (or reasonably foreseen).

FACTS: Shayne was injured when he was pushed from the balcony by a crowd surging for the exits after a boxing match. Adequate precautions for policing the crowd had been taken. "Was the operator liable for my injury?" asked Shayne. **YOU'RE THE JUDGE!**

DECISION: A panic would not be a foreseeable danger, unless the negligence of the owner or operator had created the condition. Recovery was denied.

The duty to care for a spectator's safety also requires warning of dangerous conditions.

IT'S CROWDED!

Will an owner or operator of a sports facility be liable for an injury to a spectator resulting from a crowded facility?

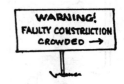

FACTS: Kallish explained, "I was injured when another spectator fell on me in an aisle." The club had oversold the game and additional spectators were seated in the aisles. Was the operator liable? **YOU'RE THE JUDGE!**

DECISION: The court found, "The injury was due to the unforeseeable, unexpected and unpreventable conduct of the spectators, not their numbers or presence in the aisles.

However, a duty to prevent crowding may arise where where such a condition has led to problems in the past.

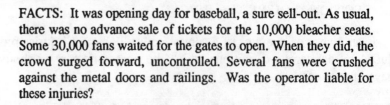

FACTS: It was opening day for baseball, a sure sell-out. As usual, there was no advance sale of tickets for the 10,000 bleacher seats. Some 30,000 fans waited for the gates to open. When they did, the crowd surged forward, uncontrolled. Several fans were crushed against the metal doors and railings. Was the operator liable for these injuries?

DECISION: **YOU'RE THE JUDGE!**

At a wrestling match a spectator, Camp, was injured when, "The crowd surged backward in anticipation of a wrestler being thrown from the ring." The promoter was found liable for "not bolting the seats to the floor, as required by law." Had they been bolted, the crowd could not have surged backwards.

WRONG PLACE!

Determining what is proper care for the protection and safety of spectators may, in part, depend on the nature of the sport. The more dangerous the sport, the more care that is required. Also, where a sport (not particularly dangerous), may create danger when played in a different place, more care may be required.

FACTS: The operator of a fair allowed baseball to be played away from the usual field, close to a picnic area. Two picnickers were injured; one by a thrown ball, the other by a player who was chasing a foul ball. They sued the operator for negligently allowing the game in an improper area. The operator claimed that the picnickers assumed the risk of injury. Who was liable? **YOU'RE THE JUDGE!**

DECISION: Although some picnickers may have been spectators, those who were not did not assume the risk of injury where they were not given notice or warning of the danger. They had the right to expect that the picnic area was safe. The operator, by allowing the game in an improper location, and otherwise failing to protect those using the picnic area, was liable for the injuries.

HAVE A SEAT!

The owner or operator of a sports facility has a duty to inspect the premises from time to time to see that they are safe. He may be charged with knowledge if a reasonable inspection would have disclosed a defect.

FACTS: Fredericks complained, "I broke my leg when I fell from the bleachers. I stumbled on a loose board."
The school in charge of the facility made inspections of the seats

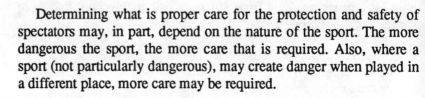

two or three times a year. They defended that Fredericks contributed to his injury by using a seat which he knew or should have
known was defective. Fredericks charged that the school breached
its duty to discover the defect. Was the school liable? **YOU'RE
THE JUDGE!**

DECISION: The school was liable. A reasonable inspection for
such a defect, which could not have happened over night, but only
over a period of time, would have revealed it.

The duty is to furnish seats both safe for ordinary seating and that
will withstand rough usage by spectators.

Sweikert was injured at a racetrack from a fall when a rotten
board in a bleacher seat gave way. The court held that the track's
owner had a duty to maintain the seats in reasonably safe condition—not only as seats but also as 2 steps—where evidence showed
that seats were customarily used as steps.

What if spectators were injured when a railing they had been sitting on gave way?

FACTS: Juan and several other boys stood on the top seat of the
bleachers. All of the other seats were taken. When they sat on the
railing, it broke and they fell to the ground. Juan, injured, alleged
that the school was liable for "not securing the railing." The school
alleged that Juan was guilty of contributory negligence. Who was
liable? **YOU'RE THE JUDGE!**

DECISION: The school district had met its duty to care for the
safety of the spectators. Even if it had been aware, or should have
been aware, of such use of the railing, it could not be held to know
that it would give way. Could Juan recover from the manufacturer
of the bleachers?

In some cases, a higher degree of care is required, such as at an
amusement park.

FACTS: An inspection of seats on an amusement park ride, "The
Snake," revealed them to be in reasonably good condition. But, because one of the seats was a bit loose, Jackson was thrown off the
ride and injured. The park operator asked, "Was I liable?"
YOU'RE THE JUDGE!

DECISION: As the risk of injury from an amusement park ride is
much more probable, a higher degree of care is required. The operator was liable.

A spectator, although noticing a slight defect, may still use a seat
and not be guilty of contributory negligence. A spectator has no duty

to inspect his seat. He may assume that the operator has exercised reasonable care for his safety. However, using a seat in an abnormal manner may be contributory negligence, which will relieve an operator of any liability.

> FACTS: A contestant, "Chubby," claimed, "I was in a national lap-sitting contest. I broke my hip when a chair collapsed and the twelve girls who were sitting on my lap fell on me." Did Chubby assume the risk of such an injury? **YOU'RE THE JUDGE!**

> DECISION: Chubby was found guilty of both contributory negligence and assumption of the risk from such a use of the chair.

Also, recovery was denied where a spectator, without permission, chose to sit in an unassigned seat which he should have seen was in need of repair.

THE THING SPEAKS!

The doctrine of **res ipsa locquitor**—the thing speaks for itself—may be applied to find an operator liable for an injury to a spectator where the injury does not normally occur unless someone is negligent, the thing causing the injury was under the control of the owner or operator and the spectator was not at fault.

> FACTS: At an indoor tennis match, a folding chair, under ordinary use, collapsed, injuring Gurney. Could he recover for his injury? **YOU'RE THE JUDGE!**

> DECISION: Yes. The court ruled, "In the ordinary course of things, such seats or bleachers do not collapse if proper care in their construction and maintenance is used. Their collapse is reasonable evidence, in the absence of explanation by the operator, that the accident arose from a lack of care."

PUBLIC WAYS

The risk of injury to those neighboring a sports facility requires that reasonable precautions be taken for their safety. An owner or operator of a sports facility may be liable if it is shown that harm ought to have been foreseen, either because of past experience, inadequate barriers or a dangerous location.

> FACTS: The operators of several baseball facilities had ample notice that baseballs were frequently knocked into adjacent public streets. At one facility, the fence wasn't high enough. At another, there was no fence or backstop. At still another, the distance to the

sidewalk was too short. Several passersby were injured by batted balls. Were the operators liable for the injuries? **YOU'RE THE JUDGE!**

DECISION: Yes. "The playing of baseball itself, on land next to a public way, does not create a nuisance. It is the failureto tkereasonble preautios here it s knwn or should be known that balls frequently fly out of the stadium and into the public way," commented one court.

Suppose that one of the passersby regularly walked by the field and was well aware of the risk. Would he then have assumed the risk of injury?

Liability will not be found where it could not be anticipated that a ball would be knocked from a field into a public way, where it happened infrequently or where the injured was aware of the risk.

May a player or his team be held liable for an injury to a passer-by?

IT NEVER HAPPENED BEFORE!

FACTS: When the Double Play Tavern's left fielder dropped a high pop fly, the winning run scored. In anger, the fielder picked up the ball and threw it out of the park. The ball struck and injured Betty as she was walking across the street. Was the player or his team liable for the injury? **YOU'RE THE JUDGE!**

DECISION: The court, in a questionable decision, decided, "The player was acting within the scope of his employment for the Tavern and, therefore, the Tavern was liable for Betty's injuries." Was the fielder hired to throw baseballs onto a public way?

Those traveling by car or on foot next to golf courses have also been injured by errant golf balls.

YOU'RE THE JUDGE!

FACTS: One golfer explained what happened. "I sliced a ball onto the street next to the course. The ball struck the windshield of a car, injuring the driver, Walton."

Walton sued for his injury. The golf course defended that Wilton assumed the risk of injury by using the road and by having notice of the possibility of such an occurrence by a posted warning sign. Was the golf course liable? **YOU'RE THE JUDGE!**

DECISION: Yes . The operator of the golf course knew or should have known, of the risk of injury to those using an adjacent public way. The particular hole was too close to the way and there had been similar accidents previously.

A golf course, without proper barriers to prevent balls from reaching a public way, may be a dangerous condition. Those using the way have a right to assume that they may do so free of risk of injury from an errant ball.

FACTS: Wylie, standing on a public street, explained what happened. "I stopped to stare and was hit by a golf ball. I lost five teeth and my nose was broken."

Wylie sued the club, which defended that he assumed the risk, as might a paying customer. Did he? **YOU'RE THE JUDGE!**

DECISION: Wylie did not assume the risk of such an injury. The judge noted, "It is the legitimate pleasure of a pedestrian to stop and stare. He had no cause to foresee that he was in danger." The club was liable for the injury.

Likewise, where a club permitted a dangerous, defective condition—by not having a fence to protect persons using a parking lot from golf balls—then liability may also be found.

But, there will be no liability when it is not likely that a ball will be knocked onto a public way, and sufficient barriers are in place.

BASEBALL

A spectator generally assumes those risks common and ordinary to the game, and any contention that he was ignorant of such risks will be rejected. It is common knowledge that "baseballs are thrown and batted with great force and swiftness, and that they often enter the stands."

Will a spectator who voluntarily chooses an unprotected seat, with full knowledge of the risks and dangers of the game, be guilty of contributory negligence if injured?

FACTS: Crane said, "I chose an unprotected seat so that I could avoid any annoying obstructions. I was then hit by a foul ball."

Other fans were injured by batted balls while sitting in box seats, the upper deck, (down the foul line) and standing behind a fence along the third-base line. Could any of these fans recover for their injuries? **YOU'RE THE JUDGE!**

DECISION: No . The clubs were not negligent in failing to protect all of the seats. It was enough to screen the most dangerous seats. Fans assume the ordinary risks of the game. Furthermore, if injured while sitting or standing in unprotected areas, they will be guilty of contributory negligence.

If an injury occurs (during pregame practice or a game) while a spectator is in the aisle, moving to or from a seat, or where a passageway or seating area is crowded, will the fan still assume the risk for any injury resulting from batted or thrown balls?

FACTS: Baker was injured when struck by a foul ball while being lead by an usher through an aisle to his reserved seat in the un-screened section of the stadium. Should the usher have waited until play was halted? Could Baker recover for his injury? **YOU'RE THE JUDGE!**

DECISION: The court found that Baker had assumed the risk of such an injury. It is "well settled that a spectator at a baseball game assumes the risk of being struck by a foul or wildly thrown ball when sitting elsewhere than behind the screen in back of home plate."

Another court commented, "If a plaintiff knew, or should have known, of the risk of injury from a batted ball while in an unprotected seat, then he should have known of the same danger in the aisle by which he approached his seat."

Similarly, a spectator assumed the risk of injury when, although requesting a seat behind the screen, she agreed to the usher's suggestion that she sit in an unprotected place.

Entrance & Exitways

FACTS: Olson explained, "I was seated behind the screen at a baseball game but while leaving at an exit not in the screened section, was injured by a batted ball." Did Olson assume the risk of such an injury? **YOU'RE THE JUDGE!**

DECISION: There is a duty to provide a reasonably safe means of entering and exiting a screened area without having to walk through an unscreened area. The operator of the facility was liable for the injury.

Liability for an operator was also found where a spectator was struck by a ball while standing in a walkway. At the spot where Jones was injured, she could see neither home plate nor the ball coming towards her. She could not assume the risk of injury from a risk not ordinary to the game—faulty construction or inadequate supervision, for example. Was the stadium manufacturer also liable?

Screen

While a screen is not needed for all seats, there is a duty to provide screened seats for spectators desiring such protection. The duty is only to provide as many of these seats as may reasonably be expected to be needed. Only the most dangerous section of the ballpark (generally behind home plate) must be screened.

FACTS: Tony snarled, "I was hit in the head while seated behind home plate. The screen went straight up, but didn't extend overhead. A foul ball came down on my head!" Should Tony have been warned of the dangers of the game? Was the operator liable

for Tony's injury for not providing a screen extending overhead? **YOU'RE THE JUDGE!**

DECISION: "The timid may stay away!" commented the judge. The lower screen protected the fans from the most dangerous foul balls, subjecting them to no more risk than the rest of the fans.

Another court remarked, "It would be absurd, and no doubt resented by many spectators, if a ticket seller, or other employee, had warned each person entering the park that he or she would be imperiled by errant baseballs."
What if there was a hole in a protective screen?

FACTS: A spectator at a Mets' game, explained how she was injured. "I was struck by a foul ball while sitting behind the home plate screen. The ball went through a hole in the screen!" "Can I recover for my injury?" she asked. **YOU'RE THE JUDGE!**

DECISION: The court held, "A spectator, while seated behind a screen, has a right to receive protection from a foreseeable danger such as a foul ball. The team was negligent under the theory of res ipsa loquitor—the acts speaks for itself." It was not necessary for the plaintiff to show that the team knew, or should have known, of the defect.

Bullpen

Maynard, while seated near the third base dugout watching a game, was struck on the head by a ball thrown by a pitcher warming up in the bullpen. Could he recover damages against the player or his team?
The court found the team negligent for locating the bullpen in a dangerous place—along the left field line, close to the grandstand—and for allowing the pitcher to experiment with new pitches while in the bullpen. It noted, "A spectator does not assume the risk of every batted or thrown ball, only from those which are ordinary to the game."
What if a player intentionally throws a ball which injures a spectator?

FACTS: Grimes, a pitcher, was warming up in the bullpen during a game in Boston. Fans seated behind the wire mesh fence next to the bullpen heckled him continuously. Grimes then threw a pitch at an angle of 90 degrees from the mound to home plate. The pitch passed through the mesh fence and struck a fan who then sued Grimes and his team, the Orioles. Were the pitcher and the team liable for the injury? **YOU'RE THE JUDGE!**

DECISION: Yes. The court found that Grimes was within the scope of his employment when he threw the pitch, attempting to stop the interference with his doing his job. Both he and the Orioles were liable for the injury.

However, where a player left the field to assault a spectator in the stands who had "ragged" him and criticized his play, the assault was not committed within the scope of the players duties, but was a personal act. Although the team was not held liable, the player could be.

I Can't See!

FACTS: Janice, attending a baseball game at the Astrodome, was struck in the face by a foul ball. She claimed that, "The glare conditions inside the domed stadium kept me from following the flight of baseballs hit toward the stands."

Smith, sitting in the left field stands at another game, was injured when he also couldn't follow the flight of the ball. A number of the lights were out. Did Janice and Smithy assume the risk of such injuries? YOU'RE THE JUDGE!

DECISION: As to Janice, the court found no liability by the operator of the facility. She assumed such a risk. However, in the case of Smith, where there was insufficient lighting, the operator was found liable.

Extraordinary Risks?

A spectator's broken arm was caused by the rough play of boys hired to pick up seat cushions and backs after a baseball game. The owner had warned them against such rough play. Was the owner liable for the injury?

The operator was liable. This was a breach of the duty to exercise reasonable care for the safety of the spectators. It was foreseeable that rough play might endanger a spectator. Such conduct was not a risk common to the game.

FACTS: Margaret testified, "While sitting in my seat, I was struck in the head by a canvas banner." She argued that the team failed to exercise due care when they permitted the banner in the spectator area and failed to supervise and control the spectators.

Mary received severe and painful burns during a scheduled fireworks display when a firework landed near her box seat. She claimed that the Pirates were negligent for "permitting a dangerous and explosive display of fireworks too close to the spectators." Did the operators breach their duty to exercise reasonable care for the protection and safety of the spectators?

DECISION: **YOU'RE THE JUDGE!**

Ordinary Risk?

A spectator at a major league baseball game was struck in the face by a foul ball while sitting behind first base. In a suit for damages, the court held that the team failed to show that it provided a sufficient number of screened seats, but damages were not awarded.

FACTS: Loren, 11, was struck by a foul ball at a major league baseball game. She suffered a broken facial bone and an eye injury.

A 12 year-old boy was left brain damaged when he was struck by a foul ball. Could they recover damages for their injuries? **YOU'RE THE JUDGE!**

DECISION: A jury award in Loren's favor was overruled. "Spectators will assume the risk of injury from an ordinary or inherent risk of that sport," held the courts. It was held that a foul ball was an ordinary risk.

GOLF COURSE

The owner or operator of a golf course has a duty to exercise ordinary or reasonable care for the protection and safety of spectators. Although not insurers of the safety of the spectators, they may be liable for a spectator's injury where they create new hazards not common to the sport.

FACTS: Mary explained how she was injured. "While watching a golf tournament, I stepped in a hole in the cart path and broke my foot. The hole was hidden by overgrown grass." Did Mary assume the risk of such an injury? **YOU'RE THE JUDGE!**

DECISION: The operator of the golf course was found liable. The hole, there for a long time, should have been tended to.

In holding that another spectator could not recover for an injury, the judge commented, "It is common knowledge that golf balls do not always go where aimed. This is the very challenge of the game which spectators come to see. Errant shots will happen, and, on occasion, will land in an area where spectators are to be expected." This is a common and ordinary risk of the sport, and one which a spectator assumes the risk of.

FACTS: Greene, a spectator at a golf tournament, was struck by a ball where balls did not normally land. Another spectator was injured when a player overhit a green. Still another was hurt when he ran inside a roped off area and was struck by a ball. Could these spectators recover for their injuries? **YOU'RE THE JUDGE!**

DECISION: No. All of the spectators assumed the risk of injury.

Spectators have the right to assume that those in control exercised their duty to best protect the spectators, and that they are reasonably safe, except for an occasional errant shot.

FACTS: Duffy was struck by a golf ball at a pro golf tournament. She charged, "The sponsor of the tournament and the golf club were negligent in placing a concession stand in a dangerous position between two fairways."

The defendants claimed that the spectator assumed the risk of being hit by an occasional errant shot. A member of the club testified, "Balls had been hit daily in that area in the past." Did Duffy assume the risk of her injury? **YOU'RE THE JUDGE!**

DECISION: The spectator assumed the risk of injury from an occasional errant shot, but not while standing in an area where she expected to be safe. The judge suggested, "Sponsors have to redefine areas where spectators can go."

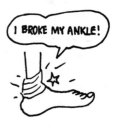

Another spectator assumed the risk of injury where she tripped over a rock concealed by tall grass and broke her ankle while walking down a rocky hill instead of on a well-defined pathway, as instructed. Similarly, another spectator assumed the risk of injury when, in broad daylight, she slipped and fell on a stone covered parking lot.

A major network was found negligent where a spectator tripped on a TV wire laid across a walkway and suffered permanent injuries. "Proper precautions must be taken to ensure the safety of the spectators," cautioned the court.

AUTOMOBILE RACING

FACTS: Carlton and Joanne, while videotaping their son in a demolition derby, were killed when a car spun out of control and into the barrier where they were filming. Allegedly, security had asked them and others to move from the area. Was the operator of the track liable for allowing spectators to remain in a known dangerous area?

DECISION: **YOU'RE THE JUDGE!**

The owner or operator of a racetrack has a duty to exercise reasonable care for the protection and safety of spectators, and to keep the racetrack and adjacent premises in a reasonably safe condition. This duty includes timely inspections to ensure their safety.

FACTS: Several spectators were injured when a race car went out of control. The car skidded when it ran into oil and debris, left on the track from a previous accident. Was the operator liable for the injuries?

DECISION: **YOU'RE THE JUDGE!**

An operator also has a duty to erect sufficient protective barriers between the track and spectators. In cases where the only barriers were a row of automobiles, a four foot fence or one that collapsed, or empty barrels, liability was found where spectators were injured as a result of such negligence in not providing sufficient barriers. This would be especially so where there had been previous injuries caused by such a lack of protection.

However, an operator of a racetrack is not an insurer of a spectator's safety. Spectators will assume the risk of injury by knowing and appreciating a danger.

FACTS: McPherson was injured while attending a stock car race when a car went out of control and crashed into the infield and pit area where he was standing. Did he assume the risk of such an injury? **YOU'RE THE JUDGE!**

DECISION: The court held, "One, knowing and comprehending danger and who voluntarily exposes himself to it, assumes the risk of such injury." Even though the protection in the infield area was less than that of the stands, he cannot recover.

What if there were no warnings? An owner or operator of a racetrack has been found liable for injuries where spectators were permitted to enter dangerous areas without being given proper warnings.

FACTS: Sisco, while walking from the pit area of a stock car racetrack, was struck by a pickup truck and killed. There were no speed limit signs, no lines denoting passenger lanes or pedestrian crosswalks and no other controls over traffic. The driver of the pickup had been drinking and unknowingly, drove through an unattended gate into the pit area. The estate of Sisco sued the track and the driver. Was the track liable for not controlling the area? Was the driver liable?

DECISION: **YOU'RE THE JUDGE!**

Negligence by an owner or operator of a racetrack has also been found where there was a failure to make a safety inspection of a race car (which later crashed and injured spectators), Also, where another race car was not equipped with a required safety shield to prevent the scattering of parts (which also caused an injury after a crash), negligence was found.

Liability for an operator of a racetrack may also exist where injuries are the result of a crash caused by the improper design of a track.

FACTS: A race car went out of control when it couldn't negotiate a turn. It crashed into the stands, injuring several spectators. The cars were traveling far in excess of the speed cars traveled when the track was built. Was the operator liable for running the race on a track not designed for such speeds?

DECISION: **YOU'RE THE JUDGE!**

A racecar driver may also be held liable for injuries to spectators where he or she acts in a negligent manner.

FACTS: One bystander told what happened, "In preparation for a race, O'Neil was doing a 'burnout'—revving the engine and spinning the tires—when the car went out of control and crashed into a concession stand, killing one and injuring other spectators."

The burnout was performed at the entrance to the track, instead of on the main race track, where it was usually performed. There were no guardrails or other barriers separating the entrance area from the stands. Was the operator of the track liable for a lack of barriers? Was the driver liable for negligence in performing in an improper area?

DECISION: **YOU'RE THE JUDGE!**

HORSE RACING

The owner or operator of a horse racing track has a duty to keep his premises in a reasonably safe condition for the protection and safety of spectators.

FACTS: Spectators at racetracks were injured by horses where there was: no entrance attendant; a lack of sufficient barriers or warning for a passageway across the track or other area leading onto or from a track; an attendant who invited a spectator to attempt a crossing; or an attendant who gave assurance that the track was clear. Did any of these situations create liability for the track operators? **YOU'RE THE JUDGE!**

DECISION: These were negligent acts for which the track operators were found liable for the spectators' injuries.

In holding that a spectator will not assume the risk of injury for not constantly watching for horses along a track or entry area, one

judge remarked, "This is very different from merely crossing a public highway. There, the person crossing, unlike a spectator at a horse track who has a right to expect that reasonable efforts have been made for the spectators' protection and safety, has no assurance, but from his own careful observation, that the way is clear."

What if an injury to a spectator is the result of an unforseeable accident?

> FACTS: Several spectators were injured at a racetrack when a horse bolted over a seven foot barrier fence and another fence six feet behind that.
>
> The track president exclaimed, "I've never seen anything like it. I've talked to a lot of old-timers who have been around longer than I and they have never seen anything like it either!" Was the track operator liable for the injuries? **YOU'RE THE JUDGE!**
>
> DECISION: Where the fence or rail was reasonably safe and suitable, there will be no liability for such an unforeseeable accident.

However, where it was a more common occurrence for horses to bolt over a particular fence, or through an opening, liability may be found for the failure to construct a fence or railing of sufficient height to protect spectators.

HOCKEY

The owner or operator of a hockey rink or team has a duty to exercise reasonable care for the protection and safety of spectators. This may not only include providing sufficient barriers where necessary, but may also include a duty in the selection or control of players.

Spectators will assume the risk of injury from the ordinary risks of the game or open and obvious dangers.

> FACTS: While watching an ice hockey game, Kennedy (with knowledge and appreciation of the risks and danger inherent in the game), was injured by a flying puck. Could he recover for his injuries? **YOU'RE THE JUDGE!**
>
> DECISION: Recovery was denied. Kennedy was sitting in the fourth row and the wooden dasher and plexiglass only protected spectators in the first three rows. He had attended many games before and was aware of the risks involved.

But where another spectator, Riley, was struck by a puck while seated in the first row of the balcony, he could recover. There were no signs warning of danger, and danger would not be apparent to one sitting so far from the ice.

Does it matter if a spectator had ever been to a hockey game before?

FACTS: The Pucksters were playing their first hockey game ever in Ft. Lauderdale. John, who had never attended a game, was injured when he was struck by a puck. Barbara was similarly injured, but she had been to many games before. Could they recover damages for their injuries. **YOU'RE THE JUDGE!**

DECISION: Although recovery has been denied where a spectator lived in an area where hockey was extensively played, recovery may be had where there was unfamiliarity with hockey and its dangers. It is expected that the puck will be batted along the surface, not in the air as in baseball.

Protective Barriers

Liability has been found where spectators were injured by pucks where screens or other protective barriers were not high enough, nor extended far enough. If protective devices were improperly maintained and boards collapsed, or where the safety glass broke after players crashed into it, liability may also be found.

One court, in finding for an injured spectator, held that the failure to provide adequate protection to spectators at a hockey game "constituted a dangerous condition that presented a foreseeable risk of injury."

Another spectator recovered for an injury received when struck by a puck while walking along the promenade. He did not know of the risk; the owner did. And where a spectator had a seat in a protected area, there was a duty to provide a safe and protected entrance and exit from that seat.

What if an injury was the result of an unforseeable accident?

FACTS: A spectator, Rich, was injured by a hockey stick which flew out of the hands of one of the players when the player collided with an opponent. Did Rich assume the risk of such an injury? **YOU'RE THE JUDGE!**

DECISION: Yes. The court held that such an occurrence was very rare since, in the course of the game, the stick was not intended to leave the hands of a player. And, as this was unforseeable, the duty to protect spectators was not violated.

Were The Players Controlled?

A team or league which encourages or condones improper behavior, or that is otherwise negligent in hiring or supervising players, may be liable for any resulting injury to spectators.

FACTS: A spectator at a hockey game complained, "I was intentionally hit in the head by a hockey stick after shouting obscenities at a player."

Another spectator, Walter, was injured when a player "thrust his hockey stick through a screen and struck me." The injuries were alleged to have occurred due to the encouragement by the team and hockey association of improper behavior. Could the spectators recover for their injuries? **YOU'RE THE JUDGE!**

DECISION: Both spectators recovered in settlements with the player and the hockey association. Spectators only assume the ordinary risks of the game.

Where a team or league does not condone or encourage improper behavior, then a player will not be acting within the scope of his duties where such acts are not done in furtherance of a his job. Thus, **respondeat superior**—holding a team liable for the acts of its employees—will not apply.

Where a player acts in self-defense of himself or another, will intentional contact with spectators be permitted?

FACTS: At the conclusion of a hockey game between the Bruins and the Rangers, an on the ice argument erupted into a brawl which grew to involve a few of the fans. Several spectators claimed, "We were hit with hockey sticks, assaulted, punched, kicked, choked and stepped on by the players who climbed into the stands."

The league and team were charged with negligence in condoning and encouraging violence, and for having inadequate security.

The players maintained that by climbing into the stands, "We were acting in self-defense and in defense of our teammates, who were being attacked by the fans." Were the players liable? Was the team or league liable for the acts of their players?

DECISION: **YOU'RE THE JUDGE!**

BOXING & WRESTLING

The duty of the owner or operator of a boxing or wrestling facility also includes maintaining the premises and equipment in a safe condition, warning of hidden hazards, and policing participants as well as spectators.

A spectator may assume the risk of injury or be guilty of contributory negligence where he knew, or should have known (from past experience), that wrestlers or boxers will leave the ring, but nevertheless sat in a front row seat and was injured. But, that is not always so.

FACTS: DeSilva, a spectator at a wrestling match told what happened, "I had a seat in the first row from the ring. One of the wrestlers picked up his opponent and threw him over the ropes. He landed on me, breaking my arm."

DeSilva had never observed a wrestler knocked out of the ring into the spectators. He sued the operator for not exercising proper care for his safety. Did DeSilva assume the risk of or contribute to his injury by sitting in a seat next to the ring when other safer seats were available? **YOU'RE THE JUDGE!**

DECISION: The risk of being struck by a wrestler or boxer leaving the ring was not an ordinary and inherent risk of the two sports. The operator was negligent for failing to warn DeSilva of such danger and for failing to place the front row seat a safer distance from the ring.

Similarly, where a wrestler struck a referee, who then fell from the ring and injured a spectator, the spectator could recover.

When a wrestler and a referee jumped from the ring and assaulted spectators in reaction to insults, although the wrestler or referee could be found liable, the promoters were not. The assaults were held to be outside the scope of the wrestler's or referee's employment. They were not employed to assault spectators.

FOOTBALL

FACTS: Mary, a spectator at a football game, was standing on the sideline when a player crashed into her and injured her. She sued the stadium operator and the player's team for negligence in not providing a barrier and not giving special warnings and protection. "Who was liable?" asked the team. **YOU'RE THE JUDGE!**

DECISION: As with any sport, a spectator assumes injury from the ordinary and inherent risks of the game, especially where the spectator chooses to sit or stand at an unsafe place despite the availability of a safer place. Mary assumed the risk of her injury.

Other spectators similarly injured have also been denied recovery. One court reasoned, "Football is a rough and rugged game requiring much brawn, physical effort and contact. The ball carrier is constantly forced out of bounds by the defense, and cannot avoid this. As a result, accidents may occur. The plaintiff was, or should have been, aware of such conditions. He knowingly placed himself in a position of danger and, therefore, assumed the risk of, and contributed to, his injury."

What if the injury was from an act by a player that was not part of the game?

FACTS: Rowan, a photographer, suffered neck injuries when he was struck in the head by a football that had been spiked into the

ground by a Patriots player. He alleged that the act was not one ordinary to the game, therefore, the team and the player were negligent.

The team argued, "Rowan was familiar with the risks of covering sports events and, furthermore, he was warned." Was the team or the player liable for the injury? **YOU'RE THE JUDGE!**

DECISION: The jury found that Rowan assumed the risk of, and contributed to, his injury by placing himself near the action.

However, where a cheerleader was similarly injured at a Patriots game, she recovered damages after settling her suit. Was it more foreseeable that a cheerleader would be in such a place than the reporter and, thus, more care should have been taken to insure her safety?

May a team or one of its players be held liable where one fan injures another?

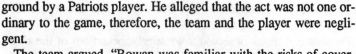

FACTS: Lenny, celebrating his game winning TD reception, threw the ball into the stands. In a wild fight for the ball, Irene was trampled and injured. She said, "I was just sitting there." Did she assume the risk of such an injury? **YOU'RE THE JUDGE!**

DECISION: Throwing a football into the stands is prohibited as a safety measure. The player was fined and the team liable for the injury.

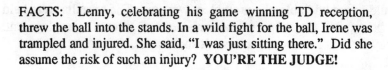

Injuries to spectators have also been caused by "tools" of the sport.

FACTS: John was attending a pro football game. During a half-time demonstration, a radio controlled model airplane went out of control, striking and killing him. His family sued the team and stadium operator for negligently and carelessly selecting halftime entertainment that was "highly dangerous and hazardous," and for failing to adequately supervise the demonstration or warn the fans of the potential danger. Was the team or the operator liable?

DECISION: **YOU'RE THE JUDGE!**

BASKETBALL

Spectators at a basketball game generally assume the risk of injuries which might occur from an errant ball, or from being run into by an out-of-control player where the acts were unintentional. A spectator near a court, other safer places being available, may also be guilty of contributory negligence.

But what if a player intentionally runs into a spectator or throws the ball into a crowd?

FACTS: A basketball player for the Globetrotters, while clowning around in one of the team's acts, faked a pass and deliberately threw the ball into the stands, striking a spectator in the face and injuring her. Was the defendant liable? **YOU'RE THE JUDGE!**

DECISION: The court found that if the ball was negligently thrown towards the audience, and that as a result the plaintiff was injured, liability would attach. "The plaintiff had no choice between a protected and unprotected seat as she might have had at a baseball or hockey game. Also, there is no real danger of injury to spectators at a basketball game from balls entering the crowd in the usual course of a game."

SKIING

Spectators injured at ski areas have assumed the risk of, or contributed to, injuries from: falling on snow or ice, being struck by a loose ski, and from injury caused by a falling skier. Also, where the operator provided a roped off area and a spectator was injured while standing along the rope, operators were not found liable.

But liability may be found where there is a failure to provide a reasonably safe barrier to protect or adequately warn spectators of a danger, such as from snowmobiles.

BOWLING

FACTS: A bowler, Kirk, struck and injured a spectator by taking a practice swing in the open area between the alleys and the ball storage room. There were no warning signs prohibiting such practice. Was the operator liable? Was Kirk liable? **YOU'RE THE JUDGE!**

DECISION: Although the bowler may be liable, the owner could not be found negligent. The act was entirely unanticipated and unforseeable. Nor was there negligence for failing to post a sign prohibiting such practice.

SOCCER

Spectators at a soccer game, while standing on the sidelines, will assume the risk of injury as ordinary to the game (such as from an errantly kicked soccer ball).

However, where protective barriers provided are insufficient or non-existent, liability may attach.

FACTS: Wilson asserted, "There was a three-foot barrier surrounding the indoor soccer field. A ball struck and injured me. I was in the third row." "Should I have provided a higher barrier for the protection of spectators?" asked the operator. **YOU'RE THE JUDGE!**

DECISION: The barrier was of insufficient height to protect the safety of those spectators closest to the playing area,and the most likely spot for an injury to result from an errantly kicked soccer ball. The operator was liable.

TENNIS

Spectators unintentionally struck by a tennis ball, racket or player, are generally held to have assumed the risk of or contributed to any such injury. This is especially so where a fan is near the court, other safer places being available.

SWIMMING

As in the other sports, a spectator will assume the ordinary risks of the sport.

FACTS: "I slipped near the pool while going to my seat at a swim meet," said a spectator, Tom. At another meet, a contestant, late for the meet, ran into a spectator, Kena, who was standing next to the viewing stands. Both Tom and Kena were injured and sued the pool operator. Could either recover for their injuries? **YOU'RE THE JUDGE!**

DECISION: Tom assumed the risk of such an injury. It is common knowledge that water will leave the pool. Furthermore, he contributed to his injury by walking too close to the pool.

Kena was in an area of expected use for spectators. The operator was found liable for not protecting spectators with a proper set-off area for contestants to enter the pool area.

SKATING RINK

Where an owner or operator of a skating rink does not take proper precautions for the protection and safety of spectators, such as by having sufficient barriers, liability may be found.

FACTS: The owner of a skating rink allowed spectators to stand around the edge of the ice to view speed contests. One contestant, out of control, barreled into an unsuspecting spectator. Was the owner liable? **YOU'RE THE JUDGE!**

DECISION: Yes. Although a spectator might be held to be aware of such a possibility, the owner may be found liable for not prohibiting the spectators from what he knew or should have known was a dangerous area.

A spectator has a right to expect that the area that he is allowed into is a reasonably safe one. However, if a spectator stays in such an area after being on notice of a risk of injury, contributory negligence and assumption of the risk may prevent any recovery.

ODDS & ENDS....

Sky Diving

At a sky diving exhibition, one of the parachutists landed on a stack of loudspeakers placed on the perimeter of the landing area. The speakers toppled and landed on a spectator, Susan, injuring her. Susan was standing in an area designated for the spectators. Did Susan assume the risk of such an injury? Was the operator of the premises liable for the injury?

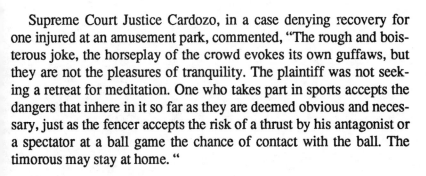

Supreme Court Justice Cardozo, in a case denying recovery for one injured at an amusement park, commented, "The rough and boisterous joke, the horseplay of the crowd evokes its own guffaws, but they are not the pleasures of tranquility. The plaintiff was not seeking a retreat for meditation. One who takes part in sports accepts the dangers that inhere in it so far as they are deemed obvious and necessary, just as the fencer accepts the risk of a thrust by his antagonist or a spectator at a ball game the chance of contact with the ball. The timorous may stay at home. "

But should spectators, especially those unable to realize or protect themselves from the dangers involved, continue to be held to assume the risk of injury from balls which might be traveling in excess of 100 m.p.h.?

Should proprietors of sports facilities be required to take better precautions for the protection and safety of spectators—such as by signs warning of the dangers, by advising fans that they have a right to a protected seat, or by extending or adding protected areas?

Should spectators, short of not attending, have a right to assume that they will be protected from hazards that they in no way could avoid, except by not attending?

25

YOU WAIVE THE RIGHT....

WHAT'S IT ABOUT?

You Waive The Right.... depicts attempts by those in charge of sports activities to have spectators waive any right to recover damages for an injury which is the fault of those in charge. Also discussed is product liability and improper warnings and instructions concerning the use of sports products which may injure a spectator.

Do you know when manufacturers may not waive any liability on their part?

WAS THERE A WAIVER?

A **waiver** is an intentional or voluntary surrender of a known right (the right to recover damages for an injury) with both knowledge of its existence and an intention to relinquish it. If valid, it will relieve another of an obligation to exercise care for one's protection.

FACTS: A ticket to most any sporting event has on the back of it a waiver of liability provision:

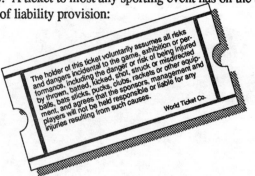

Do you think that by accepting this ticket that spectators would be prevented from recovering damages for any injury to them caused by the sponsors, managements or players' negligence?

DECISION: **YOU'RE THE JUDGE!**

For any waiver by a spectator to be valid in preventing liability by those in charge of sports activities, it must be voluntary.

> FACTS: For the annual company outing, employees were required to purchase several tickets each. The tickets had waiver of liability provisions.
>
> If an employee was injured while watching the events, would the purchase of such a ticket be considered a voluntary waiver of any right to recover damages? **YOU'RE THE JUDGE!**
>
> DECISION: No. The waiver is not voluntary if it comes out of a relationship with unequal bargaining power, such as between an employer and employee. Such a waiver is invalid.

For a waiver to be enforced in preventing liability, it must be shown that the spectator had or should have had knowledge of the waiver.

> FACTS: John, a spectator at a hockey match, said, "I didn't read the waiver of liability provision on the ticket." When John was hit by an errant puck and injured, he sued.
>
> "John knew or should have known of the waiver on the ticket," insisted the promoter. Did John know of the waiver? **YOU'RE THE JUDGE!**
>
> DECISION: John could be held to have had knowledge of the waiver. However, before liability could be waived, it would have to be determined whether or not he intended to waive his right to recover for any injury Even if the waiver were not valid, John may have assumed the risk of his injury.

It must also be shown that a spectator had the intention to waive any right to recover damages for an injury.

> FACTS: Jason's ticket to the boxing matches had a waiver of lia-bility provision. "I read and understood it," he admitted.
>
> Kiwi's and Toni's tickets to a baseball game also had waiver of liability provisions. Kiwi read the waiver, although he didn't un-derstand it. Toni didn't read it, but answered, "Sure!" when asked if he would abide by all of the provisions on the ticket. "I thought the usher was referring to sitting in the seat that the ticket was for," said Toni. Did Jason, Kiwi or Toni intend to waive any right they might have to recover if they were injured? **YOU'RE THE JUDGE!**
>
> DECISION: No. Ignorance negates a waiver as does consent giv-en by mistake or through a misunderstanding. Oversight or thoughtlessness does not create a waiver. Neither does reading and understanding the waiver, by itself, prevent a claim for injuries where there was no intent to waive any right to recover damages.

Where substantial rights, such as the right to recover damages for injuries caused by the negligence of another, are involved, will it be necessary to support any waiver with consideration for it to be valid?

FACTS: "Flash," a photographer, admitted, "I agreed to a waiver of liability provision on my admittance card in return for being able to sit up front to take pictures of the World Wrestling Championships." When a wrestler was thrown from the ring and fell on Flash, he sued. "Was the permission to be up front consideration for the waiver?" asked the promoter. **YOU'RE THE JUDGE!**

DECISION: The permission to get up close to the action, only granted to Flash, was consideration for the waiver, which consideration was necessary to support the waiver. Flash couldn't recover for his injury.

RACETRACKS & WRESTLING

Kotar, a paying spectator at a racetrack, signed a waiver in order to enter the "pit" area. The waiver released the track operator from liability for any injury. When Kotar was injured and sued the track, the court held, "In the absence of any concealment or false representation as to the contents of the waiver, the operator was not liable. The consideration for the waiver was admittance to the pit area."

What if a spectator were injured after being given a free pit pass?

FACTS: Lee, a spectator at an auto racetrack, was given a free pit pass. He was then injured due to the negligence of the operator. He had signed a waiver form. "Can I recover?" asked Lee. **YOU'RE THE JUDGE!**

DECISION: The operator was not released from liability, even though Lee had signed a waiver form. There was no consideration for the waiver. The pass was free to anyone who held it.

May more than ordinary negligence by those in control of a race also bring liability?

FACTS: Jack, attending an auto race, signed a waiver releasing the track from liability. When a car went out of control and struck an empty barrel (which was supposed to be filled with water to make it stable and thus protect those in the pit area), the barrel flew in the air, striking and killing Jack.

His wife sued, charging, "The sponsor was negligent in not filling the barrels. That caused Jack's death." Did the waiver release the track from liability? **YOU'RE THE JUDGE!**

DECISION: The waiver only released the track from ordinary negligence. The jury found that the sponsor, who testified that the sport was "perhaps the most dangerous in the world," was guilty of willful and wanton negligence for telling his subordinates, "Don't worry about filling all of the barrels with water."

In another case involving a waiver of liability provision, three spectators were injured when a car skidded into the pit area of a race-track. The promoter sought to avoid liability for not having proper protective barriers on the basis of a release in the pit passes issued to the spectators. It provided that spectators "release every and any claim for injuries."

The court, in holding, "The release did not waive any claims for negligence," questioned whether public policy—the best interests of the public—would permit enforcement of a provision printed in such small type and designed to permit a wrongdoer to shift the risk of injury to the victims.

Do other spectators have the right to demand the exercise of ordinary and reasonable care for their protection and safety?

FACTS: Wright explained, "I was injured when the wrestlers carried the match from the ring to the aisles where I was sitting. I was knocked to the floor." His ticket had a waiver of liability provision on it. Did the waiver prevent Wright from recovering for his injury? **YOU'RE THE JUDGE!**

DECISION: No. The court, in ruling that Wright could recover damages for his injury, reasoned, "The waiver of liability on the ticket was no more than an attempt to whittle away at spectators' given rights to demand the exercise of ordinary and reasonable care for their protection and safety."

Wright had not, without any other conduct, voluntarily released, with knowledge and intent, his right to hold another liable for the other's negligence.

Because of this overriding policy against any attempt to have spectators waive their rights, personal injury claims by spectators are generally defended by alleging that an injured spectator voluntarily assumed the risk of injury, apart from the printing on the ticket.

An operator or promoter of a sporting event owes a duty to exercise ordinary and reasonable care for a spectator's safety and protection. However, he is not an insurer of a spectator's safety.

Where a spectator can be held to have had knowledge and appreciation of a risk, and then voluntarily encountered that risk and was injured, may recovery be denied?

FACTS: Billy Joe bought a ticket to the drag races. The ticket had a waiver of liability provision on it which Billy read and understood When asked by the operator if he would "waive the right to recover for ordinary negligence," he answered, "Yes."

Billy Joe was then injured when a car crashed, spewing parts into the air, one of which carried over the barrier and struck him. Could Billy Joe recover for his injury if the barrier was inadequate? **YOU'RE THE JUDGE!**

DECISION: Billy Joe read the language, understood it, and then voluntarily gave away the right to be compensated for injuries due to another's negligence. He could not recover.

PRODUCT LIABILITY

"**Caveat emptor**"— buyer beware—once put the burden on a buyer to be aware of any defects in a product which was bought. The buyer, in effect, waived any right to recover damages for an injury arising out of the use of that product.

Now, manufacturers and sellers must use reasonable care to make certain that their products do not harm users. If they do, then there may be **product liability**—liability of a manufacturer or seller of a product for an injury caused by their product.

What is the manufacturer's duty? A manufacturer has a duty to make products that are safe and fit for their intended or reasonably foreseeable uses. Any breach of that duty which causes injury and damages may be negligence.

FACTS: James, a spectator at a baseball game, explained, "I was cut by a piece of the bat which broke off when the batter swung." James alleged a breach of duty by the manufacturer of the bat to provide a safe product. "Was the manufacturer liable for my injury?" asked James. **YOU'RE THE JUDGE!**

DECISION: The judge commented, "It is common knowledge that bats frequently break, and immaterial that a properly made bat ordinarily will splinter with the grain while one made of defective wood may break across the grain. The risk of injury is not materially altered. James assumed the risk of such an injury."

Although the court didn't comment, should the manufacturer have been liable if the bat broke across the grain, inferring a defectively made bat?

Use, Instructions, Warnings, Upkeep & Old Age

A user of a product may waive any right to recover damages for any injury arising out of the use of a manufacturer's product in the following cases where: the product was used improperly, instructions or warnings were not followed, improper changes were made, proper maintenance was not given, or there was predictable deterioration.

FACTS: John injured a spectator at a golf tournament when, after an errant drive, he smashed his club against a tree. It snapped and hit the spectator.

Several other spectators and Bobby were injured when Bobby blew his engine and crashed his street car while drag racing. Could the spectators and Bobby recover for their injuries by alleging product liability—that the products were defective? **YOU'RE THE JUDGE!**

DECISION: A manufacturer will not be liable for injuries caused by uses other than those for which the product was intended. Bobby was guilty of contributory negligence. He could not recover. Both John and Bobby were liable to the injured spectators.

Is there a duty to warn of obvious dangers? Although a manufacturer or seller of a product has a duty to warn of hidden dangers, there is no duty to warn of obvious dangers, or of a danger entirely under the control of the buyer.

Judy failed to follow explicit instructions in setting up and using a home gymnastics weight set. She was injured when she used too much weight and it collapsed on her leg. She could not recover in a suit for damages.

John failed to follow a bold warning recommending that the pitching machine be run through a few cycles before inserting balls. It malfunctioned, hurling several balls in rapid succession, hitting John. The manufacturer was not liable for injuries caused by John's failure to follow the warning or instructions.

What if a user alters a product, or fails to adequately maintain it, and injury then results?

FACTS: Peter admitted, "I altered the engine in my new car." When the car went out of control, Peter broke his collarbone and leg. He sued, contending, "The vehicle should have been made to take the change without affecting performance."

"A snowmobile went out of control and crashed, breaking a spectator's arm," said Jan, the driver. The steering had been loose for some time. Could Peter or Jan successfully allege that the manufacturers were liable for product liability? **YOU'RE THE JUDGE!**

DECISION: A manufacturer will not be liable for injuries caused by subsequent changes in a product or by improper maintenance. Peter was guilty of contributory negligence. He could not recover. Jan was liable to the injured spectator.

What if a product was just simply old? Brent was injured when several spokes broke and his 10-year-old bicycle collapsed. When he sued, the court held that the manufacturer was "not liable for injuries caused by predictable deterioration of a product at the end of its useful life." Brent assumed the risk of such an injury.

TESTING 1...2...3

A manufacturer's duty to make products that are safe and fit for the ordinary uses of such products may include a duty to test the products.

> FACTS: The Get Strong Co. made a product designed to test the strength of different muscles. Testing of the product was minimal. Jim, the supervisor, and Alex, who was being tested, were injured when a spring snapped.
> When sued, the company defended, "They should have known that the product was unsafe by inspecting it." Was contributory negligence a valid defense? **YOU'RE THE JUDGE!**
>
> DECISION: No. Contributory negligence is not a defense when such negligence consists merely of a failure to discover a defect in a product or to guard against the possibility of its existence. The company had a duty to test the product.

The buyer or user of a product has a right to expect that a product will perform as intended or may be reasonably expected.

STRICT LIABILITY

Strict liability is liability without regard to fault. Liability here is based upon the unreasonably dangerous nature of a product, not a manufacturer's conduct. If a defectively manufactured product causes an injury where there was a duty to make it safe, strict liability will attach.

Where strict liability applies, a manufacturer may not waive this liability for any negligence on his part.

> FACTS: A chair lift at a ski resort malfunctioned, throwing and seriously injuring spectators being brought up the slope to view a race. The bull wheel which guided the lift's cable—and which had been inspected and certified safe—collapsed, causing the cable to snap like a rubber band.
> Was the operator or manufacturer liable? Will res ipsa locquitor (the act speaks for itself), or strict liability, apply—either of which would allow recovery without regard to fault?
>
> DECISION: **YOU'RE THE JUDGE!**

When a product (such as a car or motorcycle) is sold, a seller may avoid strict liability by giving proper instructions and warnings which, when followed, make the product safe.

ODDS & ENDS....

FACTS: Sports Inc., a manufacturer of sports products, was sued when several athletes were injured by the company's products. The company was found not liable.

During the trial, Sports Inc.'s attorney asked the owner, "In evaluating the effectiveness of a product's design, and in attempting to prevent injury and avoid liability, what are your considerations in making a product?" **YOU'RE THE JUDGE!**

DECISION: "Considerations may vary depending upon the product. The following questions should be asked and satisfactorily resolved prior to actual sales.
- What type of sport is the product for? Is physical contact involved?
- What type of injury is the product, or any warning, designed to prevent?
- How durable is the product?
- Will the risk of injury be increased if the product is defective?"

The more a product is designed to prevent injury, such as a football helmet, the greater is the care that is required in its manufacture, and the need for warnings and instructions as to its proper use.

Spectators do not assume the risk of all injuries received at sports events, as is insinuated by the use of a waiver on the back of most tickets

26

THAT'S A NUISANCE!

WHAT'S IT ABOUT?

You have a right to the quiet enjoyment of your property. Any interference with that right may be a nuisance. *That's A Nuisance!* explores nuisances—private and public.

Do property owners have a special duty to help prevent injuries to children?

You have a right to the unrestricted, "quiet enjoyment" and use of your property—free from any unreasonable risk of harm. This right protects you not only from trespass by uninvited persons, but also from certain acts that cause excessive annoyance, interference or injury.

These are called **nuisances**—the creation of a condition that will or may result in an interference with the rights of others to enjoy their property.

There are two kinds of nuisances —private and public.

PRIVATE & PUBLIC NUISANCES

A **private nuisance** is one that interferes with your interest only.

FACTS: An unusually high number of soccer balls were being kicked onto your property from an adjacent field. Several windows were broken. When the kids wouldn't stop, you asked, "What are my remedies? Was this a nuisance?" **YOU'RE THE JUDGE!**

DECISION: Your remedies are an **injunction**—court order preventing someone from beginning or continuing an offensive conduct—and damages for any harm caused by the nuisance. The court enjoined the playing of soccer at the field, at least until a fence could be built, and also awarded you damages for the broken windows.

Where a nuisance is a public one, laws may prohibit the activity causing the nuisance. A **public nuisance** is one that may affect or interfere with the general public, not just you.

FACTS: S&W Co. opened a driving range for its employees. One employee explained what happened: "Sea gulls, apparently mistaking the golf balls for shells (and in attempting to break them open), began swooping down, scooping up the balls and dropping them on unsuspecting neighbors and nearby streets." Was the range a public nuisance? **YOU'RE THE JUDGE!**

DECISION: Yes. After losing 500 balls thinking that the "golfers were hitting them all over the place!" the owner then realized, "People in their right minds wouldn't hit them there," and closed the range—at least until a solution could be found.

How will a court determine whether a condition is a nuisance?

The court will "balance the interests"- balancing the social value of the land use and the impracticality of preventing an invasion of another's rights against the harm and burden placed on an injured person. If the seriousness of the harm outweighs the usefulness of the condition, then an injured party may seek relief and damages for a nuisance.

A **mixed nuisance** is one that may interfere with both private and public interests, such as a drag racing strip.

STADIUMS & BALLFIELDS

Complaints charging that a ballfield or stadium is a nuisance generally involve situations where there is glare from lights, excessive noise or where balls leave the facility.

FACTS: Mrs. Kunerth filed for an injunction to halt play at the park next to her house. "The baseballs were sailing onto my property," she complained. "They caused damage to my house and injured someone in my yard!" Was she granted an injunction? **YOU'RE THE JUDGE!**

DECISION: Evidence showed that batted or thrown balls entered Mrs. Kunerth's yard fairly frequently, causing damage and injury.

An injunction was granted to halt the play of baseball at the park—at least until a higher fence was constructed to afford adequate protection.

May a passerby, injured by an errant ball, recover damages? Where batted or thrown balls often land on a road, and there have been insufficient precautions, a passerby may recover for injuries.

Generally, though, courts have concluded that baseball—even if close to a public roadway—does not constitute a nuisance which would make the operator of the field an insurer of the safety of persons lawfully using their property or the public roadway.

FACTS: "I was working in my garden next to the public ballpark. I was struck by a ball," John groaned. He brought suit, seeking an injunction preventing baseball from being played there, and for damages for his injuries. Evidence showed,"Only a few balls had landed in his yard since he moved there years ago." Was this a nuisance? **YOU'RE THE JUDGE!**

DECISION: No. Because the intrusion was an infrequent occurrence, a nuisance was not established. There could be no injunction or recovery of damages.

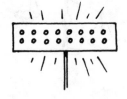

Neither will baseball be judged a nuisance where it was unforseeable that a ball would reach a roadway, (or did so) but infrequently.

Night Baseball

FACTS: Landowners next to a baseball park sought to enjoin, as a nuisance, the use of the park for night baseball. They alleged that the floodlights created "glare." All games were over by 10:30 and there was no undue noise or rowdyism. Was an injunction granted? **YOU'RE THE JUDGE!**

DECISION: The court observed that the field was used for the "sound development of boys." Night games were permitted as long as the glare could be reasonably eliminated by a screen. If not, an injunction would be granted.

Would a court view such a case differently where a professional team sought to build next to homeowners, or add lights to an existing field?

A court will balance the interests of homeowners—"Our property values will be diminished by lights and noise, and this will interfere with our comfort and enjoyment."—and the interests of the team—"We need a place suitable for playing, and which may benefit the community as a whole, bringing in fans and revenue."

FACTS: A Chicago ordinance prohibited professional sports contests at night in open stadiums, containing more than 15,000 seats that are located in a residential neighborhood.

In an attempt to install lights for night baseball, the Cubs challenged the law. Wrigley Field, the oldest in baseball, is located in a predominately residential neighborhood. Traffic to games flows through the neighborhood of people who supported day baseball, and felt, "The lights, traffic and noise would infringe on our right to peace and enjoyment, and would deteriorate the neighborhood." Was the ordinance reasonable? **YOU'RE THE JUDGE!**

DECISION: The court, in holding that the ordinance was reasonable and valid in preserving individual and community rights, joked, "Justice is a southpaw, and the Cubs just don't hit lefties."

But when the Cubs were offered the 1989 All-Star game, to be played at night, the Chicago City Council voted to allow a limited number of night games.

What if a landowner's property is "trampled" or littered on?

A ballfield may be a nuisance where neighboring property is continually trampled on by spectators or participants going to or coming from the ballfield. This could be corrected by erecting a fence or other suitable barrier. And where "rash was continually dumped on another landowner's property, the operator of the field had to clean it up or be subject to an injunction preventing the sale of products causing the problem.

FACTS: A ballfield was constructed with the backstop too close to homeplate and the bleachers too close to the field. Were these nuisances interfering with the rights of the players and fans to have a facility which wouldn't endanger their safety? Would they assume the risk of any resulting injury?

DECISION: **YOU'RE THE JUDGE!**

GOLF COURSES

Relief for injuries from errantly hit golf balls may be sought against a golf facility on the basis that it is a nuisance.

FACTS: Poorly hit golf balls landed in Lynn's yard once or twice a week. However, no one had been hit by a ball on the property for twelve years. Was this a nuisance? **YOU'RE THE JUDGE!**

DECISION: This did not constitute a nuisance to the landowners next to the golf course. It happened too infrequently. No injunction would be issued, nor could there be recovery for injuries. "The

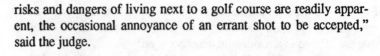

risks and dangers of living next to a golf course are readily apparent, the occasional annoyance of an errant shot to be accepted," said the judge.

Neither would an injunction be issued to prevent the construction of a miniature golf course. The court held, "Neither lights nor noise from traffic or crowds constitute a nuisance when done at reasonable times and kept at reasonable levels."

Where it is shown that an injury was the result of a deficient layout of a golf course, could the injured recover damages?

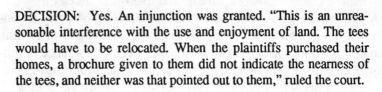

FACTS: At two tees—where play continued from 6 a.m. until twilight—crowds collected while waiting to tee off. The residents next to the tees said they were "constantly annoyed, endangered and restricted in the use of our property by the golfers who demanded absolute silence and immobility of everything in sight when teeing off." They asked, "Are the tees a nuisance?" **YOU'RE THE JUDGE!**

DECISION: Yes. An injunction was granted. "This is an unreasonable interference with the use and enjoyment of land. The tees would have to be relocated. When the plaintiffs purchased their homes, a brochure given to them did not indicate the nearness of the tees, and neither was that pointed out to them," ruled the court.

Similarly, where many golf balls were hit onto other private property, a nuisance was found. The purchasers of the property did not agree to assume the risk of injury to themselves or their property. The builders would have to construct a suitable fence to keep the balls off of adjacent landowners' properties.

Does a passerby have a right to the free and unmolested use of a roadway?

FACTS: Bob was driving a taxi cab along a public street near the 13th tee of the St. Augustine Golf Course. An errant tee shot broke his windshield, causing the loss of an eye. Was the hole a nuisance? **YOU'RE THE JUDGE!**

DECISION: Yes. Balls from that tee had frequently landed on the highway and, on several occasions, struck other vehicles. The risk of balls being sliced onto the highway was a danger and a nuisance. It interfered with the right of the public to pass safely. Bob recovered for his injury.

Fairways that are too close to a roadway—including one that cuts across a golf course between two adjacent fairways—will be a nuisance if they interfere with the public's right to free and unmolested use of the roadway.

RACETRACKS

Where racing activities result in an unreasonable and foreseeable risk of injury to persons or property near a racetrack, may a nuisance be found?

FACTS:

Various residents, businesses and churchgoers, who lived and worked near racetracks, complained of the following: squealing brakes; yelling and screaming crowds (heard up to three miles from the track and requiring residents to close their windows); pollution from exhaust fumes and dust clouds; smells from burnt motor fuels and tires; glaring lights; horns and roaring engines, and; shouting over the public address system.

They contended that such behavior and activities were nuisances that turned their properties into a "defening whirlpool of sound." Did the court grant injunctions to prevent racetracks from such conduct?

Did the court grant injunctions to prevent racetracks from such conduct? **YOU'RE THE JUDGE!**

DECISION: Yes. The racetracks were mixed nuisances, interfering with both private and public interests They disturbed the peace, enjoyment, comfort, health, safety and welfare of passersby as well as residents, and depreciated the resident's property. The residents had a right to the full use and enjoyment of their property—free from any such annoyance or interference.

Where noise from a track is minimal and the distance to residences an acceptable length, a nuisance will not be found.

One court commented, "No one is entitled to absolute quiet, but only to the comfort prevailing in that neighborhood. Where one lived in a quiet neighborhood—as opposed to a noisy and busy one—a nuisance would be more likely to be found. And where one builds next to an existing track, he may assume the risk of the accompanying interferences."

Does racing on public streets constitute a nuisance?

FACTS: Some of the local kids raced their cars on the public streets. Nancy (who was racing) and John (a pedestrian), not involved in the racing, were injured when Speedy hit a pothole and went out of control. Both alleged, "The accident was due to improper control of the racing and maintenance of the streets." Was this a public nuisance? Did either Nancy or John assume the risk of or contribute to their injury? **YOU'RE THE JUDGE!**

DECISION: A nuisance was found for the interference with John's right to enjoy the public ways without undue risk. John did not assume the risk of, or contribute, to his injury; Nancy did.

SWIMMING POOLS

A swimming pool may be a nuisance where it deprives adjacent landowners of their right to the full use and enjoyment of their property. Such would be the case where there is excessive noise, glare from lights, traffic congestion, or the pool is frequently a source of annoyance and irritation to the adjoining landowners.

FACTS: Mike and Marion Wilson lived next to the town swimming pool. In the summer, the pool—open until 9 P.M.—was lighted, crowded and noisy. Would the court enjoin the use of the pool at night for being a nuisance? **YOU'RE THE JUDGE!**

DECISION: No. As with other potential nuisances, where the rights of the parties are balanced and the inconvenience and any annoyance is minimal, especially when compared with the purpose of the pool to promote public health, happiness, and welfare, there will be no nuisance.

WAS IT AN ATTRACTIVE NUISANCE?

Attractive nuisance applies to a situation where a child on another's property is injured by the condition, nature or use of the property. If an injury occurs, recovery is usually sought on the basis that the landowner has created a nuisance that attracts children—an attractive nuisance.

FACTS: Grega Co. had dug a large hole for a new watering system for some football and baseball fields. The hole was left without a barrier or warning. A neighborhood child, Tommy, 10, playing there (as was his custom), whined, "I fell in the hole and broke my leg!"
   Grega Co. also had a pond on the premises which the kids used as a swimming hole. After the company dumped some chemicals in the pond, several of the kids swimming there became ill. Was the property an attractive nuisance? **YOU'RE THE JUDGE!**

DECISION: Both of the situations were attractive nuisances.

The attractive nuisance doctrine holds that one who maintains a condition which is dangerous to children (generally those under age 12) because of the children's inability to appreciate the danger, and which may reasonably be expected to attract them to the premises, is under a duty to exercise reasonable care for their protection and safety.

Attractive nuisance subjects a possessor of land to liability for injuries to children where: (1) the possessor knows or should know that children may trespass, and that a condition on the land may create an unreasonable risk of death or serious bodily harm to such children; (2) the children, because of their youth, do not discover the condition or realize the risk; (3) the burden of eliminating the danger is slight, and; (4) the possessor of the land fails to exercise reasonable care to protect the children.

FACTS: Larry, 7, was injured when he was hit by a golf ball. Susan, 10, was injured when she cut herself swimming at a pond next to a privately owned golf course. There were warning signs posted on a broken down fence. Children often played on the golf course and at the pond, and their presence was known by golfers and the owners.

Tim explained how his brother Jay, 8, was hurt. "He was cut by a broken bottle. It was in the broad jump pit next to the playing field." Were the golf course, pond and field attractive nuisances? Could the children recover damages for their injuries? **YOU'RE THE JUDGE!**

DECISION: All were attractive nuisances. The golf course owner had a special duty to care for the protection and safety of those who they could foresee using their property. The children played there often. The warning may have been beyond the children's comprehension. The owner was guilty of negligence and even golfers (in certain situations) may be held liable.

Jay's use of the broad jump pit was also foreseeable. There was a breach of the duty to maintain the premises by adequate inspection to prevent such an injury. All could recover.

What if the children were older? Could they still recover damages?

The age of a child and the obvious nature of any risk may prevent the use of the attractive nuisance doctrine. For example, where a 13-year-old child was injured while diving in a neighbor's pond, where it was obvious that the water was too shallow, he was held to have both contributed to, and assumed the risk of, such an injury. He could not recover damages from the neighbor.

ODDS & ENDS....

Would you want a bunch of tough guys fighting in your neighborhood?

FACTS: You lived next to Kendrick Field which was used for sports by the local high schools and neighborhood kids. On occasion, the city granted a permit for an outdoor concert at the field.

The town newspaper's headline read: TOUGH MAN CONTEST AT KENDRICK FIELD. Men would fight until one of them couldn't continue. The contest was to take place two nights a week over a two month period.

You would like to have the contest enjoined as a nuisance. You alleged, "It will attract an evil public gathering—those of idle, vicious and criminal habits—who will contaminate the youth and disturb the peaceful pursuits and happiness of citizens unwilling to attend such an event."

Will the court grant an injunction, stopping the contest as being a potential nuisance?

DECISION: **YOU'RE THE JUDGE!**

May an animal be considered to be a public nuisance?

FACTS: Harvey, who lived in an apartment next to a golf course, complained, "Those roosters just strut around the course making noise." Harvey claimed that the roosters were a nuisance. Were they? **YOU'RE THE JUDGE!**

DECISION: The state attorney threw the case out. The roosters only bothered Harvey, not the public—and the noise was too infrequent.

───────────────

You have a right to the "quiet enjoyment" and use of your property, free from any unreasonable intrusions.

27

HERE'S MY PROPERTY

WHAT'S IT ABOUT?

When you leave your bicycle, tennis racket or other sports equipment at a shop to be fixed, or your car at a parking lot while attending a sports event, a **bailment**—a contract to deliver personal property for some purpose—is formed. *Here's My Property* discusses bailments and who may be liable for any damage to such properties.

If you find personal property, do you have a duty to protect it and try to find its owner?

BAILMENTS, BAILORS & BAILEES?

FACTS: Frank admitted, "I was trying to fix Wally's bicycle and baseball glove and ruined them."

Bernie fumed, "While at the health club, I left my clothes in a locker and my valuables in the safe. They were stolen. Both services were provided as a courtesy." Could Wally or Bernie recover damages?

Suppose that you borrowed your friend's golf clubs, or loaned him your boat, and they were returned damaged? Or, suppose that you left your golf cart in the repair shop, rented fishing equipment, parked your car at a garage while at a game, rented a room, or checked your baggage or clothing, and....

What would everyone's rights and responsibilities be if any of these properties were damaged?

DECISION: **YOU'RE THE JUDGE!**

All of these situations involve a **bailment**—a contract providing for the delivery of personal property by its owner to another for some specific use or purpose.

The owner of the property is called the **bailor;** the person who receives the property is called the **bailee.** Only possession is transferred. Title and ownership are retained by the owner.

> FACTS: You brought your tennis racket to a repair shop and your son's baseball uniform to the cleaners. Both shops were busy. In a hurry, you left the racket and uniform on the counters. When you called later, both were missing.
>
> You sued, charging, "The tennis shop and cleaners were negligent bailees, they breached their duty to take reasonable care of our property." Could you recover for the loss of the racket and uniform? **YOU'RE THE JUDGE!**

> DECISION: No. A bailment does not arise until you deliver possession to the bailee, and he accepts. Leaving the property on the counters did not create a bailment.

Bailments fall into three classes: those for the benefit of the bailor; those for the benefit of the bailee, and; those for the benefit of both.

BENEFIT OF BAILOR

The promise to fix the bike and glove, and the leaving of clothing in the locker room and valuables in the safe were all for the sole benefit of the bailor—the owners of the property.

If a bailee gets no compensation for the services he renders to a bailor's property, then he is a gratuitous bailee—merely undertaking to do it as a courtesy to the bailor.

If the bailee gets no compensation, can he be held to his promise? Not unless he accepts possession of the bailor's property. Once he has accepted possession of the property, he is required to perform.

> FACTS: You, as the bailee, undertook to fix the bike and glove. The health club, also as a bailee, accepted your clothes and valuables. Did either of you owe a duty to care for the property that was entrusted to you? **YOU'RE THE JUDGE!**

> DECISION: A duty was now owed by the bailees—you and the health club—to use reasonable care to prevent reasonably foreseeable harm to the property.

What if the bailed property were lost or used improperly by the bailee? If bailed property is lost, stolen, damaged or destroyed, a bailee would be liable for the loss if he failed to use proper care. Likewise, if the harm was sustained during an improper use of the property by the bailee, he would also be liable. Otherwise, the bailor bears the loss.

FACTS: "I left the glove and bike in my unlocked garage. They were stolen," you sadly reported. The health club burned to the ground. It was caused by an arsonist. Who was liable for the properties? **YOU'RE THE JUDGE!**

DECISION: You were liable for the glove and bike. You didn't use reasonable care. You should have either locked the garage or put the equipment in a safe place.

    The club was not liable for the clothes and valuables. They took reasonable care of your property. The loss was caused by the willful act of a third person. Even if the fire were no one's fault, or a third person's negligence, the club would bear no responsibility. However, the club may be covered by insurance.

A bailee may not use property left with him unless it is necessary for its proper care, or unless the bailor grants permission. Such permission does not, however, relieve the bailee of liability for any failure of his duty to exercise reasonable care for the property. The bailee has a duty to return the identical property.

FACTS: After fixing the bike, you decided, without permission, to test it out. You rode it into a parked car. Were you liable for the damages to the bike? If the bike couldn't be repaired, could you replace it with another used bike?

DECISION: **YOU'RE THE JUDGE!**

A bailment for the benefit of the bailor may be terminated by either the bailor or the bailee. However, if a bailee agreed to keep the property for a certain time or to transport or deliver it, he must complete his requirement or be responsible for any resulting damages.

FACTS: After fixing John's glove, you delivered it as promised to the field, leaving it with a teammate. It was stolen before John arrived. "Was I liable?" you asked.

DECISION: **YOU'RE THE JUDGE!**

BENEFIT OF BAILEE

In a bailment for the sole benefit of the bailee, a bailor delivers property to be used and then returned by the bailee. If you promised

o lend out your bike, your neighbor has no right to it—and there is
no bailment—until you surrender possession and he accepts. Because
the bailor gets no compensation, he can not be held to his promise.

Any departure from an agreed upon or expected use is at the peril
of the bailee.

> FACTS: After using your friend's golf clubs and tennis racket,
> you loaned them to Joe. He lost one of the golf clubs and used the
> tennis racket to play racketball, damaging it against a wall. "Who
> was liable for the damages?" asked Joe. **YOU'RE THE JUDGE!**

> DECISION: A bailee is required to exercise great care in using
> and keeping property loaned to him. He is responsible for any loss
> caused by his negligence and will only be absolved of liability for
> loss, damage or theft, if he can show that it was not due to any neg-
> ligence on his part. You should not have loaned the equipment to
> Joe without your friend's permission.

MUTUAL BENEFIT

What is a mutual benefit bailment? Renting a sports car or taking
your snowmobile to a repair shop would be bailments for a mutual
benefit. One party is given possession of another's property for a
specific purpose, time and for a mutual advantage—you get the benefit of using the car or getting your snowmobile repaired, the rental
company or repair shop gets money.

The bailee, required to use ordinary care, is responsible if he is
negligent in his care of the property. What if a loss occurs which is
beyond his control?

> FACTS: Fires damaged both your snowmobile in the shop and
> your clothes in the cleaners, you lost the fishing equipment that
> you rented, your baggage was misplaced by a hotel, and your car
> was stolen from a secured parking garage. "Was I liable for these
> damages?" you asked. **YOU'RE THE JUDGE!**

> DECISION: The loss of the snowmobile and clothes was not due
> to the negligence of the bailee. However, he may have been cov-
> ered by insurance. The bailee was liable for the car and the bag-
> gage. You were liable for the fishing equipment.

If due to his negligence, a bailee injures another with bailed property—such as by running into another with a motorcycle—the bailee
is liable as though he owned the property. A bailee is not liable for
any injury caused by a thief who steals bailed property even though
the theft was possible because the bailee was negligent. May a bailor
be liable for an injury?

FACTS: Without giving proper warning, you, the bailor, entrusted a bailee with your golf cart, knowing that he was ignorant of the danger, and that he was reckless. The cart was not in good repair. Were you liable when the bailee injured another in an accident? **YOU'RE THE JUDGE!**

DECISION: You, the bailor, were liable. However, if the bailee were injured, he would assume the risk or be contributorily negligent if, in spite of knowledge of a defect, he made use of the property and was injured due to the defect (bad brakes).

If a bailee fails to complete the work on your property by the time promised, your damages are minimal unless you can show that it was understood that time was of the utmost importance.

A bailee is given a lien or the right to retain possession of bailed property until he has been paid for any storage or repairs.

A PAWN?

A **pawn** is a pledge or bailment of personal property by the bailor to the bailee to secure a loan from the bailee to the bailor.

FACTS: Randy exclaimed, "I needed money to pay the rent. So I took my golf clubs to the pawn shop where I got money for them. When I went back to pay the loan and get my clubs, they had been sold." Was the pawn shop liable for Randy's loss? **YOU'RE THE JUDGE!**

DECISION: The bailee or pawnbroker must exercise reasonable or ordinary care for the property, or be liable for any loss. However, if Randy did not pay the money back within a specified time, the pawnbroker could sell the clubs, upon any necessary notice to Randy.

Is a storekeeper responsible if a customer's property must be removed to try on merchandise, and then was misplaced or stolen?

FACTS: You went to a pawn shop looking for a fur coat to wear to a football game. Your coat, which you left on the counter while trying on the fur coat, was stolen. "Was the pawnbroker liable?" you asked. **YOU'RE THE JUDGE!**

DECISION: The pawnbroker was liable for the loss. He had a duty to exercise reasonable care for your coat, which necessarily had to be removed.

Are arenas or restaurants responsible for clothing left there by a patron?

Arenas, restaurants and the like are ordinarily not responsible for a patron's clothing, even if it was left at a place provided for such clothing, and even if someone employed there helps. However, liability may attach where there is a failure to take reasonable precautions to safeguard a patron's property, and this may be so despite any waiver of liability on a claim check.

BAILMENT FOR HIRE

A **bailment for hire** is an agreement by which a bailor rents out his property to the bailee for a specific purpose and warrants that the article is fit for the purpose intended.

> FACTS: You rented a tractor from Andy's Store to work on your new golf course. There was an unknown defect in the tractor which caused it to go out of control. It damaged a new green and injured you. Who was liable for the damages and injury? **YOU'RE THE JUDGE!**

> DECISION: The bailor, Andy's Store, was liable for any breach of his warranty or for any damages resulting from that breach. The manufacturer may also be liable.

A bailee is responsible for necessary repairs (tune-up), while a bailor is responsible for extraordinary or special repairs (transmission).

Another type of bailment for hire is where a bailor leaves personal property to be serviced by a bailee—repaired, altered or made into another product.

In the following example, who would be liable for any loss or destruction of the property?

> FACTS: "I left cloth with the Brown Uniform Co. to be made into softball uniforms. A fire then destroyed the factory," said Marv. Who was liable for the loss? **YOU'RE THE JUDGE!**

> DECISION: Ownership was still with the bailor, Marv. Only possession was with the bailee company. Therefore, unless the bailee was negligent, the loss was the bailor's. However, the bailee may be covered by insurance.

SPACE FOR RENT!

Where space is rented from a bailee to store personal property of a bailor, the bailee performs no service other than storing the bailor's property.

FACTS: Rich said, "I rented space in a self-service storage area to store my boat for the winter. I kept the keys and had the exclusive right to use the space." If Rich's property were damaged, who would be responsible? **YOU'RE THE JUDGE!**

DECISION: The renting of space in a locker or building does not constitute a bailment. Here, there is no delivery, merely rental with no liability to the owner of the space (other than that arising from gross negligence).

What if the owner of a storage area keeps a key to each storage area—does he then have some responsibility?

Where an owner of a space for rent has some control over that space—as by having a key to the storage area—then a bailment is formed. Then, there is a duty to exercise reasonable care to protect the property. Any breach may result in liability to the bailee, unless the loss is not due to his negligence, such as from a fire.

TRUNKS & BACK SEATS

In the absence of an express disclaimer, articles normally found in a vehicle are regarded as bailed. That is, a bailee—such as a parking garage—may have a duty to safeguard not only any vehicle parked there, but also to safeguard the vehicles contents, unless the garage clearly indicates a refusal to do so.

If an article is not normally found in an auto and its presence is unknown, then there is no bailment of the article, hence, no duty to safeguard.

FACTS: "I parked my car at the local garage," testified Wilma. "There were valuable drawings and sports equipment on the back seat and in the trunk. Everything was stolen." Who was liable for the loss? **YOU'RE THE JUDGE!**

DECISION: Although the parking of the car constituted a bailment—contract providing for delivery of personal property (car) by the owner to the garage for safekeeping—there was no bailment of valuable drawings or equipment left on the back seat that was not visible from outside of the car.

When a car is bailed with the trunk locked, there is ordinarily a bailment of whatever is locked in the trunk. Wilma was liable for the valuables left on the back seat; the garage was liable for the car and the valuables left in the trunk.

Some courts have held that the operator of a parking lot has a duty of reasonable care for the protection of the auto regardless of whether or not there is a bailment.

PASSENGERS & BAGGAGE

A private carrier of passengers operates on the basis of a contract with the people whom he transports. Since he does not offer his services to the public, he has the right to choose with whom he will do business.

A common carrier of passengers serves the public. Does a common carrier have the right to to choose with whom he will do business?

> FACTS: After a football game, the fans headed for the buses. Infuriated by his team's loss, one driver refused to allow any fans of the winning team on his bus. Could he do so? **YOU'RE THE JUDGE!**
>
> DECISION: No. The driver may not discriminate. As a common carrier, he must carry all persons who request his services, only refusing those whose behavior is objectionable or who do not pay.

A person becomes a passenger when he enters the premises intending to use the carrier's services. And this is so even though he has yet to purchase a ticket.

A carrier has a duty to provide reasonable care for the protection and safety of his passengers. Is a carrier responsible for any delay in service?

> FACTS: The Tigers' football fans wanted to reach the stadium for the kick-off. The carrier, knowing that there would be a delay, but wanting to sell his service, promised, "You'll be there on time." When the fans didn't arrive until the second quarter, they demanded a refund. "Weren't we entitled to one?" they asked. **YOU'RE THE JUDGE!**
>
> DECISION: Although a carrier is not ordinarily responsible for any delay in service, this carrier was liable because of his knowledge of the probable delay and his promise.

A carrier is responsible for checked baggage, but not for baggage carried by a passenger. Passengers have a duty to declare excess value.

Any attempt to limit liability by a waiver of liability printed on a ticket or baggage claim check will not be binding where it was not brought to the passenger's attention and his proper consent obtained to waive any right to recover.

INNKEEPER

A hotel, motel, inn or other place of boarding is a public place—open to all. Accommodations are furnished to all who request them and who comply with reasonable rules, including payment.

FACTS: Mary requested accommodations at the Sportswomen's Club. While waiting in line to register, her luggage was stolen from the lobby. Was she a guest of the club? Was the club liable for the loss? **YOU'RE THE JUDGE!**

DECISION: A traveler requesting accommodations at a hotel becomes a guest immediately, even before registering or entering the building.

In the absence of a valid limitation, the management of a hotel generally insures the safety of goods of a guest and is liable for any loss due to its negligence, unless the loss was due to an act not under the control of the hotel—such as an act of God or negligence of the guest.

Innkeepers may limit liability by bringing any limitation to the attention of the guests—by posting such limitations and providing a safe. Liability for valuables left in a hotel safe may also be limited by the management.

FACTS: A sports equipment salesman, Eddy, lost his job after, "The company's receipts were stolen from the safe of the hotel where I was staying." Could he recover his lost wages because of the hotel's negligence? **YOU'RE THE JUDGE!**

DECISION: Even where the hotel may have been liable for the loss of the receipts, the hotel was not liable for lost wages.

A hotel or inn has a lien on any property brought in by a guest for all charges owed and may hold that property as security for such charges.

ODDS & ENDS....

"I Found It!"

FACTS: Andy found Joe's Super Bowl watch. What if he tired of keeping the watch and threw it in the trash? What obligation did Andy owe to Joe? **YOU'RE THE JUDGE!**

DECISION: Andy had no duty to keep the watch, but once he decided to, he only had the right to possess it. He had a duty to keep it safe. Treating it as trash, when it clearly had great value, was gross negligence.

Andy's duty was to search for the true owner, holding the watch until there was no reasonable expectation of the true owner showing up.

The more expensive the watch was, the longer Andy would have to hold it and search for the owner before he could throw it away or keep it.

FACTS: Andy admitted, "I wore the watch while swimming, had it cleaned, and then loaned it to a drunk." Would Andy be liable if the watch were damaged?

DECISION: **YOU'RE THE JUDGE!**

The care required of a finder is slight. This is because of the slight benefit to a finder. But, the degree of care owed may rise as the benefit goes from slight to something more—such as if the watch had diamonds in it and it appeared that the owner would not be found.

If Andy wore Joe's watch while swimming, he would be liable for any damages that resulted. Andy could undertake reasonable expenses to preserve the watch and charge them to Joe if he later claimed his watch.

If Andy loaned the watch to a drunk who then broke it, he would be liable for any loss in value or cost of repair.

FACTS: If Joe showed up to claim the watch, what procedure should Andy use to determine if Joe was the true owner? **YOU'RE THE JUDGE!**

DECISION: Andy would not have to give up the watch on demand. He could ask questions as to the identity of the watch in order to meet his duty to safeguard it for the true owner. Depending on the answers, Andy may be able to withhold the watch from Joe, at least until a court decided otherwise.

Understanding bailments is instrumental to protecting your personal property, and knowing your responsibilities towards the property of others.

IN CLOSING

Well folks, that's it! There is no more. I trust that you thoroughly enjoyed *You're The Judge!*

I have fallen in love with sports and the law and hope that you have too. My sincerest wish for you, and my reason for writing this book is that it will increase your knowledge, understanding and appreciation of the law—and how it concerns not only sports, but your everyday life.

This will help lead to a lifetime of enjoyment of sports. Furthermore, you will be able to apply this new knowledge to better protect the safety of yourself and others while appreciating how the law, rules and regulations are used to mete out justice. You will begin to better understand how this body of law, applied to sports, is the same law that touches so many non-sporting aspects of your life.

Give yourself time to understand the legal concepts in *You're The Judge!* Keep it in a handy spot; refer to it as needed or desired.

Remember that laws, rules and regulations may change as people's attitudes and the needs of society change. And a judge or jury may rule differently on similar facts. Remember also that any decision or information given in *You're The Judge!* is not intended to to be a substitute for proper legal or other advice. Use the book as an informational guide only; then seek out competent legal or other advice as necessary.

Your decisions, comments, thoughts and suggestions are welcomed.

WORDS & TERMS

rds & Terms contains definitions of the important legal and other words and terms used in *You're The dge!* To assist the reader, these may be defined as they relate to sports or athletic activities. For a further cussion, see the page reference indicated in the definition. Words or terms that appear in SMALL CAPI-LS are defined elsewhere in *Words & Terms.*

:eptance, 213 Receiving a thing that is offered, :h as with the intention to make a contract.

quisition, 259 Obtaining possession of profes-nal sports teams by one league, whereby the ac-red teams and its league cease to exist. Also, see :RGER.

t Written law formally passed by legislative wer. See LAW; STATUTE.

tion, 13 Judicial proceeding to enforce or protect ight, or to prevent a wrong. See SUIT.

ult Person who has attained the age of majority :nerally 18-21), and is entitled to the manage-:nt of his own affairs and to the enjoyment of mmon rights.

:nt, 229 Person, with consent, authorized to act r another (principal), such as a professional orts agent who represents an athlete or player in gotiating a contract for the athlete's or player's rvices. See PRINCIPAL.

:eement Meeting of minds for a thing done or to done; mutual obligation. See CONTRACT.

:egation Formal written statement by a party to a :al action, telling what is expected to be proven. :e CASE.

:nateur, 19 Athlete competing in athletic activity a hobby, not as an occupation. Must compete for :n, not for pay. Also, see PROFESSIONAL.

:swer, 13 Document answering a complaint and :ntaining any denial and defenses. See COM-_AINT; DEFENSE.

:titrust Practices designed to prevent full and :e competition, such as by: illegally monopoliz-; a sport, restraining and preventing players or :letes from competing, or stifling competition. :e MONOPOLY; RESTRAINT OF TRADE.

:titrust acts, 255 Laws protecting commerce and :de from monopolies and illegal restraints of :de.

:peal Taking of a case to a higher court for a cor-:tion or reversal of a lower court's decision.

:bitration, 13, 220, 246 Process where parties, :h as professional team owners and players, sub-mit a dispute to an arbitrator for resolution.

arbitrator Private, impartial person(s) chosen by parties to a dispute to resolve the matter.

assault, 81 Unlawful, intentional threat or attempt, with force, to do physical harm to another. See BATTERY.

assumption of the risk, 88, 137 Defense to a charge of negligence where one injured is held to assume the risk of injury from a known and appre-ciated danger by voluntarily proceeding anyway. See NEGLIGENCE.

attractive nuisance, 193, 430 Rule holding that one maintaining on his premises a condition which is dangerous to young children (generally those un-der the age of 12) because of their inability to ap-preciate danger and may reasonably be expected to attract them to the premises, owes a duty to exer-cise reasonable care to protect them against such dangers. Also, see NUISANCE.

B

bailee, 435 Person receiving personal property of another under a bailment.

bailment, 435 Contract to deliver personal proper-ty by one person (bailor) to another (bailee) for a special purpose, such as delivering to be repaired, or renting, sports equipment.

bailor, 435 Person who owns and delivers personal property to bailee under a bailment.

battery, 81 Unlawful use of force by one person upon another without consent. See ASSAULT.

blackout, 263 Practice by professional sports leagues and others permitting them to prohibit the broadcast or televising of certain sports events which they control.

blue laws, 11 Laws regulating religious and per-sonal conduct.

bona fide, 28 In or with good faith or honesty, as in good faith bargaining.

boycott, 258 Agreement refraining or refusing to deal as a means of coercion; sometimes called a group boycott.

breach Failure to perform a promise, warranty or duty.

breach of contract, 226 Failure to perform any or all terms of an agreement.

breach of warranty Failure to perform a promise or guaranty, such as by a manufacturer to make a product safe.

burden of proof, 16, 82 Duty to prove those facts necessary to win a judgment by a clear majority of the believable evidence.

C

case General term for an action or suit at law or in equity. See SUIT.

case law, 11 Law based on earlier court decisions. See PRECEDENT.

cause of action Facts which if proved in a suit would, in the absence of an effect defense, enable a plaintiff to obtain a judgement.

caveat emptor, 165, 418 "Let the buyer beware." Principle under which a buyer was held to have assumed all risks of injury from any defects in a product.

charitable immunity, 136 Immunity of charitable organizations and other non-profit organizations from being sued. See IMMUNITY.

civil action See ACTION; SUIT.

Civil Rights Act, 74 Act entitling all persons to full and equal enjoyment of any public place without discrimination or segregation on the grounds of race or color. See DISCRIMINATION.

claim, 13 Demand for something due or believed due, such as damages or a right.

Clayton Antitrust Act, 258 Act opposing unlawful restraints and monopolies so as to protect trade and commerce.

coercion To enforce or attempt to enforce by threat.

collective bargaining, 241 Process of negotiations between employers (professional sports team owners, league) and employees or others (player's association) concerning wages, hours and other terms and conditions of work.

collective bargaining agreement, 242, 261 Agreement reached between employers (owners) and employees (player's association) or others which regulates terms and conditions of work.

commission, 57 Group of officials authorized to perform certain acts or duties, such as an athletic commission authorized to promote and protect the interests of the public.

commissioner, 301 Person appointed by a spo and given authority to regulate and oversee the be interests of that sport, particularly concerning reso lution of disputes and the conduct of teams and pa ticipants.

common law, 10 Law developed from custom, tr dition and decisions by judges and juries, rathe than from written laws.

comparative negligence, 90, 139 Defense whe the negligence of the plaintiff is compared to tha of the defendant. Any damages are based on th comparison. See NEGLIGENCE.

complaint, 13 Initial pleading in a suit, settin forth facts on which plaintiff bases claim for relief See PLAINTIFF; SUIT.

consent, 81, 367 To give approval or permissio Also, see INFORMED CONSENT.

consideration, 213 Thing given or done, or r frained from, from one party and intended as th inducement to another to perform his part of a co tract. See CONTRACT.

conspiracy Combination by two or more individ als or businesses (teams) for the purpose of illega ly restraining trade or commerce.

Constitution, U. S. Fundamental laws and princ ples that determine the powers and duties of th government, which along with its amendmen (Bill of Rights) guarantees certain rights to the pe ple. Also, see DUE PROCESS; EQUAL PROTEC TION.

contract, 212 Agreement to do or not to do a pa ticular thing; offer, acceptance of that offer, ar consideration, such as an agreement between a pro fessional sports team and player.

contract, express Agreement, the terms of whic are openly declared, either by written or oral la guage.

contract, no-cut, 219 Contract under which player's salary, generally, will not be affected his condition or performance, even if cut from t roster.

contract, no-trade, 220 Contract under which player may not be traded without his consent.

contract, personal services, 215 Contract e changing personal services (play) of an athlete fo a promise to pay.

contributory negligence, 90, 138 Defense to a charge of negligence where one injured is held to have contributed to his injury by knowning of and appreciating a danger or risk, but then voluntarily proceeding anyway. See NEGLIGENCE.

copyright Author's or owner's exclusive legal right to reproduce, publish or sell literary, musical or artistic work.

counterclaims, 14 Claim alleged by a defendant that seeks to reduce plaintiff's claim or provide grounds for a judgement in favor of the defendant. See CLAIM.

court, 13 Governmental body whose function is to administer justice.

---

damages, 16, 89 Compensation for a loss or injury suffered.

decision Judgment of a court or jury of a legal dispute before them. See JUDGMENT.

defamation, 366 Statement that injures a person's reputation or character by false and malicious statements. See LIBEL; SLANDER.

defendant, 13 Person against whom plaintiff's complaint is brought. Also, see COMPLAINT.

defense Answer by a defendant; that which is offered to diminish or defeat plaintiff's complaint.

defense of others, 81 Defense in negligence where force used in defending others is that force the others could have used to defend themselves.

defraud To cheat, trick or swindle another out of property.

depositions, 14 Testimony of a witness recorded outside of court for use at trial. See TESTIMONY.

discovery, 14 Disclosure of facts, documents and the like to use in presenting a case to the court.

dismissal Order or judgement by a court terminating a suit without a complete trial. See TRIAL.

discrimination, 63 Failure to treat all people equally. Attempts to discriminate or differentiate in favor or against athletes or others in sports on the basis of prejudice because of race, sex, color or disability are illegal. See EQUAL PROTECTION.

draft, 273 System used in professional team sports whereby, generally, teams select players eligible for play in their sport in the inverse order of how the teams finished in the previous year's standings.

due process of law, 54, 65 Phrase used in 14th Amendment to the U.S. Constitution limiting a governments power to deprive a person of life, liberty or property without notice and an opportunity to be heard and to defend oneself—a fair and impartial hearing.

duress, 213 Unlawful coercion in forcing one to do something which he otherwise would not have done. See COERCION.

E

eminent domain, 291 Power of a state to take private property for public use.

endorsement, 340 Advertising message which consumers are likely to believe reflects the beliefs of the endorser, such as a professional athlete.

enjoin To command or prohibit, by court order, some act. See INJUNCTION.

equal protection of the laws 55, 65 Phrase used in the 14th amendment to the U.S. Constitution requiring every state to extend to all persons within its jurisdiction equal treatment and protection. It is intended to insure that all persons similarly situated shall be treated alike.

Equal Rights Amendment (ERA), 69 Amendment declaring that equality of rights and responsibility shall not be denied or taken away on account of sex. See DISCRIMINATION.

equity, 227 Justice administered by a court according to what is fair.

evidence Anything that gives or tends to give proof at trial of an issue, such as testimony of witnesses, documents and objects.

expert, 343 One who, because of education, training, knowledge or experience, has acquired special skills.

exploitation, 59 Unjust or improper use of another person for one's own profit or advantage.

express Clear, explicit or definite, such as an express warranty. See WARRANTY.

F

fair comment Statement by a writer in an honest belief of truth, even though it is not, relating to acts that are official, newsworthy and of public interest. See DEFAMATION.

financial aid See SCHOLARSHIP.

foreseeable Ability to see or know in advance,

such as that an injury may result from an existing danger.

fraud, 213 Intentional act of trickery, deceipt or misrepresentation intended to induce another to part with a right or something else of value. See MISREPRESENTATION.

free agent, 245 Professional sports team player who plays out his option, thus becoming free to negotiate and sign with any team concerning his services. Compensation (player, draft pick, money) to the team losing a free agent may be required.

functional, 347 Feature of a product necessary for the product's use, and which cannot be protected by a trademark. See TRADEMARK.

G

good faith Honest effort and intention.

good faith bargaining, 243 Mutual obligation between labor and a union (professional sports team owners and player's association) to meet at reasonable times, make relevant information available and confer with honest effort and intention over mandatory subjects. See MANDATORY SUBJECTS.

guardian, 34 Person who is legally assigned care of an individual not competent to act for himself, such as a minor.

H

hardship rule, 274 Rule allowing undergraduate athletes to give up their remaining amateur eligibility and enter the National Basketball Association (NBA) draft.

hung jury, 85 Jury so divided that it is unable to agree upon a verdict. See VERDICT.

I

imminent danger Term used regarding self-defense. Denotes immediate danger that must be instantly met and cannot wait upon the assistance of others or the protection of the law. See SELF-DEFENSE.

immunity Freedom or protection from legal action or duties which the law generally requires others to perform. See CHARITIBLE IMMUNITY; SOVEREIGN IMMUNITY.

implied Suggested or understood, but not directly or clearly stated, such as an implied warranty. See WARRANTY.

independent contractor Person working on his own without control of another, except as to the result of the work.

informed consent, 203 Consent given by a patient after a reasonable disclosure by medical personnel of any available alternative procedures and the dangers, advantages and disadvantages to the patient.

infringement Violation of a law or regulation; invasion of a right.

injunction, 259, 425 Order of a court directing a person or business to do, or refrain from doing, a particular thing, such as an illegal activity.

injury See PERSONAL INJURY.

intent State of mind with which one acts.

interrogatories, 14 Written questions used in judicial examination of a party or witness.

interstate commerce, 257 Commerce or trade among more than one state.

issue Single essential point to be decided at the conclusion of a trial. See TRIAL.

J

judgment Final decision or order of a court upon the rights and claims of parties to a suit. See SUIT.

jurisdiction, 13 Power of a court to hear and decide a claim. See CLAIM.

jury, 10 Group of people selected to hear evidence and decide a legal matter before them.

K

knowledge Truth or condition of knowing, being aware of, or understanding something.

L

laches, 14 Unreasonable delay in filing a complaint to the harm of a defendant.

last clear chance, 90 Defense holding that a person who has the last clear chance or opportunity to avoid injury to another is liable if he does not. See DEFENSE.

law, 8 Rule to be followed or obeyed, subject to legal penalty.

lawsuit See SUIT.

lease, 292 Agreement for the exclusive possession use and enjoyment of land or property for a specific period of time, such as a sports facility.

•gislation Power to make laws.

•tter of intent, national, 34 Letter signed by student-athlete, parent or legal guardian making nown the athlete's intent to attend a certain college.

ability, legal Obligation or responsibility for amages for an intentional or negligent act.

able Obligated or responsible according to law or quity.

•bel, 366 Form of defamation made in writing, pictures or other graphic representation that damages a erson's reputation by holding him up to public dicule, contempt, shame or disgrace. See DEFAMATION.

•berty, 52 Freedom from bodily restraint; freedom ɔ be educated and of opportunity.

•ckout, 250 Act by professional team sports ownrs of refusing to allow players to practice or play s a means of forcing them to agree over some matɛr.

V1

ajority See ADULT.

alice, 90 Intentional and wrongful conduct, without proper cause or excuse, with an intent to harm nother. See DEFAMATION.

nalicious prosecution, 371 Misuse of law or ourts, without proper cause, with the desire to inlict injury on another.

nandatory subjects Collective bargaining sub- ɛcts covered by wages, hours, and other terms and onditions of work. See COLLECTIVE BAR- ҊAINING.

nerger, 259 Joining together of professional sports ɛagues into one, whereby the other then ceases to xist. Also, see ACQUISITION.

ninor Person under the age of legal majority. See ₊DULT.

nisrepresentation, 213, 223, 353 Statement by ɤords or other conduct that misleads the person to ɤhom made. See FRAUD.

nistake Unintentional act or omission done out of ɡnorance or misunderstanding.

nistrial, 85 Trial that has no legal effect, such as ɒne cancelled due to error or misconduct.

nonopoly, 256 Exclusive right, power or control

to carry on a particular business or trade, such as manufacturing products or providing services (sports activities).

municipality City, town or other governmental branch.

N

National Collegiate Athletic Association (NCAA), 20 Voluntary organization of major colleges and universities, formed to regulate and supervise collegiate athletics in the U.S.

National Labor Relations Act (NLRA), 239 Act giving employees (professional athletes) the right to form a union or association (player's association), to bargain collectively, and to engage in other activities for their aid and protection. Also, see PLAYER'S ASSOCIATION.

negligence, 88, 166 Failure to exercise the standard of care which a reasonable person in the same or similar circumstances would exercise, and which breach causes an injury and damages. See BREACH.

nuisance, 424 Creation of a condition that annoys or disturbs one in possession of his property, rendering its ordinary use uncomfortable. Also, see ATTRACTIVE NUISANCE.

O

offer, 213 Promise to do a thing, such as to make a contract, which if accepted creates the contract.

opinion Decision reached by a judge or court detailing the reasons upon which a judgment is based. See JUDGMENT.

option clause, 226 System giving professional sports team owners the right to renew a player's services without consent for one year after the player's present contract expires. See CONTRACT; PERSONAL SERVICES.

P

parol evidence rule, 216 Rule prohibiting change, in the absence of fraud or mistake, in an agreement where the parties intended to merge all oral agreements into a written one.

pawn, 438 Bailment of personal property to secure a loan. See BAILMENT.

per se By itself or taken alone.

per se rule, 259, 275 Rule holding that certain agreements or practices, because of their deadly effect on competition, are per se illegal.

personal injury Hurt or damage to a person's body, as distinguished from injury to one's reputation or property. See DEFAMATION.

plaintiff, 13 Complaining party bringing a legal action. See ACTION; COMPLAINT

player's association Group of professional sports team players, organized to bargain with their employer (team owners) concerning wages, hours, grievances and other terms and conditions of work.

precedent, 11 Utilization of previous court decisions in judging a court action with similar facts.

premise liability, 179 Liability of the owner or operator of land and buildings, such as a sports facility, or place of public amusement or entertainment, to exercise reasonable care for the safety and protection of patrons. See LIABILITY; REASONABLE CARE.

preponderance of evidence, 16 Evidence by one party to a suit, which when fairly considered, produces the stronger impression and is more believable.

president, 301 Person appointed by a sport and given authority to regulate and oversee the best interests of that sport, particularly concerning resolution of disputes and the conduct of team or participants.

price discrimination, 258 Policy where a different price is charged to similarly situated buyers. Also, see CONSPIRACY.

principal Employer of an agent; the source of authority or right. See AGENT.

privacy, right of Right to let alone, free from unwarranted publicity or public scrutiny.

privilege Right, benefit or power enjoyed by a person or business, but not enjoyed by all.

procedure, 12 Method for enforcing legal rights and seeking damages for an injury

product liability, 165, 418 Liability of a manufacturer or seller of a product for an injury caused by their product. See LIABILITY.

professional Person working or competing in a profession for pay, not as a hobby, such as a professional athlete. Also, see AMATEUR.

proof Establishment of a fact by evidence. See EVIDENCE.

property Something exclusively owned or possessed, including rights.

property interest, 52 Claim or right in property such as a right to participate in athletics.

property right Right to control some property, do with as the owner desires, such as the right of team or league to control the broadcast of the games.

proximate cause Negligent conduct without which an injury would not have happened. See NEGLIGENCE.

public figure, 355, 367 Person who has achieved fame or notoriety, and who commands substantial public interest, such as an athlete.

punitive damages, 84 Damages intended to serve as a deterent to, or to make an example of, the defendant or others for evil behavior. See DAMAGES.

pure accident, 90 Accident that is unforseeable that could not be prevented by reasonable caution. See UNFORSEEABLE.

R

rational basis test, 55 Requires that any rule classification, such as to regulate athletics or athletes, must be reasonable so that all persons similarly situated are treated alike.

reasonable care That care which an ordinary, reasonable and cautious person would exercise under the same or similar circumstances.

reasonable doubt Apprehension or suspicion which would make a reasonable man hesitate act or accept the truth of a claim or accusation.

redshirting, 26 Intentional retention or keeping back of athletes, generally to extend athletic eligibility.

regulate To control or direct; to subject to rules laws.

Rehabilitation Act, 73 Act holding that no otherwise qualified handicapped individual shall, solely by reason of a handicap, be excluded from participation in, be denied benefits of, or be subject discrimination in athletics. See DISCRIMINATION.

remedy Legal means used to enforce a right, compensate for, or prevent, an injury, such as money damages or an injunction. See INJUNCTION.

reply See ANSWER.

res ipsa locquitor, 394 "The thing speaks for i

lf." Expression inferring negligence where the efendant had exclusive control of that which used an injury and, further, that the injury would ot ordinarily happen without negligence. See EGLIGENCE.

escind To annul, make void or cancel, such as a ontract or agreement. See CONTRACT.

eserve clause, 226 System giving a professional ports team owner the right to reserve a player's ervices for an indefinite period. Unless agreed to, eserve clauses are no longer allowed.

espondeat superior, 146 "Let the master answer." Expression holding employers responsible or the negligent acts of their employees, such as a ity or school's responsibility for the acts of its eachers and coaches.

estraint of trade Contract or conspiracy which ends, or is designed, to stifle or eliminate competition—illegal monopoly, such as restrictions on a rofessional team player's ability to trade his services with other teams. See CONSPIRACY.

ight of first refusal, 282 Right of a professional ports team to sign a free agent they are about to ose for the amount agreed upon between the layer and another team. See FREE AGENT.

ight of privacy, 355 Right to be left alone, free om intrusion of one's private life.

ight of publicity, 360 Right to a recognizable and arketable personality, such as a professional athete.

isk Danger or hazard, such as which a person may nowingly accept, thus preventing recovery for any jury suffered as a result. See ASSUMPTION OF HE RISK.

ule Established legal standard or regulation directg or prohibiting certain conduct. See LAW.

ule of reason, 260 Rule holding that the legality f restraints on trade is determined by weighing ertain factors. See RESTRAINT OF TRADE.

ave-harmless statutes, 136 Laws permitting or equiring schools to protect, indemnify or grant imunity from prosecution to teachers and coaches rom financial loss in cases alleging negligence gainst them. See IMMUNITY.

calping, 377 Practice of generally selling a ticket a sports event for a price higher than the original rice of the ticket.

scholarship, 21 Authorized funds to a student by a college—grant-in-aid, loan or on-campus work—such as an athletic scholarship.

scope of employment Responsibility assigned to an individual by superiors or employer.

self-defense, 81 Conduct to protect or defend one's person or property against injury attempted by another. See PERSONAL INJURY.

settlement, 13 Agreement settling a matter without further need for a decision by a court.

sex discrimination, 64 Discrimination based solely on sex. See DISCRIMINATION.

Sherman Antitrust Act, 256 Act opposing unlawful restraints and monopolies so as to protect trade and commerce.

slander, 366 Oral statement of false and malicious words that injures another's reputation. See DEFAMATION.

sovereign immunity, 135 Freedom or protection from legal action for municipalities and schools. See IMMUNITY.

specific performance, 226 Performance of a contract according to the precise terms agreed upon. See CONTRACT.

stare decisis, 261 Practice whereby a court does not disturb previous case rulings.

state action, 49, 51 State involvement in providing public education, such as to public schools. These schools are bound by the requirements of the Constitution. See DUE PROCESS; EQUAL PROTECTION.

statute, 110 Act or law of a legislature declaring, commanding or prohibiting something. See ACT; LAW.

Statute of Limitations, 14, 134 Statute limiting the time in which a suit must be brought. See SUIT.

strict liability, 166, 420 Absolute liability, regardless of any fault or improper care by a product's user, will apply if a potentially dangerous, defectively manufactured product causes injury. There is an absolute duty to make it safe. See LIABILITY.

strict scrutiny test, 56 Requires that where a suspect class (race, sex, color) or fundamental interest (marriage, interstate travel) is involved, any rule, such as to regulate athletics or athletes, will be unconstitutional unless there is a compelling interest to be protected or promoted.

strike, 250 Act of refusing to work as a means of forcing an employer to give in to employees' demands, such as professional team players demanding of team owners less restrictive free agency or better work conditions. See FREE AGENCY.

suit Proceeding in a court where the plaintiff seeks compensation for injury or enforcement of a right.

T

tampering, 223 Improperly interfering with another's rights, such as a professional sports team's rights to one of its player's services.

testify, 15 To give testimony—evidence or statement—as a witness.

tort, 81 Private or civil wrong or injury. See PERSONAL INJURY; DEFAMATION.

trademark, 346 Distinctive word, name, mark or other symbol of authenticity through which products of one manufacturer may be distinguished or identified from those of others.

trademark infringement, 346 Act of using, without consent, a registered trademark which use is likely to cause confusion with the public.

trial, 14 Legal proceeding of issues before a court that has jurisdiction. See ACTION; SUIT.

U

unavoidable accident See PURE ACCIDENT.

unconstitutional In violation of the constitution and, therefore, unenforceable or illegal.

undue influence Improper or wrongful persuasion which induces one to do something which he would not do if acting freely.

unfair labor practice, 242 Practice where an employer or employees refuse to bargain, or bargain in good faith, such as where a professional sports team owner interferes with a player's associations' right to organize or encourage membership, or refuses to bargain. See COLLECTIVE BARGAINING.

unforseeable Not expected, seen or known of advance.

union, 238 Group of people (association player's association) organized to bargain w their employer (team owner or others) concerni discipline, wages, hours, grievances or other ter and conditions of work. See PLAYER'S ASSOC ATION.

V

valid Legally sufficient or binding.

venue, 13 Geographical place where a trial must held; place where the plaintiff files a complaint.

verdict, 16 See JUDGMENT.

vicarious liability, 86 Liability for another's neg gent acts.

voidable Capable of being voided—no legal for unenforceable—such as a contract. See CO TRACT.

Voir dire, 14 Method by which a jury is selected

volition, 115 Voluntary; acting or done of on own free will or choice.

W

waiver, 123, 414 Voluntary surrender of a ri; with both knowledge of its existence and an int tion to surrender it, such as a right to recover da ages for a personal injury. See PERSONAL INJ RY.

warranty, 168, 169, 207 Promise or guarant such as warranties given by a manufacturer or s er regarding the condition of their products.

witness, 15 Person who personally testifies to w he has seen, heard or observed.

workmen's compensation statutes, 110, 321 St utes providing that employees (professional te athletes and others), with certain exceptions, m receive compensation for injuries related to th employment.

INDEX

Bold page references indicate where topics are defined and discussed. See *Words & Terms* for a complete list of definitions with page references of important legal and other words and terms used in *You're The Judge!*